A REVENUE HISTORY OF THE SUNDARBANS

The Sundarban stretches from the brackish waters of the broad Hooghly on the west, to the fresh waters of the still broader Meghna to the east; the turbid waters of the Bay of Bengal on its southern limits, to the zamindari or pargana lands on its northern extremity and includes in its southern fringes the dense natural mangrove forests, it is famous for.

The revenue history of Sundarbans is linked up with its riverine and coastal networks to its strategic location at the head of the Bay of Bengal which made it a natural protective barrier for the densely populated city of Calcutta. The massive transformation combined with the changed physical structure of Sundarban influenced society and economy on the one hand and invited settlers to establish their control in that region on the other.

The text of Pargiter focuses on the revenue history of a larger part of Sundarbans, viz., Jessore, Khulna, Bakarganj and some parts of 24-Parganas since the inception of the colonial rule in Bengal. It has also been shown how the colonial administrators took various types of measures for collecting revenue by the way of land reclamation.

The introductory note by the editor analyses the revenue settlement policies which had been implemented on different occasions to ensure the revenue maximization policies of the British Raj on the one hand and to establish an human settlement in the deltaic region on the other.

Frederick Eden Pargiter born in 1852, was the second son of the Rev. Robert Pargiter. He was educated at Exeter College, Oxford and was a Boden Sanskrit scholar in 1872.

He passed the Indian Civil Service exam and was sent to Bengal in 1875, where he served for thirty-one years and retired in 1906. Pargiter died at Oxford on 18 February 1927.

Ananda Bhattacharyya is Assistant Director of the West Bengal State Archives. His many publications include *Sir William Wilson Hunter: Bengal MS Records – A Selected List of 14,136 Letters in the Board of Revenue, Calcutta, 1782-1807, with an Historical Dissertation and Analytical Index*, 4 vols (2018); *A History of the Dasnami Naga Sannyasis* (2018); *Adivasi Resistance in Early Colonial India* (2017); *Remembering Komagata Maru: Official Reports and Contemporary Accounts* (2016); *Notes on the Races, Castes and Trades of Eastern Bengal* (2016) and *Sannyasi and Fakir Rebellion in Bengal: Jamini Mohan Ghosh Revisited* (2014).

FREDERICK EDEN PARGITER

A Revenue History of the Sundarbans

FROM 1765 TO 1870

Edited with an Introduction by
ANANDA BHATTACHARYYA

Routledge
Taylor & Francis Group
LONDON AND NEW YORK

MANOHAR
2019

First published 2020
by Routledge
4 Park Square, Milton Park, Abingdon, Oxon OX14 4RN
605 Third Avenue, New York, NY 10017

First issued in paperback 2023

Routledge is an imprint of the Taylor & Francis Group, an informa business

Publisher's Note
The publisher has gone to great lengths to ensure the quality of this reprint but points out that some imperfections in the original copies may be apparent.

Print edition not for sale in South Asia (India, Sri Lanka, Nepal, Bangladesh, Pakistan or Bhutan)

British Library Cataloguing-in-Publication Data
A catalogue record for this book is available from the British Library

Library of Congress Cataloging-in-Publication Data
A catalog record for this book has been requested

ISBN: 978-1-03-265442-3 (pbk)
ISBN: 978-0-367-43774-9 (hbk)
ISBN: 978-1-003-00569-8 (ebk)

DOI: 10.4324/9781003005698

Typeset in Adobe Garamond Pro 11/13
by Ravi Shanker, Delhi 110 095

MANOHAR

To

Professor Rosinka Chaudhuri

Contents

Preface

The revenue history of Sundarbans is linked up with its riverine and coastal networks. The strategic location of the Sundarbans at the head of the Bay of Bengal has also made it a natural protective barrier for the densely populated city of Calcutta to its north: the mangrove barriers are the first to absorb and reduce the direct impact of the cyclonic storms and accompanying surges moving in from the Bay of Bengal. The Sundarbans was a large forest region studded with swampy marshes here and there from the Hooghly (Hughli) in the west to the Meghna in the east. It lay to the south of the then cultivated zamindari lands of the districts of the 24-Parganas, Khulna and Bakarganj. The most lucrative and the most interesting of the temporarily-settled properties in Bakarganj is the Sundarban forest, which lies on the sea coast in the southern part of the district. There are divergent opinions among the scholars on the etymology of the name, 'Sundarbans'. It is, however, generally agreed that the name Sundarbans, or more correctly, the Sundarban, is derived from *sundri* trees, which are the commonest ones in the forest. There is also a view that Sundarban comes from the word 'Samudraban' meaning a forest by the sea. The Sundarban is a large area which is fertilised by different branches of the river Ganga eventually falling in the Bay of Bengal. The northern part of the Sundarbans is considered as fertile land for the growth of rice. The Port of Calcutta has suffered constantly from the loss of navigality. Here lies the importance of the river Hooghly. The massive transformation combined with the changed physical structure of Sundarban influenced society and economy on one hand and on the other invited settlers to establish their control in that region. The most extensive land reclamation took place during this period comprising the Haroa, Kulpee, and Bhangar Police Stations in the 24-Parganas. Although it was substantially progressing in other Police Stations like – Canning, Mathurapur, Hingalganj, Sagar, Minakhan, Jaynagar, etc., but it was very slow during the period 1780-1873. Many maps of Sundarbans were prepared delimiting the Sundarban Delta during 1810-50. The maps showing the boundaries of different plots or 'Lot's in the Sundarbans were prepared by Lieutenant W. E. Morrieson during 1811-14. His brother Hugh Morrieson later modified the map in 1818. Prinsep completed the survey of Sundarban during 1822-23. In 1828, W. Dampier & Lt. A. Hodges was appointed as the Commissioner of Sundarban. Under the Directorship of W. Dampier & Lt. A. Hodges, a survey was done during 1828-32. There is a detailed explanation of its reason in the accounts of Frederick Eden Pargiter and official correspondences.

Frederick Eden Pargiter was the second son of the Rev. Robert Pargiter, and was born in 1852. He was educated at Taunton Grammar School and Exeter College, Oxford, where he obtained a first-class in mathematics both in Moderations in 1871 and in the Finals in 1873. He was also a Boden Sanskrit scholar in 1872. He passed the Indian Civil Service and was allotted in 1875 to Bengal, where he served for thirty-one years, becoming Under-Secretary to the Government of Bengal in 1885, District and Sessions Judge in 1887, and Judge of the High Court, Calcutta, in 1904. He retired in 1906.During his Indian service he was author of the *Revenue History of the Sundarbans from 1765-1870*; *Bengal Municipal Acts*, and a revised edition of the book, *Land Acquisition Acts*, written by his father-in-law, Mr. Beverley. He also devoted much of his spare time to the Asiatic Society of Bengal, Calcutta, of which he was Secretary 1884-5, and President 1903-5. He became in 1905-6, a Fellow of the Calcutta University.* The originality of the text has been made and there are no changes in the spelling, composition and in other aspects .

In order to bring out the reprint edition of Pargiter's *Revenue History of Sundarbans* I am highly indebted to Professor Rajat Kanta Ray, Professor Sirajul Islam, Professor Deba Prasad Chaudhury and late Professor Ratna Lekha Ray for providing me new insights in

* Obituary Notice, 'F.E. Pargiter', *The Journal of Royal Asiatic Society of Great Britain and Ireland*, no. 2 (April 1927): 409-11, Cambridge University Press, Oxford.

studying the agrarian history of Bengal. Prolonged discussion with Dr. Ramchandra Guha in the National Library, Kolkata, helped me a lot to write a detailed introduction of the Pargiter's volume for which I am highly indebted to him. Professor Vinita Damodaran's thoughtful discussion on the forest and forestry helped me a lot to rectify my errors for which I am also indebted to her. I am also indebted to West Bengal Secretariat Library, Writers' Buildings, Government of West Bengal, The National Library, Calcutta and the staff and Archivists of West Bengal State Archives, Kolkata. Special acknowledgement is due to Miss Anwesha Ghosh of Toronto University and Sri Saibal Datta for providing me some published documents. Miss Ankana Ghatak, M. Phil of Rabindra Bharati University, Calcutta, provided me some rare items from Archives and libraries for which I am highly indebted to her. I am also thankful to Smt. Rina Sinha, Assistant Archivist of West Bengal State Archives, Kolkata and Shri Partha Sarathi Das, Assistant Librarian, National Library for giving me access to the first edition of F.E. Pargiter's account of the Revenue History of Bengal and valuable data for preparing the biographical notes of F.E Pargiter. Finally, I am duly indebted to Shri Ramesh Jain of Manohar Publishers & Distributors, who kindly agreed to bring out the reprint edition.

ANANDA BHATTACHARYYA

Introduction

ANANDA BHATTACHARYYA

Sundarban did not form a separate administrative unit with revenue, magisterial and civil administration of its own as most of the proceedings were sent from Jessore and Bakarganj. This explains the reason of exclusion of Sundarban as a separate unit. In view of the facts it appears that the Collectors of the 24-Parganas, Jessore and Bakarganj exercised control with the local commissioners in the revenue matters of the Sundarbans simultaneously. The climate also in such parts is less insalubrious than in the others, but boundary disputes between border zamindars arising, and the Board not being equally sanguine of the eventful success of the project as the originator thereof, they shortly (in 1790) abolished in *toto* the establishments maintained at the three *ganjs* or bazaars, started within the Sundarbans, viz., Kochua on the Bhairab ('Dreadful river'), Chandkhali on the Kabadak; and Henckellganj, on the Kalindi. The first two are well known places in the present day, and the last is still known, though its identity has almost been lost by being written as 'Hingalgunj' in the Revenue Survey Map. The reclamation of the Sundarban then retrograded for a brief space of time, after which it again progressed, due to the indefatigable exertions of Mr. Henckell. Since the Sundarban forest zone was the property of the state and as such was exhausted from the Permanent Settlement of 1793, the boundary areas, which were undefined, became subject to ownership conflicts.[1] In reality, many

[1] The promulgation of the Permanent Settlement did not change the Sundarbans scenario for the better. Mukhopadhyay has rightly commented that 'Under this Act, the East India Company vested land ownership in a class of landlords who were required to pay to the colonial government a fixed tax proportionate to the size of their holding. In the event of their inability to pay the required revenue, their land

people had cleared the jungle themselves and had established a strong sense of interest and control over the land.[2] Similar legal problems were also registered in the active delta zone in association with settlement and ownership rights to ascertain land. Here the problem was further complicated by the fact that there was always more than one claimant for the new alluvial land. It was always very difficult to ascertain ownership of newly emerged land – whether it belonged to the estate to which it may have been annexed, to some other riparian proprietor upstream who had lost his land due to erosion, or even to people on the bank of the river. Inhabitants of both banks of the river, therefore, often became very quickly involved in disputes, which at times led to battle and bloodshed for the disputed land.[3] The Sundarban[4] stretches from the brackish waters of the broad Hooghly on the west, to the fresh waters of the still broader Meghna on the east; the turbid water of the Bay of Bengal from its southern limits, and zamindari or pargana lands its northern extremity and includes in its southern fringes the dense natural mangrove forests, the Sundarbans. River Raimangal forms the eastern boundary of the Sundarbans Estuarine Programme

---

would be taken away and sold to another bidder. The Settlement did not resolve the status of those extensive "waste" land or jungles, which were not as yet cleared or cultivated in the eighteenth-century Bengal' (Amitesh Mukhopadhyay, *Living with Disasters: Communities and Development in the Indian Sundarbans,* Cambridge University Press, New Delhi, 2016: 27-8.).

2 R.W. Nicholas, 'Village Factions and Political Parties in Rural West Bengal', *Journal of Commonwealth Political Studies'* II, Routledge, Taylor & Francis (November 1963): 17-32; W.W. Hunter, *A Statistical Account of Bengal,* Volume 1: *Districts of the 24-Parganas and Sundarbans,* Trübner and Co., London, 1875.

3 C.E. Haque, *Hazards in a Fickle Environment: Bangladesh,* Springer- Science, Business Media, Kluwer Academic Publishers, The Netherlands, 1997: 146.

4 Sugata Hazra et al., 'Sea Level and Associated Changes in the Sundarbans', *Science and Culture,* vol. 68, nos. 9-12, 2002. Indian Science News Association, Calcutta: 309-21; Anil Chandra Banerjee, *History of India,* A. Mukherjee & Co., Calcutta, 6th edn., July 1995: 433-41; Frederick Eden Pargiter, *A Revenue History of the Sundarbans from 1765 to 1870,* Calcutta, Supdt. Government Printing, 1934: 36; Hunter, op. cit: 1. 'The Sunderbans ... are a network of tidal channels, river, creeks and islands. Some of these Islands are mere swampy morasses, covered with low forest and scrub wood jungle, but those to the north, which are embanked, grow rich crops of rice.... This seaboard area is a typical specimen of new deltaic formation. It exhibits the process of land-making in an unfinished state....' (Hunter, op. cit.: preface)

(SEP) and river Ichhamati, an easterly distributary of the Ganga situated in the North 24-Parganas, the two southernmost districts of the state of West Bengal. The northern limit of the Sundarbans is defined by the Dampier–Hodges Line, an imaginary line that is based on a survey conducted during 1829-32 of River Ichhamati. All the rivers of the 24-Parganas Sunderbans have now been deprived of upland water carrying silt except the Hooghly and the Ichhamati during the rainy season. All the rivers of this area have thus become more or less tidal channels and new land formation is dependent almost wholly on tidal action. Tidal influences are so woven into the fabric of life in the Sundarbans that it is referred to as the *Bhatir Desh* or 'tidal country'.[5] Ratnalekha Ray is of opinion that that the area Bhati means Sundarbans including tracts along the Meghna in Dacca and contiguous districts.[6] The Bhagirathi–Hooghly had always been an important shipping route used for trade between India and

[5] Henry Beveridge, *The District of Bakarganj: Its History and Statistics*, Bakarganj District Council, Md. R. Ali Mia, Habib Press & Publications, Barisal, 1970 (rpt); *Akbarnama*, vol. I; Translation of the original work by Abul Fazl (in Persian), Asiatic Society of Bengal, Calcutta. 1897; N.R. Roy, *Manikchandra Rajar Gan* (folk song of Bengal) (*Bhatiali*); in *Bangalir Itihas, Adiparba* (in Bengali), Dyes Publishing (8th edn.), Calcutta, 1420 B.S./A.D. 2014: 104; Amitav Ghosh, *The Hungry Tide* (it captures some of the dimensions of the region's historical experience, constituted by man, beast and nature. Ghosh has an anthropologist's fascination for local mythologies that subvert the official religious and national versions of history. He is oft found investigating the 'local reality', and with it, critiquing the official version of history. Here in the novel of our discussion, the local reality is that of the Sundarbans, a densely populated archipelago in the Bay of Bengal, which straddles West Bengal and Bangladesh. The tide country people have an epic narrative of origins that they have passed on orally from one generation to another.) Harper Collins, Delhi, 2004; Ranjan Chakrabarti, 'Local People and the Global Tiger: An Environmental History of the Sundarbans Global Environment' Kluwer Academic Publishers: The Netherlands 72-9 http: //www.globalenvironment.it/. 2009. The significance of Abul Fazl's work was that while the empire was still being established. Shireen Moosvi described the processes by which the imperial secretariat had collected daily diaries and oral histories even before Abul Fazl was ordered, in 1589, to write a formal history (Sumit Guha, 'Rethinking the Economy of Mughal India: Lateral Perspectives', *Journal of the Economic and Social History of the Orient*, vol. 58, no. 4, Leiden, Brill, 2015: 532-75).

[6] Ratnalekha Ray, *Change in Bengal Agrarian Society c. 1760-1850*, Manohar, New Delhi, 1979: 15.

the rest of the world. It was, however, the rapid development in the eighteenth century of the port and metropolis of Calcutta, which further increased the importance of the river, making it a well-known name globally. Situated on the east bank of the Hooghly about 145 km. north of its mouth at Sagar Island, the Port of Calcutta, the then most important international port, serving a vast Indian hinterland and the Asian colonies of the British Empire,[7] is still one of the major ports of India.[8] From the very beginning of its establishment in the late eighteenth century as a port of call for deep draft vessels, the port of Calcutta has suffered constantly from the problem of loss of navigability. Meandering over nearly 46 per cent of its length, the geometry of the Hooghly estuarine channel is made more complicated by the existence of as many as 10 shifting sandbars that exist in the 70 km. stretch between the port of Calcutta and Diamond Harbour lying to its south. Constant changes are observed in the tidal axes, bank-line migrations, and erosion in various sections of the river. These

[7] C.A. Bayly, 'Inland Port Cities in North India: Calcutta and the Gangetic Plains, 1780-1900', in *The Rise and Growth of the Colonial Port Cities in Asia,* ed. D.K. Basu, Berkeley: University Press of America, 1985: 13-17; A. Ray, 'The Calcutta Port: The Present and Future', *The Living City*, ed. Sukanta Chaudhuri, Calcutta: Oxford University Press, vol. 2, 1990: 123-7; Tan Tai-Yong, *Port Cities and Hinterlands: A Comparative Study of Singapore and Calcutta; Political Geography,* Elsevier, Amsterdam, 2007, 26(7): 851-65.

[8] Radhakumud Mookherjee, *Indian Shipping: A History of the Sea-borne Trade and Maritime Activity of the Indians from the Earliest Times*, Longmans, Green & Co., Bombay, 1912) points out that Chandecan (Sagar Island) was one of the chief centres of Hindu naval activity during Man Singh's viceroyalty. By far the most important seat of Hindu maritime power of the times in Bengal was that established at Chandecan or Sagar Island, by the constructive genius of Pratapaditya. In the East Bengal tracts formerly held by the *bara bhiyas*, numerous petty zamindaris and *taluqs* sprang up after the fall of the *bhiyas* and their position came to be regulated, in theory at any rate, by official rules (Tapankumar Raychauchaudhuri, *Bengal under Akbar and Jehangir: An Introductory Study in Social History*, A. Mukherjee & Co., Calcutta, 1953: 20-1). Because of the weakness of the Mughal state in Bengal, not only did many old principalities survive, but new principalities were built up within Mughal territory by mashroom zamindars through regular warfare against neighboring magnates. A striking example was the build up of the Jessore raj, created under Mughal rule by a Kayastha soldier of Man Singh's which crushed Pratapaditya of Jessore (Ratnalekha Ray, op. cit.: 19).

changes and associated sediment load movements make the Hooghly a very dynamic estuary.[9] The strategic location of the Sundarbans at the head of the Bay of Bengal has also made it a natural protective barrier for the densely populated city of Calcutta to its north: the mangrove barriers are the first to absorb and reduce the direct impact of the cyclonic storms and accompanying surges moving in from the Bay of Bengal. Though they protect Calcutta from the impact of these surges, the Sundarbans themselves are vulnerable to them. Till the fifteenth century, the Bhagirathi–Hooghly was the course followed by the Ganga flowing into the Bay of Bengal. Owing to geological reasons, the Ganga gradually shifted eastward, so that by the sixteenth century, the Bhagirathi–Hooghly became the first deltaic distributaries of the river. Kakdwip is in the lower Sundarbans Gangetic delta. It is a part of an island belt criss-crossed by tidal rivers, rivulets and creeks. The low-lying islands were made habitable by putting up earthen embankments around them to keep out the sea water and clearing the forests there to create a vast rice-growing plain. The Saptamukhi River flowing along its eastern border sets off Kakdwip from the protected and reserved Sundarbans forest. The Muriganga River flows along its western border, across which lies Midnapore district. The border of Kulpithana demarcates it in the north: the waters of the Bay of Bengal touch its southern limits. The first diversions of fresh water from the Ganga had the immediate effect of improving the overall state of the river Hooghly.[10] Chugh[11] made a thorough study on Sagar, Diamond Harbour, and Garden Reach.

Thus a land 'covered over with impenetrable forests,[12] the hideous

[9] C.V. Gole and P.P. Vaidyaraman, 'Salinity Distribution and Effect of Fresh Water Flows in the River Hooghly', in *Proc. Tenth Congress of Coastal Engineering*, Tokyo, 2, 1967: 1412-34; Pranab Kumar Parua, *The Ganga Water Use in the Indian Subcontinent*; Water Science and Technology Library, Springer, 2010: 64.

[10] A.C. Nandy et al., 'Ecological Changes in the Hooghly Estuary due to Water Release from Farakka Barrage; Mahasagar'– *Bull. National Inst. Oceanography*, Tokai University, Japan: 16(2), 1983: 209-20; M. Sinha et al., 'Impact of Farakka Barrage on the Hydrology and Fishery of Hooghly Estuary', *Estuaries*, Central Inland Capture Fisheries Research Institute, Barrackpore 19(3), 1996: 710-22.

[11] R.S. Chugh, 'Tides in Hooghly River', *Hydrological Sciences Journal*, Taylor and Francis, London, 1961, 6, 2: 10-26.

[12] The most lucrative and the most interesting of the temporarily settled properties

den of all descriptions of beasts and reptiles' could only be improved by deforestation.[13] The ill-defined boundaries as observed by Mr. J.H. Reily, Commissioner in the Sundarban caused much litigation between the government and border zamindars. The Sundarbans region has always been 'known as a notorious abode of man-eaters.' The deities worshipped in the Sundarbans were the gods and goddesses of woodcutters, honey gatherers, bees wax gatherers, boat builders,

---

in Bakarganj is the Sundarban forest, which lies on the sea coast in the southern part of the district (J.C. Jack, *Final Report on the Survey and Settlement Operations in the Bakarganj district 1900 to 1908,* Calcutta, Bengal Secretariat Book Depot, 1915: 114). Under Muslim rule, the forest was regarded as belonging to the State and not included in any zamindari. This view was adopted by the early British administrators and the first systematic attempt to bring the forest under cultivation was made when Tincal Henckell became the Judge and Magistrate of Murli (Jessore). The plan was to lease the land to small lots to cultivating *ryots*. For a discussion on the process of land formation, see J.C. Jack, op. cit.: 1-11, 109, 114. See also, John F. Richards and Elizabeth P. Flint, 'Long Term Transformations in the Sundarbans Wetlands Forests of Bengal', *Agriculture and Human Values,* vol. VII, no. 2, Spring, 1990, Kluwer Academic Publishers,http: //www.globalenvironment.it/. 2009: 17-33.https: //doi.org/10.1007/BF01530432: 12. Forest continues to attract the attention of scholars. M. Rangarajan and K. Sivaramakrishnan, 'Introduction', in *India's Environmental History: Colonialism, Modernity and the Nation,* vol. 2, ed. M. Rangarajan and K. Sivaramakrishnan, New Delhi, Permanent Black, 2012. In more recent work (Vasant Saberwal and Mahesh Rangarajan (eds), *Battles Over Nature: Science and the Politics of Conservation,* New Delhi, Permanent Black, 2006): 267-99. Thus forests remains a site of competing ecological knowledge which in many ways shapes our larger sense of the environmental history of colonial and contemporary India. The finest and largest trees I [Pargiter] have seen almost invariably in places where the land had once been cleared; so that they had a good start before the jungle sprang up around them. There is little undergrowth in the forests, though here and there one may find cane-brakes and thickets of pickly scrub; and there is more of matted undergrowth and tropical luxuriance to be found in Sagar Island than elsewhere. Few of the forest trees display a handsome bloom, ... the prettiest is a species of *hibiscus*, which grows freely along the banks of the streams, and bears large yellow flowers which turn to crimson as they drop.... The low *golpata* palm with its immense leaves, the thickets of the *hibiscus* with its yellow and crimson blossoms, and clumps of the dark-green prickly *kewa* grow along the banks and overhang the stream, while above them the forest closes in with breaks of sunshine streaming through the foliage (Pargiter, op. cit., 1885).

[13] Goutam Chattopadhyay, ed., *Awakening in Bengal in Early Nineteenth Century: Selected Documents*, Calcutta, Progressive Publishers, 1965: 95-9.

and the most desperate cultivators.[14] Religion is thus a framework of general ideas articulated through symbols to help accommodate a range of experiences to give them a meaningful form.[15]

The Sundarbans is thus divided, commencing from the west and going east: The 24-Pargana Sundarban, from the Hooghly to the Kabadak ('Dove-eyed river'); the Jessore Sundarban,[16] from the last named river to the Haringhata ('Deer-shore river'); the Bakarganj Sundarban, from the last named river to the bank of the Meghna. The Sundarbans was a large forest region studded with swampy marshes.[17] Several historical accounts note that the emerging delta areas and a large part of southern Bengal including the Sundarbans constituted 'new frontier' in terms of extended agricultural land and new settlement.[18] The decay of the moribund flood plain, along with increasing population growth, caused the development of a migration stream to the delta frontier.[19] Migrants found motivation in

[14] A.F.M. Abdul Jalil, *Sundarbaner Itihas* (in Bengali), 2nd edn., Ahmed Publishing House, Dacca, 1986: 418-20.

[15] Dulal Chaudhuri, 'Folk Religion', in Amal Kumar Das et al. (eds.), *A Focus on Sundarbans*, Editions Indian, Calcutta, 1981: 74). About the folk culture in the Sundarbans see Sutapa Chatterjee Sarkar, *Life, Literature and Folk Deities in the Mangroves*, Occasional Paper, Nehru Memorial Museum & Library, New Delhi, 2013.

[16] Khulna was originally a subdivision of Jessore created as the first subdivision in Bengal in 1843.

[17] A.F.M. Jalil, *Sundarbaner Itihas* (in Bengali), 2nd edn., Ahmed Publishing House, Dacca, 1986: 2-5; Satish Chandra Mitra, *Jessore-Khulanar Itihas* (in Bengali), vol. II., Gurudas Chattopadhyay & Sons, Calcutta, 1329 BS/AD 1923. An ethnographic, ecological studies include the works of Amal Kumar Das, Asim Kumar Mandal and R.K. Ghosh (*Sundarban: A Socio Bio-Ecological Study*, Calcutta, Bookland, 1989); Rathindranath De (*The Sundarbans*, Calcutta, Oxford University Press, 1990), Kumudranjan Naskar and Dwijendra Narayan Guha Bakshi, (*Mangrove Swamps of the Sundarban, An Ecological Perspective*, Calcutta, Naya Prokash, 1987) mainly focussed on the flora, fauna and various castes and tribes of the delta.

[18] Hunter, op. cit.; F.E. Pargitar, *Revenue History of Sundarban, 1765-1870*, Bengal Secretariat Press, Calcutta, 1885; Robert Carstairs, *Human Nature in Rural India*, Edinburgh and London, W. Blackwood & Sons, 1895; C.E. Haque, *Hazards in a Fickle Environment: Bangladesh*, Springer-Science, Business Media, Kluwer Academic Publishers, Canada, 1997: 145.

[19] R.K. Mukherjee, *The Changing Face of Bengal: A Study of Riverine Economy*, Calcutta, Calcutta University, 1938; R.W. Nicholas, ' Ecology and Village Structure in Deltaic West Bengal', *The Economic Weekly*, 15, Special Number, July 1963: 1185-

the availability of new opportunities provided by rivers for transport and commerce and in the availability of fertile alluvial soil. To the Muslim historians of the eighteenth century, the coastal strip from Hijli (Midnapore) to the Meghna in the east was known as *Bhati*, meaning lowland.

The early Mughals did not interfere with the land system rather they were involved in assessment and collection of land revenue. Like the pre-Mughal period, land revenue collection was left to zamindars. With the decline of Mughal power, the farmers were allowed on payment of the predetermined sum to appropriate the revenue for their own use.[20] Prince Muhamad Shuja had tried to reclaim it in AD 1658 through the creation of Sarkar *Murad Khana* or *Jeradkhana*[21] but without success. By the time of the Viceroy Shah Shuja, who made a new revenue settlement of Bengal, 15 more sarkars and 688 more parganas had been added to the older divisions.[22] Attention of the Company's government in Bengal then turned to the vast uncultured Sundarbans tract, which even the Mughals, did not include in the revenue roll. The repeated efforts of the government to lease out forest lands for revenue purposes in the late eighteenth and early nineteenth centuries were successfully foiled by the stubborn and concerted resistance of the zamindars while the east, west and southern sides of this forest-covered area were bounded by the river and the sea. Dispute, however, soon arose over the demarcation of its northern border with the permanently

---

96, idem, 'Ritual Hierarchy and Social Relations in Rural Bengal', *Contributions to Indian Sociology* (n.s.), 1, 1967: 56–83, idem, 'Structure of Politics in the Villages of Southern Asia', in M. Singer and B.S. Cohn (eds.), *Structure and Change in Indian Society*, Chicago: Aldine Publishing Company, 1968: 243-84.

[20] T. Hussain, *Land Rights in Bangladesh: Problem of Management*, University Press Limited, Dhaka, 1995; see also, Selim Raihan et al., 'Access to Land and Other Natural Resources by the Rural Poor: The Case of Bangladesh', *South Asian Network on Economic Modelling*, Department of Economics, University of Dhaka, Bangladesh, June, 2009 Online athttp: //mpra.ub.unimuenchen.de/38621/MPRA Paper No. 38621, dated 7 May 2012.

[21] L.R. Fawcus, *Final Report on the Khulna Settlement, 1920-1926*, Calcutta, Bengal Secretariat Book Depot, 1927: 55.

[22] Atul Chandra Roy, *History of Bengal, Mughal Period (1526-1765)*, Calcutta, Nababharat Publishers, 1968: 339.

settled zamindari lands.[23] The zamindars apparently claimed the Government grants as part of their permanently settled estates, which the Government frowned upon. The colonization process of new land confined two routes (i) land reclamation, cleaning and cultivation, especially in the Sundarbans, and (ii) claims between peasants over new accretion or dispositional land in the riparian areas of the active delta zone.[24] The northern part of the Sundarbans is considered as fertile land for rice cultivation and due to the poor of navigability port towns developed there. Here lies the importance of the river Hooghly.[25] The massive transformation combined with the changed physical structure of Sundarban influenced the society and economy in one hand and on the other invited the settlers to establish their control in that region.[26] Bengal offers a nearly endless frontier where land continues to be made afresh in the delta.[27] The work of reclamation drew the attention of a Geographer like R.K. Mukherjee 'from the fifteenth century, man has carried out the work of reclamation here fighting with the jungle, the tiger, the wild buffalo, the pig and the crocodile, until at the present day, nearly half of what was fortunately an impenetrable forest has been converted into gardens of graceful palm and fields of waving rice'.[28] The region has been focussed on as being largely a forest, but human settlements have been grafted on to forests, which were systematically cleared to make way for human habitation.[29] O'Malley

[23] Paula Banerjee, 'Bengal-Bangladesh Borderland: Chronicles from Nadia, Murshidabad and Malda', in Paula Banerjee and Anasua Basu Ray Chaudhuri, eds., *Women in Indian Borderlands*, Sage, Delhi, 2010: 1-23.

[24] K.G. Lotiful Bari, ed., *Bangladesh District Gazetteers, Khulna*, B.G. Press, Dacca, 1972: 300.

[25] L.S.S. O'Malley, *Bengal District Gazetteer, 24-Parganas*, Calcutta, The Bengal Secretariat Book Depot, 1914: 2-8.

[26] John F. Richards and Elizabeth P. Flint, 'Long-Term Transformations in the Sundarbans Wetlands Forests of Bengal', paper presented in *The Commons in South Asia: Societal Pressures and Environmental Integrity in the Sundarbans*, the workshop held at Smithsonian Institution, Washington DC, 20-21 November 1987.

[27] Ibid.

[28] Mukherjee,1938: 137.

[29] Amitesh Mukhopadhayay, op. cit.: 27.

and Hunter[30] had shown that before the coming of the English in Bengal attempts were made for land reclamation in that region. During the sixteenth century under the Mughals, Sufi saints from various lineages carried out extensive land reclamation and cleared

[30] O'Malley: 26-9; Hunter, op. cit.: 327. Hunter describes the state of the Sundarban at the end of the eighteenth century when the then Governor of Bengal imposed a rule bringing the forest outside permanent settlements under Government control. The Commissioner of the Sundarbans was charged with the task of 'regulating and managing the waterlogged forests and swamps of the lower delta' and 'to ensure that private landowners cleared, settled and reclaimed Sundarban forests and swamps for rice cultivation' (Richards and Flint: 1990). For understanding of a conceptual and epistemological outlook of colonial rule in India scholar should consult the works of Chatterjee (Partha Chatterjee, *The Nation and its Fragments: Colonial and Postcolonial Histories*, Delhi, Oxford University Press, 1995), Bayly (C.A. Bayly, *Empire and Information: Intelligence Gathering and Social Communication in India, 1780-1870*, Cambridge, Cambridge University Press, 1996), Cohn (B.S. Cohn, *Colonialism and Its Forms of knowledge: The British in India*, Delhi, Oxford University Press, 1997) and Dirks (N.B. Dirks, *Castes of Mind: Colonialism and the Making of Modern India*, Princeton, Princeton University Press, 1997). Hunter *quotes* the Court of Directors as saying: 'that a Statistical Survey of the country would be attended with much utility; ... steps to be taken for the execution of the same' (Hunter, op. cit.: xxiii). The objective behind such statistical account was to 'gain exhaustive knowledge about the land and deploy it for the purposes of colonial rule'... and 'was to produce exact local knowledge for administration of Bengal' (P. Greenough, 'Hunter's Drowned Land: An Environmental Fantasy of the Victorian Sundarbans', in *Nature and the Orient: The Environmental History of South and Southeast Asia*, ed. R.H. Grove, V. Damodaran and S. Sangwan, Delhi, Oxford University Press, 1998: 238). Thus Amitesh Mukhopadhyay admitted the fact that 'Hunter tried to resolve the major dilemma that confronted the colonial administrators at various stages of the Sundarbans reclamation, namely, whether to convert the wasteland to a cropland through reclamation and settlement or deny people's claims to this land by declaring it a forested wasteland and, therefore, the state property' (Mukhopadhyay: 33). Thus Hunter's emphasis Sundarban as a 'waste' has been critically examined by Guha (Ramchandra Guha, 'An Early Environmental Debate: The Making of the 1878 Forest Act', *The Indian Economic and Social History Review*, New Delhi, Sage, 27 (1): 65-84.) in this way that the concept 'waste' 'was being readied by colonial policy makers to deflect native claims to the vast forests of India in order to move towards their exploitation', whereas, Greenough's observation 'Hunter's Victorian sensibilities led him to engage with the landscape and geography of the Sundarbans' (Greenough, op. cit.: 240) was reflected in Hunter's own version where he commented ' So great is the evil fertility of the soil, that reclaimed land neglected for a single year will

forests for wet-rice cultivation.[31] Eaton[32] has given a graphic picture of the Sundarbans under colonial rule 'at the advent of the British rule in 1765, the Sundarbans forests were double their present size.... During early British rule, zamindars, or landholders, were allowed to continue reclaiming as much of the jungle bordering their plots as they had been doing under the Mughals.' The East India Company having acquired the *diwani* of civil administration of Bengal in 1765 took the Sundarbans as its property, it being an uncleared forest. It appears that this uncleared forest region of the Sundarbans was not under Clive's *jagir*. This constituted a 'no man's land' and was taken to be the property of the State. In Rennell's time (1764-72) the forest appears to have regained on the cultivation, and extended north of the Chandkhali Khal (canal) and Menus River.[33] The Manas River is a transboundary river in the Himalayan foothills between southern Bhutan and India. It is named after Manasa, the serpent god in Hindu mythology. 'Very little had been brought under cultivation either over the marsh tracts, or to the south between them and the Sundarbans'. In fact, the uninhabited marshes and Sundarbans were then united between the Jubboonah River and the Baro (now Roopsheah Khal) or Pussur River.[34] On acquiring these lands, the British saw this area

---

present to the next year's cultivator a forest of reeds (*nal*). He may cut it and burn it down, but it will spring up again almost as thick as ever' (Hunter. op. cit.: 52). Hunter devotes an entire book to the Sundarbans where, after writing at great length about the forest and wild animals, he only mentions the people in passing, referring to a 'few wandering gangs' and 'classifying them after long lists of wild animals and plants' Hunter, 1875: 317. Greenough identifies Hunter as inaugurating a tradition that continues to this day (1998: 240).

[31] Debjani Bhattacharyya, *Empire and Ecology in the Bengal Delta: The Making of Calcutta*, Cambridge, Cambridge University Press, 2018: 47. For an account of eleventh-century archaeological evidence (Sayantani Pal, 'Religious Patronage in the Land Grant Charters of Early Bengal (Fifth-Thirteenth Century)', *Indian Historical Review*, Indian Council of Historical Research, Sage, New Delhi, 41, no. 2, 2014: 184-205. Pal cites two copper plates for religious land grants.

[32] R.M. Eaton, *Rise of Islam and the Bengal Frontier, 1204-1760*, Berkeley, CA, University of California Press, 1993: 207-11.

[33] J.E. Gastrell, *Geographical and Statistical Report of the Districts of Jessore, Fureedpore and Backergunge*, Office of Superintendent of Government Printing, Calcutta, 1868: 24.

[34] Ibid: 23.

as uncharted and unmapped forests and waste lands waiting to be reclaimed and brought under the Company's revenue rolls.[35]

The first rules on forest grants were issued by the Board in 1817 except when they limited the area to be granted to 10,000 *bighas.* Government approved a form of lease (*patta)* on 24 March 1825 with a security bond. The terms of the lease permitted a rent-free period of seven years for the whole grant and an exemption of one quarter from any revenue in perpetuity. In Bakarganj three grants were made under these rules by the Collector to the Maghs which were surrendered. These rules were revised on 25 March 1830 by which the revenue-free period was extended to 25 years, the revenue was fixed at 8 *annas* a *bigha* from the 24th year in perpetuity, but the grants were to be cancelled if a quarter of the forest was not cleared within five years. These rules remained in force until 1853, the only changes made during this period were that the grants were made by public after 1846 and that where a grant was forfeited for inadequate clearance, and the portion cleared was after 1848 settled with the grantee in the ordinary way. In 1852 seven grants were made in Bakarganj. This slow progress was due to the want of an internal survey in the forest in Bakarganj. Rough surveys were made from time to time, but they were very inaccurate and the work of one surveyor largely employed in Bakarganj was condemned as untrustworthy. He had indeed measured the area of Jnanpara as 19,800 *bighas,* when it actually contained over a lakh of *bighas*. The Bakarganj forest was never really surveyed until the Revenue survey of 1862-3, but it was nearly covered by Smith's survey in the east in 1854-5, and Mr. Gomees's survey along the Baleswar in 1852-7. The whole policy in respect of forest grants came under consideration in 1852, when the Board of revenue submitted an important report of 14 December, in which they reviewed the system of forest grants since their commencement and observed that many of the grants had been abandoned, Revenue was to seek and clearances had been less than were anticipated. The failure was due partly to speculation, but chiefly to the 8 *annas* rate, which they held

[35] Sutapa Chatterjee Sarkar, 'Bengal's Southern Frontier, 1757 to 1943', *Studies in History*, Jawaharlal Nehru University, Department of History, Sage, New Delhi, 28, no. 1(2012): 69-97.

was chiefly double the rate originally contemplated. They proposed a rate of 4 *annas* (but in Bakarganj 5 *annas)* to be reached after fifty-five years, which should contain a rent-free period of ten years, and they combined with this proposal for the limitation of grants to 3,200 acres, exemption of one quarter from any assessment and a clearance. They further proposed that the old grants should be admitted to the new terms, but not the 'resumed *mahals*' whose circumstances were entirely different. The Government accepted the Board's review of the position and the grantees view of the proper terms. According to Jack 'The paramount object of Government had been the reclamation of the Sundarbans'[36] and 'The improvement of the revenue was altogether of subordinate importance'. The terms offered should be such would attract acceptance 'and there would be no security bond, no limitation in size and no higher assessment in Bakarganj'. In the case of more than two applicants for the same grant, it should be knocked down to the highest bidder at a public sale. The terms of the existing grants could be commuted into these terms dating from the commencement of their existing leases, provided that all lands already brought under assessment should bear the full assessment of 2 *annas* a *bigha*. In Bakarganj all the existing grants were commuted into grants under these rules and 25 new grants were immediately made, as there was great competition.[37] The whole of the Bakarganj forest was leased under these rules. The exact terms were published in the *Calcutta Gazette*.[38] Of the grants made in Bakarganj only

[36] Jack, op. cit.: 121.

[37] It appears from the collectorate records that one of these (*Tauzi* no. 1243) was not regularly made and is really a terminable *ijara* for ninety-nine years. It is significant that although the Governor- General in Council directed that 'resumed mahals' were not to have the benefit of these rules, 90 years grants were actually made in respect of nine 'resumed mahals', in six of which the entire area had already been reclaimed and in the other four of which reclamation was already considerable.

[38] 8 October 1853 and are known as the 'Forest Grant Rules of 1853'. The terms were as follows: (i) One-fourth of the whole grant to be forever exempt from assessment, (ii) The remaining three-fourths to be rent-free for 20 years, to pay half-an-*anna* per *bigha* from the 21st year, one *anna* from the 31st, one *anna* and a half from the 41st and two *annas* from the 51st year, (iii) After the 99th year grant to be re-assessed at a moderate assessment, but the proprietary right and the right of engagement to remain with the grantee, (iv) one-eighth to be cleared and rendered fit

twenty-one survive, of which seven were grants under the old rules which had been commuted. Many of these grantees were European capitalists who found Bakarganj too distant a field for their attention. While the Bengali capitalists soon exhausted their capital some of the forest grants were thrown up and some were forfeited by failure to fulfil the clearance conditions. Of those which survived, a few escaped any inspection of the amount of clearance and others obtained a false certificate that the clearance conditions had been fulfilled. At the district survey fifty years after the grants were made, none of the surviving grants had cleared and rendered fit for cultivation the three-fourths which the terms provided; but that survey gave much fillip to reclamation that some succeeded before the survey was concluded. Governments were prepared even to grant *jagirs* to induce capitalists to turn their attention to the Sundarbans. In April 1862 the issue of further grants under the rules of 1853 was stopped and the new policy of revenue-free grants was brought into force. The policy was originally mooted by the Government of India in 1858 with the object of promoting the settlement of Europeans in India.

Regulation III of 1828[39] then declared that these tracts of land had always been government, not private property (notably under the Mughals) and that therefore they should remain so.[40] Controversy persists between the colonial surveyors and historians[41] and the

---

for cultivation at the end of the 5th year, one-fourth at the end of the 10th year, one-half at the end of the 20th, and three-fourths at the end of the 30th year. On failure of any one of these four conditions, the grantee to forfeit all right and interest in the lands.

[39] By this Regulation a regular survey of the Sundarban forests was necessary.

[40] Pargiter, op. cit., 1934: 22. This was indeed a logical step after the segregation of the entire forest into blocks. Each block comprised of lots which were to be sold/auctioned off. This period of reclamation was much more dynamic in nature and yielded better results in terms of both the total amount of land reclaimed and the total amount of colonial revenue collected. This dynamism is best portrayed by the fact the rules for land reclamation got changed three times in this period of 50 years.

[41] It includes Gastrell, op. cit., Westland (James Westland, *A Report on the District of Jessore: Its Antiquities, its History, and its Commerce*, 2nd edn. (Bengal Secretariat Press, Calcutta, 1874) and Beveridge, (op. cit.), who believed that there was no civilization of worth which had existed in the Sundarbans.

nationalist group of regional historians[42] as regard the existence of a well-civilized condition of Sundarban before the coming of the British in Bengal. The idea, that the Sundarbans were at one time densely populated, and that cities flourished where now liquid mud a few inches above the mean sea-level alone is to be found, is doubtless founded on the fact; that the surface of the Sundarbans has sunk more than once below the level of the ocean there can be no doubt that they will ever be re-populated in their present state is highly doubtful, that the present forest will ever be destroyed by clearance is also very doubtful, as the present northern limit of forest closely represents the southern limit of fresh water in the North-Eastern monsoon, or when the salt water is at its lowest level. Even Henckell described the Sundarbans as having been 'in the finest state of cultivation at the time of the Mogul Government' and ascribed the desertions to the ravages of the Maghs; but this is only true which has been shown in Rennell's map of the Sunderbans to the east of the Beckhallee River in the eastern Sunderbans and not in the other parts of Sundarbans. The fact that the Sundarbans were inhabited, is stated in the *Asia of De Barros*, who describes it as a populated country in the commencement of the sixteenth century (1510-20) or nearly 500 years ago. He mentions the names of several towns and villages, particularly one which he calls Satigam on the east mouth of the Ganges, and Chatigam on the west. Even, we find in Major James Rennell's *Atlas*, published in 1781, a number of villages is shown on the east bank of the Kabadack, and south of the Coirah rivers which was noticed by Mr. Dampier and found that these villages were deserted. In the proceedings of Board of Revenue dated 3rd February 1829 it was stated that 'some of the villages had been deserted twelve, ten, eight, and some so recently as three years . . . he had seen but two hundred beeghas of land, under cultivation with ten or twelve houses'. He ascertained from

[42] Mitra, op. cit., vol. 1: 54-78, and Kalidas Dutta, ed., *Dakkhin Chabbis Parganar Ateet* (in Bengali), vol. I, Baruipur, Sundarban Anchalik Sangrahashala (Sundarban Regional Collections), 1989, vol. 1: 23-50) firmly believed 'that the Sundarbans was a well-civilized and densely populated region'.

the inhabitants 'that the cause of this desertion was the salt water'.[43] The country was in perfect forest, and hardly distinguishable from the oldest Sundarbans. The revenue survey found it impossible to penetrate the jungles to lay down the old forest boundary. In this tract of land amounting to about 8,400 acres, fruit trees, tanks, and other signs of habitation was found. It is learnt from the report submitted by Dampier that 'the Kaburtuk [Kabadack] river ceased to be a sweet water river, within the last thirty or forty years. The two branches of the river shown in Rennell's map, the one joining the Jelinghee, and the other the Ganges near Commercolly, are now dry; and the waters which used to flow through them have found an outlet through the Goraie River into the Bulissur. Thus we find that the silting of the head of the river was followed by the desertion of the country. As the influence of the tides prevailed the salt water found its way further north; and we find it is only as far as the influence of salt water is felt, that the country has become a desert, and trees peculiar to the Sundarbans forest have sprung up. Further south, we observe the same changes to have taken place, only at an anterior period, and there the traces of habitation are neither so recent nor so numerous. In most places, there is an absence of fruit trees, but the more permanent marks of habitation are still to be found in lot No. 211 of Hodges map, we find the ruins of a palace and a fort, and the evident traces of a large and populous town. In lot No. 165, Major Smyth has already described the remains of the old city of Goomghur, and ancient Jessore.[44] Satish Mitra in order to establish his nationalistic opinion mentioned a map pointing out five famous ports in the Sundarbans area, named Pacauly, Cuipitavaz, Noldy, Dapara and Tipara. Mitra also mentions that prior to Mughal invasion of Bengal, in 1128 BS the lands of Sundarban were in the finest state of cultivation and the villages in general were populated. There was also a vast cultivable area.

[43] Ralph Smyth, *Statistical and Geographical Report on the 24-Pargunnahs District*, 'Calcutta Gazette' Office, Calcutta, 1857; James A. Longridge, 'Report on the Calcutta and South-Eastern Railway from Calcutta to the River Mutlah', *The Calcutta Review*, Thacker Spink and Co., Calcutta, 1781: 385-410.

[44] Letter from Presidency Commissioner to Sunderban Commissioner, No. 141, dated 15 July 1854 (Colletorate Records of 24-Parganas, Letter Issued) and Received).

But in the early period of the eighteenth century, population began to decrease mainly because of (i) a change in course of main part of Ganga (ii) and predatory activities of the Portuguese. On the available terracotta images, earthen pots, copper coins and some jewellery in the deep forest of Chamta and Chandkhali, Biswanath Ray,[45] has come to the conclusion that 'these signify human inhabitants in the area in the periods of Palas and Senas'. In order to strengthen his argument he also said that 'In Kakdwip area ruins of big buildings, images of Ganesh and earthen seals written in Bengali of Sen's age were found. . . . In a word it is a fact that in ancient times the cultural and social systems of Sundarban were quite developed.' Thus Beveridge's contention of wearing loin-cloth as indicative of uncivilized people has been negated by Satish Mitra 'on the ground that in a tropical country, this was usual and normal'. An interesting aspect of the early settlers of the flood plain frontier is their ethnic composition. Mukherjee[46] traces the movement of at least three predominant Hindu castes into the delta area, the Mahisyas, Namasudras and Pods, whose traditional occupations included cultivation, boating and fishing. Nicholas analyses spatial distribution of these people. He finds that the Mahisyas and Namasudras were dispersed all over Bengal, with a concentration in the eastern and south portions of the delta (Bakarganj, Faridpur, Khulna and Jessore); the pods were settled in the central eastern (24-Parganas) and south-central (Khulna and Jessore) part of the delta. Besides the Adivasis have a long history of cultural assimilation to the dominant communities in the Sundarbans. If they appear to consist of only 17 per cent of the population of the Sundarbans at the beginning of the twentieth century, this is because 60 per cent of them, even at that time, returned themselves as 'Hindu' on the census.[47] Eaton describes in detail the history of human colonization of the Sundarban from AD 1200 to 1750 and Richards and Flint

[45] Biswanath Ray, 'A Study on Economic Problems of Sundarban', in *West Bengal Today: A Fresh Look*, ed. Biswanath Ray, Mittal Publications, New Delhi, 1993: 107-23.

[46] 1938: 279

[47] O'Malley: 69.

provide details of the transformation of the Sundarban thereafter under British rule, whereas Presler[48] discusses the management of the Sundarbans until 1952.

The economy and tenurial patterns of Sundarbans require unbiased modern interpretation.[49] The British colonial government saw the Sundarbans as a resource to be developed in order to increase the productivity of the Bengal countryside. Management of the Sundarbans involved land reclamation and settlement.[50] Though Pargiter's account has been criticized by the Sutapa Chatterjee Sarkar[51] as 'monotonous and uninteresting' but Chatterjee Sarkar had to admit Pargiter's *Revenue History of Sundarbans 1765-1870* 'provided basic introductory reading on the subject and deal exhaustively with British efforts at land reclamation in this area in the eighteenth to mid nineteenth centuries'. This does not detract from their importance as detailed accounts of land settlements and narratives of putting into cultivation the vast uncultivated tract of the Sundarban area. Since there is no full-fledged account on the revenue history of Sundarban till today the scholars had to admit not only the importance of Pargiter's book but make it more enriched by utilizing the vast unexplored

[48] F.A. Presler, 'Forest Management in the Sundarbans, 1875–1952', in J. Seidensticker, R. Kurin and A.K. Townsend (eds.), *The Commons in South Asia: Societal Pressures and Environmental Integrity in the Sundarbans*, Washington, D.C.: The International Center, Smithsonian Institution, 1991.

[49] K.R. Naskar, *Ecology and Environment of Indian Sundarbans in West Bengal*, (Department of Information and Culture, Government of West Bengal, 2000), emphasized on diversity of species in Sundarban and suggested several measures for their conservation in consideration with socio-economic conditions of the region. He advocated for development of transport network and sustainable development. He also provided a glossary of several species and other relevant information on forest and aquatic resources of Sundarban.

[50] Pargiter, op. cit., 1885: 22; for a note on the zamindars' claim over the tracts of the Sundarbans that adjoined their permanently settled states and the government's negative response to such claims, see James Westland: 107-10.; for a discussion of colonial revenue management in the Sundarbans, see Richards and Flint, 1990: 17-33.

[51] Chatterjee Sarkar, op. cit.

treasure troves of West Bengal State Archives[52] and vernacular literature.[53]

The 24-Parganas part of the greater Sundarbans comprised the land between the Hooghly and the Jamuna. Although, the region did not find mention in Todarmal's assessment roll,[54] and the area was depopulated several times in the past due to land subsidence as suggested by geologist Oldham[55] and by the plunder and depredation carried on by the Portuguese and Maghs[56] in seventeenth and early eighteenth centuries.[57] The Portuguese had one major naval base in the Sagar Island on the bank of the Baratala River, besides two small rendezvous: one at Kulpi on the Hooghly and the other at Tardaha on

[52] Presidency Commissioners, Sundarban Records (1829-58) (West Bengal State Archives, Kolkata). Prior to the creation of this series of records of the Land Revenue Miscellaneous Proceedings are available in the Board of Revenue Proceedings for the period 1784-1829. Letters received by the Presidency Commissioners (1829-58) containing in 23 bundles, besides Draft of Letters issued by the Presidency Commissioners (1830-58) throw mines of information as regards the land reclamation policies pursued by the administrators from time to time, the settlement of Kharee in the 24-Parganas (1830-58), *pattahs, kabuliyats* of Choto Basdia, Boro Basdia & Chowk Tatiboonea, the settlement of cultivated lands of Mehal Khowleah, Barishal and *mauza* Ouleapur and lots 217-19 (1834-57) and the property belonging to the Nawab Nazim of Bengal (1836-57) are tips of the iceberg for understanding the economic as well as revenue history of the delta Sundarban.

[53] For details see the Bengali books included in Bibliography.

[54] The settlement of Todar Mall has been explained in the settlement account of Jessore (M.A. Momen, *Final Report on the Survey and Settlement Operation in the District of Jessore, 1920-1924,* Calcutta, Bengal Secretariat Book Depot, 1925: 4, 86-7) and Blochmann's account (H. Blochmann, 'Geographical and Historical Notes on the Burdwan Presidency Divisions of Lower Bengal', in Hunter, op. cit., rpt. 1973: 355).

[55] R.D. Oldham, *A Manual of the Geology of India. Chiefly Compiled from the Observations of the Geological Survey. Stratigraphical and Structural Geology*, 2nd edn., Calcutta and London, 1893: 434.

[56] In the year, 1771, Mr. Rennell's map showed a number of forts marked in Bakarganj area of the Sundarbans mentioned that the whole area of the Sundarbans was 'depopulated by the Maghs' and later on by the Portuguese. The Bay of Bengal trade route was lucrative to them. Thus the collaborative raids hampered the social and economic life of the whole of Bengal, the Sundarbans in particular.

[57] J.J.A. Campos, *History of the Portuguese in Bengal with Maps and Illustrations, with an Introduction by F.J. Monahan,* Calcutta, Butterworth & Co, 1919: 169.

the Bidyadhari River.[58] But some parts of the forest land at least had once rich habitation, is amply proved by the archaeological evidence. One interesting historical feature of the forest is the presence of certain large tanks, masonry structures and high embankments. Their significance is disputed. In some accounts they are seen as evidence that the region in earlier times enjoyed a degree of prosperity and was formerly a widespread civilization which was ultimately destroyed by pirates. In other accounts they are relics of the Portuguese and Magh pirates who 'displaced' the 'original' population of the Sundarbans and lived off salt-making and piracy, preying on the numerous merchant ships which passed through the region.[59] *The Calcutta Review*, July

[58] O'Malley: 34.

[59] Campos, op. cit.: 105; Rathindranath De (op. cit.: 12-13) and the earlier accounts of Francois Bernier (*Travels in the Mogul Empire, 1656-1668*, trans. and ed. A. Constable, Archibald Constable & Co. Ltd, Westminster, London, 1891) and Rennell's (James Rennell, *An Account of the Ganges and Burrampooter Rivers*, Proceedings of the Royal Society of London, London 1781: 87-117) (who travelled through the region during the 1600s and 1700s). The area concerned that is the Sundarbans was called by Mughal emperors 'the paradise of the kingdom', and soon became forested after aggression of different nature that played havoc on its topography. And this beautiful forest tract finally fell to the colonial settlers. (Madhumita Majumdar, 'The Other – The Sundarbans: A Land of Dangers', *The Creative Launcher*, vols. II, IV (October 2017). But simultaneously she was of opinion that when the tank was dug on the Morellgunge estate the traces of inhabitant were found there. Walter Hamilton went on to say that due to the penetration of Maghs of Arakans there were 'many clearings' (Walter Hamilton, *A Geographical, Statistical, and Historical Description of Hindostan and the Adjacent Countries*, vol. 2. John Murray, London, 1820: 84-5). Even though Hamilton's venture in the early twentieth century is documented, little is known about the human history of those people who were either brought there or those who were living in the vicinity of the forest prior to the coming of the British. Sutapa Chatterjee Sarkar echoed the same view and said that 'these people had crossed over from the Arakan coast and being fearless in nature penetrated deep into the islands, cleared the forests and began cultivating the soil to grow rice'. (Sutapa Chatterjee Sarkar, *The Sundarbans Folk Deities, Monsters and Mortals*, Social Science Press, New Delhi, 2010: 17). Citing Walter Hamilton it was her firm conviction that 'Sundarbans have always been regarded as peculiarly adapted for the reception and concealment of river pirates' (fn. 42: 27). It may be coincided with the view of Westland that Maghs settled in the southern portion of Bakarganj and which had been reclaimed by the latter. But Westland had doubts about the Maratha menace that they forced the locals 'to run away and seek shelter

1889, was happy to report the second explanation of the potentially prestigious ruins: 'these two facts [piracy and salt making] go some way to explain the existence of many masonry remains without resorting to the theory of a former widespread civilization'.[60]

An intensive study on the land reclamation policy by the early British rulers[61] and later on by the Colonial Raj demonstrates a graphic design of the extent of colonial penetration in the life and culture of the deltaic region. On the acquisition of the district of 24-Parganas by the East India Company as a grant from the Mughal Emperor the country even in the vicinity of Calcutta Claude Russell was appointed as Collector for the period 1770-3.[62] Sundarbans and thus the vast wild and uncultivated land were divided into several

---

elsewhere'. Beveridge, while writing the history of Bakarganj, particularly the agrarian and economic aspects, had confusion in his mind about the population capacity and cultivation factor. In order to establish his arguments he referred to the quantities of salt manufacture, which, according to Chatterjee Sarkar, was that 'Evidences suggest that large quantities of salt were manufactured in Sandwip. This militates against the view of extensive cultivation, for salt could not have been made without the great expenditure of fuel and this of course implied the existence of large tracts of jungle. .. and was always a great obstacle to the clearing and colonizing of the *chars* and islands in Bakarganj and Noakhali'(Chatterjee Sarkar, op. cit.: 18). The infiltration of the Portuguese pirates became an additional scourge in the sufferings of the common inhabitants. This chaotic situation came into the notice of Westland while he was writing about Jessore. The British in 1770, who hoped to derive revenue from the reclaimed land, ensure public peace by driving out dacoits from the area and to increase rice production.

[60] De: 51.

[61] The British colonial policies towards the reclamation of the Sundarbans are found in the Records of the Presidency Commissioner, Sundarban, well maintained in the record room of West Bengal State Archives, Kolkata. It appears from the records during the period under review, that, the reclamation of the Sundarbans between the Presidency Commissioner and the Sundarbans Commissioner, while for the period, 23 December 1844 to January 1846, the correspondence is between the Presidency Commissioner and the uncovenanted Deputy Collector in the Sundarbans.

[62] Anil Chandra Lahiri, *Final Report on the Survey and Settlement Operations in the District of 24-Parganas, 1924-1933*, Alipur, Supdt. Govt. Printing, 1936: 107. For a general history of the settlement of Sundarban, see (Manindranath Jana, *Sundarbaner Samaj O Sanskriti* (in Bengali), Kolkata, Dipali Book House, 1984).

'lots'[63] that was reclaimed and used for human settlement. The process of reclamations of the 'uncultivated' land was begun in the adjoining areas of Sundarbans and granted farming of uncultured jungle lands of the 24-Parganas in the vicinity of Calcutta to private individuals. The Sundarbans, along with other lands lying outside the area of cultivation and settlement, fell under state ownership.[64] Claude Russell allowed 1 rupee 8 *annas* per acre leases. These lands were called the *patitabadi taluks* or the tenures for the reclamation of wasteland.[65] The *patitabadi*[66] *taluk* system faced two major problems by way of unclear demarcation of reclaimed land and the need for embankment to keep the paddy land safe from the brackish river waters. In this first phase of unregulated deforestation, much of the revenue came from forest products including timber. However, it was gradually declining and the need for conservation was voiced from within the administration. Consequently, the first initiative for conservation was also mooted under the British rule. In 1790, the decennial settlement was made, which was declared permanent in 1793.[67] The Permanent Settlement was not followed in practice in the Sundarbans. There is a detailed explanation of its reason in the account of Pargiter[68] and official

[63] This was indeed a logical step after the segregation of the entire forest into blocks. Each block comprised of lots which were to be sold/auctioned off. This period of reclamation was much more dynamic in nature and yielded better results in terms of both the total amount of land reclaimed and the total amount of colonial revenue collected. This dynamism is best portrayed by the fact the rules for land reclamation got changed three times in this period of 50 years.

[64] Pargiter, *A Revenue History of the Sundarbans from 1765 to 1870*: 1934: 1.

[65] Hunter: 318.

[66] '*Patitabad*' or waste land which paid no rent to Government enabled them to draw *ryots* from zamindar in late nineteenth century (N.K. Sinha, *The Economic History of Bengal: From Plassey to the Permanent Settlement*, vol. II, Calcutta, Firma K.L. Mukhopadhyay, 1962: 108). In *patitabadi taluqs*, lessees made much progress and the neighbouring zamindars also promoted cultivation – so that for the next forty years the area was cleared almost to Sagar Island on the south, and Canning town on the east.

[67] Anil Chandra Banerjee, *History of India*, A. Mukherjee & Co., Calcutta, 6th edn., July 1995: 433-41; Pargiter, *A Revenue History of the Sundarbans from 1765 to 1870*, 1834: 36.

[68] Pargiter: 3-14.

correspondences.[69] The Board of Revenue papers[70] also affirmed that the whole of the Sundarban react except Henckell's *Taluks* and *Pattitabadi Mahals* were excluded from the zamindaris. In 1793, Cornwallis, the British Governor-General of Bengal imposed a new rule of landed property for Bengal under the terms of the 'Permanent Settlement.' Meanwhile, the old zamindari cultivated areas of the upper delta had been permanently settled in 1793. The Proclamation of the Permanent Settlement is reproduced in Regulation 1 of 1793. It may be read in two parts: first, recognition of the *status quo* of the zamindars as directed by the statute, and second, limitation of the public demand for ever to the amounts then fixed.[71] The Permanent Settlement of 1793 incorporated the Zamindari system in the legal structure.[72] Even in the first few years of the settlement of 1793, there were instances of transfer of mercantile fortunes to land purchases.[73] The Sundarbans area remained outside the Permanent Settlement of 1793 but it made many changes in the boundary of Jessore, Nadia and Pabna, as they pertain to the final boundary settlement. In 1796, the boundary between Jessore and Nadia was demarcated by the Administrative Order of 1796.

[69] It was also found in the correspondence written to J.C. Erskine by Commissioner of Sundarbans of the Presidency Commissioner Sundarban Records, 1829-58 (West Bengal State Archives) and also of the Copy Book of Letters Received dated 8 April 1836 and 20 August 1838 where in Dampier writes '... I must say that I consider many Proceedings to have been extremely injudicious but that the several of this form appear to me to be most erroneous and likely to produce serious loss to the Government. There are lands of which the farmer has not acquired possession but cultivates them and does not pay any rent to the government'.

[70] Letters from President and members of Board of Revenue to Governor-General in Council, dated 28 October 1814.

[71] Rai Bahadur M.N. Gupta, *Analytical Survey of Bengal Regulations (And Act of Parliament Relating to India, Up to 1833)*, Calcutta, University of Calcutta, 1943: 278-9.

[72] Binay Bhushan Chaudhuri, Rajat Kanta Ray, Ratnalekha Ray and Chittabrata Palit, *Banglar Krishi Samajer Garan* (in Bengali), Calcutta, K.P. Bagchi & Co., 1996: 76-7.

[73] Dharma Kumar and Tapan Ray Chaudhuri (eds.), *The Cambridge Economic History of India*, vol. 2, Delhi, Orient Longman in association with Cambridge University Press, 1984: 113.

In the second phase it was followed by Tilman Henckell,[74] for the area between the Haringhata or estuary of Baleswar River on the east and the Raimangal River on the west, who submitted certain proposals to Warren Hastings, the Governor-General on 20 December 1783 and pressed to grant leases of the forest land in the Sundarbans to people and settle the boundaries of estates with local landlords.[75] Labourers were hired from the Chotanagpur Plateau, present day Orissa and Arakan coast to Myanmar to reclaim the mangrove wetlands of the delta.[76] This large-scale migration that happened in the Sundarbans during colonial rule was not the first of its kind. Prior to the eighteenth and nineteenth centuries, these mangrove wetlands were inhabited in semi-permanent ways by fishermen, woodcutters, pirates and cultivators.[77] The scheme provided that the grantees or *talukdars* should receive a large portion of the land leased to them rent-free, and pay rent for the remainder after a certain number of years, at the rate of 2 *annas* per *bigha*, to be gradually increased to 8 *annas* per *bigha*, which was the maximum amount to be levied. The tenures thus created were evidently intended to be of a permanent character. The process began with Jessore, Bakarganj, Khulna and 24-Parganas. During this period an interesting socio-economic development took place as well with the birth of the *talukdar* in the

[74] He was appointed as Judge and Magistrate of Jessore in 1781, with Mr. Richard Roche as his assistant. The story goes that when Henckell's agent was clearing parts of the Sundarbans, he was very much disturbed by tigers which attacked his people. He accordingly affixed to the place the name of Henckell, expecting that the tigers, dreading that name, would no more disturb him (Westland, *District of Jessore*: 106). To avoid the loss of lives of salt manufacturers the Company rulers declared prize money for tiger-killing at the rate of Rs. 10 per tiger increasing to Rs. 200 in 1909. Ghosh has rightly commented that with Hunter, the colonial discourse of ' civilizing Sundarban' was gradually legitimized (Aditya Ghosh, *Sustainability Conflicts in Coastal India: Hazards, Changing Climate and Development Discourses in the Sundarbans*, Cham, Springer International Publishing AG, 2018: 73; Board of Revenue, 20 July 1789).

[75] Pargiter, 1885. According to H.J. Rainey ('Famines in Bengal and the Reclamation of the Sundarban as a Means of Mitigating Them' (*The Calcutta Review*, Thomas S. Smith, Calcutta, vol. 59: 330-49) that the first scheme for the reclamation of the Sundarban dates as far back as the 4 April 1784.

[76] Amitesh Mukhopadhyay: 5.

[77] Annu Jalais, *Forests of Tigers: People, Politics and Environment in the Sundarbans*, New Delhi, Routledge, 2010: 183.

Sundarbans.[78] This social group was the by-product of the constant disputes between the colonial state and the local landlords. The tenures thus created were evidently intended to be of a permanent character. A scheme of arrangement was drawn up for cultivation in the reclaimed area – 'Cultivation in the Sundarbans – Jessore. Collector was directed to submit a separate report on the present state of affairs, and to furnish information how far the original objects of the plan had been attained, together with an account of receipts and disbursements from the commencement of the undertaking to the present period.'[79] A man of great ability, Henckell's chief aim, not, like most others, was to consider only the commercial interests of the Company. In the Sundarbans, Henckell inaugurated a system of reclamation, which, has converted large areas of forest into fertile rice fields. After explaining how the forest trees have to be cleared away and the thick brushwood hacked down, Westland went on to say unless the greatest care is taken of the land so cleared it will spring back into jungle and become as bad as ever. So great is the evil fertility of the soil, that reclaimed land neglected for a single year will present to the next year's cultivator a forest of reeds (*nal*). He may cut it and burnt it down, but it will spring up again almost as thick as ever, and it takes about three eradications to expel this reed when once it has grown. The soil, too, must be cultivated for ten or twelve years before it loses this tendency to cover itself with reed jungle. When a sufficient number of people are gathered on a new clearing they tend, of course, to form a settlement, and to remain permanently where they are. But the furthest advanced parts of the cultivation, and some also of those which are not new or remote from old lands, are carried on upon a different principle. A large number of husbandmen, who live and cultivate lands in the regularly settled districts to the north, has also lands in the Sundarbans, which they hold under different landlords. He remodeled the police force, to develop the Sundarbans, and to originate the plan for reclaiming them by granting plots of land to persons undertaking to bring them under cultivation. Mr. Henckell's

[78] Sarkar, 2010.

[79] Board of Revenue, 18 March; 19 April 1790, West Bengal State Archives, Kolkata.

plan was also to lease plots of land to *raiyats* who would clear his 'own plot of land' by employing wood cutters and migrated labourers. But successive efforts by the Board of Revenue and the Collector of 24-Parganas to lease out distant forest lands for reclamation and settlement did not succeed because of the ever increasing claims of neighbouring zamindars over the reclaimed lands. Tilman Henckell,[80] drew up an ambitious plan in 1783 of bringing into cultivation a vast tract of forest land by leasing out small plots to *raiyats* and creating a body of independent peasant proprietors holding directly under the government did not succeed due to opposition from the neighbouring zamindars.[81] In 1786, Henckell marked off by bamboo stakes the line which he took to be the northern limit of the Sundarbans and the southern boundary of the zamindari land.[82] Mr. Henckell expressed a conviction that if the boundaries of the lands held by the neighbouring zamindars were settled, the number of grants would at once increase; but the Board of Revenue had grown lukewarm about the whole scheme and in 1790, it was practically abandoned. Several of the old grants forthwith relapsed into jungle. [83] Henckell had led

[80] In 1781, Mr Tilman Henckell came to Murali as Judge and Magistrate. His jurisdiction then extended over the tract now comprising the present districts of Jessore, Khulna and Faridpur. In 1786, a new collectorate was formed with Jessore as its headquarters. In 1787 Faridpur was excluded from the magisterial jurisdiction of Mr. Henckell (Momen, op. cit.: 2).Henckell's policy towards land reclamation faced stiff resistance from the local magnates considering it as an 'encroachment on their rights'. O'Malley (O'Malley, op. cit.: 41) and Sengupta (Rabindra Kumar Sengupta, 'Importance of the Sundarbans region in West Bengal's Economy', in Kanan Gopal Bagchi, Sunil Kumar Munsi and Rabindranath Bhattacharyya (eds.), *The Bhagirathi-Hooghly Basin,* Calcutta, Calcutta University, 1944), classified the Bengal delta and identified the Sundarban region as the active delta region. He had dealt the matter in length which apparently provided the *ryots* rent-free tenures that by virtue of other migrants of various districts cleared the land, constructed embankments and planted rice in the alluvial soil.

[81] Anil Chandra Lahiri: 107.

[82] Ibid.

[83] Sarit Kumar Mukherjee, *Islands of India*, Publications Divisions, Ministry of Information and Broadcasting, Government of India, 1992; Gautam Kumar Bera and Asok Kumar Mukhopadhyay, 'Syncretism at Sundarbans – Anthropological and Linguistic Dimension', in Gautam Kumar Bera and Vijoy S. Sahay (eds.), *In the Lagoons of the Gangetic Delta*, Mittal Publications, New Delhi, 2010: 9-24.

to the inception of a system of reclamation which led to the conversion of forest to fertile paddy fields. He wanted to create a group of peasant proprietors directly under the government. With this purpose in mind he granted about 150 leases in 1785. He established three *ganjes* (stations) in the heart of Sundarbans and in such places where clearings had been made in order to assist in their development by providing markets for sale of produce. One was situated at Henckellganj,[84] now known as Hingalganj and the other two at Khulna. These markets helped the sale of produce and supplies to boatmen traversing the waterways. He devised measures for the protection of the boat routes. Reclamation of the lands were brought about by demarcation of the lots bordered by streams, construction of embankment along the banks of streams which surrounded the lots, subsequent construction of strong dams across the mouths of smaller streams which ran into the block in order to keep the saline water out of reach. After the completion of these works, deforestation of the tracts, digging of tanks and construction of huts for future cultivation were followed. Initially this process of reclamation was very successful owing to high production of paddy and fishes. Prior to land reclamation the entry of saline muddy water through the tidal creeks during high tides used to raise the level of the lands, facilitating the land building process.[85] The government drew an estimate of 6 lakhs *bighas* of land that would be under cover of cultivation and would help derive revenue in tune of 7.5 lakhs in seven years. Colonial literature does mention that human activity in the Sundarban region was scarce. It is true that as far as the study of the history of this locality is concerned, we remain grossly and largely dependent on the English. It was the development of capitalistic economy that initiated the exploitation of the Sundarbans. The European settlement in the Sundarbans was practically a capitalistic settlement. Mr. Henckell was also appointed

[84] Mr. Henckell's native agent named the place after Mr. Henckell in the hope that the local tigers would no longer molest people in the area out of respect and fear of the name of the first English Magistrate of Jessore. However, reports of tiger attacks continued to reach the district headquarters with usual regularity.

[85] Karabi Das, 'Sundarban Embankments: A Study Along Suryaberiya River, Sambhunagar Island, Gosaba, West Bengal', *International Journal of Current Research*, vol. 8, Issue 5, May 2016: 32187-95.

in 1784 'Superintendent for the Cultivation of the Sundarban' and devoted himself to the extra duties imposed upon him at his own request. In the first four years nearly 50,000 *bighas* were leased out (because clearer and cultivators in such places are supplied with pure drinking water and have not to procure it from a distance) besides, substantial or experience bunds or embankments, to keep out the salt water from the rice crop, are necessary. In 1792, these had all disappeared except sixteen and in their case the character of the scheme had been modified for the lessees developed into *talukdars,* their lands being called Henckell's *taluks.*[86] This seems to have been the result of the severe struggle to which they were subjected and which eliminated the worker leases. Many of the original grants were amalgamated and the influential men who survived could not be called *ryot*s. Probably the grants were always too large to be cultivated by a *ryot*; and in any case those were not days in which a small man could stand alone. Henckell spent a lot of time and energy in settling and bringing change in the deltaic region. Tilman Henckell tried on reclamation of land for cultivation and rehabilitation of salt manufactures in the Sundarbans and for which he was very much confident of grand success. He hoped of huge lease of reclaimed land by zamindars and *talukdars*, but in reality it did not happen as it appeared as Utopian Scheme. He tried his best to overcome the hurdles faced for the

[86] Few of Henckell's grants survived the confusion which followed his retirement and the hostility of the zamindars after the Permanent Settlement. Those which survived had changed their character and came to be known as Henckell's '*Taluks*' and were even designated parganas. In fact instead of being cultivators, the leases had 'acquired the name and status of *Talukdars*'. Three of these grants survived in Bakarganj, Kaleran Chandipur, known as Pargana Bijainagar, on the extreme east of the district and two islands in the Meghna Estuary, Ram Hari Char and Char Kalmi. Henckell's three grants were actually for 256 acres and a revenue of Rs. 348.This can be very well understood from a different source that the amount of forest land being leased out fell progressively from 21,000 *bighas* in 1785 to just 1,603 *bighas* in 1789 (Haraprasad Chattopadhyaya, *The Mystery of the Sundarbans*, Calcutta, A. Mukherjee & Co., 1999). Muhammed Sami, Rajballabh Rai, Ram Ratan Mitra, Rani Sankari Dasi and Owen John Elias were the foremost among the land grabbers in the Sundarban. Rajballabh owned extensive estates in the 24-Parganas, Nadia and Jessore. Henckell defined the limit of the forest by planting bamboos as far as east as Bazrugmedpur. This line was well known as Henckell's '*bansari*' (Jack, op. cit.: 114).

reclamation scheme of the Sundarbans. Tilman Henckell proposed in a letter, dated 26 March 1790, a statement made of the progress of the scheme as following – in 1785, 7,000 acres, in 1787, 4,364 acres, in 1788, 2,704 acres; and in 1789, 534 acres and revenue from the grants of reclaimed land first became payable in 1788. But the members of the Board of Revenue were not satisfied by the statements and probable areas of the newly-cleared lands, rather they then expressed more stress on salt manufacture than cultivation, though the Board were convinced at the first time and agreed in favour of the scheme proposed by Tilman Henckell, Collector of Jessore.[87] He also tried to protect the *mahindars* or salt boilers from the clutches of the *malangis* or middlemen. Salt Agency entered into contracts for the supply of salt. The *mahindars* took advances from the *malangis* and thus fell under their servitude the *malangis* had not only the powers to drive them to work, but also insisted on receiving Rs. 20 for every Rs. 4 advanced. Henckell's measures though initially of much help to the lessees could not check the zamindars that proved too strong for the new settlers. In 1792 they all disappeared, except for 16 and for them the character of the scheme was modified because the lessees had developed into *talukdars*, their lands being called Henckell's *taluks*.

In each phase of land reclamation, people have neglected the vital role played by the tidal channels and creeks, i.e. the nerves and veins of the largest estuarine delta. A distinctive feature in the reclamation and cultivation of the Sundarban lands is the embankment of the water inlets. The banks of the rivers are higher than the lands further removed from them, and the whole of the Sundarbans may be regarded as an aggregation of basins where the higher level of the sides prevents the water from coming in and flooding and spilling over the interior. Many of these basins are so formed that left to themselves they would remain under flood, as they communicate with the surrounding channels by

[87] 'The Sunderbans', *The Calcutta Review*, vol. XXXI, 1858: 385-411.

Mr Timan Henckell's report refers only to the Eastern Sunderbans which are as follows:

1816 Mr D. Scott; 1817 Mr. A.T. Lind; 1820 Mr. R. Hunter; 1821 Mr. J. Mills; 1822 Mr. D. Dale; 1823 Mr. R.D. Mangles; 1825 Mr. J. Lewis; 1827 Mr. W. Dampier; 1835 Mr. C. Grant; 1836 Mr. M. Gilmore; 1837 Mr. G.T. Shakespear; 1839 Mr. F.B. Kemp; 1841 Mr. M.A. Shawe; 1842 Mr. Baboo Umakanth Sen.

means of *khals* or small water courses, which penetrate the bank; and a great part of reclamation work consists in keeping out the water and thus bringing under cultivation the marsh land.

In employing this method, all the inlets from the surrounding channels were embanked, and smaller channels, called *poyuns*, were opened round their ends. The inlets themselves were too big to be kept under control, but these *poyuns* can easily be so kept. This embanking was usually done in November, after the rivers had gone down. When the tide was low, the channels were opened, and the water from the inside drains off;when it was high, the channels were closed.Always the floods in this delta have been thought only as a curse and rivers as its agent here. Neither have they enlightened the need of evaluating these tidal channels or creeks as a resource which makes shelter for the rare species, nor have they given much time to the newly formed immature floodplains to be matured for agricultural success for future generations here. In recent days, reckless expansion of the built-up area in the restricted core and active deltaic part became a common issue in the so called Sundarban Reserved Forest. After the departure of Henckell his successor in March 1790 pronounced the scheme to be a failure due to non-availability of data for determining what was Sundarban. The Board and Government discouraged, the scheme was abandoned on 20 August 1790, and it was more than a century before another attempt to settle the Sundarbans directly with the cultivators was made. After the failure of Henckell's attempt to deal direct with the cultivator, the accepted policy was to find a capitalist who would undertake the task of reclamation; and eighty years were spent in devising terms which would not only attract the capitalist, but also compel him to reclaim. Captain Robertson surveyed the main water-routes from the Hooghly to the Noakhali district in 1810. In 1813-14 Lt. Blane surveyed a portion of the sea coast, east of the Hooghly. Lt. W.E. Morrieson surveyed the Sundarbans with the exception of the sea face which formed the basis of all subsequent maps of the Sundarbans.[88] On 24 October 1814, the Court of Directors expressed their views on the subject of reclamation and settlement of Sundarban lands. The Directors approved the general

[88] Lahiri, op. cit.: 107.

principle that lands not included within the boundaries of permanently settled estates, where the property of the Government and liable to such assessment as the Government might think fit to impose. Even in the later period an enquiry was conducted by Smelt, Assistant to the Collector of Jessore in 1815 for assessment of excess land and unauthorized cultivation. Simultaneously D. Scott was empowered for surveying of reclaimed lands and assessment of collecting revenues, the details of which are found in the Regulation IX of 1816.[89] In 1816 a 47-mile long canal was proposed from Calcutta to Channel Creek, the underestimated cost being put at only Rs. 10 lakhs. These focused on Sundarbans and many surveys were carried out. Even a report on the state of affairs in Jessore (modern Khulna) drawn up by the members, Messers. Rocke & Colebrook was forwarded by the Board of Revenue to the Government on 17 May 1814. Certain recommendations were made by the members for disposal of Sundarbans lands. On 11 June 1814 the Governor-General affirmed the principle that all lands were liable to assessment and approved the Board's proposals for settlement of such lands. D. Scott was then appointed to determine the claims of the zamindars. His main jurisdiction extended over the 24-Parganas. He was also entrusted with the determination of the boundaries between the zamindary lands and the Sundarbans with reference to the title deeds. He was also directed to consider the question of resumption of lands held under invalid title. Starting his operation from Chingri Creek Scott was to proceed towards parganas Hatiaghar, Shahpur and Khari to the south. Mr. Scott completed the assessment of excess lands of 122 *taluks* in 11 parganas. In 1817 the Sundarban Commissioner was entrusted with the investigations of forty-eight *katkina taluks* and twenty *pattitabadi taluks*.[90] Mr Pargiter wrote, 'The *patitabadi* mahals extended from the salt water lake (modern Dhapa area) along the edge of the Sundarbans jungle to the south-west corner of the district below Kulpi; but the line was broken in four places by *katkina* or zamindari lands., viz., Bhagabanpur, Nalua, Ranaghata and Khari'.[91] In order to

[89] Letter from President, Members of Board of Revenue to Sundarban Commissioner: Board of Revenue Proceedings, dated 20 August 1816.

[90] Lahiri: 108.

[91] Pargiter, 1934: 16

determine the extent of the (i) lands the property of the State and re-claimed, and (ii) the lands claimed by individuals but believed to be the property of the State, a survey was ordered for the whole of the 24-Parganas Sundarbans from the river Hooghly. D. Scott, the first Commissioner began inquiries and measurements in the area south and east of Calcutta. It was seen that encroachment and reclamation were carried on, partly by the lessees, partly by the zamindars and partly by other authorized persons. Such lands were held without paying revenue to the state and the proposal to levy revenue met with opposition from interested persons, specially the zamindars, who claimed the whole of the forest. A separate administration of revenue matters for the Sundarbans was first initiated in 1816 with the creation of the office of the Commissioner in the Sundarbans under Regulation IX of 1816[92] with all the duties, powers and authority of the Collector of land revenue. He helped to bring about the 'Permanent Settlement' of Bengal by information he was able to give to Cornwallis when making inquiry into the land revenue of the Presidency, when the settlement was made, 1789, Henckell had left Jessore to become Collector, Judge and Magistrate of Rajshahi, was succeeded by Richard Roche, the rule of these two men covers the period 1781-93, when Lord Cornwallis' reforms were completed.[93] Leases were granted to *ryots,* since Permanent Settlements were discarded as unsuitable for the diffuse territory. The leases granted by Claude Russell originated the *patitabadi taluks* of 24-Parganas; Henckell's leases originated the

[92] By Regulation IX of 1816, an officer under the appellation of Commissioner in the Sundarbans was appointed with the duties, powers and authority of a Collector of land revenue subject to the control and superintendence of the Board of Revenue. Revenue administration of Sundarbans as guided by Regulation IX by 1816 was changed by Bengal Act of 1905 and Sundarban was parcelled out in 3 parts – one was amalgamated with Bakarganj district, one with 24-Parganas and the third with Khulna. The Collector of these three districts since then managed all matters connected with revenue administration of the tract lying in their regulative Jurisdiction and the holders of the estate in Sundarbans paid the land revenue fixed at periodical settlements into the treasury of Barishal, Alipur, Khulna, the headquarter stations of the three districts concerned. But exploitation by poor peasants remained same almost.

[93] C.E. Buckland, *Dictionary of Indian Biography,* London, Swan Sonnenschein & Co., Lim., 1906: 198.

taluks of Jessore and Bakarganj.[94] Of that year, and covenanted officers, (among whom we may mention the name of the late Mr. William Dampier, father of Mr. H.L. Dampier, B.C.S.) continuously filled that post up to 1844.[95] From a return furnished by A.M.G. Shaw, B.C.S., in 1841, or three years previous to the Sundarban ceasing to be under the direct sway of the members of the Civil Service, we find the gross collections of the Sundarban then amounted to Rs. 1,27,910, and establishment charges, including Commissioner's salary and boat allowance, to Rs. 24,390, leaving a balance of favour of Government of over Rs. 1 lakh. This officer was charged with demarcating and managing the water-logged forests and swamps of the lower delta. He was to regulate and encourage extraction of timber and fuel wood for the growing needs of Calcutta and other towns and cities in Bengal. It was the duty of the Commissioner in 1816 to define the southern boundary of the districts of 24-Parganas, Nadiya (Nadia), Jessore, Dacca, Jellalpur and Bakarganj so as to enable the government to fix the limits of the country to be placed under his authority .But it involved a lot of uncertainties as it was difficult to assess the length of cultivable land towards south resulting the passing of Regulation XXIII for defining the right of the government 'to the revenue of the lands not included in the boundaries of estates for which Permanent Settlement was made in the districts' already mentioned. The

[94] Fawcus, op. cit.: 88.

[95] The Presidency Commissioner in his letter no. 195, dated 19 September 1843 recommended to the Board for the abolition of the office of the Sundarban Commissioner on the ground that the distribution of the jurisdiction among the Collectors would secure a saving in expenditure, greater convenience to the public, and a more efficient check on the tehsildars. The Board supported the proposal and the Government abolished the office. The abolition took effect from 1 May 1844 but from 3 May 1844 the Presidency Commissioner continued to correspond with the late Commissioner in the Sundarbans till the end of the following December. An uncovenanted Deputy Collector was retained as special officer in the Sundarbans of the 24-Parganas and Jessore under the Collectors of those districts and the Bakarganj portion was placed under a Deputy Collector subordinate to the Collector of that district. This system did not work well and the Presidency Commissioner, again, recommended for the revival of the Sundarban Commission in 1845 in the form of an independent uncovenanted Deputy Collectorate over the whole of the Sundarbans, the Bakarganj portion being brought back under his charge. The Board supported the proposal and Government re-established the office in December 1845.

Commissioner had to embark upon a periodic survey and assessment in the district of 24-Parganas where such frequent encroachments were noticed. However, the Commissioner was above all to ensure that private landowners cleared, settled and reclaimed Sundarbans forests and swamps for rice cultivation. Regulation XXIII of 1817 sought to put a stop to this litigation. Maintaining the government's 'inherent title' to a share of the produce of all lands cultivated in the Sundarbans, it re-classified these lands as 'encroached' upon by the zamindar landowners. Despite this, many landholders persisted in advancing claims. By Regulation XXIII of 1817 Government expressly declared that the Sundarbans was the property of the State and asked for the revenue of lands not included within the boundaries of estates for which a settlement had been made. It, however, began to entertain misgivings as to whether it was not debarred by the Permanent Settlement from dealing with such lands. In 1821 the Sundarbans offices was reconstituted though not till 1830 the rules for the grants of the forest was issued. The applicants were mostly European residents of Calcutta.

Regulation VII of 1822 made it obligatory for the district administration to provide record of rights to the *raiyats* and the leaseholders.[96] To cope with this formidable task, the enormous responsibility of the Commissioner was reduced by transferring the duty of revenue collection to the Collectors.[97] Since it was difficult to collect revenue from the newly settled land in 1817, Regulation asserted the legal claim of the share of the government of the produce of all lands of Sundarban but the problem continued for which the Commissioner of Sundarbans surveyed the lands belonging to the jurisdiction of 24-Parganas and later in 1822-3 by virtue of Morrieson's map the forest lands were divided into blocks and thus began the introduction of Sundarban Lots.[98] It appears from the letter

[96] A.C. Lahiri, *Final Report*: 121.

[97] A.C. Guha, *A Brief Sketch of Land System in Bengal and Bihar*, Calcutta & Simla, Thacker Spink & Co., 1915: 203.

[98] Letter from the Governor-General to President Members of Board of Revenue dated 11 November 1817 and 23 March followed by 28 May, 20 July, 3 September 1822 and 29 January and 23 August 1823. There is large number of files out of which a tip of the iceberg is mentioned here.

of the Presidency Commissioner to Sundarban Commissioner that the 'grantee of lot applied to have the boundary defined, and surveys were made.' The Presidency Commissioner . . . held that the matter was one for the civil court alone, but the Board here ruled in 1857 that no suit having been instituted, the Sundarban Commissioner had power to and should decide the dispute under section 2, clause (6) and the 33 following sections of Regulation VII of 1822 applied to all Sundarban lands, whether under settlement or not.'[99] Mr. Gomees then surveyed and reported that the disputed law, and the litigation was protracted till 1880, when the Privy Council finally adjudged the land to lot. In 1822, Ensign Prinsep was directed by the Sundarban Commissioner to survey the cultivated area and the forest. Mr. Dale himself undertook to measure the *patitabadi mahals*. Twenty-eight *taluks* were measured by him in 1822. He also made an elaborate survey of the strip of the jungle bordering the cultivation from the river Bidyadhari to the Hooghly. In November 1823, the Sundarban Commissioner Mr. Mangles proceeded with the investigation of the claims of the individuals in the *patitabadi* and Sundarban lands. In October 1824, the Sundarban Commissioner Mr. Mangles drafted a Jungleburi lease form which was approved by the Government and the Board of Revenues in 1825.[100] The survey of *patitabadi mahals* situated in parganas Muragacha and Medanmalla could not be finished by Ensign Prinsep and were taken up by Lieutenant Mallock in 1828. The year 1827 appears to have been spent in deliberations about the right of the State in the Sundarbans. The existing Regulations were insufficient to safeguard the interests of the State in the Sundarbans and it was considered necessary to introduce new legislation defining the right of property of the State in the Sundarbans. With that end in view Regulation III was enacted on 12 June 1828. In 1828, however, the British assumed the proprietary right to the Sundarbans and, in 1830, began leasing out tracts of the forests 'for undertaking the clearing operations preparatory to planting paddy. Then followed forty-five years of rapacious reclamation until 1875-6 when the

[99]Letter from the Presidency Commissioner to Sundarban Commissioner, No. 34, dated 3 March 1857 (Collectorate Records).

[100] Board of Revenue to Sundarban Commission, dated 5 April 1825.

government declared unleased forest reserved and placed it under the jurisdiction of the Forest Department'.[101] In the year 1828,[102] W. Dampier and Lt. A. Hodges were appointed as the Sundarbans' Commissioner and Surveyor[103] respectively to demarcate this land and to ensure that revenues could flow from those uninhabited and newly reclaimed parts of the wetlands which were not included in the arrangements of Permanent Settlement and in order to earn more revenues from such wetlands, the government came up with a new scheme in 1829 by which it was declared that lands free of any taxes to the government for twenty years were made available to wealthy persons who had the capacity to carry on reclamation with the motive to attract new grantees and reduce the burden on the colonial exchequer of reclaiming the remote parts of the Sundarbans wetlands. To establish their exclusive right over the Sundarbans, the Government brought in Regulation III of 1828, declaring that 'The uninhabited tract known by the name of the Sundarbans has ever been, and is hereby declared still to be, the property of the State'.[104]

[101] R.M. Eaton, 'Human Settlements and Colonization in the Sundarbans 1200-1750' Paper presented at the workshop on The Commons in South Asia: Societal Pressures and Environmental Integrity in the Sundarbans, held at Smithosonian Institution, Washington DC, 20-1 November 1987. Reclamation and expansion of human settlement into the Sundarbans 'started with a conflict between the colonial state desirous of making inroads into these wetlands for the purposes of revenue earning and the landlords or cultivators exerting their proprietary right on the ground that the wetlands belonged to them' (Amitesh Mukhopadhyay, op. cit.: 27).

[102] F.D. Ascoli, *A Revenue History of the Sundarbans from 1870-1920*, 1934: 4.

[103] This survey was recorded in a series of *rubakaris* which mentioned its course and names the villages, estates and streams which lay alongside it. Rivers usually formed its limit. The proceedings were conducted in the presence of the zamindars and their agents and all other parties interested. Hodges map was published by Mr. Wood in 1831. The land included within the Dampier-Hodges line consisted of reclamation and forest, as the line was meant to demarcate the boundary of the forest at the time of the Permanent Settlement. In Bakarganj reclamation had proceeded and was reported to have been most active in the east, where the Maghs had colonized not only the Rabnabad Islands, but Lalua, Baliatali and other portions of the mainland as well. The Dampier-Hodges line was conclusive that all land to the south of it was not included in the Permanent Settlement, but it did not end the attempts of the Sundarbans Commission to resume.

[104] Commissioners of Revenue and Circuit were appointed throughout Bengal by

By 1828 the State received all the lands surreptitiously encroached on and all the forest in 24-Parganas. Regulation III of 1828 then declared that these tracts of land had always been government, not private property (notably under the Mughals) and that therefore they should remain so.[105] The Sundarbans were proclaimed the property of the state – and as having in no way been alienated from landholders, as the area had lain 'waste' at the time of the Permanent Settlement of 1793, and therefore not included in its provisions for zamindar landownership.[106] Regulation III of 1828 also declared the right of the state over the recent cultivation and the forest. It enacted that the boundary of the Sundarbans forest should be determined by the Sundarbans Commissioner and lay down by correct survey. In order to proclaim the Sundarbans as the property of the state Regulation III of 1828 was carried out by William Dampier and Alexander Hodges to bring the lands under cultivation between the Permanent Settlement and 1828.[107] The allotments made by Prinsep in the 24-Parganas were incorporated in the map and the same system was continued by Lt. Hodges as far as the River Pasar in the modern Khulna district. He

---

Regulation I of 1829 and the Sundarban Commissioner was placed in subordination to the Revenue Commissioner of the Presidency Division, then called the Commissioner of Revenue and Circuit for the 18th or Jessore Division (see also, Eaton, op. cit.).

105 Pargiter, 1934: 22. Jack has commented that the 'The provisions of Regulation III of 1828 were very trenchant. The boundary of the Sundarban forest was to be laid down by accurate survey on the spot and could only be impugned by an appeal to a Special Commissioner on the single ground that a specific quantity of land included within the boundary was in the effective possession of the appellant at the time of the Permanent Settlement' (op. cit.: 115).

106 Ibid: 12. The right of the state had been established after long controversy and the claims of the zamindars overthrown. The Board of Revenue advised against the claim on the ground that it would be prejudicial to bonafide colonists and the Government decided in 1828 that the border zamindar should have an exclusive right to settlement, but other things being equal might be allowed a preference as an act of grace.

107 Presidency Commissioner, Sundarban Records, 28 August and 30 October 1828. For a comprehensive study on land reclamation policies followed in the Sundarbans scholar should consult Chatterjee Sarkar (*The Sundarbans*, op. cit.). She has rightly commented that 'these changes partly reflected wider currents in official policy and ideology and partly the increasing cost and difficulty of reclaiming remote Sundarban tracts' (Chatterjee Sarkar, *The Sundarbans*, op. cit.: 78).

revised the numbering of the allotments consecutively. The whole of the coast from the Hooghly to the Meghna River to a depth varying from 5 to 10 miles was copied from Major Rennel's *Atlas* of 1779. As many as one hundred and sixty-three lots were further subdivided to facilitate speedy reclamation. The Jungleburi Rules of 1825 did not work out well as it was anticipated. Only four lots were granted under these Rules. The land grants, which were opened for individuals for carrying out reclamation, according to Pargiter, 'In the bestowal of the grants, however, the European residents of Calcutta largely predominated, and few, if any, were given to the border Zamindars.'[108] Thus a distinct improvement in the administration of the Sundarbans was inaugurated by this all-embracing enactment which left no doubt about right of the State in the ungranted Sundarban tracts. The *patitabadi taluks* were the dividing barrier – a sort of buffer estates mostly Daimi settled, between the Katkina zamindari lands and the Sundarban forests.

Taking advantage of flaws in the *Patitabadi* terms and the ill-defined character of the territories which were covered by these and another set of leases prevailing in the 24- Parganas district at that time known as Katkina Taluks, continuous boundary disputes and extension of claims towards lands in the south became common. The need for a boundary delimitation by survey arose out of this situation.

The territory was finally surveyed by 1830 and the surveyed area was demarcated off into numbered lots. Grants were made in lots, and those who took the lots on lease came to be known as *lotdars.* The *lotdars* had to reclaim their lots and bring them under cultivation within five years. Permanent revenue of 8 *annas* per *bigha* (i.e. Rs. 1.50 per acre) was charged. But the scheme was a failure, many *lotdars* forfeiting their land on account of this time limit, which was too short for the conditions of an area like the Sundarbans, and the high rent. The rules were therefore changed, and the Rule of 1853 (September) gave land to the highest bidder on a 99-year lease. The earlier grants which had not been forfeited were converted into lease. Graduated reclamation was mandatory. The first 20 years of the 99 years were rent-free; for the next 30 years the rent would be a maximum of

108 Chatterjee Sarkar, 2010, op. cit.: 23.

2 *annas* per *bigha*; and for the remaining period of the assessment was to be according to the nature of the land. Prinsep surveyed the line of forest from the river Jamuna to the Hooghly in 1822 and 1823 and with the help of Morrieson's map he divided the forest lands between those rivers into blocks and numbered them. Thus the Sundarbans 'lots' came into being. 'Prinsep's line' and 'Hodges's line' are the authoritative limits of the then Sundarbans forest, while the map prepared by Lt. Hodges in 1831 from surveys made by himself and his predecessors has been the standard map of the Sundarbans. He, too, like Prinsep divided all the forest as far as the river Passur into blocks and revising the numbering, reduced the whole of his and Prinsep's blocks into a series numbered from 1 to 236.

The assessment of the Sundarban forest concerns the terms upon which reclamation grants in the forests were made and the concerns like methods by which the land was assessed. Such land was technically known as a 'resumed mahal' which the Board of revenue defined as 'a mahal... within the boundary of the Sundarbans ... and not falling within the operations of the decennial settlement ... but which have been resumed in favour of Government under the provisions of the resumption laws'.[109] When the Rules of 1830 were introduced for

[109] Jack, op. cit.: 117. Such operations had been very extensive in Bakarganj and Mr. Dampier was entrusted to assess all resumed *mahals* in the years 1830-4 immediately after resumption. The Sunderban area was demarcated from the rest of the 24-Parganas district in 1831 by means of what is known as the Dampier-Hodges line. It comprises an area of 3,089 square miles of which 1,630 square miles are controlled by the 24-Parganas Forest Division. The area strictly under Forests is 303.4 square miles. The outstanding physical facts about the 24-Parganas Sunderbans is that the land is unstable and the water-course are shifting and ill-defined. The total area of the 'resumed mahals' was 1,62,120 acres, but this included about 25,000 acres of forest, which was partly scattered in the midst of reclamation and partly on its borders. In all these estates subinfeudation had been very extensive; at the top was a *talukdar*, who had got an *abadkari* grant from the zamindars and was often one of the zamindars themselves; below him were the *osat talukdars*, amongst whom he had divided his grant, retaining two or three of the most fertile *osat taluks* in his own possession; below the *osat talukdars* were the *haoladars*, whom Mr. Dampier found to be the true reclaimers, since they cleared the forest at their own expense and divided the lands when cleared amongst a lower class of men, *nim-haoladars*, who were at first genuine cultivators, but the improvement in the country and the rise in the value of land enabled them in turn to sublet their lands to *karshas* (ploughmen). Mr Dampier

the settlement of uncultured tracts of the Sundarbans, the task of the Commissioner increased enormously. During 1830-1, ninety lots were granted, and twelve more during the next five years, with a total area of 5,51,520 acres. It was stipulated that one-fourth of the area should be rendered fit for cultivation within five years failing which grants were liable to be forfeited to Government . In 1839 about half of the forfeited grants were leased out again besides some twelve new lots. Accordingly, James Reily and McClintok were appointed as assistants to the Sundarbans Commissioner. Similarly, to lessen the burden of the Collector in revenue matters, Regulation IX of 1833 created the post of Deputy Collector in the district. This uncovenanted office was declared open to the Indians by Lord William Bentinck. Bentinck created several divisions, each of which was placed under a Commissioner who exercised general control over the conduct of affairs within his division. The greater Sundarbans and as such the 24-Parganas Sundarbans was under the Commissioner of the Presidency division. At first the office of the Presidency Commissioner was stationed at Jessore and later, after the Mutiny, it was transferred to Alipore. Eaton has shown that in between 1830-43, one hundred thirty-eight grants had been given to ninety-five persons who had an interest in reclaiming and converting reclaimed lands into the rice-fields.[110] On the basis of

---

did not admit the nim-*haoaladars* into the rent-roll (*jamabandi*) as he pronounced their rights to be non-heritable (*ghair maurasi*), in as much as they were unable to transfer their lands and were wholly dependent on the *haoladars*, who had transferable and heritable rights and were the only substantial and responsible occupants. Mr. Dampier found that the local theory regarding rent in the system of subinfeudation was that each grade was entitled to keep as its profit one quarter of the rent paid by the next lower grade. These rates differed in different *mahals* and different parganas (Jack, op. cit.: 117-18.). There were three classes all bitterly hostile to each other, the *talukdars,* the *haoaladars* and other intermediate tenure-holders and the cultivators. The assessment was first taken up by a Deputy Collector, who exposed the cause of the cultivators, fixed a reasonable rate of rent for them and fixed reasonable revenue by reducing the profits of the *talukdar* and intermediate tenure-holders. Mr. Pargiter, being the Commissioner of Sundarbans, was entrusted with a fresh assessment to be based upon the recognized *ryots* in each estate. In the face of Mr. Dampier's proceedings Mr. Pargiter most unwillingly found himself compelled to accept the *haoaladars* as '*maurasi raiyats*' and to ignore their under tenants (Jack, op. cit.: 119).

[110] Hazaribagh was a major stronghold in Eastern India for supplying woodcutters and coolies. Hardworking labourers from Santhal, Oraon, Munda categories of tribal

the statistical data Eaton has come to the decision that in ninety-six grants inspected by the surveyor, out of an area of 14,22,792 *bighas*, 2,01,910 *bighas* had been brought under cultivation and 28,450 *bighas* were low jungle, while other grants were all forest. The lands granted in the 24-Parganas were surrounded by small creeks but the lands near the sea did not have any advantages. Mukhopadhyay had to admit that 'On the whole the reclamation advanced, stood still or receded much according to the individual nature of the grant and the circumstances under which the grantee carried out reclamation and cultivation.' About 1840 several schemes were broached for the implement of Calcutta Port. One was to reclaim Sagar Island; another was to construct wet docks at Diamond Harbour.

In 1844, the office of the Commissioner in the Sundarbans was abolished. However, it was restored soon on its former basis.[111] To foil lease-holders' attempts to exploit the wood and leave the land UN-reclaimed, rules were stipulated in 1853 by which the grantee was required to reclaim one-eighth of his land in five years, one-fourth in ten, one-half in twenty, and the whole in thirty years. Also, to make the deal more attractive, land tax was reduced to a fourth of what it was previously and grants were leased for ninety-nine years to the highest bidder. Due to the slow progress in the land reclamations, the government announced revised rule for land grants in the Sundarbans in 1853. On 24 September 1853 under 'Grant of Wasteland Scheme' out of one hundred seventy-eight plots, thirty plots were given to the Europeans, one plot to an Armenian, two plots to Christians, thirty plots to Muslims and the rest to Hindus.[112] *The Survey and Settlement*

---

communities were taken mainly from Hazaribagh, Singbhum, Manbhum and Ranchi districts for the purpose of commencement of human habitation and settlement in the Sundarbans. Cultivators and *lotdars* from the neighbouring district of Midnapore settled first at the reclaimed zone of the Sagar Island, Namkhana and Patharpratima. The duration of the human habitation in the Sundarbans region is never more than 115 years. The first tube well for drinking water facilities was sunk in 1950 in the newly settled and reclaimed zone considered for human habitation (Gautam Kumar Das, op. cit.).

[111] W.W. Hunter, *Imperial Gazetteer of India*, vol. XVI, Oxford, Clarendon Press, 1908: 106.

[112] Ray, op. cit.: 107-23.

Report[113] summarises the distinctive noteworthy features of the rules of 1853:

(i) Grants were made for ninety-nine years, and were sold to the highest bidders

(ii) the revenue assessed on them was reduced to about 6 *annas* per acre and did not become fully payable till the 51st year after a long and gradual enhancement. The earlier grantees had the option to give up their old leases and take fresh leases under the new rules to protect the interest of the salt agencies, new clauses were prescribed by the government.

In 1857, the task of resettling the entire Sundarbans was rested in the Commissioner. Again, the following year, the Presidency Commissioner was empowered to hear the complaints against the Commissioner's orders regarding settlement and resumption.[114] But administrative imbroglios and rules of 1853 and 1863 (Waste Land Rules of 1863) resulted in a much decreased rate of reclamation till 1870.[115] The mission's success, however, reverberated through colonial texts as one of the visitors in 1827 wrote: 'It is pleasing to reflect that what was once only a den of wild beasts is now made to yield to not a few their "daily bread". . . reflecting a strong penchant for modernization[116] of the region.' Such eulogies marked the beginning of opening the Sundarbans up as a public resource, which continued through the century as Hunter in 1875 described the 'Sundarban Plan' a 'great success'. The centralized but separate system of revenue administration for the Sundarbans region continued till the end of the nineteenth century. The office of the Commissioner in the Sundarbans was finally abolished in 1905.[117] Since then, the 24-Parganas district and its part of the Sundarbans began to be administered as a single unit under the authority of the district Collector and Magistrate. During the period of Lord Dalhousie, the aggregate realization increased to

113 Lahiri, op. cit.: 112-13.

114 Ascoli, *A Revenue History of the Sundarbans from 1870-1920*: 4.

115 Mandal, 2003; Ghosh, op. cit.: 73.

116 Richards and Flint 1990: 19.

117 Ibid.

Rs. 4,17,570 while the expenditure was Rs. 18,300, and, as regards the extent of clearance, the total area under cultivation is said to be about 1,100 square miles. Lord Dalhousie considered the paramount object of Government in devising rules for the disposal of lands in the Sundarbans should be to effect a clearance of that 'pestilent jungle, in the shortest possible period, and to remove the stigma which most justly attaches to the existence of such a nuisance almost within sight of the capital of the empire. Lying between the Bay of Bengal', his lordship remarked, 'and the inhabited parts of the Delta, this dense forest with its accumulated and perpetually exhaling malaria, urged by the 'south-west monsoon, spread disease and death over the whole country, the tract swarms with tigers and other wild beasts whose ravages cause wide destruction of life and property, it affords convenient shelter for smugglers and river pirates, and it presents to the sea-ward a line of coast upon which those who are ship-wrecked, are sure, or nearly sure, of death by hunger, thirst and exposure. To remove or abate this source of so much material suffering, and to afford employment for hundreds of thousands of cultivators is undoubtedly the first object of Government'. 'The improvement of the revenue', . . . 'is an object of secondary importance, and . . . hinders the accomplishment of the former. Heretofore it has been thought that improvement of the revenue might keep pace with the clearance of the jungle, without materially impending it; but this opinion is now proved to be fallacious. That increase of revenue will ultimately follow the clearance of the jungle is certain; but the mistake has been in looking for a return too soon. . .'. The rules for the grant of Waste Lands in the Sundarban, promulgated during the administration of Dalhousie, were on the whole fair and liberal, and gave an impetus to private enterprise for reclaiming the Sundarban, the numbers of grantees were increased considerably thereby, and a large extent of forests cleared and cultivated. The rules were concise and simple, only four in number, and in this, as well as in other respects, contrast with the absolutely intricate and lengthy rules that have been subsequently promulgated. They shortly provided that to have an application for a grant being made to the Commissioner of the Sundarban, it should be advertized in the *Calcutta Gazette* for a week, and then reported to the Board of Revenue, but if there have two or more applications for the same grant, it was to be similarly advertized for a further period of 15 days, sold to the highest bidder of them. If the Board approved of the grant being given to the sole applicant or the highest bidders among the applicants, he was entitled to a *Pata,* specifying the boundaries, the number of the lot, estimated area, on the following terms, to wit, one-fourth of the entire lot to be forever exempt from any assessment; the remaining three-fourths to be rent free for twenty years, thereafter to be subject to a rental of half an *anna* per *bigha* from the thirty-first to the fortieth year, one and a half *annas* per *bigha* from the forty-first to fiftieth year, and two *annas* per *bigha* from the fifty-first to the ninety-ninth year after which it was to be re-assessed. It was also subject to certain conditions as to clearance, in order to effectually ensure that the grantee would use his best endeavour to clear, and cultivate the lot. These conditions were that one-eighth of the grant was to be cleared and rendered fit for cultivation at the end of the fifth year, one-fourth at the end of the tenth year, one-half at the end of the twentieth year, and three-fourths at the end of the thirtieth year; and if any of the above stipulations was not fulfilled, the grant was to be resumed, and the land found in cultivation was to be measured and settled with the actual cultivators or under-tenants thereof, to the exclusion of the grantee. The above rules were unexceptional, as it was singularly hard indeed on such grantees as failed to carry out the contract. In such cases, surely they were equitably entitled to have such lands settled with them, of course, at an enhanced rate of rent, and subject to the leases they may have created with the settlers or actual cultivators, who were entitled to have their rights under the grantees guaranteed to them, in order to protect their interests. This would inflict no hardship to the government, the grantees, or their tenants, and ensure all of them to be fairly dealt with.

Various schemes were drawn up for the location of a port, and several surveys of rivers and the suitability of areas in the Sundarbans were undertaken. The area had become highly attractive since the creation of a vast network of railway lines across India from 1853 onwards required unprecedented amounts of timber. In 1858 Port Canning was set up along the river Matla and a municipality was established there with a big scheme to develop a township. The lands on the river bank were the town lots, and all the rest remained agricultural lands. The leasehold right in the town lots was sold at public auction for a term of sixty years, and was largely brought up. Attempts were made to raise public loans for the improvement of the town and port, but they were not attended with success. A railway connecting Port Canning to Kolkata was constructed in 1862. Soon, however, the British had to abandon their plans. The once-thriving Diamond Harbour port lost four-fifths of its population in 1864 and in 1867 the Canning port and town was reduced to nothing when a huge tidal wave and storm destroyed the whole place. Also, the Matla River started rapidly silting up and the few farmers and grant holders who had taken up residence there left the place and stopped investing in the Sundarbans. In the face of these events, the British soon became dissatisfied with their ventures in the Sundarbans. An appropriate revenue system had not been found and levying revenue on the cultivable lands soon became too cumbersome. On the whole, cultivation in the Sundarbans yielded such mixed results that the British administration abandoned the idea of reclaiming the south-west portions of the Sundarbans for agricultural purposes and concentrated instead on tapping it for timber for railroads and fuel resources.

The agent of the Port Canning Company, however, endeavoured to improve the lot of their tenants by introducing in their allotment finer qualities of rice which would attract a higher price in the market than the prevalent inferior variety.[118] In the late nineteenth century it became clear that the Port Canning project had failed, and Governor-General Lord Canning ultimately abandoned it partly because of the river regime in the Matla that constrained the prospects of navigation, coupled with several shipwrecks that dampened the interest of investors. Portraitist Khitish Bishal, a resident of Canning, showed me his private museum collection that contains rare artifacts of the Sundarbans. In his repository he had the bricks used by the Port Canning Company to build the Port that could not be operationalized because of problems caused by siltation and strong gale in the Matla. The fate of Diamond Harbour in the mouth of the Hooghly River has turned out to be the same.

[118] T.D. Banerjee, *Zamindars and Raiyats in Bengal*, Calcutta, W. Newman & Co., Caxton Printing Works, 1883: 57.

About the year 1853 the idea of making a subsidiary port to Calcutta on the river Matla was thought of and that river was surveyed by Lieutenant Ward . On 5th July 1853, Government bought lot 54 with an area of 25,000 *bighas* for Rs. 11,000 for the construction of a ship canal and railway connecting the Matlah and Hugli rivers. During 1854 the lands were measured and the cleared portion, 3,883 *bighas* settled provisionally.[119] In 1855 the river frontage of the lot, where part had been cleared, was surveyed by Mr. Gomess under the Board's orders for six miles, and marked out into roads and lot's for the construction of the new town and port, a site being chosen near the Malikhal for the railway station. The clearance of the lot was begun by contract. Rs. 4,000 being sanctioned for the clearance of the river frontage and the excavation of two tanks.[120] In 1860 the management of the Government property there was made over to the Sunderban Commissioner,with instructions to clear the jungle, lease out the land to rice cultivators, keep the embankments in repair, and collect the rents of the town. About Rs. 38,000 would seem to be spent on the clearance to the Matla lots during Years 1860-1863 from a fund called the "Matla Town Improvement Fund." In 1864 a map of lot 54 was submitted to Government with an explanatory report by Mr. Casperaz, Sundarban Comissioner.[121] The establishment of the port named Port Canning began about 1858. The lands on the river bank were the town lots, and the rest was agricultural land leasehold rights in the town lots were sold at public auction for a term of sixty years, and largely bought up. Matla is a safer river for commercial purposes than the Hooghly; it has greater depth, the navigation is easier; it has more accommodation for ships, and there are no shifting sands, bores or freshes. In 1862 the Port Canning Municipality was formed and formally obtained from the Government its property in the town

[119] Letter from Sunderban Commissioner to Presidency Commissioner, No. 333, dated 7 August; and Presidency Commissioner to Sundarban Commissioner, No. 56, dated 22 Septembers 1854.

[120] Letter from Sundarban Commissioner to Presidency Commissioner, No. 560, dated 31 December 1855; and Presidency Commissioner to Sundarban Commissioner No. 252, dated 1 February 1856.

[121] Sunderban Commissioner to Presidency Commissioner, No. 43, dated 16 June 1862.

lands. In March 1866, a loan of 4½ lakhs without interest for five years on the security of their land and other property – the port dues, however, being retained in the hands of Government. In connection with the scheme a company was started, called the Port Canning Land Investment, Reclamation and Dock Company Limited for purchasing and reclaiming the waste lands on the river Matla. The Company bought seven lots and held ten others in grant, and it contributed largely to a debenture loan that the municipality succeeded in raising in 1865. When half had been repaid, however, the property of the municipality was attached to by the civil court in execution of a decrees obtained by Government in respect of the loan of 4½ lakhs, and the Collector of the 24-Parganas was appointed ex-officio in manager of the estate. The net income was reckoned at about at Rs. 20,550, and was employed in paying the dividends due to Government and private debenture-holders who were 20 in number. During the years 1877 to 1881 Government took steps to buy out these debenture-holders, offering them 50 percent of the per value of their bonds. Seventeen accepted the terms and the sum paid to them was Rs. 56,915, while three remained to whom the full amount due was Rs. 25,157. In 1881 the Government resolved to execute the decrees it held by bringing the estate to sale, and to buy it in. Government thus acquired the right, title and interest of the municipality and became the proprietor of the whole property with the exception of the free-hold town lot.[122] A railway was constructed between Calcutta and Port Canning, but the port failed to attract trade and the scheme failed. In 1862 Port Canning Municipality was formed but it fell into hopeless pecuniary difficulties, which at length brought it into costly litigation with the Port Canning Company and with Government. The final result was that many of the lease-holders of the town lots, who held large quantities of the municipality's debentures, commuted their debentures for the free-hold right in their lots; and Government bought up the whole of the property of the municipality in the Civil Court and paid off all the other debenture-holders. A Sundarban Development Committee in

[122] Government of India Resolution No. 251, dated 5 March 1866; Government of Bengal to Government Government of India, No. 536 A ., dated 15 August 1882; No., 483 A., dated 2 June 1884; No. 763 dated 1 September 1884; No. 90 A, dated 27 October 1884; and No. 155A., dated 18 February 1885.

1849 reported that the improvement of the Sundarbans depended much on the carrying out of the Ganga Barrage Project and the reform of the land tenure system by which the large number of profit earning zamindars could be eliminated. The Committee suggested some steps for economic improvement in transport facilities by increasing number of ferries, ferry points, constructing more roads, rising of deep water and salt resistant varieties of paddy with an improvement in fodder, fisheries and forest produce.

Port Canning now wears an appearance of stagnation. No shipping visits the port. Firewood and other articles are carried by the railway to Calcutta, but the line does not convey the produce that is brought by country boats from Eastern Bengal round through the Sunderbans. A mill is the only place in the town that displays any signs of industry. The Government spent at least six lakhs, but the amount can scarcely have been comparable with the expenditure.

At the same period that the Port Canning scheme was set on foot, other measures were taken to improve the navigation and trade in the Sunderbans. There were two alternative routes for boats between Calcutta and Eastern Bengal, and two routes existed more or less during the past. One is inner route, running through the cultivated tracts; and the other is a more southerly one, and passes in places through the forest. The latter is very largely used in the cold season, when the weather was ordinarily calm and there was no fear of storms or floods.

In the Island of Sagar, which lies upon the extreme edge of the Deltaic basin, consequently lying higher than the centre of the Delta, the remains of tanks, temples and roads were seen, showing that it was once more densely populated than the former and its past history says that Sagar Island was inhabited for centuries.

About 1810, it was proposed to clear Sagar Island in order to benefit the navigation of Hooghly. Two persons tried in turn, but failed, and many others applied for grants in the island, but it appeared they had no real intentions of clearing the land, and only wanted to secure a nominal property that might become valuable later. The island was surveyed in 1813-14 and the Collector of the 24- Parganas, Mr. Trower, began clearing in a central portion, which was named as Trower land and a company, called the ' Sagar Island Society' with a capital of more than Rs. 2 lakhs was founded for beginning of cultivation. The Society made satisfactory progress at Mud Point, Trowerland, Ferintosh and Shikarpur until May 1833, when a great gale and inundation occurred destroying almost everything and compelling the society to throw up the scheme in despair. Four gentlemen, Messers. Hare, MacPherson, Hunter and Campbell, then bought the four northern portions and carried on the undertaking. The Government also conferred on them the privilege of making salt, from which, and from rice cultivation combined, they reaped a lucrative return. During the operation of clearing Sagar Island in 1822 to 1833, and later when clearing away the jungle for the Electric Telegraph in 1855-56, remains of buildings, tanks, roads and other signs of inhabitation were brought to light. Again upon the Eastern portions of the Sundarbans, where the country has been cleared of forest, mud-forts were found in good numbers, erected most probably by the then occupiers of the soil to ward off the attacks pf the Maghs, Malays, Arabs, Portuguese and other pirates who depopulated this part of the country. The Maghs even advanced so far to the Westward as to Haringhata and Rabanabad channel. The storms and cyclones of 1842, 1852, 1864, and 1867 forced attention to the necessity of providing means of safety and protection of embankment in such a manner that no habitation should ordinarily be built more than a mile from the place of refuge, and that embanked paths should be made connecting the places of refuge with the houses.

Hence, for them the Sundarbans represent an area where struggles have been played out and where those who 'had nothing to lose' were ultimately the only ones to stay on. The image of the Sundarbans as a locale not fit for humans has thus had important repercussions in the way the contemporary islanders of the Sundarbans feel that, both for the state and for those who live outside the Sundarbans, they are at best 'illegitimate' inhabitants of the area, or at worst mere 'tiger food', invisible in official colonial records, listed in a secondary position after the (literally) 'natural' inhabitants of the area – the local flora and fauna – and the unimportant remnants of a forgotten lot for successive leaders of *bhadralok* politics. Since the first settlements in the Sundarbans in 1770, the population of the West Bengal Sundarbans has risen by 200 per cent to its present population of around five million. The sea level in the Sundarbans has increased by an average rate of 3.14 cm a year over the past two decades, while the global average has increased by only about 2 mm a year. Indeed, it has been foreseen that, if the sea level rises by just one metre, 1,000 sq. km of the Sundarbans will be inundated. Colebrooke explained this situation very succinctly:

> Some of the islands, before they have acquired a degree of stability which might enable them to resist the force of the stream, are entirely swept away; but whatsoever, by the repeated additions of soil, they appear to be sufficiently firm, the natives then no longer hesitate to take possession of them, and the new land becomes an immediate subject of altercation and dispute. The new settlers bring over their families, cattle, and effects... These islands will continue a number of years, and may last during the lives of most of the new possessors; as they are, in general, liable to destruction only by the same gradual process of undermining, and encroachments, to which the banks of the river are subject.[123]

[123] Colebrooke: 4-5, cited in Aditya Ghosh, op. cit.

BIBLIOGRAPHY

Primary Sources

West Bengal State Archives

(a) Presidency Commissioners, Sundarban Records (1829-58), West Bengal State Archives, Kolkata.
(b) Letters received by the Presidency Commissioners (1829-58) containing in 23 bundles.
(c) Draft of Letters issued by the Presidency Commissioners (1830-58).
(d) Proceedings of the Board of Revenue (1784-1858).

Collectorate Records

Collectorate Records (24 Parganas) 1855-1858 (Letters Issues and Received).

Secondary Sources

Banerjee, Anil Chandra, *History of India*, A. Mukherjee & Co., Calcutta, 6th edn., 1995.

Banerjee, Paula, 'Bengal-Bangladesh Borderland: Chronicles from Nadia, Murshidabad and Malda', in Paula Banerjee and Anasua Basu Ray Chaudhuri (eds.), *Women in Indian Borderlands*, Sage, New Delhi, 2010.

Banerjee, T.D., *Zamindars and Raiyats in Bengal*, W. Newman & Co., Caxton Printing Works, Calcutta, 1883.

Barman, Pradip Kumar, *Sundarban Bishoyak Sangkalan* (in Bengali), Jiyan Kathi Prakashan, Mayachauri, 2012.

Bayly, C.A., 'Inland Port Cities in North India: Calcutta and the Gangetic Plains, 1780–1900', in: *The Rise and Growth of the Colonial Port Cities in Asia*, ed. D.K. Basu, University Press of America, Berkeley, 1985.

________, *Empire and Information: Intelligence Gathering and Social Communication in India, 1780-1870*, Cambridge University Press, Cambridge, 1996.

Bera, Gautam Kumar and Asok Kumar Mukhopadhyay, 'Syncretism at Sunderbans – Anthropological and Linguistic Dimension', in Gautam Kumar Bera and Vijoy S. Sahay, eds., *In the Lagoons of the Gangetic Delta*, Mittal Publications, New Delhi, 2010.

Bernier, Francois, *Travels in the Mogul Empire, 1656-1668*, trans. and ed. A. Constable, Archibald Constable & Co., London, 1891.

Beveridge, Henry, *The District of Bakharganj: Its History and Statistics,*

Bakharganj District Council, Md. R. Ali Mia, Habib Press & Publications, Barisal, 1970 (rpt).

Bhattacharyya, Debjani, *Empire and Ecology in the Bengal Delta: The Making of Calcutta*, Cambridge University Press, Cambridge, 2018.

Blochmann, H., 'Geographical and Historical Notes on the Burdwan Presidency Divisions of Lower Bengal', in W.W. Hunter, rpt. 1973.

Buckland, C.E., *Dictionary of Indian Biography*, Swan Sonnenschein & Co., Lim., London, 1906.

Carastairs, R., *Human Nature in Rural India*, William Blackwood & Sons, London, 1895.

Campos, J.J.A., *History of the Portuguese in Bengal with Maps and Illustrations*, with an introduction by F.J. Monahan, Butterworth & Co., Calcutta, 1919.

Chakrabarti, Ranjan, 'Local People and the Global Tiger: An Environmental History of the Sundarbans; Global Environment', Kluwer Academic Publishers: The Netherlands 72-9 http://www.globalenvironment.it/. 2009.

Chaudhuri, Dulal, 'Folk Religion', in Amal Kumar Das et al. (eds.), *A Focus on Sundarbans*, Editions Indian, Calcutta, 1981.

Chatterjee, Partha, *The Nation and its Fragments: Colonial and Postcolonial Histories*, Oxford University Press, New Delhi, 1995.

Chatterjee Sarkar, Sutapa, *The Sunderbans Folk Deities, Monsters and Mortals*, Social Science Press, New Delhi, 2010.

———, 'Bengal's Southern Frontier, 1757 to 1943', *Studies in History*, Jawaharlal Nehru University, Department of History, Sage, New Delhi, 28, No. 1(2012).

———, 'Life, Literature and Folk Deities in the Mangroves', Occasional Paper, Nehru Memorial Museum & Library, New Delhi, 2013.

Chattopadhyay, Goutam, ed., *Awakening in Bengal in Early Nineteenth Century: Selected Documents*, Progressive Publishers, Calcutta, 1965.

Chattopadhyaya, Haraprasad, *The Mystery of the Sundarbans*, A. Mukherjee & Co., Calcutta, 1999.

Chaudhuri, Binay Bhushan et al., *Banglar Krishi Samajer Garan* (in Bengali), K.P. Bagchi & Co., Calcutta, 1996 .

Chugh, R.S., 'Tides in Hooghly River', *Hydrological Sciences Journal*, Taylor and Francis, London, 1961, 6, 2.

Cohn, B.S., *Colonialism and Its Forms of Knowledge: The British in India*, Oxford University Press, New Delhi, 1997.

Das, Amal Kumar, Asim Kumar Mandal and R.K. Ghosh, *Sundarbans: A Socio Bio-Ecological Study*, Bookland, Calcutta, 1989.

Das, Karabi, 'Sundarban Embankments: A Study Along Suryaberiya River, Sambhunagar Island, Gosaba, West Bengal', *International Journal of Current Research,* vol. 8, issue 5, May 2016.

De, Rathindranath, *The Sundarbans,* Oxford University Press, Calcutta, 1990.

Dirks, N.B., *Castes of Mind: Colonialism and the Making of Modern India*, Princeton University Press, Princeton, 1997.

Dutta, Kalidas, ed., *Dukkhin Chabbis Parganar Ateet* (in Bengali), vols. I-IV, Baruipur, Sundarban Anchalik Sangrahashala, 1989.

Eaton, R.M., 'Human Settlement and Colonization in the Sundarbans, 1200-1750', paper presented at the workshop on The Commons in South Asia: Societal Pressures and Environmental Integrity in the Sundarbans, held at Smithosonian Institution, Washington DC, 20-1 November 1987.

________, *Rise of Islam and the Bengal Frontier, 1204-1760*, University of California Press, Berkeley, CA, 1993.

Fawcus, L.R., *Final Report on the Khulna Settlement, 1920-1926*, Bengal Secretariat Book Depot, Calcutta, 1927 .

Fazl, Abul, *Akbarnama,* vol. I, translation of the original work (in Persian), by Asiatic Society of Bengal, Calcutta, 1897.

Gastrell, J.E., *Geographical and Statistical Report of the Districts of Jessore, Fureedpore and Backergunge*, Office of Superintendent of Government Printing, Calcutta, 1868.

Ghosh, Aditya, *Sustainability Conflicts in Coastal India: Hazards, Changing Climate and Development Discourses in the Sundarbans*, Springer International Publishing, Cham, 2018.

Ghosh, Amitava, *The Hungry Tide*, HarperCollins, Delhi, 2004.

Gole, C.V. and P.P. Vaidyaraman, 'Salinity Distribution and Effect of Fresh Water Flows in the River Hooghly', in *Proc. Tenth Congress of Coastal Engineering*, Tokyo, 2, 1967.

Greenough, P., 'Hunter's Drowned Land: An Environmental Fantasy of the Victorian Sunderbans', in *Nature and the Orient: The Environmental History of South and Southeast Asia*, eds. R.H. Grove, V. Damodaran, and S. Sangwan, Oxford University Press, New Delhi, 1998.

Guha, A.C., *A Brief Sketch of Land System in Bengal and Bihar*, Calcutta & Simla, Thacker Spink & Co., 1915.

Guha, Ramchandra, 'An Early Environmental Debate: The Making of the 1878 Forest Act', *The Indian Economic and Social History Review* 27 (1), New Delhi, Sage.

Guha, Sumit, 'Rethinking the Economy of Mughal India: Lateral Perspectives', *Journal of the Economic and Social History of the Orient*, vol. 58., no. 4, Leiden, Brill, 2015.

Gupta, Rai Bahadur M.N., *Analytical Survey of Bengal Regulations (And Act of Parliament Relating to India, Up to 1833)*, University of Calcutta Press, Calcutta, 1943.

Hazra, Sugata et al., 'Sea Level and Associated Changes in the Sundarbans', *Science and Culture*, vol. 68, nos. 9-12, Indian Science News Association, Kolkata, 2002.

Hamilton, Walter, *A Geographical, Statistical, and Historical Description of Hindostan and the Adjacent Countries*, vol. 2, John Murray, London, 1820.

Haque, C.E., *Hazards in a Fickle Environment: Bangladesh*, Springer- Science, Business Media, Kluwer Academic Publishers, The Netherland, 1997 .

Hunter, W.W., *A Statistical Account of Bengal*, Volume I: *Districts of the 24-Parganas and Sundarbans*, Trübner and Co., London, 1875.

———, *Imperial Gazetteer of India*, vol. XVI, Clarendon Press, Oxford, 1908.

Hussain, T., *Land Rights in Bangladesh: Problem of Management*, University Press Limited, Dhaka, 1995.

Jack, J.C., *Final Report on the Survey and Settlement Operations in the Bakharganj District 1900 to 1908*, Bengal Secretariat Book Depot, Calcutta, 1915.

Jalais, Annu, *Forests of Tigers: People, Politics and Environment in the Sundarbans*, Routledge, New Delhi, 2010.

Jalil, A.F.M. Abdul, *Sundarbaner Itihas* (in Bengali), 2nd edn. Ahmed Publishing House, Dacca, 1986.

Jana, Manindranath, *Sundarbaner Samaj O Sanskriti* (in Bengali), Dipali Book House, Kolkata, 1984.

Kumar, Dharma and Tapan Ray Chaudhuri (eds.), *The Cambridge Economic History of India*, vol. 2, Orient Longman in association with Cambridge University Press, New Delhi, 1984.

Lahiri, Anil Chandra, *Final Report on the Survey and Settlement Operations in the District of 24 Parganas, 1924-1933*, Supdt. Govt. Printing, Alipur, 1936.

Longridge, James A., 'Report on the Calcutta and South-Eastern Railway from Calcutta to the River Mutlah', *The Calcutta Review*, December, 1858, Thacker Spink and Company.

Lotiful, Bari K.G. ed., *Bangladesh District Gazetteers, Khulna*, B.G. Press, Dacca, 1972.

Majumdar, Madhumita, 'The Other–The Sunderbans: A Land of Dangers', *The Creative Launcher*, vol. II, IV (October 2017).

Mandal, Asim Kumar, *The Sundarbans of India; A Development Analysis*, Indus Publishing, New Delhi, 2003.

Mitra, Satish Chandra, *Jessore Khulanar Itihas* (in Bengali), vol. II, Gurudas Chattopadhyay & Sons, Calcutta, 1329 BS/AD 1923.

Momen, M.A., *Final Report on the Survey and Settlement Operation in the District of Jessore, 1920-1924*, Bengal Secretariat Book Depot, Calcutta, 1925.

Mookherjee, Radhakumud, *Indian Shipping: A History of the Sea-borne Trade and Maritime Activity of the Indians from the Earliest Times*, Longmans, Green & Co., Bombay, 1912.

Mukherjee, R.K., *The Changing Face of Bengal: A Study of Riverine Economy*, Calcutta University, Calcutta, 1938.

Mukherjee, Sarit Kumar, *Islands of India*, Publications Divisions, Ministry of Information and Broadcasting, Government of India, New Delhi, 1992.

Mukhopadhyay, Amitesh, *Living with Disasters: Communities and Development in the Indian Sundarbans*, Cambridge University Press, New Delhi, 2016 .

Nandy, A.C. et al., 'Ecological Changes in the Hooghly Estuary due to Water Release from Farakka Barrage; Mahasagar', *Bull. National Inst. Oceanography*, Tokai University, Japan, 16(2), 1983.

Naskar, K.R., *Ecology and Environment of Indian Sundarbans in West Bengal*, Department of Information and Culture, Government of West Bengal, Calcutta, 2000.

Naskar, Kumudranjan and Guha Bakshi, Dwijendra Narayan, *Mangrove Swamps of the Sundarban, An Ecological Perspective*, Naya Prakash, Calcutta, 1987.

Nicholas, R.W., 'Village Factions and Political Parties in Rural West Bengal', *Journal of Commonwealth Political Studies*, II (November 1963).

________, 'Ecology and Village Structure in Deltaic West Bengal', *The Economic Weekly*, 15, Special Number, July 1963.

________, 'Ritual Hierarchy and Social Relations in Rural Bengal', *Contributions to Indian Sociology* (n.s.), 1, 1967.

________, 'Structures of Politics in the Villages of Southern Asia', in M. Singer and B.S. Cohn (eds.), *Structure and Change in Indian Society*, Aldine Publishing Company, Chicago, 1968.

Obituary Notice, 'F.E. Pargiter', *The Journal of Royal Asiatic Society of Great Britain and Ireland*, no. 2 (April 1927), Cambridge University Press, Oxford.

Oldham, R.D., *A Manual of the Geology of India: Chiefly Compiled from the Observations of the Geological Survey, Stratigraphical and Structural Geology*, 2nd edn., Calcutta: Government Press, 1893.

O'Malley, L.S.S., *Bengal District Gazetteer, 24 Parganas*, The Bengal Secretariat Book Depot, Calcutta, 1914.

Pal, Sayantani, 'Religious Patronage in the Land Grant Charters of Early Bengal (Fifth-Thirteenth Century)', *Indian Historical Review*, Indian Council of Historical Research, Sage, New Delhi, 41, no. 2, 2014.

Pargiter, F.E., *Revenue History of Sundarban, 1765-1870*, Bengal Secretariat Press, Calcutta, 1885.

———, *Revenue History of Sundarban, 1765-1870*, Supdt. Government Printing, Calcutta, 1934.

Parua, Pranab Kumar, *The Ganga Water Use in the Indian Subcontinent: Water Science and Technology*, Springer Science & Business Media, Berlin, 2010.

Presler, F.A., 'Forest Management in the Sundarbans, 1875-1952', in J. Seidensticker, R. Kurin, and A.K. Townsend (eds.), *The Commons in South Asia: Societal Pressures and Environmental Integrity in the Sundarbans*, The International Center, Smithsonian Institution, Washington, D.C., 1991.

Rainey, H.J., 'Famines in Bengal and the Reclamation of the Sundarban as a Means of Mitigating them', *The Calcutta Review*, Thomas S. Smith, Calcutta, vol. 59.

Rangarajan M. and K. Sivaramakrishnan, 'Introduction', in *India's Environmental History: Colonialism, Modernity and the Nation*, vol. 2, ed. M. Rangarajan and K. Sivaramakrishnan, Permanent Black, New Delhi, 2012.

Ray, A., ' The Calcutta Port: The Present and Future', in *The Living City*, vol. 2, ed. Sukanta Chaudhuri, Oxford University Press, Calcutta, 1990.

Ray, Biswanath, 'A Study on Economic Problems of Sundarban', in *West Bengal Today: A Fresh Look*, ed. Biswanath Ray, Mittal Publications, New Delhi, 1993.

Ray, Ratnalekha, *Change in Bengal Agrarian Society c. 1760-1850*, Manohar, New Delhi, 1979.

Raychauchaudhuri, Tapankumar, *Bengal under Akbar and Jehangir: An Introductory Study in Social History*, A. Mukherjee & Co., Calcutta, 1953.

Roy, Atul Chandra, *History of Bengal, Mughal Period (1526-1765)*, Nababharat Publishers, Calcutta, 1968.

Roy, N.R., *Manikchandra Rajar Gan* (folk song of Bengal, Bhatiali), in *Bangalir Itihas (Adi Parva)* (in Bengali), Deys Publishing (8th edn.), Calcutta, 1420 B.S./A.D. 2014.

Rennell, James, *An Account of the Ganges and Burrampooter Rivers*, Proceedings of the Royal Society of London, London, 1781.

Richards, John F. and P. Flint Elizabeth, 'Long Term Transformations in the Sundarbans: Wetlands Forests of Bengal', paper presented in The Commons in South Asia: Societal Pressures and Environmental Integrity in the Sundarbans, the workshop held at Smithsonian Institution, Washington, DC, 20-1 November 1987.

———, 'Long Term Transformations in the Sundarbans Forests of Bengal', *Agriculture and Human Values*, vol. VII, no. 2, Spring 1990, Kluwer Academic Publishers, http://www.globalenvironment.it/. 2009: 17-33. https://doi.org/10.1007/BF01530432: 12

Saberwal, Vasant and Mahesh Rangarajan (eds.), *Battles Over Nature: Science and the Politics of Conservation*, Permanent Black, New Delhi, 2006.

Selim, Raihan et al., 'Access to Land and Other Natural Resources by the Rural Poor: The Case of Bangladesh', *South Asian Network on Economic Modelling*, Department of Economics, University of Dhaka, June 2009 Online athttp://mpra.ub.unimuenchen.de/38621/MPRA Paper No. 38621, dated 7 May 2012.

Sengupta, Rabindra Kumar, 'Importance of the Sundarbans Region in West Bengal's Economy', in Kanan Gopal Bagchi, Sunil Kumar Munsi and Rabindranath Bhattacharyya (eds.), *The Bhagirathi-Hooghly Basin*, Calcutta University Press, Calcutta, 1944.

Sinha, M. et al., 'Impact of Farakka Barrage on the Hydrology and Fishery of Hooghly Estuary', 19(3), 1996.

Sinha, N.K., *The Economic History of Bengal: From Plassey to the Permanent Settlement*, vol. II, Firma K.L. Mukhopadhyay, Calcutta, 1962.

Smyth, Ralph, *Statistical and Geographical Report on the 24-Pargunnahs District*, 'Calcutta Gazette' Office, Calcutta, 1857.

'The Sundarbans' (by an anonymous writer), *The Calcutta Review*, vol. XXXI, 1858.

Tai-Yong, Tan, *Port Cities and Hinterlands: A Comparative Study of Singapore and Calcutta; Political Geography*, Elsevier, Amsterdom, 2007, 26(7).

Westland, James, *A Report on the District of Jessore: Its Antiquities, its History, and its Commerce*, 2nd edn., Bengal Secretariat Press, Calcutta, 1874.

A REVENUE HISTORY OF THE SUNDARBANS

FROM 1765 TO 1870

FREDERICK EDEN PARGITER

CHAPTER I

Early History
1765-1816

1. The Sundarbans: Introductory: The Sundarbans[1] are the southern portion of the Ganges delta, extending from the Hugli on the west to the Meghna on the east, through the present districts of 24-Parganas, Khulna, and Bakarganj, and their limits on the north are the permanently-settled lands of those districts. In 1772 a settlement was made for five years of the land revenues of the zamindaris in Bengal, and on its expiration they were adjusted from year to year. In 1790 the decennial settlement was formed, which was declared permanent in 1793. The zamindaris that bordered on the Sundarban forest had no constant boundaries on that side, but cultivation advanced and receded according to the general circumstances of the country and the capabilities of the landowners. The forest was the property of the State and was not included in the Permanent Settlement; but its extent could not be defined during the early period, while the southern boundaries of the zamindaris were undetermined, and it was not till

[1] The derivation of the word Sundarban is undecided. Several derivations have been suggested, but only two appear to me to deserve attention. One is sundari, "the sundari tree", and *ban,* "forest", the whole meaning "the sundri forests;" and the other samudra (through its corrupted and vulgar form samundar), "the sea", and *ban,* "forest", the whole meaning "the forests near the sea." There are two arguments in favour of the former—first, that the sundri is the commonest tree there, and secondly, that the word is sometimes locally pronounced *Sundariban.* There is one argument in favour of the second derivation, viz., that the same name is given to similar forests in the south of the Chittagong district, where, 1 am told, sundri trees either do not grow, or are rare. I believe, too, though I cannot recall any passage, that I have met the word *samudravana* in Sanskrit authors as meaning large forest tracts near the sea. The second derivation seems to me the more probable.

about the year 1838 that the claims which the zamindars asserted to the forest were decided and the confusion dissipated.[2]

2. Origin and Description of the Patitabadi Taluks in 24-Parganas, 1770-93: On the grant of the 24-Parganas to the East India Company, the country, even in the Vicinity of Calcutta, was in a wild and uncultivated state. With the object of reclaiming it, leases were granted by the Collector-General, Mr. Claude Russell, to individuals during the years 1770 to 1773 on certain conditions, of which the following were the most important.[3] The lands were to be held free of rent for seven years, generally[4] after which they were to be subject to a yearly progressive assessment up to the full rate of 12, 8 or 6 annas[5] per bigha,[6] according to their quality, which was to be determined by a survey made on the expiration of the free period. On the first two classes of land 75 per cent, and on the third class 70 per cent, of the jama was to be paid as revenue to Government. Lastly, a measurement was to take place every ten years, and the assessment to be adjusted on the area then found under cultivation, according to the rates already fixed. Such grants were called patitabadi taluks.[7] Measurements appear to have been made in 1182 BE (1775-76) and 1186 (1779-80); but the first was valueless, as the amins received their wages from the talukdars, and could not be trusted; and the circumstances of the country rendered it extremely doubtful whether either measurement was real.[8] The grants were first properly measured

[2] Various surveys and maps will be mentioned in the course of the history. These are useful especially as regards details, but the best map for general reference is the map of the Sundarbans of 1873 by Mr. Ellison, Deputy Collector. It is published by the Survey Department.

[3] Bd. Rev. to Govt., letter dated 5 July 1816. Some particulars have been gathered elsewhere. There was, however, considerable variety in the leases.

[4] The Board, in the letter referred to, say one, two, or three years; but see no. 20 of the regulations relating to patitabadi lands, dated 16 Apr. 1781 (annexed to Bd, of Rev.'s letter to Sbn. Commr, dated 28 May 1819).

[5] The coinage was always sicca until 1836 (Govt.) to Accountant-General, no. 1267, dated 30 Dec. 1835).

[6] The bigha in the 24-Parganas seems to have been 40 yards square always.

[7] *Patitabad* means the cultivation of waste or fallow land.

[8] Bd. Rev. to Govt., dated 15 June 1827, a most valuable review of all matters up to that date.

in 1783 (1190 BE), when a general measurement of the 24-Parganas district was carried out. On that measurement was effected the decennial settlement of the district in 1790 (1197 BE). That settlement extended, as regarded the patitabadi mahalls, in reality to those lands only which were recorded as cultivated in the measurement papers of 1783, and the other conditions of the lease, as regarded the assessment with revenue of increased cultivation, still held good.[9] But in fact the mahalls were classed indiscriminately with the ordinary zamindari lands, and, except for an isolated reference by the collector in 1803,[10] the rights of Government dropped out of sight and lay dormant until 1813.

3. Mr. Henckell's Scheme of Sundarban Reclamation in Jessore, 1783-84: With the objects of securing the peace of the country against the dakaits that infested the Sundarbans, and of bringing the Sundarban waste into cultivation, Mr. Tilman Henckell, Judge and Magistrate of Murli (or Jessore), submitted certain proposals to Warren Hastings, the Governor-General, on 20th December 1783, for granting out leases of the forest lands. His plan was to lease out plots of land to raiyats, and create a multitude of occupants. Each raiyat would clear his own "little spot," and hold it directly under Government, free from the interference of "zamindar, farmer, sazawal, or any one immediately invested with the management of the collections." Cultivation would drive out the dakaits and also facilitate the salt manufacture. That the scheme was feasible was proved, he urged, by the former prosperous cultivation of the Sundarbans during the Mughal Empire, the fertility of the soil, and the proximity to the markets of Calcutta. Population had multiplied in the province, and the excess numbers would flock in for means of subsistence. The natural products of the soil—timber, firewood, wax, and shell-lime—would furnish the raiyat with means of support during the labour and expense of clearing the ground, but it would be indispensable that Government should protect him in his tenure. He proposed to grant out the lands two years free, and thereafter subject to a fair assessment. He asked for permission to

[9] See Patitabadi regulations cited above, and the notes on them by the Committee of Revenue and their Assistant, Mr. Touchet in 1782.

[10] Collr. of 24-Parganas, to Bd. Rev., 5 Dec. 1803.

carry out the plan which, he felt persuaded, would prove beneficial to the country and also to the Company. Difficulties there would be, but perseverance and assiduity would overcome them. The Governor-General's approval was accorded on 7th February 1784, and Mr. Henckell revised the terms and fixed them thus on 3rd April 1784.[11] The grants, with boundaries specified, were to be held free of revenue for the first three years, and at a rental of 2 annas sicca per bigha[12] in the fourth year on whatever land was then brought into cultivation; 4 annas in the fifth year, 6 annas in the sixth year, and 8 annas—the full rate—from the seventh year in perpetuity. Provision was made for the assessment at those rates of increased cultivation, and a deduction of one-sixth was allowed for expenses on the land under cultivation. On the same date also he defined the boundaries of the Sundarbans under his superintendence to be these:

South—Bay of Bengal.
East—Haringhata river.
West—Raimangal.

North—Village of Dulyapur.	Kalinga river (branch of Raimangal)
Ditto Kagrighat.	Jabuna river.
Ditto Chingrikhali.	Kabadak river.
Mouth of Dhaki creek.	Marjata river
End of Dhaki creek.	Pahdor river [Bhadar river ?]
Village of Serpatalya.	Daudkhali river.
Ditto Kachua.	Baleswar river.

At the same time he drew up an estimate, in which he conjectured that 6,00,000 bighas would be taken, from which Government would derive a revenue of 7½ lakhs in seven years. The government approved the terms on 16th February 1785. Proclamations were published notifying the terms, and applications were received, in which the

[11] See minute by Mr. Rocke. President of the Board of Revenue, dated 17 May 1814, which contains a history of Mr. Henckell's scheme; Mr. Henckell's letter dated 20 Dec. 1783; and also Bd. Rev. to Govt., dated 15 June 1827. A few particulars have been gathered elsewhere.

[12] The bigha was 55 yards square. This measure was current in Jessore, and generally used there until 1849 (see paragraph 173).

boundaries of the land asked for were specified, and its area stated by estimate. As "Superintendent of the Sundarbans", Mr. Henckell accordingly gave away, from April to October 1785 (1192 BE), 144 grants, comprising 64,928 bighas, between the rivers Raimangal and Haringhata, where his jurisdiction lay.[13] The boundaries were defined in "chihnit-namas," or descriptive schedules, and the terms of the grants provided for the ascertainment of the extent of cultivation by measurement. But certain areas, generally small, were expressed to begin with, and the assessment computed thereon, while the holders were still liable to pay an increase when larger areas were brought under cultivation.

4. Account of the Scheme, 1784-88: Mr. Henckell took active measures to ensure the success of his scheme. In 1785-86, at the same time that he made the grants of waste lands, he established three Government outposts in central positions, and placed a Gomashta with a small establishment in charge of each, for the purpose of defining the boundaries of the Sundarbans, encouraging reclamation, preserving the police, and assisting passengers; they were Henckellganj (named after him, and subsequently corrupted to Hingalganj) on the west bank of the Jabuna, at its junction with the Kalindi, in the west of his jurisdiction; Chandkhali on the river Kabadak, in the middle; and Kachua, at the junction of the Baleswar and Bhairab rivers, in the east. The surrounding lands were cultivated, and the stations were at length firmly established, though at considerable expense. They were known as "khass abads." Having defined, as above-mentioned, in 1784, the boundary between the zamindari lands and the Sundarban forest,[14] Mr. Henckell called upon the zamindars to prefer their objections thereto; but they remained silent though allowed a period of nine months. After the grantees, however, had got their leases and commenced reclamation, the zamindars lodged claims to their lands as lying within their own estates, and the Committee of Revenue directed him in 1786 to inquire into the claims as a matter of equity, though not of right. He took up the inquiry, but was hindered by want of knowledge of the boundaries and the inattention of the zamindars to

[13] See list dated 25 Oct. 1785.

[14] Mr. Henckell had Major Rennell's atlas of 1779 to consult—see Sbn. Commr. to Presdy. Commr., 8 Dec. 1834.

the parwanas issued; and they were besides clandestinely extending their cultivation, while he was endeavouring to define their boundaries. He deputed persons, in company with the kanungo's officers, vakils, and others, to ascertain and fix the northern limits of the Sundarbans, and at his request the Committee of Revenue published fresh notices, allowing a fresh period of nearly two months in which the zamindars were ordered to present their claims to lands within the limits that were being defined.[15] Under the orders of Government, dated 25th April 1786, the Huzuri mahalls (those which paid their revenues in at Calcutta) were divided into collectorships : Jessore was made one of them, and Mr. Henckell was appointed the Collector. On 19th July 1786 he drew up a list of the parganas that bordered on the Sundarbans in the three districts of Nadiya, Jessore, and Buzurgummedpur. The party deputed to fix the boundary demarcated it by means of bamboos planted at short distances all along the banks of rivers, agreeably to a chart approved by the committee of Revenue.[16] The undertaking appears to have been carried out in May 1786, but not to have been completed till about August. The line was called Henckell's Bansgari. His proceedings do not appear to have been definitely reported to or approved by the Board of Revenue.[17] The demarcation seems to have introduced some degree of certainty, and the scheme began to succeed. By July 1787, 21,000 bighas were brought into cultivation,[18] and during that year (1194 BE) Mr. Henckell granted away fresh leases for 13,000 bighas.[19]

5. Account Continued, 1788: On 9th April 1788, the Government enquired how far the plan had been carried into effect, and how far it might be extended before the end of the year. Mr. Henckell submitted his report on 16th May. Applications had been made for a very large quantity of land, but leases could not be granted as the limits of the

[15] Collr. to Committee of Revenue, 15 May 1786.

[16] There seems to have been a plan of the lands by a Mr. Cooke, see Sadr Bd. Rev. to Sbn. Commr.. 6 Feb. 1835.

[17] The Board of Revenue replaced the Committee of Revenue on 12 June 1786

[18] This is doubtful. It seems that out of the 64,928 bighas granted in 1192, *leases* for 21,000 bighas only were in force in 1788, see paragraph 5.

[19] There is a register of Henckell's "Chihnit-namas, which contains 207 entries, but is not completed.

Sunderbans had not been marked out till about August 1786, and the zamindars claimed much of the land in those limits as part of their estates. In consequence of the confusion attaching to the boundary and the zamindars' opposition, and also in some cases the neglect to ascertain the situation of grants before their bestowal, the greater number of those who had received pattas in 1785 returned them and relinquished the scheme, so that out of the pattas given away in 1192 and 1194, 60 alone remained in force in 1788, with a total area of 34,000 bighas. But these lands, too, were claimed by the zamindars. The full assessment would be due in 1200 BE (1793-94), by which time the aggregate realizations would, he estimated, amount to Rs. 63,500. He proposed to grant away that year (1195) leases for 1,00,000 bighas, while he still retained applications for two lakhs of bighas, the situation of which he had not then ascertained. He estimated that the financial results of the leases for 34,000 bighas would stand thus at the end of 1202 (1796)—aggregate revenue Rs. 2,72,500; expenses Rs. 94,776; net gain to Government Rs. 1,77,724. No advantages had been yet gained, nor had the objects been in any considerable degree accomplished; still he did not despair of success, especially as the recent union of the Raimangal Salt Agency to his district had already proved beneficial to the scheme.[20] The only impediment was the zamindars. Their claims reached to the sea, though the jungle lands had not been included in their hastabuds and formed no part of their estates. They had desisted somewhat from their hostility, but still neglected to define their boundaries: hence at his desire a last notice was issued by the Board in July 1788, ordering them to define their boundaries within three months, on pain of forfeiting their titles to lands within the limits fixed in 1786, a penalty being necessary to remedy the dead-lock to which matters had been well-nigh brought.

6. Results of the Scheme, 1788-90: The notice appears to have aroused the zamindars, for till then their titles were mere assertion and were not established in any instance. But during 1789 Mr. Henckell was engaged in deciding a number of their claims to lands comprised in the 1192 grants. Their claims were founded on hastabud

[20] Jessore Collr. to Bd. Rev., 16 May 1788 and statements appended; also Bd. Rev. to Govt., 27 June 1788.

accounts, depositions of raiyats, or pattas stated to have been conferred previous to the grants. In those documents places often bore different names, and could only be ascertained to be the same as the grants, by the depositions of people brought by the zamindars. In the cases of Babupur (including Banchanagar and Basharatpur), Kalidaspur, Chandpur, and Mohammedabad, the zamindars established their titles, and the lands were restored to them on 15th September, 1789; but fresh grants were given instead in the new localities where they now lie, viz., the east side of the Kabadak, and these grants went under the same names. The new Chandpur, however, was found to be comprised in Mohammedabad, and was consolidated with it. In Asmatpur and Pranpur the zamindars' claims were dismissed, and the grantees retained possession. In Ballabhpur, Gokulnagar, Bhairabnagar, Gobindapur, Bansipur, and Ismailpur there appeal' to have been no counter-claims. Chandipur and Ramzannagar also survived. The first collections were made in 1195 (1788-89), and the grantees, though in numerous instances out of possession, yet paid the revenue in the hope of regaining their lands. But when the quarrels with the zamindars still subsisted, the collections became impracticable except in the few cases where no disputes arose. In this way a large number of grants disappeared, until there remained about 25 only in 1790.[21] The plan, too, appears to have become modified. Instead of raiyats holding immediately under Government, as Mr. Henckell propounded in his original letter, the lessees acquired the name and status of talukdars, and their grants were called taluks. This seems to have been the result of the severe struggle to which they were subjected. The weaker lessees were eliminated, and only the influential men survived, who, however, could not be designated raiyats.

7. End of the Scheme, 1789-90: Mr. Henckell left Jessore in September 1789, and was succeeded by Mr. Rocke, who experienced much difficulty in completing the scheme. He reviewed it in March 1790, and held that it had failed, not from inherent defects, but from want of data for determining what was Sundarban land. Although the zamindars had been yearly cultivating lands exclusive of their hastabud, yet the revenue of almost every pargana had been in a

[21] Jessore Collr. to Bd. Rev., 26 March 1790 and 28 May 1791.

declining state since 1773. The disputes between the zamindars and the Sundarban talukdars might be easily adjusted if the former defined their boundaries; but, claiming as they did all the lands as far as the sea, he urged that Government should fix some criterion for determining their rights, as otherwise the plan could never be perfected, for no one would embark his property in such a venture. He therefore proposed the following rule for the decision of all disputes then and in the future—The settlement of 1179 BE (1772-73) should be decisive as to the zamindars' rights to any land under the denomination of hastabud or malguzari, and all other lands situated within the boundaries of the Sundarbans fixed in 1786 should belong to Government, with the following exception, viz., that any land cultivated by a zamindar, not being hastabud, should be confirmed to him as a separate taluk, provided he should establish his claim thereto within three months from the date of a proclamation, which should be made previous to giving the grantee possession; but in default this land also should devolve to Government. Mr. Rocke asked the Board for the issue of a parwana to that effect, guaranteeing that it would prove successful. Government was, he urged, pledged to help the grantees who had invested on its encouragement. Very little of the grant-lands had, in his opinion, been included in the hastabud of 1179. He submitted what he considered to be a trustworthy estimate of the result of the scheme, in which he computed that Government would have a net profit of Rs. 1,57,701 at the close of 1203 (1797), and a yearly revenue thenceforward of Rs. 71,955, exclusive of the benefits that might accrue from future leases, for which he had a large number of applications then. But the difficulties encompassing the scheme, and the discouraging pecuniary results (the expense having largely exceeded the receipts[22]), induced the Government, on the recommendation of the Board, to abandon it on 20th August 1790.

8. Permanent Settlement in Jessore, 1790-92: It fell to Mr. Rocke's duty to make the decennial settlement of Jessore in 1790. The assessment of the Sundarban taluks required thorough revision; for, owing to numerous relinquishments that had been made both

[22] The receipts were Rs. 5,332, and the expenditure Rs. 53,132, Rs. 718 per month, having been allowed for it.

before and after the demarcation in 1786, the jamas assessed on the taluks were in a great degree nominal. Under the original terms the full assessment would be attained in 1198 (1791-92); but on account of the long disputes and various changes the principles of the plan had been superseded, and the revenue collected on no regular system. The talukdars were discouraged, and their lands had in a large measure relapsed into jungle. Mr. Rocke had therefore to devise reasonable rasads and jamas on equitable grounds, according to the then condition of the taluks. That was done for the surviving grants of 1192 BE., though at the cost of some decrease in the revenue. Besides that, the continued trial of the zamindars' claims resulted in the release of further lands. Thus six mahalls—Anandapur, Dattpukhuriya, Gauripur, Khanpur, Malliknagar, and Prasadnagar—lying on the borders of pargana Salimabad, and claimed by the zamindar, were inquired into by the Collector of Dacca Jellalpur,[23] to whose district they seem to have appertained. He deputed his head assistant, Mr. Middleton, to make a local investigation in 1789-90, and it seems that the zamindar's claim was substantiated and the mahalls relinquished to him. In three other cases—Jaynagar, Jayrampur, and Udaypur—situated in that neighbourhood the talukdars, through dispossession by the zamindars, or neglect to cultivate, lost all their rights. Those taluks which had never been brought into cultivation and had paid no revenue were struck out. Sundarkhali fell in and was amalgamated with Asmatpur. The khass abads had been encroachments on the zamindari lands, so Mr. Rocke proposed to restore them to the zamindars, provided they entered into agreements for the jama. Kachua appears to have been disposed of in that way, but Henckellganj and Chandkhali remained khass, as the zamindars recused. As regards the grants of 1194 BE, the claims of the zamindars were investigated during 1791, and were decided by 1792 : all the grants appear to have been lost except Gutlakati. In concluding the decennial settlement, it seems that the released lands were united to the zamindaris to which they appertained, and their jama engaged for by the zamindars in addition

[23] The district of Bakarganj was formed in 1817 (?) by the separation of a part of the Dacca district. The decennial settlement of Dacca was concluded during 1198 to 1206 (1791-1800).

to the former hastabud. The settlement as regards the Sundarban taluks was reported by Mr. Rocke to the Board on 26th July 1792.

9. "Henckell's Taluks", 1792: The few grants that survived were reassessed and included in the decennial settlement, not, however, on the same terms, as the zamindaris, but at progressive rates, according to the terms of their leases, until the full assessment on the whole land was reached, while no rights were conferred on them extending beyond the land described in the leases; and the stipulations as to future assessment on increased cultivation remained unaffected.[24]

Their revenue was Rs. 1,363 in 1790, and rose gradually to Rs.3,120 in 1795—the full assessment on the areas mentioned in their leases. They were known by the name of "Henckell's taluks", and were 16 in number. Their names and the areas stated in their pattas were these—

	Bighas	
Pranpur	301	Lying about the river Jabuna
Ramzannagar	101	
Bhairabnagar	301	
Bansipur	202	
Gutlakati	301	
Ismailpur	201	
Gobindapur	201	
Babupur	1,815	Lying on the east side of the rivers Kabadak and Kayra.
Banchanagar		
Basharatpur		
Mohammedabad	5,029	
Kalidaspur	2.908	
Asmatpur	1,001	On the east bank of the river Pasar.
Gokulnagar	201	Between the Mangla and Bhola rivers.
Ballabhpur	201	
Chandipur	352	At the junction of the Baleswar and Kocha rivers.

Besides these there were the two khas abads—Henckellganj and Chandkhali—which, especially the latter, were also frequently classed

[24] Bd. Rev. to Govt., 15 June 1827.

as "Henckell's taluks".[25] The mahalls appear in Mr. Henckell's early lists under the names of smaller chaks; and it seems that some of them, as Mohammedabad, Kalidaspur, and Chandipur, were made up of more than one of the original grants. Banchanagar and Basharatpur soon became absorbed into Babupur. The mahalls were sometimes designated parganas, and in the case of Henckellganj the original name was superseded by the vulgar one of Bangalpara.

10. Sketch of Sundarban Matters in Jessore, 1792-1813: The next 20 years present few matters of importance. In 1796 the Board refused to grant new applications for forest land. In 1798 the Raja of Nadiya sued in the civil court to get possession of Henckellganj as appertaining to his zamindari of Okra, and, gaining a decree in March 1801, held possession for three years; but the appellate court decided on 2nd march 1804 that, as its jama was not included in his zamindari tahud at the decennial settlement, the mahall should remain khass under Government until he agreed to pay the jama, Rs. 169. He still recused, and the mahall was farmed out in 1805 for ten years, 10 per cent, malikana being given him. Chandkhali also was farmed out in 1809 for five years.[26] In 1802 the Collector commenced an investigation into lands reclaimed posterior to the decennial settlement, intending to assess new cultivation which should appear liable, and believing that a very large increase of revenue might be obtained. He advertised for information regarding various kinds of land which had been excluded or omitted from assessment at that settlement, and, some informers having come forward, he seems to have begun measurements,[27] but his proceedings appear to have been stopped by the Board. Partial remeasurements were made in Henckell's mahalls in 1799 and 1803-4, on the latter occasion increased cultivation being found in the eleven mahalls in the west and east. The assessment was readjusted thereon according to the fixed terms, until, in 1812, the area was 9,129 bighas and the full revenue Rs. 4,077.[28] In 1803

[25] Registers of measurements and settlements in 1816. by Messrs. Smelt and Steer; and Donnelly to Sbn. Commr., 3 July 1832. Smelt gives the original area of Ismailpur as 302 bighas.

[26] Presdy. Commr. to Jessore Collr., No. 1603, dated 9 Aug. 1834.

[27] Jessore Collr. to Bd. Rev., 16 Nov. 1802.

[28] Ibid., 24 Sept. 1812.

the question of Sundarban reclamation was raised by the Court of Directors, but the Board considered it best to leave matters alone, and they expressed the same opinion, for fear of checking reclamation, in 1808 when the collector reported the results of the remeasurements in Henckell's mahalls, and wished to assess lands estimated at 40,000 bighas which had been brought under cultivation without leases. In 1808, however, a patta was granted to Mohammed Sami and another person, under the Board's authority, for land nominally in Jessore that the Collector reported to be waste; but, in consequence of claims to it by the zamindars and illegal exactions by the lessees, Government, on the Board's motion, annulled it on 25th November 1808 as having been granted without the indispensable sanction of Government itself. The lessees thereupon carried the matter into the civil court. On 22nd January 1810 the Collector sent the Board a list of Sundarban pattas, beginning from Henckell's time and containing several which had been granted by succeeding Collectors on their own authority. It contained all "Henckell's taluks" (except Mohammedabad), the two khass abads,[29] 114 pattas granted by Mr. Henckell which were null and void, as the grantees had not cultivated the lands, ten pattas granted by him in 1192 and transferred in 1196 to Dacca Jellalpur, one patta for Pasar granted by the Collector with the Board's permission in 1808, another for Atharabanki granted without approval in 1804-05, three pattas (including Mohammed Sami's lease) granted, but subsequently cancelled, and two prepared but never bestowed. Soon afterwards he forwarded fresh applications for leases to the Board, but they decided, on 5th June 1810, that the pattas were illegal, and prohibited the bestowal of leases without the express sanction of Government. They would not interfere with those already granted, but they would give no new leases. In September 1812 the Collector supplied the Board with a statement of the Sundarban leases which were then in force, and mentioned that of late years individuals as well as landholders

[29] Kalidaspur was purchased by Govt, when sold for arrears of revenue in 1798, and was farmed out in 1811. Mohammedabad was leased out in 1811 with an area of 6,461 bighas and permanent jama of Rs. 1,183. Henckellganj was at length settled with the zamindar in 1814 at a jama of Rs. 873 Presdy. Commr. to Jessore Collr., no. 1603, dated 9 Aug. 1834.

had cultivated immense tracts under leases obtained from the adjacent Zamindars.[30] The civil suit by Mohammed Sami was decided in 1811, the appellate court upholding, the order of Government. Thereupon the Board ordered an enquiry into his case. The boundaries mentioned in the patta were—north, Teoria and Sherabariya; east, Kulya and Raimangal; south, Atharabanki; and west, Kanchdiya and Badartala; that is, the grant comprised the country lying between Bansra and Hoseinabad in the 24-Parganas district. The area was measured and found to comprise between 80,000 and 90,000 bighas, of which 25,000 bighas at the south-west were in cultivation, and some 4,000 in process of reclamation by various zamindars: while the land west of the Raimangal and south of the Bidyadhari was in the possession of Raj Ballabh Rai, and the remainder to the east was jungle, to which the zamindar, Owen John Elias, had no valid claim.[31] The Board called upon the holders in 1812 to establish their titles and prove that the lands were included in the decennial settlement of pain, in case of failure, of paying the past and future revenue at the usual Sundarban rates. And when they produced no documents to support their claims, the Board, in 1813, directed the measurement and attachment of their lands, unless they entered into agreements to pay the revenue. The question thus developed into the necessity of measuring the whole of the border lands, inclusive of "Henckell's taluks", and assessing such as were paying no revenue.[32]

11. Sundarban Matters in 24-Parganas, 1793-1813: The rights of Government in the patitabadi mahalls were revived in 1813, when, on application being made for land at Diamond Harbour for wet docks, the Collector reported that the land was claimed by a Patitabadi talukdar, but really belonged to Government; and he gave it as his opinion that the revenues of the 24-Parganas, Nadiya, Jessore and Dacca might be greatly increased by an investigation into the claims of the landholders to own Sundarban land. The Board called for a list of the patitabadi leases, and asked as to the best mode of settling claims to jungle lands, which the talukdars would probably

[30] Jessore Collr. to Bd. Rev., 24 Sept. 1812.
[31] Ibid., 21 March 1812.
[32] See annexure to Bd. Rev. to Govt., 15 June 1827.

assert to be included in their mahalls. The lands reclaimed were of three kinds—(1) lands reclaimed by the border zamindars; (2) lands reclaimed by the patitabadi talukdars in excess of the quantity for which they paid revenue; and (3) lands reclaimed by persons without title. The patitabadi taluks had been measured at the time of the decennial settlement and their area specified in the chittas, and the talukdars were not entitled to more land than had been then assessed. The Government authorised him to depute his Assistant to conduct the enquiry, but called for more information.

12. Rights of the State Over Reclaimed Sundarban Lands Considered, 1814: The rights of the State over reclaimed Sundarban lands in Jessore and 24-Parganas thus came to the front in 1813; but the aspect in Jessore, being far more comprehensive and important, almost eclipsed for a time that in the latter district. The position of affairs in Jessore was reported to the Government in 1814, and the Government, alluding to the survey of the Sundarbans then in progress by Lieutenant Morrieson[33], conceived that the assessments proposed by the Board could be best undertaken on a large scale, and desired the Board to consider the matter further. The Board explained that they referred merely to "Henckell's taluks", one of the conditions of which was that excess lands were liable to measurement and assessment, and in support of their views forwarded, on 17th May 1814, two minutes drawn up by the Members on the general subject of Sundarban reclamation.[34]

13. Minutes by Board of Revenue, 1814: The minutes were written by Messrs. Rocke and Colebrooke (the former of whom was

[33] The Sundarbans (exclusive of the sea-face) from the river Hugli as far as the river Pasar were surveyed by Lieutenant W.E. Morrieson during 1811-14, and his results were corrected by his brother, Captain Hugh Morrieson, in 1818. They confined their survey of Jessore to the khals and rivers between the Kabadak and Pasar rivers, and in no case surveyed forest boundary. (Captain Gastrell, Revenue Surveyor to Sbn. Commr., no. 160, dated 24 Aug. 1858.) No survey was made by them east of the Pasar, except of the water passage from the river Mangla to the river Baleswar. Captain Robertson had surveyed the main water routes from the Hugli as far as Bamini in Noakhali during 1810. The coast between the Hugli and Thakuran rivers was surveyed by Lieutenant Blane in 1813-14.

[34] See annexure to Bd. Rev., to Govt., 15 June 1827.

the officer already mentioned as having been Collector of Jessore at the time of the decennial settlement), and, though dealing in general views, were based almost exclusively on the course of events in Jessore. Affirming, as a matter of notoriety, that the whole of the Sundarban tract, with the exception of a small quantity[35] skirting the permanently-settled region, was excluded from the zamindaris and belonged absolutely to the State, the Board yet believed that since the date of the Permanent Settlement a large extent of Sundarban land had been reclaimed, which was included in no engagement, and was paying nothing to Government, but from which Government was entitled to revenue. It was desirable that the State should assert its rights to those lands. The failure of Mr. Henckell's scheme was attributed, not to inherent defects, but to the want of sufficient accuracy in defining the boundary between the zamindari lands and the forest, the encroaching claims of the zamindars, the absence of correct surveys, and the impossibility of the public officers devoting enough time to its working. Those obstacles would be overcome by the survey of the Sundarbans, which Lieutenant Morrieson was then carrying out, and by the appointment of special officers. The survey would shew what lands had been reclaimed and what still remained forest, and the Board proposed the following principles for the settlement of both classes of land. With regard to the former, they recommended (1) that all lands lying between the eastern extremity of Tolly's nullah and Soladana, which had been brought into cultivation subsequent to the decennial settlement, and which the zamindars could not prove to have been already settled with them, should be assessed; and (2) that talukdari sanads should be bestowed on the reclaimers. They drew up rules of procedure to explain and further those measures. With regard to the forest lands, their chief proposals were (1) that the western forest as far as the river Jabuna should be declared the property of the State, and, if necessary, parcelled out; (2) that applications for grants of forest land, not less than 500 bighas and not exceeding 10,000 bighas, with boundaries specified, might be made to the Collector of 24-Parganas; (3) that grants, after a revenue-free period of seven years, should be assessed at 8 annas generally per bigha on the cultivated area, the

[35] The patitabadi and Henckell's Mahalls.

holder receiving a talukdari sanad, while the unreclaimed land should be liable to resumption; and (4) that all the natural products of the land should belong to the grantee. With reference to the orders of Government, dated 20th August 1790 and 25th November 1808 (mentioned in paragraphs 7 and 10) the Board recommended that all the unauthorized leases granted before the latter date should be declared valid. As to the course of operations, they advised that the inquiries should begin at the south, where the claims would be less complicated, and proceed gradually northwards to questions of greater intricacy.

14. Orders of Government, and Appointment of Mr. Scott to Conduct Enquiries in 24-Parganas, 1814: The decision of the Government was passed on 11th June 1814. The Governor-General affirmed the principle that all lands, which were not the acknowledged property of zamindars, or were not included within the known limits of zamindaris, were liable to assessment, and approved the Board's proposals of settlement. Mr. Scott, who was then appointed Assistant to the Collector of 24-Parganas, was chosen, and directed to settle the lands reclaimed in that district, beginning at the south and working northwards as experience should recommend. Detailed instructions were drafted by the Board and approved by Government for the settlement of the cultivated lands, while the settlement of the forest was put aside till the boundaries of the zamindaris should be determined; and the Governor-General promised to take into consideration the appointment, which the Board had strongly urged, of an Assistant to the Collector of Jessore to conduct the enquiries on the eastern side of the river Jabuna.[36]

15. Instructions to Mr. Scott: The instructions given to Mr. Scott were these.[37] Lands reclaimed seven years antecedent to the year 1221 BE (1814-15) were to be assessed at 8 annas per bigha, which was the full rate; if reclaimed six years antecedent, at 6 annas; if five years, at 4 annas; and if four years, at 2 annas; with a progressive rate of assessment of 2 annas per bigha yearly up to the full rate of 8 annas; and if reclaimed three years before or less, the assessment

[36] Govt. to Bd. Rev., 17 Sept. 1814.

[37] Bd. Rev. to Govt., 4 Oct. 1814.

was to commence from the expiration of the fourth year; while cases where lands were incapable of bearing the full rate were to be specially reported. He was empowered to punish recusancy to engage and the withholding of documents or other evidence by attachment of the land under enquiry. A proclamation was issued by the Board, notifying his appointment and duties, specifying the terms of assessment and settlement, and requiring all landholders, who claimed to own lands as being comprised within previous engagements, to prove their titles, and furnish him with whatever information he might desire. No pattas had been granted by Mr. Henckell in the portion of country assigned to Mr. Scott, except in a small part of pargana Dhuliyanpur, between the Kalindi and Jabuna rivers, and they had been adjudged by the civil court to the Raja of Nadiya.[38] Hence his duties it seems were confined to the country west of the river Isamati, and he was furnished with a copy of Lieutenant Morrieson's map.

16. His Operations in 24-Parganas, 1814-16: During season 1814-15 he commenced investigations into the progress of cultivation, making some measurements and enquiring into the tenure of land and the rates of rent. He met with opposition from the zamindars, especially Raj Ballabh Rai; so the Board authorised him to impose fines on the refractory—a power which he seems to have exercised rather lavishly. He appears to have taken up his quarters at Baroipur and issued a general proclamation to the zamindars; but the Board directed him to proceed into the interior. Cultivation was found to have been chiefly effected by the molungis (salt makers) and chakdars (undertenants); but such men were often dispossessed by the zamindars when their lands had been cleared.[39] Mr. Scott's operations were too diffuse and desultory, though the Collector repeatedly urged the Board to direct that Mr. Scott should confine his attention to one patitabadi mahall before proceeding to others, for there were many important questions to be decided before he could advance to assessment. The Collector appears to have formed a correct estimate of the work that had been entered upon. He had, while at Dacca, prosecuted enquiries into Sundarban reclamation, and had proposed to survey all Sundarban

[38] Ibid., 1 July 1814.

[39] Bd. Rev., to Mr. Scott, 3 and 17 March and 28 Apr. 1815.

lands and assess the surplus; but the Board had checked him for fear of disturbing public confidence in the Permanent Settlement.[40] After acting for a time as Collector of the 24-Parganas in 1815, Mr. Scott appears to have resumed his inquiries during the early portion of the next season. Nothing solid, however, seems to have been accomplished beyond establishing the necessity for more specific and accurate investigations.

17. Appointment of Mr. Smelt to Conduct Enquiries and Measurements in Jessore, 1815: The proposal to appoint an Assistant to the Collector of Jessore resulted in the deputation of Mr. Smelt, who received orders from the Board on 18th April 1815 to measure the lands comprised in Mr. Henckell's taluks. Measurements had been made by amins, as explained in paragraph 10; but the amins had been bribed, and the results were untrustworthy. His instructions were to measure the lands with the aid of amins, to ascertain the periods when the various plots had been brought into cultivation, and to assess them at the rates and on the conditions fixed in the pattas. He was besides expected to measure all other lands that he might find to have been reclaimed from the forest. He proceeded to Jessore in July, but could do nothing till after the rains.

18. His Operations in Jessore, 1815-16: He began the measurement in December 1815 in the west of the district, employing six amins. After first testing them by independent measurements of a few mahalls, and finding their work generally accurate, he proceeded to the general measurement, putting three amins to each mahall. He closed his operations in April 1816, having measured a vast extent of land amounting to 323,252 bighas, of which 212,025 were cultivated.[41] The measurement was by blocks and not by fields—chakwari rather than daghwari and its celerity and vastness detracted from its accuracy; for, considering that he was occupied less than five months, the figures shew that, omitting the jungle, he must have proceeded at the rate of nearly a square mile a day. The jungle was generally measured nazar-andaz, or by guess-work, from

[40] 24-Parganas Collr. to Bd. Rev., 25 Apr. and 18 May 1815, and 21 June 1816.

[41] Mr. Smelt used a bigha of 43 yards square, but on objection by the talukdars the bigha of 55 yards was re-established. His figures were total 424,409 bighas, and cultivation 278,375 bighas. I have given the equivalents in 55-yards bighas.

its apparent length and breadth. The measurements naturally were rough and the details approximate; but as Mr. Smelt declared that the operations had been conducted under his personal supervision, and he felt satisfied of their accuracy, the shortcomings were scarcely admitted.[42] The operations comprised lands reclaimed by the holders of Henckell's pattas, and also lands cleared by persons who had received no authority.[43] But south of the tract measured by him there remained much cultivation which want of time prevented his touching. The operations embraced all Henckell's mahalls (Basharatpur and Banchanagar being included in Babupur) twelve other mahalls—Guabariya, Gopipagla, & c. (adjoining Saiyadkhali), Lakhikhola, Phulbari-Bigardana[44] Hoglabuniya, Mindinagar, Gobindi (with Bantalar char), Kathaltali. Iswaripur (taufir), Dharmkhan (taufir), Mauza Pranpur, and Ghoramari-Mindinagar, most of which had been reclaimed without authority—and also a large portion of pargana Asasuni containing 73 taluks with 200 chaks. It was impossible to ascertain the periods of reclamation, but as it was notorious that the lands had long been under cultivation, the Board pronounced them liable to the full assessment of 8 annas per bigha, and directed the Collector, Mr. Steer, to settle them thereat from 1815. The talukdars threatened to prove recusant, and he was empowered to attach their estates. In answer to their enquiries the Board declared that future measurements would be made according as cultivation spread (pattadars and non-pattadars being treated alike equitably), but that the assessment would be permanent on lands where it had reached the full rate, and that their talukdari tenures would secure to them all the rights and privileges enjoyed by zamindars, with an allowance of 10 per cent, malikana, but no nankar, in case of recusancy.[45] Those who had reclaimed without authority were ordered to deliver in

[42] Jessore Collr. to Bd. Rev., 13 March 1816.

[43] Bd. Rev. to Govt., 14 June 1816.

[44] Phulbari-Birardana formerly belonged to pargana Sahosh, but was separated from it in 1798 and became the property of Govt, it was farmed out in 1804, sold in 1814, and bought in by Govt, in 1815, See Bd. Rev. to Jessore Collr., 30 Apr. 1816, and Bd. Rev. to Govt., idem.

[45] Bd. Rev. to Govt., 5 Apr 1816 and Bd. Rev. to Collr. of Jessore, 5 Apr. 1816. The former allowance of one-sixth was eventually revived.

statements of their limits, areas, period of cultivation, and the authority under which they had reclaimed on main of forfeiture of their lands.[46] The zamindars had objected throughout to Mr. Smelt's operations on the ground that he was measuring their estates as Sundarban land.[47] Their contentions were very difficult to solve, but were decided by means of the Sundarban boundary fixed by Mr. Henckell in 1784. In the course of the enquiry it was found that Mr. Smelt's results were vitiated by the fact that he had proceeded on the boundaries mentioned in two early pattas (procured from the Collector's office), which had been granted by Mr. Henckell to Mohammed Safi and Ram Lochan Bhanja, but which had been annulled on the zamindars showing that portions of their lands had been included within the grantees' boundaries. Consequently a considerable quantity of the lands measured was released, either as lying outside the Sundarban limits fixed in 1784, or, if lying within them, as entitled to exemption from length of time.[48] Thus Kathaltali, Mindinagar, Ghoramari-Mindinagar were released, and also a large number of the taluks in pargana Asasuni. In some instances lands within the limits of the Sundarbans, as fixed in 1784, had been surrendered to the zamindars under decrees of court or the orders of former collectors, but the Board believed that such relinquishments could not be numerous, and that there must be much land in those limits properly appertaining to the Sundarbans, from which Government was undoubtedly entitled to revenue. They directed the Collector, in the event of the zamindars not agreeing to an equitable assessment, to attach the lands until the claimants proved their right to exemption, and the orders appear to have been carried out.[49] The talukdars also had their own objections to the measurement. They objected to the bigha of 48 yards square, which Mr. Smelt had used, instead of the 55-yard measure : the point was conceded, and the figures amended. They were also dissatisfied with the classification of the soil, alleging that the allowance for waste was insufficient: the contention was not admitted, but was parried by the exemption from assessment of 5 per cent of the cultivated area,

46 Bd. Rev. to Jessore Collr., 19 Apr., and Jessore Collr. to Bd. Rev., 6 May 1816.

47 Collr. of Jessore to Bd. Rev., 1 and 23 Apr. 1816.

48 Collr. to Bd. Rev., 13 June and 29 July 1816.

49 Bd. Rev. to Collr., 30 Apr. 1816.

and the deduction was afterwards consolidated with malikana into an allowance of one-sixth of the cultivated area. Grants of lakhiraj land constituted another subject of dispute, but the Board disallowed all except those not exceeding 10 bighas and actually supporting existent religious institutions.[50] If those concessions did not bring about a settlement, the taluks were to be farmed out for ten years; but all other questions regarding the lands were to be left for decision by the Commissioner, who was soon to be appointed to the Sundarbans.[51] The reluctant talukdars were compelled through fear of farmers, who were quite ready *to* undertake their estates at the jamas assessed, to yield, and by the beginning of August 1816, all but two had accepted the terms imposed, and those two afterwards gave in.

19. Results in Jessore: The results were these. The total area of the mahalls was 255,352 bighas, of which 156,754 bighas were cultivated. In that Henckell's mahalls had a total area of 90,596 bighas, of which 52,860 bighas were cultivated, being an increase of about 43,740 bighas. The revenue was raised to Rs. 64,338, of which Rs. 21,496 were derived from Henckell's mahalls, being an increase of Rs. 17,420 from them, and the remainder Rs. 42,842 appears to have been clear gain from lands till then unassessed.[52]

20. Orders of Government on the Operations in Jessore, 1816: Some discussion followed the report of the proceedings, but on 30th August 1816 the Governor-General ratified the terms of the settlement, sanctioning the allowances, confirming the title conveyed, without, however, the bestowal of sanads, and prohibiting remeasurements except after intervals of five years, as regarded the pattadars; but refused to advance those who had reclaimed without authority to the same footing, conceiving that they should be assessed at an equitable jama in the ordinary way, though they should be recognized as possessing the proprietary right in their lands. With regard to the imposition

[50] Bd. Rev. to Collr., 30 Apr. 1816.

[51] Ibid., 18 June 1816.

[52] The area, as they were measured in 48 yard bighas, were-total 335,274 and cultivation 205,808. Hencklell's mahalls, total 118,947 and cultivation 69,402. See register of settlements in 1816 by the Collr., Mr Steer. But Jessore Collr., to Presdy. Commr., no. 57 , dated 28 Feb. 1834, gives very different figures, the total assessment of Henckell's mahalls being there stated to be about Rs. 13,370.

of a uniform rate of 8 annas per bigha throughout the Sundarbans that the Board had strongly urged, and other questions raised, the Government, beyond ordering the publication of a notice warning all who had cultivated lands without authority that they would be liable to assessment, postponed its decision till the commissioner in the Sundarbans should have entered on his duties.[53]

[53] Govt, to Bd. Rev., 30 Aug. 1816. The correspondence regarding the operations in Jessore is rather copious but, as they were hurried through, it suggests rather than decides *a* number of important matters which received their determination afterwards.

CHAPTER II

Establishment of the Sundarban Commission and Preliminary Operations
1816-1821

21. Orders of the Court of Directors Regarding the Sundarbans, 1814: Mr. Dowdeswell, before quitting his seat at the Board of Revenue, had pointed out that large tracts of land, such as the Sundarbans, border lands in Chittagong and the frontier districts, and lands gained by alluvion, were not included within the boundaries of the permanently-settled estates, and had recorded his suggestions as to the best means of drawing a revenue from them. The subject came under the consideration of the Court of Directors, and their views were communicated to the Governor-General in their letter dated 28th October 1814. Laying it down as a general principle, that lands not included in the boundaries of permanently-settled estates were the property of Government, and liable to such assessment as the Government might think fit to impose, they expressed their persuasion that such lands, if assessed, might bring in a very considerable accession of revenue. As regarded the Sundarbans, they thought that although a survey had been begun there, a more detailed measurement, by the agency of natives, would be requisite to adjust the assessment to the capabilities of the soil; they prohibited the public sale of those lands, and directed that settlements should be concluded with the actual occupiers for the lands already brought into cultivation, whilst holding out reasonable encouragements for further reclamation, such as the concession of an initial revenue-free period; and lastly they desired that separate accounts should be kept of the revenue of such lands.

22. Regulation IX of 1816, and appointment of Mr. Scott as Commissioner in the Sundarbans: His Duties, 1816: Their instructions seem to have led to the enactment of Regulation IX on 26th April 1816, which provided for the appointment of a

Commissioner in the Sundarbans, and vested him with all the duties, powers, and authority of a Collector of land revenue.[1] On 5th July the Government appointed Mr. D. Scott, Commissioner and communicated their wishes to the Board concerning the work to be undertaken. Referring to the previous attempts to assess reclaimed Sundarbans lands and their scant success, the Governor-General explained the causes to have been that the arrangements were incommensurate with the extent and nature of the work, and that the attempts had been premature from want of the requisite data, but he augured more success under the new scheme. It was Mr. Scott's duty, after gaining experience in preliminary inquiries, to define the southern boundary of the districts of 24-Parganas, Nadiya, Jessore, Dacca Jellalpur and Bakarganj, as they existed at the period of the decennial settlement, so as to enable Government to fix the limits of the country to be placed under his authority. That would require full and minute investigations in each case, as it had been impossible up to that time to determine the boundary accurately, and it was a matter of great uncertainty, not only how far cultivation stretched to the south, but also to what extent the substantial rights of individuals attached under their title-deeds to the adjoining waste lands; for although all lands not included within the known boundaries of zamindaris would *prima facie* be liable to assessment, still sanads or other title deeds might establish the rights of zamindars to land situated on the south of that boundary. After that was accomplished, he should appoint patwaris, divide the country into parganas, and assign kanungos to each. Attention was called to the views of the Court of Directors and the declaration that there was no intention to subvert the Permanent Settlement, and the Government enjoined that their orders on Mr. Smelt's proceedings in Jessore should guide Mr. Scott in his duties. The Board were asked to consider whether some regulation providing the power of resuming, in the first instance, lands held free of revenue under invalid titles might not be necessary, and on that point it would be Mr. Scott's duty to furnish them with information.

[1] Excise and stamps were at first under his control, but his authority, being found to clash with that of the Collr. of 24-Parganas, was soon curtailed and finally withdrawn in 1829.

23. His Jurisdiction: Instructions were accordingly issued to Mr. Scott.[2] to strengthen his control over the zamindars, with whom he would have to deal, and to prevent clashing between him and the Collectors, it was resolved that those portions of the adjoining territory in their districts, where his operations would range, should be placed under his immediate authority, and that in the first place the requisite portion of the 24-Parganas should be so treated.[3] The Board directed him to take Chingri creek (close below Diamond Harbour) as his starting point, and commence on the parganas lying south therefrom in a line from west to east.[4] Under those orders he took charge in January 1817 of parganas Hatiyaghar, Shahpur and Khari,[5] which formed the southern limit of 24-Parganas district (in the portion that now constitutes the Diamond Harbour sub-division).

24. Patitabadi Mahalls Assigned to Him, 1816: In continuation of the proceedings by Mr. Scott during 1814-15, the Collector of 24-Parganas had sent the Board a number of documents explanatory of the patitabadi taluks. Thereupon the Board wrote to the Government in 1816 reviewing the history and circumstances of those mahalls. They stated that 36 taluks had been granted out, bearing a jama of Rs. 8,527, and expressed their opinion that, although it did not appear whether any remeasurement had been made, yet the cultivated area had been very greatly increased since 1783, and the excess lands, not being included within the Permanent Settlement, were justly liable to pay revenue. Hence they proposed that a general measurement of the taluks should be at once carried out, and the whole of the cultivated lands assessed, from the year in which the measurements should begin, and at the rates specified in the leases; or, if the leases were not forthcoming, at any rates agreed upon subsequently or found generally prevalent in such lands.[6] These measures were apporved by the Government.[7] The taluks fell within the country assigned the Sundarban Commissioner, and when he began his operations in the

[2] Bd. Rev. to Sbn. Commr., 20 Aug. 1816.
[3] Govt. to Bd. Rev., 6 Dec. 1816.
[4] Bd. Rev. to Sbn. Commr., 20 Dec. 1316.
[5] Sbn. Commr to Bd. Rev., 6 Jan. 1817.
[6] Bd. Rev. to Govt., 5 July 1816.
[7] Govt. to Bd. Rev., 26 July 1816.

24-Parganas, were taken in hand by him. In fact they constituted the main object of his attention for several years. At the end of 1816 the Collector sent the Board a list of patitabadi mahalls in his district; he computed their number at 122 in 11 parganas, and their aggregate revenue at Rs.4,78,054.[8]

25. Extent of His Jurisdiction, 1817: Mr. Scott received from the Collector, to begin with, 35 mahalls in parganas Hatiyaghar and Shahpur in January 1817; 33 more in those parganas, and also pargana Khari were added in July. The Commissioner's jurisdiction therefore stood thus—

		Revenue Rs.
48 Katkina taluks[9]		87,352
20 Patitabadi taluks		3,695
	Total	91,047

The patitabadi mahalls were these—Sobhanagar, Harimal, Gangadharpur, Belpukhuriya, Lakhipasa, Ramtanunagar, Lakhipur, Ramchandrapur, Sibpur, Bhairabnagar, Khudadadpur, Syamnagar, Gobindapur, Radhakantpur, Ramlochanpur, Rangaphulla, Dhankhola, Kasinagar, Bhagabanpur, and Kishtarampur.

26. His Operations, 1817 and 1818: He found the unassessed cultivated lands in that quarter to be of the following kinds—(1) encroachments by zamindars; (2) extension of cultivation by patitabadi talukdars beyond the quantity for which they paid revenue ; and (3) reclamations by unauthorised persons who subsequently procured forged documents.[10] He began by measuring the latter two kinds of land by the agency of amins, and for his guide he had the original leases or other title-deeds whenever produced, the-chittas of 1190 BE (1783), and a copy of Lieutenant Morrieson's map. There was much opposition to contend against. The zamindars were all arrayed against him, and chief among them were Raj Ballabh Rai (who owned extensive estates in 24-Parganas, Nadiya, and Jessore), Ram Ratan Mittra, and the Rani Sankari Dasi. The landholders declined to produce their documents, and, when visited with lines, offered copies of the 1190 chittas, which

[8] Collr. 24-Parganas, to Bd. Rev., 23 Dec. 1816.

[9] These were modified patitabadi taluks—see paragraph 30.

[10] Sbn. Commr. to Bd. Rev., 10 July 1817.

were found to be utterly untrustworthy, for not only were the originals often unattested by the signature of any European officer, but they had also been mutilated and tampered with in the Collector's office, and false copies had been collusively obtained therefrom.[11] The amins, too, were obstructed in their work, and the aid of the police had to be invoked, while fraud on the part of the amins themselves constituted a separate source of danger. Cases of gross and persistent opposition were punished by attachment of the lands under measurement. Mr. Scott, however, succeeded in measuring large extent of land in 1817, and the operations were continued by Mr. Lind in 1818. Their combined measurements were these,[12] of which no part was jungle—

		Bighas
Katkina taluks (parts of three)		22,763
Patitabadi taluks (19)[13]		91,059
	Total	113,822

27. Questions Involved in the Operations: Various matters of difficulty arose in the course of settling the lands. The rights and incidents of the patitabadi tenures had been broadly defined before hand, but those of the katkina taluks, where large excess areas were discovered, courted investigation; while the extent of surplus land (taufir) assessable, claims to lakhiraj, the rate of assessment and malikana, the persons who should engage for the surplus lands, and the period of settlement, all required determination: but foremost came the question of the right of Government to derive revenue from

[11] The Collr. wrote to the Board of Revenue (9 Feb. 1818): "I am sorry to say there is every reason to believe that the most fraudulent tricks have been played with the records of this cutcherry, and I could not vouch for the authenticity of any one that is not clearly attested by the Collector of the office. There is no reason to believe that, the dowl bundobast alluded to by the Commissioner is authentic, but yet I am informed, and experience confirms the assertions, that none of the chitta papers previous to 1197 were ever attested by the collectors". A flagrant instance is mentioned by Mr. Scott letter to Board, 10 July 1817) there copies of the same document were given to a plaintiff and defendant—to one as for revenue-paying land, and to the other as for lakhiraj.

[12] Sbn. Commr. to Bd. Rev., 30 July 1818.

[13] For particulars see Sbn. Commr to Mr. Prinsep, 15 March 1822. Bhagabanpur seems to be the only mahall not mentioned, but there is some uncertainty.

the increased cultivation. The consideration of these questions lasted through both years, during which the following principles were laid down.

28. Right of the State to Assess Surplus Lands: The right of the State to assess the increased cultivation was not doubted at first,[14] but it was soon called in question with reference to the policy of the Permanent Settlement, the Government being uncertain about it. The discussion continued for several years and was not finally set at rest until 1828. The question was raised in the civil court about the year 1816 in a law-suit between two of the talukdars, and the Judge denied the title of either party to certain land in dispute, holding that it belonged to Government. Referring to that case, the Board mooted the desirability of ascertaining the opinions of the law courts on the matter; but the Government held it unnecessary, as they were about to pass a regulation to remove the difficulty.[15]

29. Regulation XXIII of 1817: That Regulation, XXIII of 1817, was passed on 28th October for the purpose of defining the right of Government to the revenue of lands not included within the boundaries of estates for which a settlement had been made in the districts of 24-Parganas, Nadiya, Jessore, Dacca Jellalpur, and Bakarganj. The preamble declared "there is reason to believe that extensive tracts of land, lying within that part of the country which is ordinarily denominated the Sundarbans, and which at the period of the formation of the Permanent Settlement was entirely waste, and not included within the limits of parganas, mauzas, or other known divisions of estates for which a settlement was concluded, have been brought into cultivation and are now occupied by individuals without payment of revenue ; * * * but the inherent title of Government to a certain proportion of the produce of every bigha of land, in all cases in which it shall neither have transferred its right thereto for a term or in perpetuity, nor have limited its demand by a distinct agreement with the proprietor or possessor, has uniformly been avowed and acknowledged; and in pursuance of that principle, Government

[14] See Bd. Rev., to Sbn., Commr., 20 Dec. 1816, where the right is pronounced unquestionable.

[15] Govt, to Bd. Rev., 17 Oct. 1817, with Bd. Rev., to Sbn. Commr., 11 Nov. 1817.

are already entitled to assess all lands of the nature of those above described." The principle was applied to all lands reclaimed from the Sundarbans, and lands which lay within the limits of the patitabadi and jangalburi taluks of 24-Parganas and Jessore. The Collector after obtaining the Board's sanction, was to make a thorough inquiry into each case, measuring the lands if necessary, and to submit his opinion to the Board, who would pass the final decision; and the lands, if declared liable to assessment, were to be brought under settlement, while parties aggrieved might institute civil suits against Government within six months. Little seems to have been done towards resumption during 1817 and 1818; the measurements were indispensable preliminaries, the landholders were obstructive, and the officers were engaged in thoroughly ascertaining the history and circumstances of the land under inquiry.

30. Katkina Taluks: Their Nature, and the Orders Regarding: The results of the measurements in the katkina taluks were precisely like those in the patitabadi taluks, and shewed that the katkinadars had pushed their claims and held lands far exceeding the quantities on which they had been presumably assessed. Their titles were subjected to scrutiny, and it was discovered that the katkinadars originally held under patitabadi pattas, and were assessed at the decennial settlement without specification of the amount of land on which their settlements were concluded, and when it was declared permanent, their holdings also became permanent. That settlement being based on the chittas of 1190, the katkinadars laid claim to large tracts of jungle on the strength of those chittas, where the jungle was recorded as having been measured in their estates. But the sole original document produced shewed that the patit (fallow) and jungle had been expressly excluded, and the settlement made on the cultivation alone. These facts were urged[16] as entitling Government to deal with them like the patitabadi mahalls; but the Board, though at first inclined to that view, dissented on the ground that the original pattas appeared to have been so materially altered at the time of the decennial settlement, with regard to the limits of the estates, the rate of assessment, and other points, as to render the anterior stipulations no longer applicable; and, quoting

[16] Sbn. Commr. to Bd. Rev., 16 March, 7 July, and 19 Oct. 1818.

the resolution of the government, dated 19th June 1818, where it was laid down as an inviolable principle of the Permanent Settlement that while, on the one hand, Government had a clear-right to the revenue of all lands not included within the limits of estates for which a settlement had been made, yet, on the other hand, lands included within the limits of estates for which permanent engagements had been then taken, could not afterwards be subjected to new or additional revenue,[17] the Board held the circumstances of the katkina mahalls to fall under the latter description, and stayed all further proceedings regarding them. The Sundarban Commissioner was, however, still authorised to deal with lands which he could clearly prove not to have been comprised in the boundaries of a katkina taluk.[18]

31. Determination of the Patitabadi Area Formerly Assessed: The operations were thus restricted to patitabadi mahalls, holdings covered by no engagement, and the Sundarban forest. The right of Government to receive revenue from the excess lands and cultivation possessed by the patitabadi talukdars was emphatically affirmed,[19] but the question of defining what was excess did not admit of a ready solution. It was impossible to distinguish the new cultivation from the old, and the only method that suggested itself was to compute the former areas by means of the former jamas, since the cultivation alone had been laid under assessment and engaged for by the talukdars. With that object the former dowls or engagements were carefully examined by the Sundarban Commissioner and the Collector of 24-Parganas, and their inquiries revealed that, whenever the state of the records permitted reliance being placed on them,[20] the lands had been invariably assessed at 8 annas per bigha at the decennial settlement, and 30 per cent, deducted for malikana.[21] On this the rule

[17] Bd. Rev., to Sbn. Commr., 21 July 1818—see also Govt., to Bd. Rev., 22 May 1818, where the principle receives the widest extension.

[18] Ibid., 7 Aug., and 1 and 18 Sept. 1818.

[19] Govt, to Bd. Rev., 17 Oct. 1817, annexed to Bd. Rev. to Sbn. Commr., 11 Nov. 1817.

[20] See note 3 to paragraph 26.

[21] Sbn. Commr. to Bd. Rev., 15. Jan 1818 and Collr. 24-Parganas, to Bd. Rev., 9 Feb. 1818. The proportion mentioned in the different leases as malikana varied from 9 to 56 per cent, but could rarely be trusted; 25 and 30 per cent were most usual.

was proposed by the Board and approved by Government, that the cultivated area at the time of that settlement should be reckoned at twice the jama plus 30 per cent, and the onus of proving a different area was laid on those who objected to the calculation.[22] Lands for which no engagements could be produced required no special rules, and the Sundarban forest was dealt with separately.

32. Lakhiraj Claims: Their Character and Treatment: Claims to Lakhiraj were involved in much intricacy, and notices had to be repeatedly published before the holders would produce their title-deeds. The quantity claimed exceeded 15,000 bighas, and the grounds were of all kinds; but small grants were very numerous, and it had been a common usage to exempt 10 bighas in every 100 for religious purposes. With the exception of a few who produced sanads executed by the talukdars subsequent to 12th August 1765—the date of the Company's acquisition of the Diwani—the holders rarely had vouchers other than the chittas of 1190, which, as already explained, were open to the gravest mistrust, and were pronounced insufficient proof alone.[23] Mr. Scott asked for the extension of Regulation VIII of 1811 (which provided for the resumption by the revenue authorities of lands held free of assessment under invalid titles in the Ceded and Conquered Provinces) to the country under his charge, as the alienations were necessarily *prima facie* invalid; but the Board directed him to follow the only procedure then open, namely, to institute resumption suits in the civil court. Accordingly he began one case, the decision in which would govern all others, the claims being all substantially alike.[24] The Government, however, ordered the immediate cessation of the suits, as a regulation to remedy the inconvenience (XXIII of 1817, explained above) was soon to be promulgated, and declared that not only did the parties merit no special immunity from the ordinary restrictions regarding revenue-free land, but the grants were inadmissible, as the talukdars were incompetent to make them.[25] A very few grants were alleged to be anterior to 1765, and they presented no peculiarity,

[22] Govt. to Rev., 17 Apr. 1818. The rule is not quite accurate.

[23] Bd. Rev. to Sbn. Commr., 8 July 1817.

[24] Bd. Rev to Govt., 23 Sept. 1817.

[25] Govt. to Bd. Rev., 17 Oct. 1817, with Bd. Rev. to Sbn. Commr., 11 Nov. 1817; and Bd. Rev. to Sbn. Commr., 9 Dec. 1817.

except that they were asserted to have been specially excluded from the measurement papers of 1174 and 1190.[26] Out of all the claims to lakhiraj put in, a very insignificant portion only was confirmed by the Board.

33. Rate of Assessment, and Proposals as to Settlement: In the original patitabadi pattas, the ultimate rate of assessment had been 6, 8, or 12 annas per bigha, according to the supposed quality of the soil; but at the subsequents adjustments in 1190 and 1197, the distinctions had been given up, and the cultivation assessed uniformly at the rate of 8 annas. The jamas so fixed were to hold good in perpetuity, but the talukdars could not claim that the extensive surplus lands, which they had brought, into their possession, should be governed by the terms of their pattas, though the Board proposed to concede them that favour instead of demanding, as Government was entitled to do, the highest equitable assessment from such State lands,[27] and on that point some inquiries made by the Commissioner regarding the produce and rent of lands shewed that the raiyats were paying rent at from Re. 1 to Rs. 1-8 per bigha. The Governor-General, however, considered that any such expectations which the talukdars might have conceived had been amply compensated by the forbearance of Government till then, and that for the future, while strictly maintaining any express stipulation in the pattas limiting the State's demand, the indiscriminate assessment all around of 8 annas could not be approved after the local inquiries proved a higher rate might fairly be demanded.[28] The Commissioner was therefore directed to ascertain fully the capabilities of the lands (bringing them under his khass management, if necessary) and report the most advantageous terms he could obtain. Information on those points was gained from some estates then under his management, and by means of notices inviting offers of settlement from outsiders;[29] and the commissioner proposed to assess at Re. 1 per bigha with an allowance of 25 per cent, for malikana.[30]

26 Bd. Rev. to Sbn. Commr., 11 Sept. 1818.
27 Ibid., 23 Sept 1817.
28 Sbn. Commr. to Bd. Rev., 10 July 1817.
29 Govt. to Bd. Rev., 17 Oct. 1817.
30 Sbn. Commr. to Bd. Rev., 24 June and 30 July 1818.

34. Parties Entitled to Settlement: Proposals in Case of Recusancy: The talukdars having brought the lands into cultivation were pronounced justly entitled to settlement in all cases, provided they agreed to an adequate jama, it not being the intention of Government generally to assert any right of property in the lands.[31] They were accordingly called upon to engage, but neglected to attend, believing that government would not settle with others, and they would force Government to conclude the settlement with themselves at the old rate of 8 annas.[32] Notices were issued inviting applicants, to which several responded, and the Commissioner proposed, in the event of the talukdars proving recusant, to dispose of their surplus lands alone, either by sale to the highest bidder, by lease to the applicants, or in farm, for a period of five or ten years tentatively; though the difficulty of separating lands, strictly the property of the talukdars, from those included in the new settlements would render the measure by no means desirable.[33]

35. Results of the Measurements, 1818: The outcome of the operations in the patitabadi mahalls during 1817 and 1818 was this—

	Bighas	*Bighas*
Area assessed in the former leases		10,239
Surplus area unassessed, consisting of cultivation	54,136	
Culturable fallow	19,132	
Unculturable	7,262	
Lakhiraj, confirmed[34]	290	80,820
Total area measured		91,059

36. Regulation II of 1819: On 12th February 1819 was passed Regulation II of that year. It repealed Regulation XXIII of 1817, but re-enacted its provisions, describing the field of investigation in general and less exact terms, rearranging the rules of practice, and supplementing them in minor points. The only important change was the extension of the period for contesting the decision of the revenue authorities in the civil courts to one year, though the landowners were

31 Govt. to Bd. Rev., 17 Oct. 1817.
32 Sbn. Commr. to Bd. Rev., 16 May 1818.
33 Ibid., 21 June and 30 July 1818.
34 Ibid., 30 July 1818. The quantity was somewhat increased by later confirmations.

bound, if they wished to retain possession of their estates meanwhile, to give security within a fortnight for the payment of the future revenue, and institute a suit within ten days thereafter. Provision was also made for the investigation of civil suits regarding lands held free of assessment by the revenue officers before their adjudication by the civil courts. The efficiency of the new law, however, was marred by the omission of the declaration set out in the preamble to Regulation XXIII, that the Sundarbans had not been included in the decennial settlement and were liable to assessment by Government.

37. Operations Suspended, 1820: During 1819 the claims to hold lands free of revenue were carefully investigated under the new regulation, but after that they were relinquished, as not being cognizable until Government finally decided on the liability of the patitabadi lands to assessment.[35] The results of the measurements justified the undertaking and furnished cogent proof of the immense gain which would accrue to the State from their continuance; but, as long as the lakhiraj claims remained undecided, and the terms of assessment unapproved, the Commissioner was stayed from completing the settlements; besides which, the right of the State to enter on the surplus lands of the patitabadi taluks seems to have again undergone debate.[36] Matters were thus brought almost to a standstill in 1820. The Sundarban Commissioner was occupied with the introduction of the kanungo and patwari system, which had been started by Mr. Scott in 1817, but was resisted by the landholders, both openly and passively, from the belief that it was destined to subvert the permanent Settlement. Applications had been received all along in large numbers for grants of the Sundarban forest, but only those for lands in the 24-Parganas district were taken into consideration. Nothing definite, however, was accomplished. On 20th June 1820, the government ordered that the active prosecution of the objects for-which the Commission had been established should be discontinued, until special instructions should be communicated thereon; and so matters remained till April 1821.

[35] Bd. Rev. to Sbn Commr., 28 Dec. 1819.

[36] Ibid., 11 Jan. 1820.

38. Proceedings Regarding Forest Lands, 1817-21: The proceedings regarding forest grants had been these. The Board enjoined in 1817 that the grants should be for so much *space,* not exceeding 10,000 bighas, and should be subjected to assessment, both for the good of cultivation, and also with a view to stop the exactions levied by the landholders under the designations of bankar, jalkar, and mom-mahall, which the Board were not prepared to arrogate to Government.[37] The conditions of the grants were elaborated after discussion between the Board and the Commissioner, the old patitabadi leases,[38] the proposals recorded by the Board in 1814, and the terms offered by the applicants being all compared and considered.[39] Their conclusions were reviewed by the Government in 1819.[40] A form of lease was drafted by the Commissioner in accordance with the instructions communicated, and was sent up for confirmation,[41] but no notice seems to have been taken of it. On the receipt of applications, the procedure was to publish advertisements to discover whether the lands were unowned and available for lease, but in almost every instance the neighbouring landholders lodged objections, alleging that the lands were comprised within their estates, the most forward among them being Raj Ballabh Raj, who surpassed the rest in the magnitude of his claims, and the resistance he offered to the Government measures. Their claims were investigated, Regulation II being followed in the later cases, and were generally found to be groundless, though the absence of a definite boundary to the settled tracts[42] precluded a thoroughly satisfactory decision. No grants, however, could be leased out, pending the issue by Government of a form of patta. With regard to applications made

[37] Bd. Rev. to Sbn. Commr., 29 July 1817. Rs. 42,501 were offered as annual rent for at lease of those duties.

[38] See Bd. Rev. to Sbn. Commr., 28 May 1819, for the patitabadi regulations, dated 16 Apr. 1781.

[39] Bd. Rev. to Sbn. Commr., 17 Nov. 1818.

[40] Govt. to Bd. Rev. 19 March I819. with Bd. Rev. to Sbn. Commr., 2 Apr. 1819.

[41] Sbn. Commr. to Bd. Rev., 16 Apr. 1819. The form was nearly like that provided in 1825 (see paragraph 49) as to the clearance conditions and assessment, but no exemption of one-fourth was allowed, and the fall rate was 9 instead of 12 annas: unreclaimed land was liable to resumption: there were provisions as to measurement and lakhiraj tenures were prohibited.

[42] Sbn. Commr. to Bd. Rev., 19 Nov. 1818.

to the Collector of Jessore for jungle grants beyond the jurisdiction of the Commissioner, the Board announced in 1817 that the orders of Government of 30th August 1816, holding undecided Sundarban matters in abeyance until the appointment of the Commissioner, did not apply to the case of grants of jungle, and that the Collector was at liberty to proceed to their settlement. They gave him permission in 1818 to measure certain newly reclaimed land, which the holder was willing to engage for, and authorized the grant of a lease of jungle to one Sarfaraz Ali, provided the zamindars did not oppose it.

CHAPTER III

Completion of the Operations in the 24-Parganas 1821-1828

39. Office Reconstituted with Fresh Instructions. Mr. Dale, Commissioner, and Ensign Prinsep, Surveyor, 1821: On 16th March 1821 the Government reconstituted the Commission, with a survey party to aid it, and maturer instructions for its objects and method.[1] The first and main object was to demarcate by a distinct line public lands from private property in order to prevent future encroachment, beginning with the country between the rivers Hugli and Jabuna, which had been surveyed by Lieutenant Morrieson. In carrying that out, two descriptions of land were expected to demand attention—(1) lands, the property of the State and unreclaimed; and (2) lands claimed by individuals, but believed to be the property of the State. All cases would need careful investigation, and Mr. Dale of the Judicial Department was selected for the office. Ensign Prinsep of the Engineers was appointed the Surveyor. Their operations were to be conducted regularly and systematically towards the attainment of the first object, and the Commissioner was to found his proceedings on a careful review of all that had been done from the earliest period down to that date. Minor objects were the assessment of lands held free of but liable to assessment, the grant of jungle leases, and the case of the patitabadi mahalls. The first of these might be taken up if compatible with the primary object, but no jungle leases were to be given, until the limits of the public land had been distinctly settled and all claims decided, nor without the confirmation of Government. As regarded the patitabadi taluks, the Governor-General did not consider their nature and conditions had been perfectly elucidated with reference to the bearing of the Permanent Settlement on the limits of estates and on the rights of zamindars to adjacent waste, and the commissioner

[1] Bd. Rev. to Sbn. Commr., 13 Apr. 1821.

was enjoined to inquire minutely into the history of each taluk, using the hastabud of 1183, the chittas of 1190, khass management papers, and certain memoranda of the Revenue Committee and their Assistant, Mr. Touchet, of the years 1778-85.

40. Jurisdiction Enlarged: Mr. Dale took charge of the office on 9th April 1821. Till then three parganas only had been assigned the Commissioner, but the extent of his jurisdiction required to be increased to suit the enlarged operations sketched out, and consequently the following 21 parganas were removed from the collectors of 24-Parganas, Nadiya, and Jessore and made over to Mr. Dale—Azimabad, Calcutta, Mohammedalipur, Maida, Madanmal, Baridhati, Balinda, Bhaluka, Baliya, Paikhati, Sarfarazpur, Maihati, Birpur, Amirpur, Agarpara, Dhuliyapur, Pardhuliapur, Dumranmastafapur, Mirnagar, Pranpur, and Nurnagar—together with a number of fresh patitabadi taluks. The revenue of these lands was Rs. 3,78,326, and with that already under his charge amounted to Rs. 4,69,388.[2] The jurisdiction equalled that of a minor Collectorship, and the small establishment till then allowed was largely increased.[3]

41. Character of Operations: Measurement of Patitabadi Mahalls, 1822-23: The year 1821 was spent in preparations, which were much impeded by the resistance of the collectors of 24-Parganas and Nadiya to the reduction of their jurisdiction[4], but the operations were steadily, prosecuted during 1822 and 1823 by Messrs. Dale and Prinsep. They took up the demarcation of the line separating State from private lands and worked form Pranpur on the river Jabuna westwards; but it was found that the claims set up by the landholders to waste lands reached everywhere, so that instead of the two classes of land supposed by Government, there was only one, namely, public lands claimed by private persons. The claims besides often conflicted, and the parties evinced no inclination to state specifically or point out locally the extent of the lands claimed by them. Mr. Dale came therefore to the conclusion that no satisfactory decision could be had till the line separating the forest from the cultivation was ascertained,

[2] Sbn. Commr. to Bd. Rev., 30 Spt. 1822.

[3] At first about Rs. 400 monthly were sanctioned. The cost was now raised to about Rs. 2,500.

[4] Sbn. Commr. to Bd. Rev., 30 Sept. 1822 and 1 Oct. 1823.

surveyed, and mapped, and that he directed Mr. Prinsep to do. He himself undertook the measurement of the patitabadi mahalls, the number of which was increased by the discovery of several new tenures. During 1822 he measured, by the agency of amins, 28 taluks, namely, Arunnagar, Finga, Tona, Dusra, Bhagabanpur, Kishtapur, Ghola, Srikrishnanagar (two estates), Ramchandranagar, Simalbariya, Bantra (two estates), Lakhinarayanpur, Masamari, Kharampara, Jallasi, Durganagar, Teghariya, Panakua, Srikrishnapur, Kharamba, Santoshpur, Chandibariya, Chapna, Ban Hugli, Gopalpur, Mallikpur, and Iswanpur,[5] and during 1823, 22 more taluks, of which the only important are Gabbariya and Insulbariya.[6] The results of the measurements were these:[7]

	1822 Bighas	*1823 Bighas*	*Total Bighas*
Cultivation	63,884	21,799	85,683
Fallow	31,044	9,083	40,127
Unculturable	7,451	5,088	12,539
	102,379	35,970	1,38,349

of which only about 13,000 bighas appear to have been already assessed.

42. Prinsep's Survey of Forest Line, Patitabadi Mahalls, and Jungle Lands, 1822-23: Mr. Prinsep made a detailed survey of the forest line from Pranpur on the river Jabuna to the river Piyali during 1822, and continued it to the Hugli, a little below Culpi, during the

[5] Sbn. Commr. to Bd. Rev., 23 March, 25 May, 20 July, and 3 Sept. 1822. Srikrishnapur, Santoshpur, and the last three do not reappear at the time of settlement, though Iswaripur, it appears, was released from attachment in 1830 Sbn. Commr. to Presdy. Commr., no. 244, dated 24 May 1843.

[6] Sbn. Commr. to Bd. Rev., 29 Jan. and 23 Aug. 1823. The others were Rajarampur, Mauldari, Koldari, Raigachi, Kapashati, Taraguniya, Ramnagar, Gauri, Baggi, Salkhiya, Jagadispur, Binda. Batgucha, Tangtala, Kharimpur, Damdama, Sultanabad, Chitrasal, Nabasan, and Dadpur, but they do not reappear at the time of settlement.

[7] Sbn. Commr. to Bd. Rev., 1 Oct. 1823, and annexure to Bd. Rev. to Govt. 15 June 1827.

succeeding year, through a total distance of about 180 miles. He also surveyed the patitabadi taluks measured by Messrs. Scott and Lind, with the object of testing the accuracy of the amins' measurements as a whole, and of determining exactly the limits of the land so measured, noting at the same time new cultivation. During 1823 he surveyed the 28 taluks that were measured the previous year. He thus completed 48 taluks with a total area of 1,57,160 bighas[8] and found the amins' measurements fairly correct, except in three instances of jungle, where they had resorted to guess-work. The applications for jungle grants between 80 and 90 in number, were also made over to him for inquiry into their boundaries. Using Morriesson's map as his basis, he filled in the khals and other details during excursions by boat. The areas applied for were estimated by the petitioners at 98,500 bighas, but were found by him to exceed, 9,71,000 bighas: the gross underestimates were attributed to fraud. The quantity properly surveyed and mapped out was about 4,89,600 bighas, of which all was jungle except some 5,000 bighas that had been reclaimed within the previous three or four years. But in addition he made a full survey of the strip of jungle bordering the cultivation from the river Bidyadhari to the Hugli, with a breadth varying from one and a half to six miles, and comprising 3,24,847 bighas. His map at the end of 1823 shewed the precise situation of almost every important patitabadi taluk in the 24-Parganas district, and the exact limit (with the village boundaries inserted) to which cultivation had up to that period been carried between the rivers Hugli and Jabuna. The patitabadi mahalls extended from the Salt Water Lake along the edge of the Sundarban jungle to the south-west corner of the district below Culpi; but the line was broken in four places by katkina or zamindari lands, viz, Bhagabanpur, Nalua, Ranaghata, and Khari. From Dhosa on the river Piyali along the forest boundary to the river Jabuna, with the solitary exception of Harmul, no Patitabadi or other estate had been surveyed by Mr. Prinsep.[9] The results of his survey as regarded the jungle were exhibited in two plans, called A and B. He parcelled the jungle into separate allotments and gave them numbers;

[8] The bigha used by Prinsep was the standard of 40 yards square.

[9] See Prinsep's note appended to Mr. Mangles' memorandum of 7th Jan. 1828, paragraph 58.

but each plan had its own series of numbers. He experienced much trouble from the conflicting names given by rival zamindars to the creeks and other natural features, but he gave currency in his maps to the names which the fishermen and woodcutters on the spot used.

43. Nature and Results of Investigations under Regulation II of 1819 during 1822-23: The Government, when reconstituting the Commission, had expressed its belief that more extensive powers would be needed than were contained in the existent regulations, but wished the latter to be tested before fresh provisions were enacted.[10] The right of the State to draw additional revenue from Sundarban lands would, they thought, ordinarily rest on grounds, touching likewise the right of property in the soil, and they enjoined that if the claims of private parties were extensive or indefinite, the inquiries should be turned to those places first, where there might be a resumption in favour of Government. Mr. Dale, however, pointed out that Regulation II of 1819, under which the investigations were to be conducted, laid down the procedure to be followed in the case of lands *held* free of assessment or at an inadequate jama, where Government did not intend to deny the proprietary right of the holders; but it did not explicitly touch the case of lands where Government claimed, not only revenue, but also the soil itself as its absolute property to be disposed of at its pleasure, and where the existence or non-existence of counter-claimants was unknown. Hence he urged the necessity for fresh rules for the disposal of claims to forest lands, which were not in the *actual possession* of any one, and which applicants desired to cultivate.[11] The proceedings, however, were ordered to be conducted under that regulation, and the evidence generally taken on the spot.[12] With the Board's sanction investigations were undertaken with reference to the whole range of forest border land surveyed and mapped by Mr. Prinsep, and the surplus lands of all the patitabadi taluks that had come under measurement up to 1822. The zamindars had boundaries to their estates, the determination of which would set a limit to their claims; but the western portion of the Sundarbans under the Commissioner's

[10] See Bd. Rev. to Sbn. Commr., 13 Apr. 1821.

[11] Sbn. Commr to Bd. Rev., 30 Sept. 1822.

[12] Bd. Rev. to Sbn. Commr., 2 Nov. 1821.

jurisdiction was almost entirely skirted by patitabadi mahalls, whose owners asserted a title to large portions of the jungle, which the nature of their tenures did not preclude them from advancing. That their pretensions, however, could not debar Government from entering on the surplus lands was proved by Regulation II of 1819, Section 3, Clause 3, which expressly states that the settlement of the patitabadi and jangalburi taluks in the 24-Parganas and Jessore had not been made permanent in 1793: and the fact was shown by Mr. Dale from a variety of papers to have been acted on by the Government officers and courts of a justice, and to have been known to the talukdars themselves.[13] The jungle lands being in no one's ostensible possession, a proclamation was issued requiring all persons to put in their claims, and the investigations were directed into the whole circumstances of each block of jungle throughout the belt surveyed by Mr. Prinsep, with the view of ascertaining merely its liability to assessment. The results during the years 1822 and 1823 were not prosperous; for out of 84 cases instituted, Mr. Dale decided 35, of which one alone received the Board's immediate confirmation:[14] that was confirmed on 20th August 1823, and established the right of Government to 24,600 bighas of jungle land in pargana Maida.[15] In that case and in four others that he decided and the Board confirmed, no appeal was lodged, viz., Ramtanunagar (confirmed 31st March 1824, 200 bighas), Bhairabnagar (4th June 1824, 314 bighas), Gobindapur (22nd November 1824, 836 bighas, and Gangadharpur (25th March 1825, 2440 bighas).[16]

44. Operations, 1824-28: Mr. Dale was removed in November 1823, and Mr. R.D. Mangles succeeded him for two years, after which there were several changes until 1828. The Commissioner's attention was occupied with the prosecution of the investigations under Regulation II of 1819 mainly, and also with the settlement of the cultivated lands and the grant of jungle, where the right of Government to derive revenue therefrom was established. Mr. Prinsep

[13] Sbn. Commr. to Bd. Rev., 30 Sept. 1822.
[14] Ibid., 1 Oct. 1823.
[15] Ibid., 12 Feb. 1824.
[16] Statement dated 7 Nov. 1826.

during 1824 partitioned the jungle belt from Palta and Hoomra to the river Jabuna, and was deputed to Chittagong at the end of the year. There still remained unsurveyed 27 or 30 patitabadi mahalls measured by amins, with a gross area of about 50,000 bighas lying chiefly in parganas Calcutta, Muragacha, and Madanmal. They touched upon two patches of jungle of about 20,000 or 30,000 bighas each, which lay between Dhosa (on the river Piyali) and the Salt Water Lake, separate from the main forest. A survey of the mahalls would also furnish a boundary to the patches of jungle; but some of them were much entangled with katkina lands.[17] His establishment, however, was retained, and Lieutenant Mallock of the Engineers was appointed Surveyor in November 1826; but it does not appear that he did anything, the Commissioner being occupied in disposing of the pending investigations before proceedings to take up fresh ground.

45. Regulation IX of 1825: On 5th May 1825, Regulation IX of that year was passed. It extended the provisions of the settlement law—Regulation VII of 1822—to all lands not included within the limits of permanently-settled estates and also to the Sundarbans and all estates bordering thereon; simplified the procedure by allowing settlement operations to be carried on at the same time as investigations into the liability to assessment; and gave the force of law to previous practice by providing that where land appeared to belong to Government, and no one had *bona fide* possession, the commissioner might ensure the discovery of claims by publishing a notification to claimants, and then adjudicate on them, while the parties, if aggrieved, were limited to a period of six weeks for contesting the decision of the revenue authorities. It improved the procedure, but left the radical defects of Regulation II of 1819 untouched.

46. Investigations under Regulation II of 1819 during 1824-29: At the close of 1823 almost all the lands within the Sundarban Commissioner's jurisdiction appear to have been made the subject of investigation, and the number of cases with the quantity of land involved stood as shown in the following table;[18] but, during the

[17] Prinsep's note to Mr. Mangle's memorandum of 7 Jan. 1828, paragraph 58.

[18] Sbn. Commr. to Bd. Rev., 1 Oct. 1823, and annexure to Bd. Rev. to Govt., 15 June 1827.

subsequent years till 1827, 11 new cases were instituted, which raised the total to 109—

Cases relating to	*No. of cases*	*Total area*	*Deduct uncultur-able*	*Remainder culturable*	*Deduct already assessed*	*Net liable to assess-ment*
		Bighas	*Bighas*	*Bighas*	*Bighas*	*Bighas*
Patitabadi taluks	48	209,515	13,762	195,753	17,193	178,560
Katkina taluks	2	25,627	1,708	23,919	–	23,919
Other estates	14	11,547	671	10,876	–	10,876
Jungle lands	34	1,165,664	291,416	874,248	–	874,248
Total	98	1,412,353	307,557	1,104,796	17,193	1,087,603

The 14 cases, "other estates" were classed as patitabadi cases, but they seem rather to have related to lands cleared by persons without title. The quantity of jungle land deducted as unculturable is a mere estimate of one-fourth, Mr. Dale taking it that that portion might be roughly set aside as unculturable. Of the net area liable to assessment, 2,02,178 were already cultivated or fit for immediate cultivation, and the remainder, 8,85,425 bighas, were still uncleared. Mr. Mangles prosecuted the cases with vigour, grounding his proceedings on assiduous local inquiries. Still their disposal progressed but slowly, as the parties usually appeared by vakils, whose attendance was very remiss. During the years 1819 to 1827, 88 cases had been decided by the Commissioner and reported to the Board, of which the Board decided 54 (with an area of about 1,67,521 bighas) in favour of Government and 4 in favour of the occupants. Of the 54 cases, 27 were appealed to the provincial court of Calcutta, the talukdars having given security for a year under section 22 of Regulation II of 1819, while the estates in the other cases were attached and held khass. Clear information regarding these cases is not forthcoming, but the following facts may be mentioned: 27 cases were decided in favour of Government by the Board by the end of the year 1825-26—Lakhipasa, Kasinagar, Lakhipur, Bhagbanpur (two cases), Kristarampur, Ramlochanpur, Rangaphulla, Belpukhuriya (two cases), Nokali (two cases), Dumranmastafapur, Syamnagar, Khudadadpur, Radhakantpur, kismat pargana Paikhati, Sibpur, Dhankhola, Ramchandrapur, Bantra, Chapna, Masamari, Hatiyara (two cases), Ramchandranagar, and Insulbariya—and the rest by the end of 1826-27. Those 54 cases appear to have related to reclaimed lands, and the forest area seems to have been resumed in three other cases. One was for 3,51,200 bighas, and comprised practically all the forest south of the Atharabanki in the present Basirhat subdivision, the claimants being the zamindars Raj Ballabh Rai, Mr. Elias, and Mohammed Amir.[19] The suit was decided in favour of Government by the Board, but was carried into the civil court, where Mohammed Sami appeared as the appellant. There were two other cases for 1,46,000 bighas and 66,400 bighas, which were decreed by the Board and appealed to the civil court. They seem to have comprised the rest of the forest in the 24-Parganas. The ultimate Sadar Jama on the lands declared liable to assessment was computed by the Board at Rs. 3,32,991,[20] but it was an over-sanguine estimate of the spread of cultivation. Messers.Dale and Mangles investigated the majority of the cases, and their exertions were rewarded with handsome commissions of from 10 to 20 per cent, on the jama derivable from the lands resumed, under the instructions issued by the Government on 30th April 1819 for the active enforcement of Regulation II.[21] All the remaining cases would seem to have been decided by the end of the year 1827-28, and out of the total, 109 cases, to which the number in the above table had been increased, 96 were decided by the Sundarban Commissioner in favour of Government and 13 against. The Board confirmed his decisions in 56 of the former, and of the latter they confirmed nine and reversed one. Four more cases were appealed to the civil court, raising the number to 31, viz., the first 21 in the foregoing list of 27, and Rampur, Belpur, Shahpur, Teghariya,

[19] The boundaries were—north, Atharabanki; east. Raimangal; south, the sea; and west Badartala and Kachadiya, which partially resemble those in Mohammed Sami's patta cancelled in 1808 (see paragraph 10). See Special Commissioner's decrees for 1836.

[20] Bd. Rev. to Govt., 15 June 1827.

[21] Presdy. Commr. to Sbn. Commr., no. 2010, dated 30 Nov. 1830.

Srikrishtanagar, Sobhanagar, Shahzadapur, Ban Hugli, Kharampara, and Kharbil.[22]

47. Results of Resumptions, 1824-28: Particulars of the resumption in these cases are not forthcoming, but the general results appear to have been these. The suits for cultivated lands seem to have extended as far as the river Kabadak; those for lands between the Hugli and Jabuna were practically decided by the Sundarban Commissioner and the Board in favour of Government by the year 1828, but about one-half of them were appealed to the civil court. The suits for lands east of the Jabuna seem to have lasted a long while and were not all decided until Mr. Dampier's time, when they became associated with the proceedings regarding Henckell's and Donnelly's mahalls. The forest lands in 24-Parganas were resumed without much difficulty—about 3,76,500 bighas by the end of 1824, and the whole before 1828, for applications for them were readily entertained, and, as soon as the rules of 1829 were promulgated, grants were freely bestowed.

48. Settlements, 1823-28: The settlement work accomplished was scanty: only six estates appear to have been settled—Kishenrampur, Bhagabanpur (two estates), Ramtanunagar, Gangadharpur, and a talukdari settlement with one Sujauddin. The rates varied from 10 annas to Rs. 1-4 per bigha, and the settlement was made with the owners except in the first estate, where the talukdar's oppression induced the Board to engage with the undertenants.[23] They were, however, all revised by Mr. Dampier.

49. Jangalburi Grant Terms Sanctioned, 1825: No form of Jangalburi lease had up to that time been approved by Government. Mr. Mangles revised the form submitted in 1819 and forwarded his draft in October 1824, whereupon Government prepared and issued forms of lease and security bond on 24th March 1825.[24] The terms were these. One-eighth of the grant was to be brought into cultivation in three years, one-fourth in four, and half in six years under pain, in case of default, of a penalty of one rupee for each bigha of land unreclaimed (but this provision was not to be pressed). The land was

[22] There would seem, however, to have been other cases, viz., Sarasbariya, Kishtachandrapur & C. Sadr. Bd. Rev. to Govt., no. 342, dated 25 Sept. 1832.

[23] Bd. Rev. to Sbn. Commr., 27 July 1824, 2 Sept., 28 Oct., and 2 Dec. 1825.

[24] Ibid., 5 Apr. 1825.

to be held rent-free for seven years, thereafter one-fourth was to be exempted from assessment on account of houses, streams, unculturable land, & c, and the remainder assessed at 2 annas in the eighth year, 4 annas in the ninth, and 6 annas in the tenth; and in the eleventh year and afterwards at 12 annas less malikana of one-third, which was equivalent to an ultimate net rate of 8 annas, the terms being so stated for convenience of underletting by the grantee. He was to furnish yearly a list of his raiyats, shewing each man's area and rate of rent. All penalties were recoverable as arrears of revenue. Besides that, the grantee had to procure a surety, who was required to execute a bond for the payment of all penalties and arrears of revenue: until three-fourths of the grant were reclaimed. A few leases on these terms were authorised: 9,000 bighas (being the southern portion of the present lot 56) to Messers. Kerr, Sturmer, and Hill in equal parts; 37,650 bighas (composed of lots 55, 61 and 64) to Mohammed Sami: 10,000 bighas to Ram Ram Banerji; 11,000 bighas to Ram Narayan Banerji; and two other portions to Imamuddin and Uzir Begam, widow of Mr. Beeby; but only the first two grants seem to have been actually made,[25] though Mr. Beeby began reclamation under an amalnama in 1822-23.

50. Sundarban Commissioner's Revenue Jurisdiction, 1821-28: Mr. Dale's jurisdiction in 1821 comprised estates bearing a total revenue of Rs. 4,69,388. During 1823 additional estates with a revenue of Rs. 86,562 were transferred to him from the 24-Parganas, thus raising his revenue demand to Rs. 5,55,950; but a subsequent transfer to that district of estates with a revenue of Rs. 1,58,988 reduced it to Rs. 3,96,962, at which amount it stood in September 1826. When reviewing his operations near the close of 1823, Mr. Dale stated that he had sufficiently ascertained the course and position of the Sundarban jungle, and desired that, as the collection of the revenues was a serious burden on his duties, he might be relieved by the transfer to the Collectors of all estates except the tract skirting the forest. The same course was recommended by Mr. Mangles, and Government took it into consideration at the end of 1825; but it was strongly opposed by some of the subsequent Commissioners, especially Mr. John Lowis, and the correspondence grew acrimonious, when the

[25] Sbn. Commr. to Presdy. Commr., 20 and 22 July 1829.

Collector of the 24-Parganas espoused that course on the ground that the possession of the revenue jurisdiction would strengthen his hands in the Salt Agency, where there was considerable animosity between his subordinates and the raiyats. The matter was reviewed and decided by Government in 1827. The revenue jurisdiction of both officers was rearranged with the object of enabling the Commissioner to adjust the claims of Government over the holders of particular estates, as arising out of the terms of the settlements or the peculiarity of their position on the verge of the forest, subject to a prohibition against the breaking up of estates between the two jurisdictions—a fault which had not previously received due attention, and had produced serious mischief in the independent sales for arrears of revenue. The revenue and salt officers were instructed to work amicably together, for the reclamation of the jungle, by furnishing fuel for the salt manufacture, should secure the equal progress of the latter.[26]

[26] Bd. Rev. to Sbn. Commr., 21 Aug. 1827.

CHAPTER IV

Final Determination of the Right of the State to the Sundarbans 1827-1828

51. Board's Report on Sundarban Operations, 1827: The Government had called for a report on the operations in the Sundarbans on 28th November 1823, but the Board delayed replying until they should have been able to form a careful opinion on the fullest materials. Mr. Mangles draw up a precis of all the important correspondence that had passed, and the Board submitted a long and exhaustive report to Government on 15th June 1827. Its contents, so far as they have not been already mentioned, were as follows.

52. Right of Government to Assess Reclaimed Lands in 24-Parganas and Jessore Discussed: Since the re-establishment of the office in 1821, the Commissioner's attention as regarded cultivated lands, had been principally directed to the question of the right of the State to assess those lands in the patitabadi taluks which had been reclaimed after the decennial settlement and were not included in that arrangement; but the views entertained as to the expediency of an inquiry into that question, and they want of a sufficient surveying establishment to enable him thoroughly to sift the claims of the zamindars, had retarded his progress. That question the Board now discussed. The lands in cultivation, and still more the waste lands, claimed by the zamindars as belonging to their permanently-settled estates, were so enormously dittsproportioned to the amount of revenue paid by them that the most liberal construction recommended by the Court of Directors of the terms of the Permanent Settlement could not include them; while the evidence offered by the zamindars in support of their title to those lands was most unsatisfactory. In the 24-Parganas the documents relied on were the unauthenticated chittas of 1190 BE, and dowls of the years 1193 to 1196: the former were vitiated by all kinds of fraud and other malpractices; the latter were generally forged. In Nadiya and Jessore, where the decennial settlement had been made without a previous measurement, the documents adduced were hududbandis (schedules of boundaries) and copies of the quinquennial registers. The hududbandis had been drawn up by the zamindars at the call of successive Collectors, and naturally recorded their claims at the expense of the interests of the State, but had rarely been attested by the Collector. Their mass was too vast for the contents to have been properly examined, and they were suspected to have been often fictitious and generally vitiated by forgeries collusively interpolated in his office. The quinquennial registers were based on them and specified the areas of the estates. But however great the disproportion between the revenue and the alleged area, it was still greater between that and the quantity of land comprised within the alleged boundaries. The registers had no greater value than the hududbandis, but a fictitious weight was sought to be given them by tendering authenticated copies. The Board, referring to former papers, and especially Mr. Rocke's minute of 1814, expressed their agreement with the opinion enunciated by him and other distinguished officers with regard to the general question of Sundarban rights, namely, that the property in the soil throughout the Sundarbans belonged to the State, and that the lands reclaimed since the decennial settlement, which were not already brought on the rent-roll, could not be considered as comprised in any settlement till then made, but were open to assessment.

53. Case of Patitabadi Lands in 24-Parganas Specially Considered: The question presented little difficulty in Jessore, where the nature of Mr. Henckell's grants had never been lost sight of, and the increased cultivation had been periodically brought under assessment. In the 24-Parganas, however, the patitabadi taluks had fallen out of notice from 1790 to 1814 with one or two trifling incidental exceptions. Still that fact could not overbear the general conclusion, for the grants in both districts were marked by a similarity so close, and a nature so peculiar, that the remissness of Government in asserting its rights over the surplus lands of those taluks could be ascribed to nothing but accident and oversight. The Court of Directors considered the discussion to hinge on the question whether those taluks were included in the Permanent Settlement or not; but the Board held that view erroneous, since those taluks had been included therein according to the special conditions of their pattas, which fixed the rate, but left the aggregate assessment dependent on the quantity of land to be progressively cultivated: and the Board proceeded to discuss the only points which had been considered doubtful in India, namely, the extent in respect of the quantity of land to which the taluks had been permanently settled, and the force or nullity of the terms of the original tenures. No boundaries had been assigned in the patitabadi taluks in the 24-Parganas, for Mr. Touchet, the Assistant, in his letter of 11th January 1785 to the Committee of Revenue, observes: "It is evident from the tenor of the original grants that they were intended to encourage the cultivation of the lands bordering on the Sundarbans, and prevented the further encroachments of the salt water jungle; and had the limits within which each person taking such grants was to cultivate been fixed at the time, the intentions of Government might have been answered, and no possible inconvenience could have ensued. But the lands granted not having been pointed out, the persons to whom those grants were made, and who were then most of them employed in the parganas under the authority of Government, took possession at will of spots of land that happened not to be in actual cultivation, & c." Dismissing the measurements of 1182 and 1186 BE as valueless, the Board explained that at the measurement in 1190 BE (1783), no part of the forest could have been measured, as the agents were mere amins ignorant of *surveying;* hence no boundaries could have been fixed on the side of the forest; and in the absence of boundaries it was impossible for the estates to comprise more lands than were distinctly brought on the rent-roll in 1790; while, if they were entitled to all lands in their possession in 1827, there was no limit to the same process in the future. The proceedings of 1790 therefore related to those lands only which were then assessed, and Government was not barred from claiming revenue from subsequent cultivation.

54. Mistaken Views Regarding Patitabadi Taluks Considered: The Court of Directors considered that the patitabadi taluks had been put on the same footing as the Zamindaris at the Permanent Settlement, but the Board disproved that view by shewing that while the latter were assessed at from Re. 1 to Rs.2 per bigha and only 10 to 15 per cent, allowed them as malikana, the taluks were assessed at

12 annas in pargana Calcutta, and 8 annas elsewhere with a deduction for malikana of 25 to 30 per cent. The Court besides believed that the talukdars had reclaimed the lands in reliance on the faith of the Permanent Settlement, so that it would be equitable to hold them exempted from additional assessment; but facts controverted that opinion. Reclamation had been undertaken by enterprising men possessed of some capital, who being unable to stand alone against the powerful landholders, were compelled to enlist themselves as their tenants under the name of "chakdars". They received leases for a certain quantity of land to be held rent-free for a certain number of years, and then subject to a progressive assessment which reached its maximum about the tenth year, and a stipulation was inserted that if they reclaimed more they should pay rent in proportion. The lands therefore had been reclaimed without any labour, risk, or expense on the part of the talukdars, who had merely embraced opportunities of increasing their lands and rents with no chance of loss to themselves, and with no belief regarding the Permanent Settlement.

55. Measures Proposed for the Assessment of Reclaimed Lands: Having thus established the right of Government to assess the extended cultivation, the Board considered what means would best accomplish that end. Regulation II of 1819 was well adapted for the adjustment of the claims of Government to the revenue of lands held free of assessment, except the clauses which provided for an appeal to the civil courts. The courts, besides having an abundance of their business, were not well suited to try the questions, especially those relating to the patitabadi taluks, which from lapse of time and paucity of evidence, were very intricate. The cases, if undecided for years, would probably ruin the holders, if they gave security and retained the lands meanwhile, or might induce them to oppress the raiyats and abscond in the end. The Board therefore proposed that, after the enquiries had been perfected by the Commissioner, he should be joined with the District Judge to constitute a mufassil special commission to try the right of Government to assess the lands, and that their decisions should be submitted for further adjudication to a sadar special commission (such as had been established under Regulation I of 1821) composed of selected officers of acknowledged integrity and long experience, whose decisions again should be submitted to Government.

56. Proposals for Resumption and Demarcation of Sundarban Forest: Regulation II of 1819 would deal, the Board considered, well enough with the question of the assessment of lands held under invalid titles or not included in the Permanent Settlement, but it failed to touch cases where the State claimed the *property in the soil,* as in the Sundarbans. Section 22 shewed that the regulation applied only to persons in actual possession of cultivated lands, and not to claimants of vast forests which could not be considered as in the possession of any one, for the actual occupation of fishermen, woodcutters, and others who paid tolls to exacting zamindars could not be construed as possession by the latter or proof of their title. The Sundarbans therefore being the *property* of the State, the Board urged the necessity of supplementing that regulation by a new enactment declaring the *exclusive right* of Government to the whole of the uncultivated Sundarban waste and of speedily delineating the waste throughout the districts bordering on it. They recommended that the Commissioner should devote the whole of his time to local inquiries, and for that purpose should be relieved of all revenue collections and have his headquarters in the mufassil.

57. Memorandum by Mr. Mangles on Sundarban Operations, 1828: The Board's views were supplemented by a memorandum, dated 7th January, 1828, by Mr. Mangles, who had earned high commendation during his tenure of the Commissionership. Pointing out that the leases granted by Messers. Henckell and Claude Russell differed in no essential particulars, except that the former mentioned the boundaries while the latter did not though blanks were left for their insertion (even Mr. Henckell's boundaries, however, could not be relied on as accurate), he traced how the tenures starting together on equal terms encountered widely different fortunes, for the reason that in Jessore Mr. Rocke, who conducted the decennial settlement, included Mr. Henckell's mahalls therein on the terms of their engagements, and secured the remembrance of the rights of Government; while in 24-Parganas the patitabadi taluks were settled indiscriminately with the general mass of the district lands and their nature obscured. The conditions of the leases had been periodically enforced upon the former, and the latter had for nearly 35 years escaped increased demands; yet reclamation had not been damped in Jessore. Faith in the Permanent Settlement therefore had not actuated the abadkars of the 24-Parganas, who in fact had delegated all the risk and expense to their tenants, the chakdars, and were but too ready to oppress and oust them after the lands had been brought into cultivation. He argued strongly that the patitabadi talukdars were entitled to no indulgence beyond their fellows in Jessore, and deserved none after their persistent opposition. But, on the contrary, if they were exempted, Government was bound in equity to restore the latter to the same position. He pointed out and discussed the changes introduced by Regulation II of 1819 in its repeal of Regulation XXIII of 1817, and the grave inconveniences which had resulted,[1] and recommended the enactment of a declaratory law, in order to cut away the ground from beneath the litigious resistance that Government had itself created, and also to give the grantees a feeling of security regarding the rights they acquired from Government, for they had no confidence that the decisions of the revenue authorities would be upheld in the civil courts, and they were besides harassed by the enmity of Raj Ballabh Rai and other zamindars.

58. Note by Mr. Prinsep on the Measurements and Survey, 1827: Annexed to Mr. Mangles' memorandum was a note by Mr. Prinsep on the fieldwork that had been accomplished and still remained to be done. He summed up the results of his surveys in the patitabadi lands and forest tract, and urged that along the eastern portion of the forest boundary between the rivers Piyali and Jabuna, where, with a solitary exception, no estates had been surveyed, artificial landmarks should be constructed for the sake of certainity in the demarcation and ease of future identification. He recommended that the mahalls, measured by amins but unsurveyed, and the two patches of jungle lying between the river Piyali and the Salt Water Lake should be surveyed. Reclamation had spread beyond the measured boundary in Belpukhuriya, Lakhipur, Bhajna, and Gangadharpur, and he considered that further measurements might be needed along the line south of Hosainabad, where the zamindars based their claims to the forest on the existence in it of certain high tracts, which they alleged to be the result of cultivation, but which were in reality merely

[1] See paragraph 59.

sandbanks. After alluding to other difficulties, he recommended the measurement and survey of the belt of estates bordering on the jungle.

59. Orders by Government on the Demarcation of the Sundarban Forest, 1828: The orders of Government were passed on 14th February 1828. The Government remarked that the only error of importance into which former revenue officers had fallen originated in the too easy belief, that no claims would be asserted which were not grounded on some foundation of plausible rights, and when the Commission was re-established in 1821, it was not apprehended that the right of Government to the soil in the depths of the forest would be contested.[2] Those anticipations had been painfully disappointed, and the determined hostility of the zamindars was due to interested motives encouraged by the inapplicability of Regulation II of 1819 to lands unreclaimed and incapable of appropriation. Hence a change in the law was necessary. Under Regulation XXIII of 1817 (section 4, clauses 1 and 2, taken in connexion with the preamble) no further proof of the liability of the lands to assessment appeared necessary than the fact of their having been *reclaimed from the forest* since the decennial settlement; and, after asserting in the preamble the right of the State in the whole of the forest tract, that law contented itself with providing rules of practice. Afterwards Regulation II of 1819 was enacted to amend the rules, and in repealing the former Regulation the declaration in the preamble was accidentally forgotten and was not repeated. The omission had been productive of serious inconvenience, and six years had been spent in almost fruitless litigation. In ignorance of the persons who possessed the waste lands, it had been the custom to issue notices requiring claimants to come forward. That system, which amounted to one of advertising for claimants of valuable rights, awakened the interested passions of those who hoped for success through hardihood of assertion, fabrication of documents, and persistence in litigation. The improved provisions of Regulation IX of 1825 were inapplicable to the forest tract, and had been found inoperative. The Governor-General therefore proposed to enact a regulation declaring all those tracts of the Sundarbans, which were then waste and had not been cultivated since the Permanent Settlement,

[2] Mr. Henckell's experiences are overlooked.

to be the property of the State; and that could be safely done without fear of infringing the settlement, for cultivation had extended and not receded since then. It would be necessary to define and follow in a scientific survey the line of abutment of the forest on the cultivation from the river Hugli to the river Meghna, the revenue and salt officers accompanying and co-operating with the survey party. Part of the line had been surveyed by Mr. Prinsep, and it only remained to complete it without delay from the river Jabuna to the Meghna. With regard to the right of Government to assess the surplus lands of the patitabadi taluks and the encroachments of the border zamindars on the waste since the Permanent Settlement, which questions were pronounced of secondary importance to the determination of the forest, Government agreed with the Board, but awaited the decision of the civil courts.

60. Regulation III of 1828: The deliberations resulted in the enactment of Regulation III of 1828 on 12th June. It provided for the appointment of Special Commissioners for the determination of investigations under Regulations II of 1819 and IX of 1825, the powers of the civil courts being thereafter suspended in regard to such cases, and for the transfer from the courts to the Special Commissioners of all cases then pending. In new cases the Collector or other local officer would commence the inquiries in accordance with those regulations and record his judgement, from which either Government or the adverse party might appeal to the Special Commissioner, whose decision would be final. In cases appealed to the civil court, the decisions of the Board, declaring the liability of the lands to assessment, were to be carried into immediate execution, and the holders dispossessed if they declined to pay the assessment. In regard to the forest, section 13 enacted: "The uninhabited tract known by the name of the Sundarbans has ever been, and is hereby declared still to be, the property of the State: the same not having been alienated or assigned to zamindars, or included in any way in the arrangements of the perpetual settlement, it shall therefore be competent to the Governor-General in Council to make, as heretofore, grants, assignments, and leases of any part of the said Sundarbans, and to take such measures for the clearance and cultivation of the tract as he may deem proper and expedient." Grantees were entitled to take possession of and hold their grants without question or opposition, and if their title or right of possession were contested by a neighbouring zamindar through the courts of law, the suit was to be dismissed, if it was found that the lands when granted lay within the limit of the unoccupied jungle. Claims by the zamindars to banker, mom-mahall, &c, in the Sundarbans were to cease, and compensation was to be given instead if they were satisfactorily proved. Section 13 further enacted: "The boundary of the Sundarban jungle shall be laid down by accurate survey, as determined on the spot by the Commissioner of the Sundarbans; and any zamindar, talukdar, or party interested shall be entitled, on application made through the Commissioner, and on payment of the charge of preparing the same, to receive a copy of the survey map or of any part of the same, with the boundary marked there as so determined, together with a copy of the Commissioner's proceedings on the subject." The proceedings were always to be held and published on the spot, and parties aggrieved might contest the same before the Special Commissioner, within three months of the date of the proceedings, on the single ground that at the time of survey a specific quantity of land was in the possession of the party, which the line of demarcation included within the Sundarban tract belonging to Government. Special Commissioners were appointed under Government resolution, dated 19th June 1828, and rules of practice to regulate their proceedings were passed on 21st August 1828, and are appended to the regulation.

61. Preferential Claim of Border Zamindars to Grants of the Adjacent Forest: The right of the State to the Sundarban tract had thus been established after long controversy, and the claims of the zamindars overthrown; but the latter presented themselves in another aspect. It was suggested that the border zamindars, who had abstained from, or had withdrawn, extravagant pretensions to the Sundarban wastes, should have a prior claim to engage on the usual jangalburi terms for the cultivation of those tracts of jungle which immediately adjoined their estates; and that course was recommended, as it would diminish the apparently arbitrary character of Sundarban legislation and prevent boundary disputes. But the Board pronounced against it because it would militate against the interests of cultivating speculators, and advised that the grants should be bestowed by selection among the applicants. The Court of Directors had enunciated disinterested principles regarding the rights of the zamindars under the Permanent Settlement, and the Governor-General had put the most liberal construction thereon. The zamindars had already received advantages enough, while they had been guilty of fraud and oppression. The Government decided on 27th June 1828 that the border zamindars should have no exclusive right to the lands, but all applications should be weighed, though, other things being equal, they should have the preference in tracts immediately adjoining their estates.[3] In the bestowal of the grants, however, the European residents of Calcutta largely predominated, and few, if any, were given to the border zamindars.

3 Bd. Rev. to Sbn. Commr., no. 3724, dated 26 Sept. 1828.

CHAPTER V

Definition of the Boundary of the Sundarban Forest 1828-1833

62. Mr. W. Dampier, Sundarban Commissioner, and Lieutenant Hodges, Surveyor, 1828: Mr. William Dampier, who had held charge of the Sundarban office for some five months in 1827, was again appointed to it in February 1828, when the revised scheme was promulgated. Lieutenant Alexander Hodges was appointed the Surveyor in January 1828, and the instructions issued to him were to accompany Mr. Dampier and survey the boundary of the forest as the latter defined it, noting in during his course the khals and other natural features in order to parcel out correctly fresh allotments for speculators. His maps were to be preserved and copied, and his operations supervised by the Surveyor-General. The reason was, however, too far advanced to admit of their beginning the definition of the boundary that year.[1]

63. Definition of Boundary of Sundarban Forest in Jessore and Bakarganj, 1829-30: During the early months of 1829, Mr. Dampier defined and Lieutenant Hodges surveyed the boundary of the Sundarban forest, carrying it from the river Jabuna, at the junction of the Shura khal opposite Pranpur, as far as the river Baleswar, at its confluence with river Jeodhara. Cultivation had extended all along the line except between the rivers Kholpatua and Kabadak, along the river Kayra, and in chaks Lakhikhola, Tildanga, and Kumarkhali (the present Kamarkhola) on both sides of the river Bhadar. In those three localities lands once cleared had been deserted and had relapsed into jungle. In the two former, which fell within parganas Jamira and Talakhajra, the Board ordered that the limit of the then forest should be marked out, and also the limit of the forest as it was delineated by Morrieson in 1814, when the intermediate country had been

[1] Bd. Rev. to Sbm. Commr., 8 Nov. 1828.

cultivated, and that a record should be formed of the distance between the two lines.[2] Mr. Dampier, being unable to define the boundary positively, directed Lieutenant Hodges to take as the boundary the line shown in Morrieson's map and complete the survey up to the river Sipsa, while he himself crossed over to the opposite side and described the limits as well as he could. Lieutenant Hodges, however, made no survey of the limits of the then waste, but simply copied in his complete maps the line drawn in Morrieson's map.[3] Mr. Dampier could not proceed beyond the river Baleswar that year, as the nature of the ground he traversed compelled him to leave his elephants and the greater part of his equipage behind, and they want of good boats prevented his moving down that river, the cultivated area reaching further south on the east bank than on the west. During the following season he made arrangements about boats and completed the line, carrying it backwards from the Rabanabad Islands, at the mouth of the river Meghna, to the river Baleswar: rivers were generally the limit of the waste in Bakarganj. Reclamation had spread there most extensively along the whole border of the forest within the previous 20 years: about half those islands had been cleared, and there were large Mag settlements in Lalua, Baliyatali, and the contiguous chaks further south.

64. Mode of the Definition: The proceedings were recorded in a series of rubakaris which describe the boundary by mentioning its beginning course and ending, with the villages estates and streams that lay alongside it. By themselves they convey no vivid impression; they must be taken with Hodges' maps which were drawn *pari passu,* and exhibit his route and the limits of the forest; and the boundary then becomes clear and definite. The proceedings were conducted in the presence of the zamindars or their agents, and all other parties

[2] See Presdy. Commr. to Sbn. Commr., no. 228, dated 7 Sept. 1837, and Sbn. Commr. to Presdy. Commr., no. 430, dated 3 Oct. 1837.

[3] Sadr. Bd. Rev. to Sbn. Commr., 20 Feb. 1832 (1829?). It is said Hodges did survey the then limit of the forest, but see paragraph 65. See Mr. Dampier's remarks, when Member of the Board of Revenue in 1857, in Bd. Rev., to Presdy. Commr., no. 465, dated 2 Dec. 1857, sent with Presdy. Commr., to Sbn. Commr., no. 112, dated 7 idem. Hodges also surveyed a number of estates that fell on the line, see his letter to Sbn. Commr., 17 Aug. 1829, for the areas.

interested. The boundary laid down by the survey was never disputed nor appealed against:[4] in fact the definition of the limit of the forest scarcely admitted of disagreement. The boundary thus became final at the end of three months. The Board had enjoined that the boundary should be published in the Gazette, but that does not appear to have been done.

65. Character of the Boundary: The boundary from the river Jabuna to Gobra on the river Kabadak is plain, but from the latter place to Orabuniya abad (at the north-east of the present lot 217) there is an immense gap, regarding which Mr. Dampier says[5]: "The mauzas situated on the western bank of the river Kayra belong to pargana Jamira, and those on its eastern bank to pargana Talakhajro. From Morrieson's map and the depositions of the raiyats it appears that all the mauzas except Gobra have been overrun with jungle and left waste from the effect of the Sundarban climate. They have been deserted—some twelve years, some ten, some seven, and some two or three years. There is a little cultivation in Maliganti and Baga alone. The mauzas have become joined to the Sundarban forest, some from a distance of two kros, and others of three or four kros. The waste villages are comprised in the zamindari which contains the parganas, and cannot belong to the Sundarban forest. Consequently no map can be prepared or approved, unless the boundary of the jungle and waste lands of the several mauzas be determined; and it would be a difficult matter to define the boundary of the Sundarban forest. Hence the right course is to fix the boundary of the forest on the basis of the zamindari boundary and Morrieson's map." That was accordingly done. Hodges made no survey, though the Board ordered that the then limit of the forest should be surveyed; for there is no map of

[4] See Presdy. Commr. to Sadr. Bd. Rev., no. 350, dated 4 Aug. 1846, paragraph 9 (with Presdy. Commr. to Sbn. Commr., no. 138, dated 2 Sept. 1846).

[5] Rubakari no. 13, dated 3 Feb. 1829. Captain Gastrell, Revenue Surveyor, carefully examined Hodges' field-books in 1858, and gives an account of the survey *from the junction of the Podar Gang and Sipsa river as far as the Baleswar.* There is no gap in the survey, and it formed a continuous line, though in lot 222 and some other places he did not survey Mr. Dampier's line because the jungle prevented him. Chunkuri abad was all grass jungle, and he mentions it. Pankhali he does not mention, Gastrell, Revenue Surveyor, to Sbn. Commr., no. 1, dated 2 Oct. 1858.

this tract among his primary maps on the scale of four inches to the mile, and yet the numbering of those maps proves that there is none missing. The line of the forest in Morrieson's map was taken to be the Sundarban boundary, and Hodges copied it into his own secondary maps on smaller scales. From Orabuniya to Lakhikhola (on the west of the present lot 222) the boundary is defined in these words[6]—"On the west bank of the river Sipsa lies abad Orabuniya, and on the east bank the Badurgachi khal which flows to the river Bhadar. On the west of the Badurgachi is an embankment along the side of a plot of cultivated land; towards its north-east the Bhadar runs across it; towards the north is abad Lakhikhola."But Hodges' map depicts the forest as spreading in a large block far to the north, and his line does not tally with Mr. Dampier's description, for it travels around that block, and then passes to the south side of the river Bhadar, so as to exclude the two abads of Tildanga and Kumarkhali (Kamarkhola). Again from Lakhikhola to the east bank of the river Pasar the definition runs thus[7]—"The Maukhali Doaniya khal, which is on the east of Lakhikhola; abad Pankhali, which lies east of the Maukhali; and the river Pasar on the north-east side of Pankhali; *** Chunkuri abad; across the river Pasar towards the north-east lies abad Debraj; on the south-west of the Pasar lies dense Sundarban forest. Again, from the Pasar rises the river Pir Mangla, & c." Hodges made no survey of this portion, but copied for the boundary the line of forest shewn by Morrieson which relinquishes on the east side of lot 222 some 6,000 bighas that Mr. Dampier pronounced Sundarban forest.[8] From the junction of the Pasar and Mangla rivers to the Agunmukhi river the rubakaris and maps agree. The line was not carried through the Rabanabad Islands.

66. Hodges' Maps: The results of the survey were drawn first in a series of plans on the scale of four inches to the mile, which were worked down into another series on the scale of one inch to the mile,[9]

[6] Rubakari no. 14, dated 9 Feb. 1829.

[7] Ibid., dated 9 Feb., and no. 15, dated 11 Feb. 1829.

[8] Sbn. Commr. to Bd. Rev., no. 54, dated 27 Apr. 1882.

[9] All Hodges' maps of Bakarganj were sent to the Survey Department in 1840 under the Board's orders (Presdy. Commr. to Sbn. Commr., no. 71, dated 17 June 1856). All his original Sundarban maps and field-books are now in the Survey office.

and from the latter Hodges prepared a map (on the scale of two miles to the inch) of the whole of the Sundarbans, using Morrieson's map as the basis for the country as far as the river Pasar and Prinsep's maps for the details of the 24-Parganas. It was completed in 1831 and is known as Hodges' map of the Sundarbans. It shows the boundary of the Sundarban forest along the whole length from the Hugli to the Meghna. The allotments made by Prinsep in the 24-Parganas were incorporated in the map, and the same system was continued by Lieutenant Hodges as far as the river Pasar, which was the limit of Morrieson's detailed survey; but he revised the numbering and reduced the whole of Prinsep's and his own allotments into one series of consecutive numbers from 1 to 236 extending from the Hugli to the Pasar. A register was found of the lots by Mr. Grant and their aggregate area was computed at 51,49,820 bighas.[10] The whole of the coast from the Hugli to the Meghna with a breadth varying from five to ten miles was copied from Major Rennell's atlas of 1779,[11] but the interior details of the forest tract east of the Pasar had never been surveyed. The portion of the coast lands lying between the Hugli and Pasar was not lotted out, there being no likelihood of its early reclamation, while the system of allotments could not be applied to the Sundarban waste east of the Pasar which was *terra incognita.* Besides those particulars, Hodges' map shews the position of the patitabadi mahalls in the 24-Parganas and the principal details of the zamindari lands in Jessore and Bakarganj according to Rennell's atlas. To provide sufficient copies of the man, and render it available for the public, the Government transferred the copyright to a Mr. Wood on condition of receiving 100 lithographed copies free.[12] The map was advertised by Messrs. Black & Co. in 1830.[13]

67. Definition of Boundary of Sundarban Forest in 24-Parganas, 1832-33: After grants of the forest had been freely made in 1830 and 1831 collisons occurred in the 24-Parganas between the grantees and

[10] Sbn. Commr. to Presdy. Commr., no 500, dated 9 Nov. 1843. The bigha used by Hodges was the standard of 40 yards square.

[11] See note 4 to paragraph 12.

[12] Presdy. Commr. to Sbn. Commr., 14 June 1830.

[13] See Govt. Gazette of 6 Sept. 1830 (advertised beforehand?).

the zamindars, the latter complaining that parts of their lands had been included in the leases. Such cases arose along the forest line, especially beyond the river Piyali, where patitabadi mahalls with their well defined boundaries did not about on it. The line there had been surveyed by Prinsep, but no proceedings had been conducted under Regulation III of 1828, and the boundary was not authoritative. Hence it was necessary to give efficacy to his demarcation. Mr. Dampier was ordered to go over Prinsep's line from the Hugli to the Jabuna and define the boundary in proceedings held agreeably to the provisions of the regulation, employing Lieutenant Hodges to survey the correct boundary wherever Prinsep might have erred, and rectifying all deficiencies or ambiguities in the latter's maps.[14] That duty was carried out during season 1832-33. The portion of the boundary that most needed determination was that between Pranpur on the river Jabuna and Bhadratola on the river Bidyadhari. He investigated and settled all claims and disputes, and finding them baseless, did not require Hodges to make any survey, but maintained Prinsep's boundary, marking it here and there with bamboos, and his decision was acquiesced in by all parties.[15] There do not appear to be any rubakaris dealing with this portion of the Sundarban boundary in the same way as in Jessore and Bakarganj.

[14] Sadr. Bd. Rev. to Sbn. Commr., no. 55, dated 8 May 1832, and no. 76, dated 20 June 1832.

[15] Sbn. Commr. to Sadr. Bd. Rev., 7 and 27 Aug. 1833. Presdy. Commr. to Sbn. Commr., 10 and 24 Jan. 1539. Sbn. Commr. to Presdy. Commr., no. 82, dated 22 Apr. 1840, and Presdy. Commr. to Sbn. Commr., no. 76, dated 4 June 1840.

CHAPTER VI

Jurisdiction and Summary of Operations
1828-1836

68. Jurisdiction of Sundarban Commissioner, 1828-36: Various minor changes had been going on between the revenue jurisdiction of the Collector of 24-Parganas and the Sundarban Commissioner, for estates were retransferred to the former when their settlements were completed and confirmed, but revisions of settlements introduced considerable fluctuation. In 1828 pargana Penchakuli and other mahalls with a jama of about Rs.5,00,000 were transferred to the Commissioner. In former years he had been engaged almost exclusively in the 24-Parganas, but at the close of 1828, from which time his duties often carried him for long periods into other districts, the practice was introduced that the Collector of 24-Parganas should manage the collections during his absence. This suggested (what the Board had recommended in 1827) the expediency of revising the Commissioner's jurisdiction, and it was resolved by Government in its No. 1201, dated 24th November 1829, that his office should cease to be one of collection, and the parganas should be retransferred to the several Collectors, but that he should continue to exercise the powers of a Collector of land revenue as far as necessary to enable him to conduct the investigation of the resumption cases under Regulations II of 1819 and III of 1828, and to complete the settlement of the patitabadi and resumed lakhiraj lands, notwithstanding that they were situated within the limits of the parganas transferred to the Collectors. The establishment was reduced from Rs. 778 sicca to Rs. 376 per month, and the office, which had hitherto been sometimes at Baroipur and sometimes in the suburbs of Calcutta, was permanently located at Alipur. The whole of the revenue jurisdiction was permanently transferred to the Collectors on 1st February 1830, except in the case of estates attached or immediately under settlement, where the collections were transmitted to the Collector, though the accounts were controlled by the Sundarban Commissioner.[1] Such estates, however, were made over to the Collectors as soon as the cause for which they had been taken in hand ceased. The change was beneficial, as it allowed him to concentrate his attention on the settlement of the patitabadi mahalls, which, after the definition of the boundary had been accomplished, became his most important duty, and afterwards on the resumptions and settlements which fell in under Regulations II of 1819 and III of 1828. For, on the Board's recommendation, his jurisdiction was extended by the Government in its No. 834, dated 3rd August 1830, over all the parganas and estates contiguous to the boundary in all the districts, and he was vested throughout with the same authority as he possessed in the patitabadi mahalls, while all cases under Regulation II of 1819 within those limits were transferred from the Collectors to him, thereby also facilitating the determination of the boundaries of those districts. Besides those duties, the large khass mahalls Buzurgummedpur and Ramna Bamna, of which a detailed settlement had long been required, were placed under his temporary management,[2] During nearly ten years of great activity, however, so many estates came into the Commissioner's direct charge by means of resumptions and attachments or for purposes of settlement, that Khass management constituted a large and onerous portion of his work. Experience approved those changes, for the Board when reviewing the operations in 1832 observed that, apart from the inapplicability of the law, the grand error of the original plan had been that it constituted the Commissioner a Collector with the charge of a treasury and the performance of other duties foreign to his peculiar avocations, so that both his time and attention were wasted.[3] It may be mentioned here that the whole staff of kanungos was dismissed in 1828, except two who were employed to compile the records, and indexes for the 24-Parganas, Jessore and the Sundarbans.[4] The object seems to have been accomplished within a year or two.

1 Sbn. Commr. to Revenue Accountant, 9 Sept. 1833, and Presdy. Commr. to Sbn. Commr., no. 19, dated 13 Jan. 1830.

2 Presdy. Commr. to Sbn. Commr., no. 1437, dated 4 Sept. 1830.

3 Sadr. Bd. Rev. to Govt., no. 342, dated 25 Sept. 1832.

4 Presdy. Commr. to Sbn. Commr., 3 June 1830.

69. Appointment of Revenue Commissioners, 1829: Revenue Commissioners were appointed throughout Bengal in 1829 under Regulation I of that year. The Sundarban Commissioner was placed in subordination to the Revenue Commissioner of the 18th Division, which comprised 24-Parganas, Jessore, and Bakarganj, though, for a short time, from 1832 to 1834, Mr. Dampier was allowed to correspond direct with the Board of Revenue for the speedy disposal of the numerous and important operations that were then in hand. The district of Dacca Jellalpur,[5] which bordered on a portion of the Sundarbans, lay within the 15th or Dacca Division; but, for the sake of simplicity and uniformity, the whole of the Sundarbans was taken together and controlled by the Commissioner of the 18th or Presidency Division.[6] The present Presidency Division is composed of the greater part of the old 14th and 18th Divisions, but for the sake of convenience, the Revenue Commissioner will be spoken of as the Presidency Commissioner. The Board of Revenue was replaced by the Sadar Board in 1830.

70. Summary of Operations, 1830-36: Having defined the boundary of the Sundarbans, Mr. Dampier employed himself during season 1830-31 in investigations under Regulation II of 1819 throughout the eastern portion of the Bakarganj district adjacent to the forest, where reclamation had been rapidly progressing. He completed the investigations in pargana Chandradwip and carried them westwards as far as Ramna and Bamna.[7] Lieutenant Hodges meanwhile was occupied in surveying all the estates presumably liable to resumption in that locality east of the river Buriswar, and Mr. James Reily was appointed Assistant to Mr. Dampier to conduct the settlement of the patitabadi mahalls in the 24-Parganas. The following season Mr. Dampier was ordered to carry out enquiries under Regulation XI of 1825, section 4, regarding all alluvial lands in the district of Bulloa (Noakhali); but a delay in the communication of the intelligence to the Collector prevented Mr. Dampier's undertaking

[5] Dacca Jellalpur was abolished by Regulation V of 1833, and the boundary between the Jessore and Bakarganj districts seems to have been the Putimari river and the Bhola or Chilla Chandpai river.

[6] Presdy. Commr. to Sbn. Commr., 11 May 1838.

[7] Sbn. Commr. to Presdy. Commr., 6 Oct. 1831.

the duty that season, and he returned to Bakarganj to attend to the settlements of the mahalls that had been resumed in favour of Government; authority having been given him to complete the settlements of such lands, if the holders agreed thereto, immediately after resumption.[8] Besides the operations in Bakarganj, which were very extensive, he had to finish the settlements of the patitabadi mahalls in the 24-Parganas and undertake the resettlement of Henckell's mahalls and the settlement of the newly resumed lands in Jessore, for resumption proceedings were numerous and almost endless. To enable him to cope with the work, three Assistants were given him in season 1831-32— Mr. McClintock in 24-Parganas, Mr. Donnelly in Jessore, and Mr. Crawford in Bakarganj—and they were succeeded during season 1832-33 by Messrs. Crawford, Grant, and Tottenham respectively, of whom the latter two remained through season 1833-34, while Nar Narayan Rai Peshkar took Mr. Crawford's place. During 1832-33 Mr. Dampier defined the boundary between Bakarganj and Bulloa in company with the Collector of the latter district[9], and, taking up the postponed inquiries under Regulation XI of 1825, investigated and resumed, under Regulation II of 1819, 17 chars and islands in Bulloa from Dakhin Shahbazpur to Sandwip.[10] Lieutenant Hodges surveyed Ramna Bamna (62,326 bighas) and a part of pargana Saiyadpur (4,88,743 bighas) in seasons 1831-33, and the islands and chars in Bulloa the following season. In September 1834 Mr. Grant, the Assistant, succeeded Mr. Dampier as Commissioner, and was employed two seasons in completing and revising the work that had been in progress, especially in Jessore and Bakarganj.

[8] Presdy. Commr. to Sbn. Commr., 30 Nov. and 24 Dec. 1830.

[9] Govt, to Sadr. Bd. Rev., no. 354, dated 29 March 1833.

[10] Sbn. Commr. to Sadr. Bd. Rev., 16 July 1833. Hodges used the surveys by Captain Robertson in 1810 and Captain Blake in 1824.

CHAPTER VII

Resumptions

1828-1836

71. Early Resumption Proceedings in Jessore and Bakarganj: In the border lands from the Hugli to the Jabuna, which had hitherto been under the Sundarban Commissioner's jurisdiction, the resumption proceedings under Regulations XXIII of 1817 and II of 1819 had been conducted by him; but in the Jessore and Bakarganj districts he had no authority, and all such proceedings fell within the cognizance of the Collectors. In Jessore, where the supervision of Henckell's mahalls had frequenty drawn attention to the spread of cultivation, much interest was displayed, and, contemporaneously with the renewed activity of the Sundarban Commissioner in 24-Parganas after 1821, the Collector instituted proceedings for the resumption of new reclamation. Investigations had been begun still earlier, but few were brought to a decision before Regulation IX of 1825 was passed. In Bakarganj the subject attracted less attention, and, though proceedings were set on foot, little seems to have been accomplished.

72. State of Sundarban Lands in Jessore: Between the Kabadak and Pasar rivers, on the confines of parganas Sahosh and Malai, the zamindars had largely encroached on the forest by granting away leases for it as appertaining to their permanently-settled property; two noteworthy instances being the Lakhiraj *brit* (or estate) of Syam Rai Thakur, which had appropriated 7,000 bighas of forest, and leases given away by the zamindar of Malai for 14,075 bighas. In the case of Sahosh, which with 22 other parganas belonged to Raja Barada Kantha Rai of Jessore, there was some colour of right in the claim to the forest, for in 1826, when his property was under the Court of Wards, the Collector, looking solely at the interests of the ward, prepared *a dihbandi* (or list of villages), in which large portions of the forest were recorded as belonging to the pargana, and his action subsequently brought on a conflict between the interests of the State and those of the ward, and created great difficulty in the resumption of lot 222 and neighbouring lands between the Pasar and Putimari rivers, which latter seems to have been the eastern boundary of the district cultivation. Numerous estates had been carved out of the forest under the authority of the neighbouring zamindars subsequently to the Permanent Settlement. Besides such usurpations, lands were sometimes held by individuals under pattas granted by the collectors.[1] Between the Kholpatua and Kabadak, and about the Kabadak and Kayra rivers in parganas Jamira and Talakhajra, cultivation had retrograded after the year 1816.

73. Resumption and Settlements in Jessore, 1825-30: The Collector's method of resumption appears to have been to depute amins to make inquiries and measurements and base his proceedings on their reports; but it was unsatisfactory and entailed much confusion. Suits were instituted without sufficient previous acquaintance with the lands concerned; boundaries were inaccurately defined in the decrees; estates were at times resumed twice over; and occasionally estates already on the revenue-roll were decreed as if new clearances under different names.[2] His decisions were at first submitted to the Board of Revenue for final adjudication, and on the appointment of Special Commissioners in 1828 were appealed to the latter. His attention seems to have been chiefly directed to the encroachments by the zamindars of parganas Sahosh and Malai. Hariya (with Sankardana), Tetultala, and Dalai were resumed by the Board on 11th March 1825; and Orabuniya (near Paikgacha) on 20th September 1825; the former were settled by the Collector in 1826,[3] and the latter estate about the same time.[4] A block of land between the Shalta and Gengrail rivers was resumed by the Board on 26th September, in accordance with the Collector's opinion of 16th June 1826,[5] and it was found to comprise 11 chaks—Khagrabuniya, Koipukhuriya, Magurkhali, Parmagurkhali, Hetalbuniya, Korakata, Suargudi, Alladipur, Jharjhariya, Sibnagar (in

[1] Donnelly to Sbn. Commr., 3 July 1832.

[2] Sbn. Commr. to Sadr. Bd. Rev., 4 Feb. 1835.

[3] Confirmed by Bd. Rev., 7 Feb. 1827.

[4] Ibid., 1 Nov. 1828.

[5] In many letters the year is given incorrectly as 1825.

which were included Kataliya and Ghazinagar, and also apparently Ghuruniya and Bagarder), and Kalajangal *(alias* Parmandartala). For the last two chacks appeals were preferred to the Special Commissioner, which were not decided for ten years. The Collector leased out Jharjhariya and Korakata under amalnamas in 1830.[6] He settled the others in 1827 and 1828, Putimari (which had been resumed about the same time) in 1829, and Taltala (resumed on 27th April 1829) in 1830; and the settlements of these nine chaks and one other were confirmed by Government in its no. 519, dated 26th April 1831. The total area settled by the Collector was about 3,550 bighas, and the revenue Rs. 1,080. Other resumed estates were Harijhipatan and Khaliya (both resumed by the Board on 26th September 1826) Harikhali resumed by the Collector on 31st July 1826, Chandmukhi (three portions) resumed by the Collector on 27th December 1828, and Andarmanik on 25th January 1830. Appeals were preferred in the cases of Harikhali and Andarmanik, but were both decided by the Special Commissioner in favour of Government on 25th January 1830. Other estates were Bharbhari (including Kumibuniya), Kalmibuniya, and Bogara with Romardanga, all resumed on 15th January 1830; Nawalitala and Bashiya on 25th January 1830; Beharibhita, Singjor, and Basakhali, and also Siberbati about the same time; Samukpota (in which it seems Panna was included) and Bahirbuniya on 17th June 1830;[7] Gumantali, Jabakhali, and Betangi on 7th June 1830.[8] Bhairabghata and Bankeswar were also resumed about this time.[9] The Collector measured Harijhipatan and Harikhali in 1826, and settled them with an area of 2,534 bighas and jama of Rs. 252 in 1829.[10] The other estates were not immediately settled, and were afterwards made over to the Sundarban Commissioner. Besides regular settlements the Collector also gave away leases for the forest under the permission accorded in 1817.[11] Thus a patta on Mr. Henckell's terms appears to have been granted in 1820 by the Collector with the Board's approval

[6] Presdy. Commr. to Sbn. Commr, 5 March 1834.
[7] Ibid., 8 Aug. 1831.
[8] Sbn. Commr. to Presdy. Commr., 9 Jan. 1836.
[9] See Sbn. Commr's statement of Dec. 1831.
[10] Babu U.K. Sen to Presdy. Commr., no. 152, dated 23 Aug. 1845.
[11] See Paragraph 38.

for Kaikhali[12] (South of Pranpur) and one for Khaliya in 1826.[13] A similar patta was given for Atliya (or Talbariya, a portion of lot 166) on 10th July 1827, and a large tract of forest between the Bhadar and Pasar rivers was bestowed on one Maulavi Abdullah with the Board's approval, on the then Sundarban terms apparently.

74. Resumptions and Settlements in Bakarganj, 1805-30: Lands in the Bakarganj Sundarbans are high, embankments are unnecessary, and the rivers are comparatively sweet. These causes led to their early and wide cultivation. A few grants were made by the Collectors, notably one in 1805 to Ramdhan Chatterji for Mauzas Phuljhuri and Aila Teorkhali, which gave rise to long litigation afterwards; but the great bulk of the cultivation had been effected under leases granted by the neighbouring zamindars. Enquiries were conducted by the Collectors, and one of them, Mr. Hunter, employed a European surveyor about the year 1818.

On 14th July 1819 the Collector decided that Lalua, Baliyatali, Dhalasar, and Chapli were liable to assessment, and the Board resumed them from the zamindars of pargana Chandradwip on 18th July 1823. Grants were made of them at once to three Mags, there being large Mag colonies there, namely, in Lalua drons 199-9, Baliyatali drons 349-4, Dhalasar drons 158-9, Chapli drons 337-6, and char Chapli drons 67-5; but the settlements were ineffective, as the raiyats would not acknowledge the grantees. The zamindars appealed to the appellate court at Dacca, and on 10th January 1828 gained their case; but the decree was upset on reference to the Special Commissioner, who affirmed the Government right on 11th December 1832.[14]

75. All Resumption Proceedings Committed to Sundarban Commissioner, 1830: The deputation of Mr. Dampier to define the boundary in Jessore and Bakarganj introduced no change, for his duty merely went to the determination of the limits of the forest, and it still remained the duty of the Collectors to complete his results by prosecuting inquiries into lands which appeared open to resumption. The boundary defined was the limit of the forest, and inside it there

[12] Sbn. Commr. to Presdy. Commr., no. 36, dated 10 July 1858.

[13] Ibid., no. 391, dated 13 Sept. 1854.

[14] See Sbn. Commr. to Bd. Rev., no. 236, dated 25 Aug. 1881.

existed, with two or three exceptions perhaps, no abads or cleared lands. For cultivated lands which lay outside, but which were alleged to have been reclaimed after the decennial settlement, it was necessary to proceed under Regulations II of 1819, IX of 1825, and III of 1828. Suits were begun throughout by the Collectors in large numbers, but, before they were decided, they were all transferred to the Sundarban Commissioner in 1830 under the orders of Government, no. 8348, dated 3rd August 1830. Besides the cases so received, a large number were afterwards instituted by Mr. Dampier and his Assistants.

76. Supplementary Resumption and Settlement Rules, 1831: The provisions of the resumption laws were supplemented by further rules On 22nd February 1831 the Government ordered that no land held rent-free should be assessed until the expiration of six months from the date of the Collector's resumption decision; but the Collector was bound immediately to notify to the parties his intention to assess the land at the expiration of six months from the date of his notice, and thereafter proceed to assess, if no appeal were preferred; while, if the parties appealed, the assessment was to be stayed on their furnishing security.[15] The rule was repeated in 1836, and the occupant was protected from being dispossessed or subjected to assessment during the six months, unless the Commissioner of the division should consider immediate measures for the assessment of the land essential to the preservation of its integrity or the maintenance of its assets; and in such case the party was entitled to a sum equal to the net mufassil rental for six months.[16] Otherwise, pending the confirmation of the settlement, the lands were held khass, and this practice continued till 1846. Then, however, khass management was deprecated as entailing oppression and loss of revenue, and the Board ordered that some settlement should be made in all cases without delay, even with the late lakhirajdars at the sacrifice of some revenue.[17]

77. Surplus Lands in Patitabadi Mahalls Resumed by Special Commissioner, 1828-36: The patitabadi investigations fairly grasped the whole case for resumption in the 24-Parganas, the Jabuna apparently

[15] Bd. Rev., C.O. no. 7, dated 8 March 1831.

[16] Presdy. Commr. to Sbn. Commr., no. 261, dated 21 March 1831, and no. 128, dated 31 Aug. 1836.

[17] Presdy. Commr. to Sbn. Commr., no. 110, dated 7 Oct. 1846.

being the boundary between that district and Jessore, and the right of Government had been practically established by the decision of the Board in the resumption "suits, although some 30 patitabadi cases had been appealed to the civil court. Special Commissioners for the trial of such cases were appointed in 1828 under the Government resolution of 19th June 1828, and the appeals were transferred to the Special Commissioner of Calcutta for adjudication. All doubts were set at rest when Mr. Halhed, the Special Commissioner, decided the first case in 1829, and decreed the right of Government to assess the patitabadi taufir or surplus lands.[18] Decrees in the other cases naturally followed, and all were disposed of by the year 1832, with the exception of Ban Hugli, Teghariya, and a few others. These also were decreed before 1836.

78. Circumstances in Jessore and Bakarganj, 1830: Jessore, from the Jabuna to the Bhola, was the peculiar region of Henckell's and Smelt's operations, and the rights of Government there were involved in great obscurity, for the measurements and settlements of 1815-16 had been hasty and superficial; claims had been parried rather than decided, and many questions had been shelved until the Sundarban Commissioner could take them up. In Bakarganj, east of the Bhola, the claims were less complicated and were divided into four distinct sets by the river Baleswar, Amua Don, and river Buriswar. Between the Bhola and Baleswar lay pargana Salimabad; between the Baleswar and the Amua Don, pargana Saiyadpur; between the Amua Don and the Buriswar were contained the large khass mahalls of Ramna Bamna and Buzurgummedpur and the grant of Aila Phuljhuri; east of the Buriswar lay parganas Aurangpur, Ratandi-Kalikapur, and Chandradwip-Rafiyanagar, which were somewhat intermixed. Mr. Dampier began his resumption proceedings at the extreme east in season 1830-31 and worked westwards, and when the three Assistants were given him in the following season, he assigned Jessore to Mr. Donnelly, while his own immediate attention was devoted to Bakarganj.

79. Resumptions in Bakarganj, 1831-34: In Bakarganj all the resumption cases instituted were, with the exception of Kataliya and Pattamara, which the Collector decreed, practically carried through

[18] Sbn. Commr. to Presdy. Commr., 26 Aug. 1829.

by Mr. Dampier.[19] During season, 1830-31 he prosecuted his investigations throughout the reclaimed tract east of the Buriswar and Lieutenant Hodges at the same time surveyed it. The estates there had never paid revenue, and their liability was first pointed out by him in 1830.[20] The total area was 3,46,211 bighas, of which 2,49,280 bighas were cultivation, 11,487 bighas waste, and the remainder jungle, which lay chiefly in Rangabali, Bara Basdiya, Dhankhali, Nishanbariya, Kukua, Gerakhali, Bara Bighai, and Gulsakhali, the other estates being cleared. His enquiries were highly successful, and during the year 1831 he established the right of Government to all the Sundarban mahalls that have been resumed in that quarter, except Charwa and Ragua which he resumed on 16th May 1832,[21] and Bazarghona, Patukhali, Kalibari, Chalitabuniya, and Pakhiya, which he resumed together on 20th November, 1834. Appeals were preferred in the cases of almost all the estates situated south of the Badura river and Kukua Don, but seldom with success. Thus the Special Commissioner decreed Taktabuniya on 5th September 1832 and Pattamara on 28th November 1832 and in 1833 Bara Basdiya (28th June), Chota Basdiya[22] (27th February), Rangabali (10th September), Tiyakhali, Nishanbaniya, and Sonauta (7th August), Tepura (11th September), Char Ghila (12th September.)[23] In some instances—Bara Basdiya, Rangabali, and Tepura—Mr. Dampier released a portion of the chak as not liable to resumption, but the Special Commissioner decreed the whole to Government, being of opinion that the exemption of those portions had been obtained by fraud on the part of the landholders. A few appeals were successful, thus the Special Commissioner released Patua and Kataliya. In Dhankhali, resumed by Mr. Dampier on 1st March 1831, and Debpur (with Sibpur)and Kishtapur, both resumed

[19] Colls., Bakarganj, to Sbn. Commr., 13 Oct. 1830.

[20] Sbn. Commr. to Sadr. Bd. Rev., 14 Feb. 1833.

[21] Appeals were instituted in both cases, and decided in 1837 and 1844 respectively. Ragua seems to have been one of Henckell's patta mahalls—see paragraphs 124 and 239.

[22] Choto Basdiya includes Kuraliya which was often spoken of as a separate mahall.

[23] The dates mentioned in Sbn. Commr. to Presdy. Commr., no. 636, dated 11 Oct. 1836, appear to be wrong.

on 9th April 1831, there was no appeal.[24] These estates were all resumed from parganas Chandradwip and Ratandi-Kalikapur. In the group of estates north of the river Badura and Kukua Don, where lie parganas Aurangpur and Buzurgummedpur, no appeals were instituted, and Mr. Dampier's decrees passed in 1831 held good—Kukua, Gulsakhali (with Gajkhali), Marichbuniya, Gerakhali, Hajikhali, Kewabuniya, Barunbariya, Guabariya, Pasarbuniya, and Bara and Chota Bighai, all resumed on 18th June—nor were his decrees of 1834 in the case of Bazar-ghona and the four other estates above mentioned contested.

80. Claim to Aila Teorkhali Failed, 1830-33: When engaged in the demarcation of the boundary in Bakarganj in March 1830, Mr. Dampier discovered an instance where the right of Government to a large tract of forest appeared to be gravely imperilled. He fixed the boundary along the border of Phuljhuri and Aila Teorakhali[25], but the owner of those lands, Abdul Ghafur, appealed to the Special Commissioner for a declaration that they belonged to him, and the claim appears to have been tried in an ordinary resumption suit instituted by Mr. Dampier. Abdul Ghafur produced a patta that Mr. Battye, Collector of Dacca, with the sanction of the Government, had given to his predecessor in title. Ramdhan Chatterji, on 9th April 1805, conveying to him the talukdari right in those chaks free of revenue for seven years and thereafter at a fixed yearly rental of Rs. 349; the boundaries were specified at the foot of the patta.[26] Phuljhuri was found by survey to contain 40,000 bighas. The boundaries of Aila Teorkhali on the south and west were not clear, but if the western boundary was, as appeared from Rennell's and Hodges' maps, the river Bishkhali below the Khak Don, its area by estimate exceeded 1,00,000 bighas. The patta appeared to have been granted by the Collector on a superficial report by his naib, with the vaguest ideas regarding the extent of the land; and it was open to suspicion from the fact that Ramdhan was a relative of the then Diwan Golok Chandra Mukharji,

[24] Sbn. Commr. to Presdy. Commr., 9 Jan. 1836.

[25] Rubakaris, dated 5 and 12 March 1830.

[26] See judgement of Privy Council on appeal of Khaja Abdul Gunny *versus* Commissioner in Sundarbans delivered 26 Jan. 1870.

by whom the land was in reality held.[27] The boundaries of Phuljhuri were plain, and the lessee's right to it appeared to be beyond question; but those of Aila Teorkhali did not admit of ready identification, and Mr. Dampier instituted proceedings to try the Government right to the land claimed as belonging to it. Failing, however, to establish the right, he dismissed the suit on 19th August 1831, and his opinion was confirmed by the Commissioner of the division on 31st January 1833.

81. Resumptions in Pargana Saiyadpur, 1832-34: Having completed his investigations westwards from Rabanabad as far as Ramna Bamna during season 1830-31. Mr. Dampier continued them to the Baleswar the following season, and instituted 40 or 50 suits for newly cultivated lands there on the borders of pargana Saiyadpur.[28] Holding that the Puna and Bhagirathpur Dons were one and the same,[29] he fixed them as the line of division between zamindari lands and lands resumable. All suits for mahalls north of the line he dismissed,[30] but decreed those south of it—82 in number—to Government on 24th August 1832. Appeals for the latter were preferred to the Special Commissioner and were not decided until 1838. These mahalls were Tushkhali, & c. They were resumed according to kismats and not according to taluks. Halta and kismat Haringhata were resumed by Mr. Dampier on 24th August 1832, but for them too appeals were preferred, which were decided in 1836.[31]

82. Resumptions in Pargana Salimabad, 1832-34: Resumption proceedings were instituted for 72 chaks lying on the south-west border of pargana Salimabad, between the Bhola and Baleswar rivers and north of the Manikkhola and Ghoshkhali khals. A Mr. Middleton had been deputed by the Collector of Dacca about the year 1790 to inquire into a claim that the zamindars of the pargana had presented for remission of revenue to the amount of Rs. 33,666 on account of lands, which they asserted had been taken possession of by Henckell's pattadars.

[27] Sbn. Commr. letters to Collrs. of Dacca and Bakarganj, 7 July 1830, and to Presdy. Commr., 10 idem.

[28] Sbn. Commr. to Presdy. Commr.(?), 29 Feb. 1832.

[29] For Mr Dampier's opinions regarding the boundary river in this locality, see Presdy. Commr. to Sbn. Commr., memo no. 73, dated 22 May 1865.

[30] Sbn. Commr. to Presdy. Commr., 4 Apr. 1837.

[31] Ibid., 21 June 1836.

He considered they were not entitled to a remission of more than Rs. 5,965, but (going, it seems, beyond his instructions) he proposed to alter the Sundarban line that Mr. Henckell had laid down in 1786, and described a new one as a substitute, which would have given up a considerable Sundarban tract. His line was the rivers Panguchi, Jeodhara, and Bhola or Manikkhola.[32] Government sanctioned the remission he suggested. On those facts Mr. Dampier, believing that Middleton's boundary had been confirmed, and the decennial settlement determined according to it, came to the conclusion, using Rennell's first map as his guide, that the lands comprised in the 72 cases had been released by Government, and dismissed them all on 14th and 22nd May 1834. But south of that area lay a group of estates newly reclaimed, the right of Government to which was not so barred. The Collector of Jessore had begun proceedings against them, which Mr. Dampier finished by resuming the estates on 4th June 1834. They were Phulhata, Jeodhara, Sonirjhor, Deotala, Baharbuniya, Ghusiyakhali, Manikkhola, and Panchakaran, and their area was estimated at about 33,000 bighas,[33] though no boundaries appear to have been specified. Appeals, however, were made to the Special Commissioner, which were decided in favour of Government on 22nd September 1836.

83. Mr. Donnelly's Operations in Jessore, 1831-32: The operations in Jessore were begun by Mr. Donnelly, the Assistant, in season 1831-32. They embraced the whole tract of country between the Raimangal and Baleswar, which had been the extent of Mr. Henckell's jurisdiction, and they were more intricate than in the other districts through the confused state of boundaries and the frequent disputes about the right of occupation. He began a remeasurement of Henckell's mahalls, and inquired into the circumstances of lands reclaimed subsequently to the Permanent Settlement, and into the state of cultivation between the Pasar and Baleswar with special reference to the condition of Henckell's grants in that quarter.[34] He determined the boundaries by documents preferentially, otherwise by oral evidence, conflicting claims being left to Mr. Dampier's decision; but, in some

32 Ibid., 18 Dec. 1834, and Ross, Dy. Collr. to Sbn. Commr., 10 March 1842.

33 Presdy. Commr. to Sbn. Commr., 4 Feb. 1837, and Sbn. Commr. to Presdy. Commr., 9 Jan. 1836.

34 Sbn. Commr. to Sadr. Bd. Rev., 14 June 1832.

instances, lands after being regularly resumed were laid claim to on the strength of leases given by the Collectors, the boundaries at times being extremely indefinite.[35] Conducting his enquiries, with the aid of Smelt's proceedings, into the circumstances of all lands cultivated along the face of the forest, he discovered a number of unassessed mahalls. The people were reluctant to give information, and new clearances on the borders of permanently-settled mauzas were often disguised under the names of those mauzas or of the *bils* of those mauzas. There was much new cultivation in parganas Bhaluka, Naihati, and Bajitpur; but it all lay within the limits of those parganas as fixed at the decennial settlement.[36]

84. Mr. Donnelly's List of Sundarban Mahalls of 1832: He prepared lists of all unassessed cultivated Sundarban lands, which appeared liable to resumption,[37] nothing their boundaries, holders, and estimated areas, but the ownership was generally disputed. Between the Pasar and Baleswar he discovered 46 chaks[38] with a total area of 1,00,400 bighas, namely:

List I

Salimabad Pargana

Arjunber
Karasumon.
Alordanga
Gupli Bhadra
Bansbariya
Sonakhali
Bhatkhali
Harganti and Dhuliganti
Kumirjhop
Kalibari, Banitala, and Khandkarber
Debraj
Mistridanga
Madardiya
Mallikerber
Ghusiyakhali
Fulta
Panchakaran
Sannyasi
Bansbariya
Betkata
Betbuniya
Deotala
Jeodhara
Kalir Par

[35] Dounelly to Sbn. Commr., 3 July 1832.

[36] Sbn. Commr. to Donnelly, 16 March 1832.

[37] Donnelly to Sbn. Commr., 1 and 7 March and 3 July 1632.

[38] The list contains only 44 chaks. It seems Gokulnagar, and Tatibuniya should be added.

Hooli Pagrana
Kuntibadhan
Hagla Pargana

Rampal	Karerdanga	Binai	Tengramari
Geubuniya	Digraj	Papulbuniya	Gula
Junjuriya			Bhalniya
and Basuri	Hurka	Kalekan	
Chapra	Bagura	Mererdanga	

West of the Pasar there had been encroachments by the zamindar of pargana Sahosh and also clearances by persons who had got leases from the Collectors. Mr. Donnelly could elicit no information about them from the people, but he named 43 chaks[39] with a total area of 48,200 bighas, all lying to the south of that pargana, which appeared open to resumption. Most of them were on the border of the jungle, and in some the still visible stumps of trees attested their recent clearance. They were these:

List II

Kachur abad	Batua	Motibuniya	Nabubuniya
Tildanga	Bankhali	Kalsibuniya	Hoglabuniya
Kamarkhola (with	Rutmari	Maehaliya	Sailmari
six villages)	Bajabuniya	Telikhali	Alakdi
Jirbuniya	Sanatankhali	Batua	Pankhali
Bhagabatipur	Orabuniya	Shapa	Chunkuri
Digla	Jirabuniya	Godamara	Bota
Nottabhanga	Bujbuniya	Raihardanga	Khota
Banstala	Rajnagar	Hatbari	Digardana
Manoharpur	Kanchannagar	Hetalbumya	

West of those there was a quantity of land for which the zamindar of pargana Malai had that year given leases; it comprised 37 chaks

[39] The list contains only 38 mahalls, unless the six villages in Kamarkhola be reckoned separately.

with a total area of 14,075 bighas (the boundaries, however, not being mentioned), namely:

List III
Pargana Malai

Alakdi	Noikati	Kachiharani	Digla
Kankardono	Kankraguniya	Jinkra	Banstala
Matabhanga	Bakultala	Gochura	Sahibmari
Natarkun	Goalbatan	Banaridanga	Bullabuniya
Snpliailald	Kanaidanga	Mazinagar	Debita'a
Karaibuniya	Godardanga	DusraPutiman	Batiyaghata
Chinamalla	Matam	Jhoradanga	Mallimara
Bailahara	Poowar Our.	Hoguldanga	Ghoni
Alladipur	Chuarchuardanga	Jirabuniya	
Nangalmora	Demshakhali		

West of those in list II, and bordering on parganas Malai and Sahosh, was the lakhiraj *brit* of Syam Rai Thakur which had encroached on the jungle to the extent of 7,000 bighas. He drew up a list of the chaks composing the *brit,* amounting to 33,475 bighas. This list is not found, but it appears to be composed of the two following lists—one of 38 chaks with an area of 18,475 bighas claimed as lakhiraj on the border of pargana Malai, viz.:

List IV
Pargana Malai

Paikgacha	Baitka	Dhonaruddi	Kumibuniya
Sannyasidanga	Kotibuniya	Nagar	Singjor
Parsamari	Motbari	Nasirpur	Lottabuniya
Kakrabuniya	Pankhali	Hoglabuniya	Lashkarerber
Rarikhati	Gopalpur Idta	Knshtanagar	Daskati
Saran	Tokiya	Srikantpur	Alumtala
Rakukati	Baridanga	Kuliya	Dhamsakhali
Kusal	Bibaghi	Helakhardanga-	Kuriya
Bhaira	Molta	Parirabad	Lakhikhola
Kuttota	Howli	Bailmari	

and the other of 19 chaks adjacent to pargana Sahosh with a total area of 14,100 bighas, namely:

List V
Sahosh Pargana

Katiyabhanga	Kashiyadanga	Telikhali	Hakta
Gangarampur	Sukdhara	Saiyadkhali	Baihakta
Natgona	Madhukhali	Kalinagar	Chandghar
Kinukata	Par Madhukhali	Gopipagia	Chandipur
Dagnatala	Radhanagar	Kavakhali	

85. Resumptions in Jessore, 1830-36: Resumption suits were instituted by the Collector for lands in Jessore, and they are said to have accumulated enormously before him, so that when his jurisdiction in such matters was transferred to Mr. Dampier in 1830, something like 300 cases must have been pending.[40] Mr. Dampier is said to have disposed of 110 cases during 1830-31, 96 being in favour of Government, while there still remained 191 cases for trial at the end of October 1831,[41] and it was to help him in those inquiries that Mr. Donnelly was placed under him. It is hard to understand what or where all those resumed mahalls were, or how many of them were also decreed by the Special Commissioner; for apart from those figures it would seem that, during Mr. Dampier's time, resumption proceedings in Jessore constituted no marked feature of the administration. Mr. Donnelly's inquiries had been conducted in a preliminary and general way rather than with close regard to the circumstances of individual cases; and Mr. Dampier's attention being occupied chiefly with the important resumptions and settlements in Bakarganj, and the completion of the patitabadi settlement in 24-Parganas, affairs in Jessore seem to have been postponed for subsequent consideration, so that little seems to have been accomplished until Mr. Grant, who succeeded Mr. Dampier, was specially directed to give his attention to

40 Presdy. Commr. to Sbn. Commr., no. 1437, dated 4 Sept. 1830.

41 Ibid., no. 1331, dated 1 Sept. 1831 and no. 226, dated 16 Feb. 1832.

them in 1834.[42] The history of Jessore reclamation went back to Mr. Henckell's time, and Mr. Grant appears to have mastered it; but his researches occupied time, and when he seems to have brought matters to a satisfactory position in 1836, ill-health necessitated his departure. Resumptions during this period were therefore very few; Gumantali (including Jabakhali and Betangi) was resumed on 2nd January 1834; Tetulbariya on 19th November 1833; Perikhali on 15th July 1834;[43] Nasimabad on 23rd November 1835.

86. Resumption of Forest Lands, 1830-36: Regulation III of 1828, section 13, declared the Sundarbans to be the property of the State, and provided that its limits should be laid down by the Sundarban Commissioner. Hence it seems that, when the boundary was defined, the forest became *ipso facto* the property of the Government, and no resumption proceedings were necessary. In some instances, however, along the border suits were instituted, but the right to the forest seems to have been ordinarily tried in suits by the zamindars before the Special Commissioner under section 13, for there were a few great zamindars—Owen John Elias, Raj Ballab Rai, Ram Ratan Mitra, and Mohammed Amir—who asserted claims to the whole of the forest. The particulars of the resumption proceedings are not forthcoming, but it would seem that in the forest lands in the district of Jessore there were either no suits or the suits were speedily disposed of, for grants were freely made there during 1830 and 1831. As mentioned in paragraph 46, three suits for forest lands in the 24 Parganas, estimated at 3,51,200, 1,46,000, and 66,400 bighas, had been appealed from the Board's decision to the civil court. They were transferred to the Special Commissioner when he was appointed in 1828, and were decreed by him in favour of Government in September 1836.[44] In Bakarganj the Sundarban boundary ran through the border mahalls dividing them into part cultivation and part jungle. The mahalls were resumed by Mr. Dampier as described above, but no proceedings seem to have been taken for the chaks beyond, which were all forest, except in the case of Aila Phuljhuri, where the holder claimed under a special grant.

[42] See paragraphs 113 and 114.

[43] Perikhali, however, was released by the Special Commissioner on 3 Sept. 1845.

[44] Presdy. Commr. to Sbn. Commr., 4 Feb. 1837.

87. Policy of Compromise Proposed, 1833: In some of the patitabadi appeals, the talukdars had offered a compromise which Mr. Dampier declined, and subsequent offers, though supported by him, were disapproved by the Board and the Government. The Court of Directors, when reviewing the Sundarban operations in 1833, expressed their regret thereat, and recommended compromises, provided no great abatement was made in the Government claim; but the Governor-General, while observing that the expediency of compromising depended on the number of cases pending, doubted its advisability, since the operations had been so extremely successful, and left his decision dependent on further information.[45] At that period, however, little effect was given to the Directors' views, for the manner of compromise being that, in consideration of the landowners' admitting the Government claim, Government should demand a moderate revenue, generally in perpetuity, neither party, it seems, was inclined to yield. The only instances in which the policy was resorted to were the Kharija mahalls of pargana Buzurgummedpur.

88. Resumption Proceedings in the Kharija Taluks of Pargana Buzurgummedpur, 1831-34: The origin of the Kharija mahalls was this.[46] A batwara of pargana Buzurgummedpur was carried out by Mr. G. Thompson, Assistant Collector of Dacca, in 1792. He divided it into five shares, appointing the cultivated lands (the extent of which, however, was not recorded) between the proprietors, but leaving the uncultivated lands in their joint possession until separate arrangements for them could be undertaken. Before the contemplated division of the latter lands was carried into effect, the five shares were sold for arrears of revenue in 1206 apparently, and bought by Government, which thus became the proprietor of the whole estate as it originally stood. Subsequently several of the mahalls of which the estate was composed were sold for arrears of revenue due from the *talukdars;* and were treated as separate estates with the jamas assigned them in the batwara papers of 1792, but without any specification or proper division of the lands. These were the Kharija taluks, and in the agreements entered

[45] Sadr. Bd. Rev. to Sbn. Commr., no. 115, dated 30 Aug. 1833.

[46] Presdy. Commr. to Sbn. Commr., no. 21, dated 14 May 1842, and Sbn. Commr. to Presdy. Commr., no. 4, dated 3 Jan. 1840.

into with the purchasers, Government expressly reserved the right to assess all uncultivated lands which might afterwards be reclaimed from the jungle and brought into cultivation. They appear to have been seven in number.[47] In 1812 the pargana was farmed out for ten years at a jama of Rs. 21,310, but the arrangement continued until the pargana was made over to Mr. Dampier in 1831 for resettlement. In the course of the settlement his attention was drawn to the Kharija mahalls, and they were found to have been encroaching on the forest. Mr. Dampier proceeded against them under the resumption laws to assess the recent cultivation, and in 1831 decreed three of them, Baduriya, Sakhariya, and Sailabuniya. On appeal, however, the Special Commissioner confirmed his decision in one case and reversed it in another; the former was for lands reclaimed posterior to the decennial settlement, and the latter for lands belonging to the pargana, which were neither reclaimed Sundarban waste nor taufir of any other description: Regulation 11 of 1819 applied to the former but not to the latter. With reference to the latter lands, the Special Commissioner ruled that Government on its own zamindari could not proceed against its tenants under the resumption laws,[48] but he stated that his decision would be no bar to any claim which, as zamindar of the pargana, Government might think fit to assert against the talukdars for land held by them in excess of the right area of their separated taluks. There was no conflict in the decisions, but Mr. Dampier, believing that they were irreconcileable, desisted from prosecuting the Government claim, and, with the approval of the Government granted in March 1834, instituted fresh proceedings under section 5 of Regulation IX of 1825. That course was adopted, because the pargana was under settlement, and the talukdars though independent had long before been declared by Government liable to pay rent for increased lands that might be found in their possession, and also because it would enable him to secure compromises.[49] Compromises were accordingly made in 1834 in the cases of Baduriya, Sakhariya, Sailabuniya, Buramajumdar, Atharagachiya, and the one-fourth share

[47] See below and also paragraph 124.

[48] Presdy. Commr. to Sbn. Commr., no. 150, dated 22 Nov. 1833.

[49] Govt. to Sadr. Bd. Rev., no. 275, dated 3 March 1834.

of Auliyapur. The talukdars agreed to pay an increased revenue of Rs. 14,908 instead of Rs. 11,281, and the Government forewent its full claim.[50] The claim over the three-fourths share of Auliyapur was burked, and the fraud was not discovered till 1839.

89. Review of the Results, 1834: The results accomplished at the end of 1834 may be thus summed up. All the patitabadi cases in the 24-Parganas had, with very few exceptions, been decided by the Special Commissioner in favour of Government. From the Jabuna to the river Kabadak lay some of Henckell's well known mahalls, where the right of the State to increased revenue was beyond question. From the Kabadak to Chandkhali, Government claims scarcely found a place, for not only had those of Henckell's mahalls which were situated there relapsed into jungle, but also a considerable area of permanently-settled land. From Chandkhali to the river Bhadra, where the spread of cultivation had broken into the forest waste, the reclaimed lands had for the most part been either already resumed separately, or were comprised within tracts that had been resumed as jungle previously, so that the right of Government was practically established, though subordinate claims presented abundant confusion. From the Bhadar to the Putimari (or Bhola), which was then the boundary between Jessore and Bakarganj, Government failed to make good its claim to any cultivated lands (for cultivation seems to have made no advance there), and even lost for a time its right over the forest in lot 222. Between the rivers Bhola and the Amua Don in parganas Salimabad and Saiyadpur Mr. Dampier had released the northern and decreed the southern mahalls, but his decisions were contested in appeal on either side. Between the Amua Don and the river Bighai lay the khass mahalls Ramna Bamna and Buzurgummmedpur, where the claim of Government as zamindar was indefeasible, and Phuljhuri and Aila Teorkhali, where it had broken down. Beyond the river Bighai almost all the suits had been finally adjudicated, and the lands secured to Government. As regards the jungle, the whole appears to have been resumed, and the few appeals that were pending were finally decided in favour of Government in 1836. With the exception of pargana Salimabad, where the Special Commissioner in 1837 decreed a large number of estates that Mr.

[50] Sadr. Bd. Rev. to Sbn. Commr., 23 May, 8 July, and 20 Sept. 1834.

Dampier had released, and of the grant of Aila Phuljhuri, where Government recovered in 1870 after long litigation the fine mahalls of Bargona, Dhalua, and Naltona, no important changes were introduced in after years in the revenue features of the Sundarbans, and the jurisdiction remains at the present time very nearly what Mr. Dampier left it in 1834. Resumption proceedings were afterwards undertaken in large numbers, especially in connexion with Henckell's and Donnelly's mahalls in Jessore, but they have added very little to the Sundarban revenue area. The appeals pending in 1834 and the subsequent resumption cases were strenuously contested, and the policy of compromise seems to have been relinquished.

90. Fees in Resumption Suits, 1828: The rewards to Government officers who succeeded in resuming lands were abrogated about 1827; but, with the establishment of Special Commissioners with judicial courts, Government laid down in August 1828 a scale on which remuneration was to be granted to its agents who conducted the resumption cases before the Special Commissioners: namely, 20 per cent, of the net annual increase of revenue, if the increase did not exceed Rs. 500, but if it was more, the remuneration mounted up by a gradually diminishing series of percentages: thus for the portion of the increased revenue above Rs. 500 and not exceeding Rs. 1,000, 15 per cent; for the portion between Rs. 1,000 and Rs. 2,000, 12 per cent; for the portion between Rs. 2,000 and Rs. 5,000, 10 per cent; for the portion between Rs. 5,000 and Rs. 10,000, 5 per cent; for the portion between Rs. 10,000 and Rs. 20,000, 1½ per cent; and if the increased revenue was more than Rs. 20,000 the fee was Rs. 1,000, which was the maximum except in very special circumstances.[51] The increase of the revenue could not be ascertained till after settlement, and as that often occupied several years, the rule was added by the Board in 1838 that the commission should be provisionally reckoned at Rs. 1-14 per acre of estimated cultivation.[52]

[51] Superintendent and Remembrancer of Legal Affairs to Govt., 9 Aug. 1828, and reply, 21 idem.

[52] Deputy Superintendent of Legal Affairs to Presdy. Commr., no. 243, dated 6 Nov. 1838.

CHAPTER VIII

Grant Rules of 1830 and Grants of Forest Lands

1829-1836

91. Revised Rules for Forest Grants, 1829: By the definition of the boundary the Sundarban forest became, under Section 13 of Regulation III of 1828, available for grants. The terms fixed in 1825 were reconsidered. The rule regarding security had deterred applicants, for four persons only—Mohammed Sami and Messers. Kerr, Sturmer, and Hill—had accepted pattas. Mr. Dampier proposed to do away with it in the case of respectable persons, and substitute a simple agreement that the lands were taken for cultivation, and that the grantees would pay the revenue at the end of the free term, which he recommended should be extended from seven to ten years. The Government, accepting the proposal of the Board of Revenue, dispensed with the security when advisable, rendering instead the lease liable to cancelment, if one-fourth of the grant were not reclaimed after five years, and lengthened the free term to twenty years.[1] But the indulgence was subsequently qualified by the proviso, that applicants should shew to the satisfaction of the Sundarban Commissioner that they really possessed the means of reclamation and would at once employ them.[2] The revised terms of 1829 were these. The entire grant was to be held free of revenue for twenty years; one-fourth of the area was to be rendered fit for cultivation in five years, and in the event of failure Government had the right to resume the whole; one-fourth was exempted from assessment in perpetuity in lieu of an allowance for roads, houses, embankments, & c.; the remaining three-fourths were to pay revenue at these rates—2 annas per bigha[3] in the twenty-first year, 4 annas in the twenty-second year, 6 annas in the twenty-

[1] Presdy. Commr. to Sbn. Commr., 29 Sept. 1829.

[2] Ibid., no. 1429, dated 31 Aug. 1830.

[3] The bigha in all grants was the standard of 40 yards square.

third year, and 8 annas in the twenty-fourth year and in perpetuity; lastly, the Board were empowered to call for accounts. The kabuliyat was to the same effect, and contained an extra clause providing for a measurement at the end of the twentieth year by Government, either of its own motion or at the desire of the grantee.[4]

92. Promulgation of the Rules, 1829-30: The changes in the terms were notified to the public in October 1829, and the revised rules were published in the Government Gazette of 25th March 1830. Applications poured in, mostly from Europeans resident in Calcutta, among whom sanguine expectations were formed of the success to be gained in Sundarban reclamation. The applications were submitted to the Government along with the recommendations or remarks of the Sundarban Commissioner and Board of Revenue, and large numbers were sanctioned; but it was enjoined that the Salt Agency, which owned numerous khalaris in the Sundarbans, should be consulted in all cases before grants were made, in order to avoid conflicts between the grantees and the salt manufacturers.[5]

93. Interests of Salt Department Protected: References were accordingly made to the Salt Agents of the 24-Parganas and Jessore, and they explained what lands they wished to have set apart for their use. Eight lots were reserved in Jessore—nos. 127, 128, 131, 132, 149, 150, 151 and 152.[6] But the requisitions in the 24-Parganas were impracticable, unless all idea of extending cultivation was abandoned,[7] and were not approved, though lots 31 and 36 were subsequently withheld from lease.[8] The grants made in Jessore contained numerous khalaris, which it was impossible to exclude; but in 24-Parganas there were none. The Salt Agent on the one hand, it was laid down, had no right *to* move his khalaris from their sites to other parts of grants, nor had he a lien over sites once worked but then deserted.[9] On the other hand the grantees in some cases closed the khals that fed the salt works in order to reclaim their lands, and the Government prohibited them

[4] See first register of Sundarban pattas.
[5] Presdy. Commr. to Sbn. Commr., 6 May 1830.
[6] Sadr. Bd. Rev. to Sbn. Commr., 11 Oct. 1831.
[7] Sbn. Commr. to Sadr. Bd. Rev., 31 Dec. 1832.
[8] Collr., 24-Parganas to Sbn. Commr., 25 Nov. 1833.
[9] Presdy. Commr. to Sbn. Commr., no. 1242, dated 16 Aug. 1830.

from such acts where the khalaris were working and existed anterior to their leases; but the order seems to have been of doubtful validity and was protested against.[10] If, however, the department wished to resume operations in abandoned khalaris, recourse was necessary to the provisions of Regulation I of 1824. In 1834 two new clauses were prescribed—(1) that land occupied by the Salt Department was excluded from the grant and deserved to Government, provided the Salt Agent should demarcate it within six months from the time when he received notice of the grant; and that in default the grant should be unconditional and absolute against the department; and (2) that the Agent in his demarcation should be restricted to such fuel land nearest to the khalaris as might be indispensable to the manufacture of salt.[11] In 1835 a new clause was prescribed regarding the manufacture of salt, and the earlier grantees were called in to have their leases amended.[12]

94. Grants Made, 1830-36: A large number of applications was sanctioned by Government preference being given according to priority,[13] but the leases executed and submitted to Government for registration varied from the applications with regard to names, boundaries, area, &c, which had undergone correction, and some delay occurred before the final confirmation. The applicants were called upon to state what assurance they could give for the clearance of their lands, and inability or reluctance on the part of some led to the cancelment of their grants; while many of them evinced no haste to execute their engagements, and Mr. Dampier was at length obliged to coerce them with the threat that their grants would be cancelled if they continued recusant. Bankruptcy and alienations also introduced changes. Mohammed Sami and Messers. Kerr, Sturmer, and Hill were admitted to the benefit of the new and more favourable rules, and fresh pattas were given them. Being the earliest grantees, they had suffered from the hostility of the zamindars, who had obstructed their reclamation and harassed them with law-suits. The following new lots were granted away in 1830 and 1831—nos. 1-7, 18, 21, 22, 24-26, 28-30, 32, 33, 40, 42-50, 52-54, 56 (portion), 57, 59, 60, 62, 63,

[10] Sbn. Commr. to Presdy. Commr., 15 Sept. 1831.

[11] Sadr. Bd. Rev. to Sbn. Commr., no. 55, dated 1 Apr. 1834.

[12] Ibid., 24 Aug. 1835 and 1 Feb. 1836.

[13] Govt. to Sadr. Bd. Rev., no. 101, dated 26 Jan. 1830, & c.

65, 66, 67, (south portion), 68-77, 79, 80, 83, 86-90, 93-99, 101-11, 114-16, 122, 123, 129, 130, 133, 136, 142,143, 166 (portion), 167, 168, 172, 217-21, 224, and 225. The following appear to have been sanctioned about the same time, but the leases were not executed till after some delay—In 1832 lots nos. 84 (portion) and 137; in 1833 no. 58; in 1834 nos. 13, 84 (portion), 85, 91, 92, 100, and 169 (portion); and in 1836 nos. 78 and 135. The total area granted away at the end of 1836 was 16,68,340 bighas with an ultimate revenue of Rs. 6,25,627.[14] The principal grantees were Messers. Kerr, Sturmer, McDermott, Mackenzie, D'Costa, Betts, Clark, Hamerton, Heatly, Storm, Rogers, Campbell, Fergusson, Brae, Pigou, and Calder, Bruce and Hurry among Europeans; and among natives Radhakrishna Datt, Guru Prasad Chaudhuri, and Hafizuddin.

95. Supplementary Provisions: In making the grants special attention was directed to the subject of boundaries and area, which were to be specified with the utmost possible precision, and where that could not be done, provision was to be made in the lease for their determination when the lands were cleared.[15] As a further safeguard, the Sundarbans Commissioner put the grantees in possession by deputing his nazir to the lands. It was found in some cases that cultivation had been progressing so as to have pushed beyond the forest boundary. In such cases it was laid down as a general rule, that the reclaimed lands would not be included in the grants, but the rule was not to be enforced except in special circumstances.[16] The question, whether the right of fishery in the rivers and khals that bounded the grants belonged to the grantees, was raised by some of the zamindars and grantees each claiming it; but the Board decided in 1829 that it was not included in the grants.[17] Some uncertainty arose regarding the dates to be assigned to the grants, for, after applications had been sanctioned and possession given, the grantees in some cases neglected to execute their engagements. The Board directed that the date of

[14] These are the totals of the grants. The figures given in Sbn. Commr. to Presdy. Commr., 12 Dec. 1856 are manifestly incorrect.

[15] Bd. Rev. to Presdy. Commr., 22 Oct. 1830.

[16] Ibid., no. 3947, dated 29 Dec. 1829.

[17] Ibid.

the sanction should be adopted as the initial date, a few cases being specially excepted.[18]

96. Bakarganj Forest: Numbers of applications had been received for grants in Bakarganj, amounting to 60,000 bighas, by the year 1834, but none were sanctioned, no formal grants being practicable as no detailed survey had been made of the forest lands there. All the forest east of the Pasar seems to have been considered to belong to that district. Mr. Dampier in 1833 pronounced the revenue-free period of twenty years too long, and suggested that the terms should be modified in Bakarganj, where the work of reclamation was easier than in 24-Parganas and Jessore; but his views were not accepted by the higher authorities.[19] Unable to bestow grants there, Mr. Dampier gave amalnamas, which conveyed a provisional though informal authority to the recipients to begin reclamation in the lands specified. He did not report his action to the higher authorities, and the amalnamas never received sanction; but it appears to have been his intention that pattas properly approved should be conferred when the lands were cleared.[20] As a survey of the cleared lands would then be necessary, this method amounted to one of surveying the forest area in detail gradually and piecemeal. Thus he gave an amalnama for Gyanpara (with an estimated area of 20,000 bighas) and also for Andarmanik[21] (a portion of lot 220 in Jessore) with an estimated area of 2,500 bighas in 1832, and for the land west of the river Bhola and south of Perikhali[22] in 1834. Mr. Grant following him gave an amalnama for lots 211 and 212[23] in Jessore in 1835, and in 1836 another with a revenue-free period of twenty years to Mr. D'Silva, the ausat talukdar of Gulsakhali, for the jungle portion of it, called Eliyatiyakhali,[24] which had been excluded from the settlement of the chak made in 1834.

[18] Sadr. Bd. Rev. to Sbn. Commr., 24 Aug. 1835 and 1 Feb. 1836.

[19] Sbn. Commr. to Bd. Rev., 20 July 1829, and to Sadr. Bd. Rev. 1 Oct. 1833.

[20] For an explanation of his intentions see his remarks, when Member of the Board of Revenue, in the Board's letter to Presdy. Commr., no. 73, dated 8 Feb. 1856 (with Presdy. Commr. to Sbn. Commr., no. 267, dated 16 Feb. 1856).

[21] Babu U.K. Sen to Presdy. Commr., no. 148, dated 13 Aug. 1845.

[22] Sbn. Commr. to Presdy. Commr., 18 Sept. 1837.

[23] Presdy. Commr. to Sbn. Commr., no. 46, dated 18 Apr. 1849.

[24] Ibid., no. 469, dated 26 Sept. 1844.

CHAPTER IX

Settlement of Resumed and Other Lands

1828-1836

97. Settlement of Patitabadi Mahalls, 1828-36: Mr. Dampier took in hand the settlement of the patitabadi lands as soon as he was appointed in 1828. The progress had been extremely slow, for many cases awaited the decision of the civil court to which they had been appealed, and in others where the right of Government to assess the lands had been established, the opposition and chicanery of the owners, the claims to lakhiraj, the remeasurement of estates where cultivation had progressed, and the changes of officers had been common causes of delay. As long as the Government right remained doubtful, the mahalls were not brought on the rent-roll, but either the talukdars (as generally happened) gave security and retained possession, or the lands were managed khass and the accounts written up as profit and loss. After the year 1830, the operations were in the immediate charge of an Assistant, had were supervised by Mr. Dampier. Remeasurements were made where lands had been left out, or where cultivation had of late years been pushed further. Resumption proceedings were begun by Mr. Dampier for mahalls newly discovered and for extended clearances where the original mahalls had already been brought under resumption. New cases were Kalaburu, Dihi Batgachi, & c. The chief obstacle was removed in 1829 when the Special Commissioner, to whom all the appeals had been transferred,[1] first decreed the right of Government to assess the surplus; and the other cases naturally followed. But the uncertainty created by the protracted litigation had led in some instances to the neglect and relapse into jungle of lands once cleared. The settlements were carefully made and were based on

[1] One appeal seems to have been decided by the civil court and in favour of the talukdar.

detailed jamabandis, which Mr. Mangles had strongly pleaded for[2] as a protection to the under-tenants and raiyats, since the temptation to the talukdars to violate the terms of the jangalburi pattas given by themselves to the chakdars was very strong, for the full rates fixed in the pattas varied from 9 to 14 annas, while the lands when brought into cultivation were worth from 1 to 2 rupees per bigha: and in fact, one of the great landholders had at once set himself to violate them. The rates of assessment and the percentage of malikana were fixed in the Special Commissioner's decrees, and the Government revenue was computed thereon. But the rates of rent to be paid by the raiyats to the talukdar were determined after local enquiry by the Assistants, subject to Mr. Dampier's approval. The former rates were usually 8, 10, or 12 annas per bigha, but occasionally less. The malikana was ordinarily 20 or 30 per cent. The unculturable and waste lands were deducted from the whole area, and the remainder assessed at the above rates. From the gross jama so obtained the malikana was deducted, and the balance fixed as the Government jama. The taufir after being thus settled was united with the old assessed land, and the revenue of the whole taluk secured in one engagement,[3] which was confirmed in perpetuity by the Government, to whom all the proceedings were submitted.

98. Particulars of Patitabadi Mahalls: Precise information regarding the settlement seems unobtainable, the records being imperfect, and the proceedings having been frequently taken in hand by different officers, reopened, remanded, and revised, the causes of which would appear to have been the discovery of extended cultivation, the existence of conflicting claims, and some indecision in settlement operations.[4] Bhairabnagar was settled in 1828; in 1830 Syamnagar (with *Kistachandpur),* Rangaphulla (with *Radhanagar),* and Durganagar; in 1831 Gangadharpur, *Nokali* (with Sibpur), Lakhipasa with *Bhajna,* Panakua, *Karaibariya,* and ten small parcels of resumed land; in 1832 Gobindapur, Ramtanunagar, Ramchandrapur, Srikrishnanagar, Lakhinarayanpur, *Sibganj, Serhangampur* (or *Kerhangampur),*

[2] His memorandum, dated 7th January 1828, see paragraph 57.

[3] In some cases the method was reversed.

[4] Some idea of the character of the patitabadi settlements may be gathered from the account of Belpukhuriya, Khari, and other mahalls in chapter XVII.

Kasinagar, Khudadadpur,[5] Radhakantapur, and Lakhipur; and in 1833 *Kharbil.* By the year 1834 all the settlement proceedings appear to have been concluded in all the patitabadi mahalls, but delays occurred in the submission and confirmation of the results. In 1835 Bantra was settled; in 1836 Dhankhola, Sobhanagar, Harimul, Ramchandranagar, Simalbariya, Kharampara, Jallasi, Teghariya, Kharamba, Finga, Ghola, Chandibariya, Insulbariya, *Muragacha,* Khari (a katkina taluk), Abad Narayan Chand Bose (in pergunnah Madanmal),[6] Ramlochanpur, Arunnagar, Ban Hugli, Gabbariya, *Shahzadapur, Tegacha,*[7] and *Sarasbariya.* During the years 1833-36 the following estates appear to have been settled, after having for the most part been measured in season 1833-34. viz., Belpukhuriya, Bhagabanpur (two estates), Kishtarampur, Tona, Krishnapur, Srikrishnanagar (second estate), Masamari (two estates), Chapna, Kharamba (second estate), Sibpur (second portion), *Madhabpur, Nandanpur, Kurmamliva, and Bhurmpara.*[8] Many of the estates—those in italics—are not found in the lists of patitabadi mahalls given in paragraphs 25 and 41, but nearly all seem to have been mahalls of that description, and Karaibariya, Kharbil, and Khari came under the Commissioner's jurisdiction soon after the establishment of the office. In Hodges' map, however, the following additional mahalls are, noted down among the well known patitabadi taluks—Bhairabtala, Dhalsankibariya, Sibnagar, Mahisgot, Haldiya, Uttarpara, Harinarayanpur, Lakhinar, Adulpur, Churaghata, Karabeg, Tilpi, Maniknagar, Dhosa, and Dharmtala; but none of them appear among the records of the office as such lands. The surplus area

[5] McClintock to Sbn. Commr., 21 May 1832.

[6] Presdy. Commr. to Sbn. Commr., 1 Dec. 1836.

[7] Sadr. Bd. Rev. to Presdy. Commr., no. 268, dated 11 Nov. 1836.

[8] Sbn. Commr. to Presdy. Commr., 24 Dec. 1834. The origin of two estates of the same name was frequently this. A resumption suit was instituted by Mr. Dale for unassessed cultivation, and when that was decreed about 1830, Mr. Dampier found that the talukdar had further increased his clearances. The later cultivation was then resumed and treated as a separate estate. The resumed clearances in some cases, e.g. Chapna, consisted of small detached plots of land, which had been previously jungle intermixed with the cultivated lands of the original patitabadi taluk. Hence, no doubt, arose much of the difficulties of these settlements.

of the patitabadi mahalls thus brought under assessment was 1,99,117 bighas and the increase of revenue Company's Rs. 73,042.[9]

99. Subsequent History of Patitabadi Mahalls: The mahalls were thus definitely settled and, the State having established its right to all the waste lands beyond them, were no longer capable of expansion. The assessments were confirmed in perpetuity and the mahalls finally made over to the Collector of 24-Parganas. Their interest from a historical point of view here ends. Some of them afterwards through various causes came under the Sundarban Commissioner's control for resettlement, but they were merely dealt with in the ordinary way and present no features worthy of notice. One important class of exceptions will, however, call for future notice, namely border mahalls which had encroached on the Sundarban allotments, and in the dowls of which such usurped lands had been incorporated without specification of their peculiar character.[10] A few of the mahalls still remained under the Sundarban Commissioner's management through recusancy of the talukdars or other cause. These, however, were all transferred to the Collector's charge in 1838, it being impossible for the Sundarban Commissioner to attend to them while engaged continuously in Bakarganj.[11] When the talukdars persisted in their recusancy, they lost their rights and the lands fell in to Government as khass. With the patitabadi taluks went taraf Bansidharpur which had been a khass mahall from the beginning of the Commission, though a settlement of it seems to have been made in 1835.

100. Settlements in Jessore, 1831-32: In Jessore a number of estates had been resumed and settled by the Collector previous to 1830, as mentioned in paragraph 73. But when the Sundarban Commissioner's jurisdiction was extended throughout the districts, Henckell's mahalls and the other chaks, that had been resumed but not yet settled by the Collector, were transferred to Mr. Dampier for settlement. They were—Khaliya, Chandmukhi, Bharbari (including Kumibuniya), Kalmibuniya, Bogara (with Romardanga), Nawalitala, Bashiya, Beharibhita, Singjor, Basakhali, Siberbati, Samukpota

[9] Sbn. Commr. to Presdy. Commr., 12 Dec. 1836; but the figures cannot be relied on as accurate.

[10] See Chapter XVII.

[11] Presdy. Commr. to Sbn. Commr., 21 Apr. 1838.

(including Pana), and Bahirbuniya. This duty was entrusted to Mr. Donnelly in season 1831-32. He measured those mahalls and also began a remeasurement of Henckell's taluks. All the former except Bahirbuniya and Pana (where there were troublesome boundary disputes), Khaliya, Chandmukhi, and Kalmibuniya were settled, and also Bhairabghata and Bankeswar, at a total sadar jama of about Rs. 1,610. Char Jabuna in the Nadiya district was also settled at a jama of Rs. 8. Pranpur and Ramzannagar, two of Henckell's mahalls, were remeasured and settled, their aggregate area being 5,172 bighas and jama Rs. 2,591. Kaikhali, an out-clearance of Pranpur, was also assessed at Rs. 220.[12]

101. Settlements in Jessore, 1833-36: The operations in Henckell's other mahalls occupied a longer time and were completed by Mr. Grant, who was specially vested with the powers of a Deputy Collector in Jessore under Regulation IX of 1833 for the better discharge of his duties. Mr. Mills, the Collector, in 1834 carried out remeasurements of Gokulnagar, Ballabhpur, Bhairabnagar, Bansipur, and Chandipur. In the first two there were no lands in excess of Smelt's areas, but increased cultivation was found in the three others. Mr. Grant himself in 1835 remeasured[13] Henckellganj[14], Ismailpur, Gutlakati, and Asmatpur, also Kalidaspur (including Chandkhali), Gobindapur, and Babupur (including Banchanagar). The last two were all jungle, and no excess lands were found in the others except the fifth. In 1836 he remeasured Mohammedabad[15] (10 annas share) and found taufir there. A fresh patta was given for Gobindapur. Babupur, with the exception of portion of Banchanagar, had been taken possession of by the neighbouring zamindar, who seemed to be supported by the rubakaris

[12] Most of these settlements were confirmed by Govt., to Sadr. Bd. Rev., no. 1342, dated 18 Nov. 1833 (sent with Presdy. Commr. to Sbn. Commr., no. 1, dated 3 Jan. 1834). See Sbn. Commr. to Sadr. Bd. Rev., 14 June 1832.

[13] But see Sbn. Commr. to Presdy. Commr., 26 Aug. 1835.

[14] Henckellganj had been measured by Smelt, but the surplus lands were left unassessed with the Board's approval; it was to consist merely of the cultivation and fallow that he measured, viz., 2,945 bighas. Presdy. Commr. to Jessore Collr., no. 1603, dated 9 Aug. 1834.

[15] Mohammedabad was bought by Govt, on 18 Nov. 1823, and was partitioned into two shares of 10 and 6 annas. The former share was leased out in 1824 at ultimate jama of Rs. 739. Presdy. Commr. to Jessore Collr., no. 1603, dated 9 Aug. 1834.

under which Mr. Steer had released lands in 1816. The revenue fell into arrears, and the mahalls were bought in by Government—Babupur in 1830 and Banchanagar in 1833. The undisputed portion, comprising, it appears, chaks Banchanagar, Bejpara, and Basharatpur, with an area of about 8,000 bighas, but boundaries indefinite, was leased out by amalnama in 1836.[16] The increased cultivation in Bhairabnagar, Bansipur, Chandipur, Kalidaspur, and Chandkhali was brought under assessment by Mr. Grant in 1835, and that in Mohammedabad in 1836; so also in Phulbari-Bigardana in 1835, which had been separated from pargana Sahosh in 1798 and bought in by Government in 1815.[17] The settlements were completed at once in all except Chandkhali, Mohammedabad, and Kalidaspur, where the holders delayed executing their engagements till the end of 1838.[18] The settlements of these three were revised in 1841 with retrospective effect from 1836.[19] The area of these six mahalls resettled was 27,492 bighas of 55 yards square, and the Government revenue Rs. 6,120. Phulbari-Bigardana does not appear to have been settled. The increase of revenue to Government from the resettlements of all kinds in Jessore in 1836 was computed at Company's Rs. 6,187.[20] The bigha used by Donnelly and Grant was the 55-yard measure. Also Atliya (part of lot 166), which had been granted out in 1827 on Henckell's terms, was measured and settled—637 bighas.[21]

102. Method and Terms of Settlements in Jessore: In Pranpur and Ramzannagar Mr. Donnelly made a raiyatwari settlement, assessing the raiyats at rates varying from Rs. 1-8 to Rs. 2 per 55-yard bigha, but maintaining the fixed rate of 8 annas for the talukdars. In the settlement of Henckell's other mahalls, however, Mr. Grant dissented

[16] Sbn. Commr. to Presdy. Commr., 7 July and 12 Dec. 1835, 29 Aug. 1836; no. 240, dated 6 Sept. 1841; no. 229, dated 17 May 1843. Presdy. Commr. to Sbn. Commr., 14 May 1836, and no. 118, dated 1 July 1852. Last letter says both were bought in by Govt. in 1830.

[17] Bd. Rev. to Jessore Collr., 30 Apr. 1816, and Bd. Rev. to Govt., idem.

[18] Sbn. Commr. to Presdy. Commr, 26 Aug. 1835 and no. 498, dated 27 Dec. 1838.

[19] Ibid., nos. 218 and 219, dated 27 Aug. 1811. Presdy. Commr. to Sbn. Commr., no. 109, dated 13 Oct. 1841.

[20] Ibid., 12 Dec. 1836. But the amount cannot be relied on as accurate.

[21] Ibid., no. 116, dated 10 July 1851.

from that method, holding that, by the conditions of the lease, Government had no right to go below the talukdar, and his view seems to have been accepted.[22] He therefore merely ascertained the areas of cultivation, waste, and unculturable for each mahall, and assessed at the patta rate. But in Mohammedabad, Chandkhali, and Kalidaspur, which were khass mahalls, there was no restriction, and the lands were assessed at the revision in 1841 at rates varying from 10 annas to 1 rupee sicca per bigha. As in the patitabadi settlements in 24-Parganas, the taufir was united with the earlier lands and the revenue for the whole secured by one engagement. In the resumed mahalls the settlements by the Collector appear to have been ordinarily made thus. After deducting the unculturable from the total area, one-sixth was set apart for the settlement-holder's allowances, and the remainder assessed, sometimes at 6, but generally at 8 annas, per bigha. In the settlements by the Sundarban Commissioner, the raiyats holdings were separately measured, but no detailed jamabandis appear to have been drawn up, nor were the rents of the gantidars or other middlemen fixed in the few cases where they existed. Deducting the unculturable from the total area, the remainder was assessed at 8 annas (with rent-free and progressive periods for the jungle), and from the gross jama allowances of first 10 per cent, for expenses, and then 15 per cent, on the remainder for malikana (equivalent to a total of 23½ per cent) were given to the settlement-holder, the balance being the sadar jama. The zamindars, having done nothing towards reclamation beyond granting pattas, were generally put aside, and the settlement was made with the abadkar in possession, who was ordinarily a talukdar; the Government having laid down the principle on 8th November 1831 that the superior landholder, by whose encouragement the jungle had been reclaimed, was entitled, not of right, but in equity, to be admitted to the engagement.[23] The State by resumption became the real malik, but the distinction was not at first clearly drawn, and the allowance to the settlement-holder, whatever his status, was usually designated malikana. No periods were as a rule assigned to the settlements in the

[22] Ibid., no. 19, dated 12 Feb. 1835.

[23] In the case of Ramna Bamna; and the Board gave it general effect, Sadr. Bd. Rev. to Sbn. Commr., no. 1, dated 3 Jan. 1834.

leases, but they could not last longer than twenty years under the orders of the Court of Directors, except in special cases.[24] This Directors had prohibited perpetual engagements in the permanently-settled districts. This order, however, did not apply to cases where the proprietary right was vested in individuals, they being entitled by law to the privilege of a permanent settlement, but only to those cases where the right was vested immediately in Government.[25]

103. Settlements in Bakarganj, 1831-35: Pending the decision of the appeals before the Special Commissioner, Mr. Dampier brought the mahalls resumed in the east of Bakarganj under measurement and assessment during seasons 1831-33, viz., Rangabali, Bara and Chota Basdiya, Char Chapli, Dhalasar, Baliyatali, Lalua, Tiyakhali, Nishanbariya, Dhankhali, Debpur, Kishtapur, Sonauta, Char Chila, Tepura, Taktabuniya, and Kukua. Messers. Crawford and Tottenham were in immediate charge of the operations. The appeals were all decided in favour of Government by the year 1833, and the settlements were completed by 1834 before Mr. Dampier's departure, and were submitted for confirmation during that and the following years. They appear to have been approved for 15 years from 1238 to 1252 BE (1831 to 1846); but the sanction was delayed in the cases of Rangabali. Chota Basdiya, Tepura and Taktabuniya where he had maintained a long chain of undertenures. The settlements were agreed to, except in those four estates and in Bara Basdiya and Char Chila, all of which were therefore held khass, attempts to conclude temporary farms of them having failed. The engagements were executed for Rangabali Char Chila, and Taktabuniya in 1838, and the estates were released; but the three others still-continued khass.[26] The area of the settled portions of all the above mahalls (the dense jungle being excluded) was drons 1,081-13¼, equal to 1,40,638 bighas of 40 yards square.[27] The estates Lying on the north-west—Marichbuniya, Tafalbariya, Gerakhali, Hajikhali, Barunbariya, Kewabuniya, Guabariya,

[24] See Sbn. Commr. to Presdy. Commr., 9 Jan. 1836.

[25] Presdy. Commr. to Sbn. Commr., no. 1522, dated 11 Sept. 1830.

[26] Sbn. Commr. to Presdy. Commr., no. 390, dated 16 Sept. 1839.

[27] The kani (16 of which make a dron) is equal to standard bighas 8.2 kathas, and 12 chataks; but in Mr. Dampier's time it was taken as equal to about bighas 8-2-8. that is 8⅛ bighas.

Pasarbuniya, Gulsakhali, and Bara and Chota Bighai—were measured and assessed in season 1833-34, their total area being 21,027 bighas of 57½ yards square,[28] equivalent to 43,450 40-yard bighas. Bazarghona, Patukhali, Kalibari, Chalitabuniya, and Pakhiya, resumed in 1834, were taken in hand during the next two seasons, and their aggregate area found to be 4,564 bighas of 57½ yards, equal to 9,431 40-yard bighas. The settlements were completed in almost all the estates by 1835 and appear to have come into force at once, though they did not receive final confirmation till 1840-41. But the operations in the latter five estates needed revision and occupied some time longer. The revenue derived from all these Bakarganj settlements was computed in 1836 at Rs. 91,636[29] and was clear gain, the lands having contributed nothing before.

104. Method and Terms of Settlements in Bakarganj: The settlements were carefully and thoroughly made. In fact, these early Bakarganj settlements are models that were rarely imitated in after years. They contain also some census information. The measurements ordinarily followed the local standards of drons and kanis in the country east of the Kukua Don; but the bigha of 40 yards square was occasionally introduced in the final results, while in pargana Aurangpur west of that river the measure was the bigha of 57½ yards square. The lands had been reclaimed through a well developed body of tenantry. The zamindars granted leases to influential persons as talukdars or ausat talukdars (i.e., a class of talukdars whose status was "intermediate", between full talukdars and the lower tenants), and they portioned out their lands among haoladars (men who received charge—hawala[30]—of land for the purpose of reclamation). The haoladars were the true reclaimers, for they cleared the jungle at their own expense and divided the lands when cleared among a lower class nim-(or "half) haoladars. These latter were at first genuine cultivators, but the improvement of the country and the rise in the value of the

[28] The bigha in this locality, pargana Aurangpur, was 57½ yards square and was equal to bighas 2-1.5 of the 40-yards measure.

[29] Sbn. Commr. to Presdy. Commr., 12 Dec. 1836; but the amount cannot be relied on as accurate.

[30] It is the tendency in East Bengal to throw back the accent or stress in Hindustani words; hence hawala becomes hawala and then haola.

land enabled them in their turn to sublet their lands, for each class of undertenants in an estate had its own general rate, which was firmly established and free from fear of enhancement. The class to whom they sublet were called karshas *(i.e.,* ploughmen), who were mere labourers destitute of all rights. In most of the *eastern* mahalls in the Bakarganj Sundarbans at this time the nim-haoladars were the lowest class of cultivators; but the karshas had come into existence and were to be found in Baliyatali, Dhankhali, and apparently in the northern group of resumed estates.[31] The measurements were carried down to the nim-haolas and recorded the particulars of each holding, but the nim-haoladars were not admitted into the jamabandi, for Mr. Dampier considered their position and pronounced them to be *ghair-mourashi* (non-hereditary), inasmuch as they were unable to transfer their lands and were wholly dependent on the haoladars. The karshas being a lower grade still received no recognition whatever, unless they held directly from the haoladars, in which case their lands were measured like nim-haolas. The haoladars possessed heritable and transferable tenures, and were the only substantial and responsible occupants. Mr. Dampier pronounced them to be the "maurusi raiyats" and made them the basis of his jamabandi, leaving the rights of all below them to the cognizance of the civil courts. He investigated the value of the lands and the rents paid, and accepted as fair the rates he found current, being guided by the conclusions adopted in the patitabadi settlements in the 24-Parganas. The rates were for haoladars Rs. 2-8, Rs. 2-12, or Rs. 3 per kani according to different estates (equivalent to about 5, 5¾ and 6½ annas respectively per 40-yard bigha); for ausat talukdars Rs. 2 and Rs. 2-8; and for talukdars Rs. 1-4 and Rs. 1-12.[32] Fallow and jungle were allowed rent-free and progressive

[31] See the settlement rubakaris, and Sbn. Commr. to Collr., Bakarganj, no. 25, dated 13 Feb. 1841. In Chota Basdiya and Rangabali the jungle had been cleared by hired labour, and there were no raiyats holding lands and paying rents; but the raiyats hired themselves out and got money wages or half the crop. They seldom cultivated the same land in consecutive years. Sbn. Commr. to Sadr. Bd. Rev., 21 Sept. 1833. But there was a largely developed body of undertenants, see paragraph 105.

[32] In Baliyatali there is a special class of petao taluks between the taluks and ausat taluks: their rate was Rs. 2 per kani. The rates were for karshas Rs. 6 (sometimes Rs. 5); and nim-haoladars Rs. 3-8 and Rs. 3-12. See settlement rubakaris, and Sbn.

periods before the imposition of the full rate; but dense unbroken forest was excluded from settlement. In pargana Aurangpur the residents were haoladars, nim-haoladars, and karshas; but there too only the haoladars were put into the jamabandi, and their rate was Rs. 1-2 sicca per the 57½ yard bigha: the karsha rate was about Rs. 2-8. The lands by resumption became the property of the State, but Mr. Dampier respected the rights of all abadkars.[33] In the resumed lands reclamation, in every instance but one, had been the work of middlemen, and in pargana Chandradwip the zamindars, even when they did embark in reclamation, did so as talukdars under their co-sharer zamindars.[34] The zamindars therefore having done nothing for the lands were put aside, and the settlements were concluded on the principle explained in paragraph 102 with the talukdars or ausat talukdars who had undertaken the risk of reclamation. No deductions were made from the jama for them, for they were assessed at their own special rate, which allowed a profit on the lower rates, and the assessment at their rate was the sadar jama.

105. Orders Regarding System of Undertenures in Bakarganj: The long chain of undertenures with their liberal allowances, and the consequent small revenue due to Government in Chota Basdiya,[35] Rangabali, Tepura, and Taktabuniya raised doubts in the minds of the higher authorities regarding the propriety of Mr. Dampier's arrangements. The Board, not satisfied about the necessity for the extraordinary profit, objected to the principle on which the profit had been made to depend on the number of undertenures, and, without wishing for arbitrary interference with existing customs, inculcated caution in allowing the pernicious system of subinfeudation. In October 1833 they required him, (1) to assess the jama solely with reference to the nature and situation of the land, and the original expense and difficulty of reclamation, but not the condition of its occupation; (2) to report on the claim and merits of each tenant; and (3) where the engager had sublet part of his interests, to divide the net

---

Commr. to Sadr. Bd. Rev. 21 Sept. 1833. The theory is that each grade is entitled to keep about one-fourth of the rent paid by the next lower grade.

[33] Sbn. Commr. to Presdy. Commr., 18 March and 11 Sept. 1834.

[34] Sbn. Commr. to Sadr. Bd. Rev., 1 Oct. 1833.

[35] Including Kuraliya, which was often spoken of as a separate mahall.

profit between the several parties without diminishing the Government revenue. Mr. Dampier in reply explained his arrangements, but did not definitely answer the Board's observations.[36] The Board partially accepted his conclusions, but the Governor of Bengal did not feel satisfied that the interests of the State had been properly cared for, and called for further information regarding the tenures and rents, the method and course of reclamation, the division of profits, the rights of middlemen, and the period of settlement.[37] The inquiry on these points was committed to the Collector of Bakarganj in 1837, and he measured these four estates during the following season for that purpose.[38] Final orders were passed in 1839. The Deputy Governor did not think it safe in the then state of information to alter the settlements, as they had been in operation some years and had not worked ill, and so confirmed them for 15 years from 1831. The knowledge then obtained did not warrant the laying down of a general rule for settlements in such mahalls, but it was enjoined that settlement officers should complete the information in future, while observing a caution against heedlessly innovating upon established usages.[39]

106. Settlements in Pargana Saiyadpur, 1832-34: As mentioned in paragraph 81, Mr. Dampier resumed 82 mahalls—Tushkali, & c. —in pargana Saiyadpur in 1832 and brought them under assessment, though appeals had been instituted against the resumption. They were all small, being rather villages than mahalls. They were surveyed by Lieutenant Hodges during season 1832-33, and measured by amins the following season, the total area being computed at 81,755 and 88,179 standard bighas respectively. The lands of the haoladars were assessed at 9 (Company's) annas per standard bigha in Matbari, and 8 annas in Tushkhali and other more recently reclaimed lands; and the

[36] Sadr. Bd. Rev. to Sbn. Commr., 15 Oct. 1833, and Sbn. Commr. to Sadr. Bd. Rev., 27 Nov. 1833.

[37] Presdy. Commr. to Sbn. Commr., 2 March 1837, with Govt. to Sadr. Bd. Rev., no. 190, dated 7 Feb. 1837.

[38] Sbn. Commr. to Presdy. Commr., no. 333, dated 30 July 1840.

[39] Govt. to Sadr. Bd. Rev., no. 1623, dated 12 Nov. 1839.

sadar malguzars paid at 7 and 6⅛ annas respectively.[40] The assessment was completed in 1834 at a total jama of Rs. 50,196 and approved by Mr. Dampier,[41] but the mahalls had been attached in November 1833 and were held khass pending the decision on appeal. Halta also was measured and assessed during 1834-35, and was held khass pending the decision on appeal.[42]

107. Settlement of Buzurgummedpur, 1831-34: The large khass mahall of Buzurgummedpur was transferred to Mr. Dampier in 1830 for resettlement, as mentioned in paragraph 68. Its early history has been noticed in paragraph 88. After its acquisition by Government and the separation of the Kharija taluks, the remainder was farmed out in 1812 for ten years at a jama of Rs. 21,310, but no resettlement was made on the expiry of the term, though the area under cultivation had been yearly increasing. Mr. Dampier assumed the management on the owners of the component mahalls declining to execute engagements, and commenced the resettlement. The lands were measured and assessed during the years 1831-34 under the immediate direction of Messers. Crawford and Grant. The settlements were at first made on the detailed raiyatwari system and proceeded upwards, allowing each undertenant his profit and where no undertenants intervened, granting the talukdar (the owner of each petty mahall) a deduction of from 25 to 35 per cent, from the rents; but after November 1833 only those undertenants and raiyats were admitted into the jamabandi who paid direct to the talukdar, though account was taken of the others below in fixing the rents. The rates current were for karshas Rs. 4 to Rs. 6 per kani,[43] Rs. 5 being the general rate assumed by Mr. Grant; nim-haoladars Rs. 3, Rs. 3-8, and Rs. 4; haoladars Rs. 2, Rs. 2-8 and Rs. 3; and talukdars Re. 1, Rs. 1-4, and Rs. 1-8. All undertenures held by relatives of the talukdars were disallowed, it being a common

[40] Sbn. Commr. to Presdy. Commr., 25 July 1837 and 12 Feb. 1838. The assessment appears to have been really made on 55-yard bighas in sicca coinage.

[41] Ibid., no. 170, dated 29 May 1837. Presdy. Commr. to Sbn. Commr., 7 Aug. 1837.

[42] Sbn. Commr. to Presdy. Commr., 21 June 1836.

[43] The kani in pargana Buzurgummedpur was stated to be equal to 5¼ bighas. Babu U.K. Sen, Dy. Collr., to Presdy. Commr., no. 388, dated 18 Sept. 1845.

practice in Bakarganj to increase the profits in that way, the results were these:[44]

		Drons	*Acres*	*Rent (Rs.)*
243	petty mahalls[45]	510-5	15,390	31,377
96	chars[46]	138-3	3,807	6,153
28	salt tafalbaris	40-6	1,109	2,466
10	resumed lakhiraj	14-6	408	686
7	kharija mahalls	106-5	2,928	4,465
	Total	810-5	23,642	45,147

The settlements were completed in 1834. Where the talukdars agreed to the new jama and executed engagements, they received possession of their lands, but the majority appear to have recused, and their lands were held khass. In 1833-34, 73 of the petty mahalls were farmed out under the title of taluk to Krishna Kanta Bakhshi and another person at a sadar jama of Rs. 6,543.[47] The rest of the khass mahall was managed by the Sundarban Commissioner with the aid of a tahsildari establishment.

108. Settlement of Ramna Bamna, 1831-34: Ramna Bamna was another large khass mahall that was made over to Mr. Dampier for resettlement with Buzurgummedpur, both lying in pargana Buzurgummedpur. It had been bought by Government when sold for arrears of revenue in 1799-1800, and had been farmed out in 1805 to Mohammed Shafi, the talukdar, by whom it was still held at the same jama, though the period had long expired, and the area of cultivation had been immensely increasing.[48] Lieutenant Hodges surveyed it in season 1831-32, and found it contained 62,326 bighas. A detailed measurement was undertaken at the same time, and the area computed at drons 448-3, of which drons 443-11 were assessed at Rs. 1-4 per kani, a lenient assessment being imposed in

[44] Mr. Grant to Sbn. Commr., 10 Sept. 1834, and Sbn. Cornmr. to Grant, 11 Dec. 1832.

[45] In many of these Govt. had bought the talukdari right.

[46] See Sbn. Commr. to Presdy. Commr., 25 Aug. 1840.

[47] Ibid., no. 218, dated 16 July 1840.

[48] Ibid., 3 Apr. 1830.

consequence of the distressed condition to which the raiyats had been reduced through the talukdar's oppression.[49] Detailed jamabandis were prepared for all classes. The engagements were made with the ausat talukdars, and the heirs of Mohammed Shafi were excluded on account of their oppression, but received malikana of 10 per cent, in consideration of their talukdari right. The settlement was confirmed for ten years with a sadar jama rising from Rs. 6,972 in 1831 to Rs. 8,664 in 1840, or about double the former revenue.[50] The mahall was transferred to the Collector in 1834; he appears to have held it khass for about two years, after which the ausat talukdars paid their rents directly into his treasury.[51]

[49] Ibid., no. 181, dated 31 March 1843.

[50] Govt. to Sadr. Bd. Rev., no. 493, dated 28 Apr. 1834.

[51] Sbn. Commr. to Collr., Bakarganj, 1 July 1834. Sbn. Commr. to Presdy. Commr., no. 93, dated 27 Apr. 1840.

CHAPTER X

Resumptions and Collateral Inquiries

1834-1844

109. Sundarban Officers, 1836-44: Mr. Grant held charge of the Commission till March 1836. After a short tenure by Mr. Erskine, Mr. Shakespear assumed it in August 1836. Mr. Kemp succeeded him in January 1839, and Mr. Shawe followed from May 1841 till April 1843, when Rai Uma Kanta Sen, Deputy Collector, was put in charge of the office.[1] When Mr. Dampier left, it was thought the operations were drawing to an end and the Commission might be abolished,[2] but resumptions and settlements and other matters grew so numerous that the idea was shelved for a time. To cope with the increased work, Deputy Collectors were appointed. Mr. Herklots joined the office in March 1837 and was succeeded by Mr. Dennehey in July 1838, who was transferred the following year. Mr. Ross was appointed in December 1841 and remained until 1844, when the Commission was abolished. The services of a surveyor were also found indispensable to decide boundary difficulties. Mr. Turner served from March 1839 till his death in November 1840, and Mr. Mullins was appointed in January 1841. Mr. Dampier became Commissioner of the Jessore (or Presidency) Division in the beginning of 1838 and held the office till the beginning of 1840. His great knowledge of the Sundarbans corrected the errors that arose from the inexperience of the officers who were constantly changing and from the duplicity of their subordinates, Government appears to have called for a report on the Commission from its commencement, and much of Mr. Shakespear's

[1] Uma Kanta Babu was not acquainted with English. He managed his own sarrishta, and the English correspondence was drafted by the head clerk Mr. Pereira though during the later years Uma Kanta Babu appears to have employed a private clerk.

[2] See Sbn. Commr. to Sadr. Bd. Rev., 17 Sept. 1835.

time was occupied with it; but though voluminous statements and lists were submitted that year, no report seems to have been compiled.[3]

110. Jurisdiction: Resumption investigations along the Sundarban border had been assigned to the Sundarban Commissioner in 1830; but the Collectors—especially the Collector of Jessore—exercised similar jurisdiction over lands lying further inside their districts. The means of distinguishing their provinces, however, were not clear, and their independent jurisdiction created confusion and uncertainty, especially between the Kabadak and Bhadar rivers where the Sundarban tract stretches far to the north. Mr. Donnelly, who was Collector there in 1835, suggested a division of territory to obviate the evils and a line was proposed, apparently the then northern Sundarban boat route; but the scheme fell through.[4] Special Deputy Collectors were appointed in 24-Parganas and Jessore about 1836 to conduct the resumption inquiries in those districts concerning cultivated lands which were not encroachments on the Sundarban forest.[5] They appear to have exercised most of the powers of a Collector, a few only being excepted, such as in cases under section 30 of Regulation II of 1819 (some of which had been transferred to them from the Sundarbans office early in 1837), such cases being triable solely by the Collectors.[6]

111. Resumption Appeals in Pargana Salimabad, 1836-38: The appeals preferred against the resumption of chaks Phulhata, Jeodhara, Sonirjhor, Baharbuniya, Ghusiyakhali, Manikkhola, and Panchakaran were dismissed by the Special Commissioner on 22nd September 1836[7] as mentioned in paragraph 82. As regards the 72 other cases on the border of pargana Salimabad, which Mr. Dampier had dismissed in 1834, the Board were dissatisfied with the decision. Mr. Grant, his successor, pointed out, first, that Mr. Dampier had

[3] Sbn. Commr. to Presdy. Commr., 12 Dec. 1836. During Mr. Shakespear's tenure various reports and statements were prepared of the work past and current: they are useful, but not thoroughly trustworthy.

[4] Presdy. Commr. to Sbn. Commr., 28 Dec. 1835. Sbn. Commr. to Presdy. Commr., 8 Jan. 1836.

[5] Presdy. Commr. to Sbn. Commr., 10 Nov. 1838.

[6] Sadr. Bd. Rev. to Presdy. Commr., 18 Feb. 1827, and Presdy. Commr. to Sbn. Commr., no. 95, dated 6 June 1837.

[7] Presdy. Commr. to Sbn. Commr., 4 Feb. 1837.

erred in holding that Middleton's boundary had been confirmed by Government and fixed as the limit in the decennial settlement, for the remission of revenue sanctioned operated to the release of merely the land concerned in it, and not to the giving up of more than 200 square miles; and secondly, that Mr. Dampier had been misled by using Rennell's first map instead of his map of the Sundarban passage, and had mistakenly supposed certain rivers (not specified in Rennell's map), which cut off half of Middleton's tract, to be the rivers mentioned by that gentleman.[8] The whole of those cases were therefore taken up and appeals preferred on behalf of Government to the Special Commissioner in 1835, while Mr. Grant proposed, in the event of a favourable issue, to put forward appeals in eight other cases.[9] The Special Commissioner considered that 36 of the mahalls were open to resumption, but, before pronouncing, deputed a Mr. Houstoun to make a special local inquiry regarding the boundary line of pargana Salimabad, with the help of Lieutenant Goldie as Surveyor, early in 1837.[10] The inquiry was made, and Lieutenant Goldie determined in a rough survey the situation of the mahalls that were open to resumption. The 36 mahalls were finally decreed in favour of Government by the Special Commissioner on 29th August 1837,[11] viz., Harganti, Kaliya, Kayardiya, Nazirdiya, Abdulrasulpur, Panchamalerber, Mallikber, Bansbariya, Madardiya, Kapalibanda, Narendrapur, Jeolmari, Baintala, Betkata, Khondakarber, Debraj, Kumariyajola, Mahischaraniya, Gazaliya, Kharoikhali, Sutaluri, Gatipur, Fakirtakiya, Bhatkhali, Putikhali, Ghazirghata, Haldaha, Sannyasi, Betibuniya, Charadaha, Teliganti, Dhuliganti, Kakarbil, Kalyapara, Bistupur, and Nalbuniya.[12] The area was roughly estimated at 79,350 bighas. Other estates in the neighbourhood were also

[8] Sbn. Commr. to Presdy. Commr., 18 Dec. 1834.

[9] They were Hakimpur, Padmanagar, Jallalpur, Massampur, Sabikghata, Khutikhali, Patariya. and Betibuniya (Sbn. Commr. to Sadr. Bd. Rev. 25 July 1836). There was also another called Juniya, see Presdy. Commr. to Sbn. Commr., 18 Oct. 1837.

[10] Sbn. Commr. to Sbn. Commr., 6 Feb. 1837.

[11] Sbn. Commr. to Presdy. Commr., no. 444, dated 28 Nov. 1838.

[12] Sbn. Commr. to Goldie, 20 Nov. 1837, and Goldie to Sbn. Commr., 30 idem. It does not appear what became of the other 36 cases.

resumed: Narsinghdattber by the Special Commissioner on 24th January 1838; and Gazaliyarber on 27th August 1837.

112. Resumption Appeals in Pargana Saiyadpur, 1836-38: Appeals were lodged in the 82 cases on the border of pargana Saiyadpur that Mr. Dampier had decreed in 1832. His decision was upheld in 1838 by the Special Commissioner in 56 cases,[13] but reversed in six after deliberation by three Special Commissioners.[14] Those six mahalls were Bhagirathpur, Bara and Chota Salloa, Debipur, Bansbuniya, and Tetulbariya. Mr. Shakespear objected to the line of argument followed by the Special Commissioners in those cases on the ground that it would militate against Government in other cases, and an attempt was made to have the question reconsidered, but without success.[15] During the years 1839 and 1840, 16 other mahalls were released by the Special Commissioner on appeal.[16] Those 56 mahalls compose the present large estate of Tushkhali. Between that estate and Ramna Bamna lay a tract of 42,000 bighas, bounded on the north by a line from Amua Hat to Bhagirathpur; east by the Amua Don; south by the Bamini river; and west by the Dundua and Bhagirathpur rivers. Mr. Dampier had instituted 25 suits for its resumption , but had dismissed them, relying on a decision by Mr. Henckell of 24th February 1786 that several chaks and mauzas lying to the south of that tract were included in the zamindari of Saiyadpur, and that the river Bamini was situated on the southern boundary of that pargana. The Special Commissioner, however, in the appeals in the cases he decreed, declared that Mr. Henckell's decision was not binding on Government. Mr. Shakespear on these grounds urged in 1837 that Government should appeal in the 25 cases and sue in five similar new

[13] Sbn. Commr. to Presdy. Commr., 12 and 15 Feb. 1838.

[14] Ibid., 6 Aug. and 16 Nov. 1838.

[15] Presdy. Commr. to Sbn. Commr., 25 May 1839, and no. 181, dated 29 Oct. 1839. Tetulbariya was actually decreed to Government by the Special Commissioner on 6 Sept. 1836, but was wrongly given up to the zamindars when executing the decree regarding Sallua and Bhagirathpur. The error was discovered about 1857, and various attempts were made to regain the mahall, but without success, and the further prosecution of the claim was finally abandoned in 1862. Presdy. Commr. to Sbn. Commr., no. 91Ct., dated 20 Nov. 1857; no. 99, dated 5 Aug. 1862; and no. 34, dated 3 June 1863.

[16] Sbn. Commr. to Presdy. Commr., no. 240, dated 10 Aug. 1840.

ones, and Mr. Dampier, on being consulted, acquiesced.[17] It does not appear what happened except that the cases if instituted must have been lost. Mr. Shakespear also instituted proceedings for the resumption of the tract of country north of Tushkhali and adjoining Telikhali on the river Kocha, and measured the land north of Kalaran Chandipur with a view to similar proceedings[18]; but the results would seem to have been unsuccessful.

113. Board's Report on Claims of Government in Jessore, 1834: Mr. Donnelly's inquiries in Jessore during 1831-32 suggested more than they had accomplished. Mr. Mills, the Collector, in February 1834, in answer to a call, submitted to the Presidency Commissioner a list of Henckell's 16 mahalls, which he described as being all the jangalburi grants made by Mr. Henckell or his successors of which the recipients had availed themselves; and he went on to say that large tracts of land which had been measured by Mr. Smelt in 1816, as included in Henckell's pattas or as having been recently reclaimed from the Sundarban forest, had been released by Mr. Steer, the Collector, the claim of the State being abandoned and the lands restored to the parties whom Smelt found in possession. The orders were recorded in Persian rubakaris in which the Board's letter of 18th June 1816 was cited as the authority for the release. Mr. Mills thought the lands had been released without much investigation, and said he could not find that the Board had accorded their sanction to the release of all, though their letter was quoted as the authority. He was then remeasuring some of Henckell's mahalls and he urged that the rest also should be taken in hand.[19] The Board directed him to make careful measurements and thorough inquiries, as frauds had been perpetrated regarding the lands in Smelt's time; and they informed him that their letter of 18th June 1816 did not authorize the release of any land, or the abandonment of any claim, on the part of the State to its just revenue from lands reclaimed from the forest posterior to the Permanent Settlement.[20]

[17] Ibid., 4 Apr. and 8 June 1837, where lists of the mahalls are given; also no. 6, dated 14 Aug. 1834; and Presdy. Commr. to Sbn. Commr., no. 65A, dated 23 May 1840, with annexures.

[18] Sbn. Commr. to Presdy. Commr., no. 473, dated 7 Nov. 1837.

[19] Jessore Collr. to Presdy. Commr., no. 57, dated 28 Feb. 1834.

[20] Presdy. Commr. to Jessore Collr., no. 1602, dated 9 Aug. 1834.

About the same time the Board reported the matter to Government. They stated that the claims of the State to lands measured by Smelt had been abandoned in 1816 after a most cursory and insufficient investigation, and documents utterly worthless or irrelevant had been admitted as irrefragable proof of the right of parties to hold, as integral portions of their permanently-settled estates, lands which Smelt had measured as recently reclaimed from the Sundarban waste; while their letter of 18th June 1816, which had been cited in the rubakaris as the authority for the releases, in fact conveyed no such authority and had disappeared from the Jessore Collector. They had little doubt that Smelt had measured considerable tracts of land really permanently settled, but they suspected that the zamindars in collusion with the Jangalburi talukdars were allowed to claim lands that really belonged to the latter, on the understanding that such lands should be restored to the talukdars as soon as the close of Smelt's operations in the mufassil relieved the latter from apprehension. They asked that the measurements which were being carried out should be entrusted to an able junior officer, and the Government in October 1834, appointed as Sundarban Commissioner Mr. Grant, the Assistant, who had already acquired considerable experience in such matters in Jessore.[21]

114. Investigations in Jessore, 1834-36: These orders led immediately to the remeasurement and resettlement during 1835 and 1836 of Henckell's mahalls as described in paragraph 101; but Mr. Grant also began at once a close inquiry into the circumstances of the releases, studying the original correspondence of Messers. Henckell and Rocke which seems to have been till then neglected. The rubakaris appeared to be forgeries collusively fabricated; but Mr. Dampier, when engaged in such investigations in 1833, not being aware of the circumstances had relied on them as authentic, and dismissed five resumption suits begun in 1822 for 25 chaks—Asasuni, & c.—with an area of 24,500 bighas. Mr. Grant discovered the mistake in 1835, and an appeal was made to the Special Commissioner in 1836, but it was rejected in 1839 and the matter relinquished, Mr. Dampier's decision being correct on other grounds.[22] His investigations led him

[21] Presdy. Commr. to Sbn. Commr., no. 2357, dated 14 Nov. 1834.

[22] Sbn. Commr. to Presdy. Commr., no. 162, dated 6 June, and no. 194, dated

to the conclusion that the quantity of zamindari land that had been included in Henckell's pattas had been greatly exaggerated and too easily credited by the Government officers who had investigated, though the institution of suits without sufficient previous acquaintance with the subject had been productive of much mischief. Under the orders of the Board, issued in February 1835, he began an enquiry into the right of Government to those lands, investigating their situation, extent, and liability with the object of instituting suits for them under the regulations, if they should appear open to resumption.[23] As frauds were supposed to have been committed in the Jessore Collectorate just after Smelt's measurement, he scrutinized the cases more closely, and his researches confirmed the former impression that although Smelt had measured much land belonging to zamindars yet Government had a just claim to much.[24] During 1835-36 he deputed two amins to Jessore and Bakarganj to enquire about and sketch out the lands laid down in Rennell's and Hodges' maps. They reported 248 mahalls as open to resumption, with an estimated area of 118,355 bighas adjoining Jessore, and of 53,500 bighas adjacent to Bakarganj in the vicinity of parganas Salimabad and Saiyadpur.[25]

115. Investigations by Mr. Donnelly, Collector of Jessore, 1836: Mr. Donnelly, who was Collector of Jessore in 1836, drew up a list of Henckell's pattas—135 in number; all that he had been able to find. It contains Henckell's well known mahalls and three others—Magurkhali, Koipukhuriya and Khagrabuniya—all of which were assessed with revenue, but all the rest were new mahalls, the holders of which, he stated, had either never cultivated the lands or never paid revenue through the collusion of the amla. He proposed that resumption suits should be begun for them, as their entry among Henckell's records seemed presumptive proof of their being Sundarban land, and almost all had one or more boundaries known by which

1 July 1840. Presdy. Commr., to Sbn. Commr., no. 83, dated 10 June, and no. 88, dated 16 June, and no. 136, dated 26 Aug. 1840.

[23] Sbn. Commr. to Sadr. Bd. Rev., 10 Jan. and 4 Feb. 1835, and Sadr. Bd. Rev. to Sbn. Commr., 6 Feb. 1835.

[24] Sbn. Commr. to Presdy. Commr., 26 Aug. 1835.

[25] Ibid., no. 636, dated 11 Oct. 1836, and Presdy. Commr. to Sadr. Bd. Rev., 22 idem.

they might be discovered. He also sent copies of the lists of resumable estates that he had prepared in 1832 for Mr. Dampier. He mentioned that he had already commenced proceedings for the chaks comprised in the lakhiraj *brit* of Syam Rai Thakur, in consequence of his having begun a suit to try the validity of the tadad under which the original tenure was held; and that the lands constituting the Ramjan *brit* were *prima facie* resumable, it having been disallowed at the time of the decennial settlement. Those measures were partial, but he urged that a regular local inquiry should be set on foot regarding *all* Sundarban lands in Jessore, for it would prove very productive to Government, and he suggested a partition of the country for his and the Sundarban Commissioner's jurisdictions.[26] The list, which thenceforward became a standard one, was communicated to the Sundarban Commissioner with orders to take up the inquiry.

116. Donnelly's List of Sundarban Mahalls, 1836: Donnelly's list of 1836 was as follows:[27]

Asmatpur
Ballabhpur
Gokulnagar
Chandkhali-Kalidaspur
Mohammedabad
Gobindapur
Chandipur
Bhairabnagar
Bansipur
10 Ramzanagar*
Pranpur
Ismailpur*
Gutliyakati*
Babupur-Banchanagar*
Henckellganj*
Ujani
Karnitala
Telikhali
Gugramari
20 Purni
Bil Chamua
Bil Apna
Khudiyarkhal
Rangamari
Sundarbuniya
Sundarbuniya
Taltalardanga
Koipukhuriya
Munkiyardanga
30 Chinarmallardanga
Bagarder
Magurkhali-Kaabtalardanga
Damardanga
Miragoda
Haliya Bauna
Tetultala
Goalbatan
Iswarpur
Gobtalar Dokonda*
40 Kalikapur
Mowtowfapur
Jorpukuriya
Kabadak-nadir-do-par
Subankar Cottir uttar

[26] Jessore Collr. to Presdy. Commr., no. 382, dated 6 July 1836.

[27] No boundaries are given for the mahalls marked with an asterisk. Several of the so-called names are merely rough directions where to look for the lands.

Bhagiya Manoharpur*
Bairardanga
Barapara
Patibuniya
Lashkarkhali
50 Moscotta
Bonitaia
Chittirbaga
Baliyadanga
Chanderdiper Khal
Chinamalla
Chunmatua
Goalbuniya
Kadidhua
Kantaliya
60 Raipur gangarhula
Hoglakhaler pubpar
Telikhali
Buzurgummedpur
Matbhanga
Khonmabad
Patta
Kapalbara
Huma
Dayardakhin
70 Natherkuri
Kurear Bussoteegean
Kariyamara gram dakhin
Kantaliya
Chalua Kur, &c.
Mirzapur
Soluamardanga
Madartala
Bangamara
Lakhikhola
80 Kamarkhola
Allipur
Kirtpersob
Hatjhara
Hadirber dighirpar
Kalma
Manikdahdanga
Hetalbuniya
Sakerbhita and Rajband
Gopalkhali
90 Kasiyamara and Kamekhola
Goalibariya
Sriramba
Lalmohan ‘
Kalmichua
Teghariya-Jaynaga
Mangralikhaler do kul
Malidanga
Bankara
Haldarkhali
100 Eakchur
Boltalarchar
Jamua
Arjunbat
Hoglabuniya
Nalbuniya
Godara
Khagrabuniya
Bawaliya
Chandipur
110 Baloibuniya
Ratnodipukhiya
Patua
Nawalitala
Digia
Sonakunda
Paliyagola
Kaliya
Dhokra
Barobhumi
120 Bablasikdar Mallik
Garuimarirkunda
Garamardan
Juartapur
Chaltiyabuniya
Mausimpur
Bhimrajbari
Bhabanipur and Panchcoila and Kaoliya
Sonabuniya
Bajua and Mautopi and Tongibatiya
130 Barni
Naukhali
Jafarabad Ichakorabada
Bonsiyarhola
135 Mayjora

117. Researches among Henckell's Pattas, 1836: Besides the above data, fresh materials were unearthed by searches among the records in the Sundarban office. From old mutilated pattas, chihnit-namas and applications for leases were obtained the names of 339 chaks as having been either granted by Henckell and his successors or applied for by the petitioners most of them being in Jessore and Bakarganj, but some in 24-Parganas and Balloa (Noakhali).[28] None of them appear to have been measured by Smelt. These measures seem to have been rather reckless, everything being swept into the collection that could be connected with Henckell or his successors. The intention seems to have been to gather first without much reference to the antecedent history, and afterwards to discriminate and select or refuse. Some of Henckell's grants had never been taken possession of; others had been relinquished after being taken; and others again, noticeably in pargana Saiyadpur, had been cancelled by Henckell as having been wrongly conferred.

118. Matters for Investigation, 1836: The duties that thus awaited disposal in 1836 were the inquiry into the released lands measured by Smelt, the investigation into the 135 Henckell's mahalls of Donnelly's list and their assessment, the investigation into and resumption of lands supposed to be resumble between the Pasar and Baleswar, and the completion of the inquiries regarding the 24 mahalls in Jessore and Bakarganj mapped out by the amins.[29] These matters however, ran very much into one another and covered much the same ground: in fact they were different aspects in which the same question presented itself rather than distinct questions.

119. Investigations, 1836-37: The local investigations were conducted in season 1836-37, and when the preliminary data were obtained, suits were commenced for the resumption of the lands. But after Mr. Grant quitted the Sundarbans in March 1836, there followed a succession of officers who were unacquainted with the history and peculiar character of the operations, the proceedings were crude, and the suits were instituted often with more zeal than discretion, especially during 1837, when it became necessary to initiate resumption suits

[28] Sbn. Commr. to Presdy. Commr., no. 473, dated 7 Nov. 1837.

[29] Presdy. Commr. to Sadr. Bd. Rev., 22 Oct. 1836.

for the lands contained in the lists previously compiled. Where, as was generally the case, the boundaries were known, the identification of the lands was feasible and the subsequent steps plain. But where merely the names of the chaks had been extracted, but their locality and boundaries either could not be ascertained or were indefinite, preliminary inquiries to discover the lands were always tedious, and sometimes unsuccessful. The boundary of the Sundarban forest as depicted in Rennell's map was taken as the initial criterion. When lands lay outside of it, they were at once eliminated, and only those which fell inside were made the subject of proceedings, Mr. Shakespear instituting suits if the Collector had not already done so. Still, after the suits were started, their issue was highly uncertain; for in these later cases the Government proceeded on a presumption arising from one consideration or another that the lands were Sundarban lands reclaimed posterior to the decennial settlement, and had never been assessed with revenue; but the result depended on the evidence that the zamindars might adduce to prove the lands were included in that settlement.[30]

120. Results of Investigations, 1837: The inquiries brought out the following results in 1837. Of the 125 mahalls (as the 135 of Mr. Donnelly's list became after revision) some lay outside Rennell's boundary and were free; others had been already released after trial by Mr. Dampier or the Special Commissioner; suits had been already begun for others; and others again had been measured by Smelt, but could not be discovered. Suits were instituted for those that remained, of which some had been measured by Smelt, and the others, though not mentioned in his measurement abstract, were believed to have been measured by him.[31] All the other separate taluks measured by Smelt had been by the end of 1837 either settled by Messrs. Dampier, Donnelly, or Grant, or were pending in suits before the Special Commissioner or elsewhere. Of the 339 chaks collected by the Sundarban Commissioner, but not measured by Smelt, 49 had been already finally disposed of by resumption, release, or compromise, and

[30] Sbn. Commr to Sadr. Bd. Rev., 17 Sept. 1835.

[31] Numbers are mentioned in Sbn. Commr. to Presdy. Commr., no. 473, dated 7 Nov. 1837, but are irreconcilable.

28 were undergoing trial. In 63 no boundaries could be procured, and in 87 others the boundaries were indefinite or the situation was still unknown. Among the rest suits were begun for 12, and preliminary investigations were in progress for the remaining 100.[32] Not much advance appears to have been made in the discovery of these indistinct grants, but it was thought that as their boundaries were so vague and Henckell's chaks stretched from the Raimangal to Dakhin Shahbazpur, many of them must have been already resumed.[33]

121. Resumption Suits, 1836-43: In 1836 there were 36 suits pending, two in 24-Parganas for 760 bighas, 30 in Jessore for 58,911 bighas, and four in Bakarganj for about 23,941 bighas,[34] and one new one was added, so that at the beginning of 1837 there were 37 pending before the Sundarban Commissioner. As the result of his investigations, Mr. Shakespear instituted 117 fresh suits during 1837, and four the following year, the amount of land involved in all the suits, old and new being about 1,24,700 bighas. He decided one in favour of Government in 1837 and disposed of 26 by adjustment or withdrawal in 1838, while two were transferred to Nadiya. For 1839 there remained 129 suits to which Mr. Kemp added five in 1840. He decided during those years 19 in favour of Government and 55 against, while 15 were adjusted or withdrawn, leaving 45 pending at the end of 1840. One new suit was added in 1841, another in 1842, and three in 1843. Of these 50, eight were decreed to Government and three adjusted or withdrawn during 1843, and there remained 39 cases pending on 18th September 1843. A large number of the dismissals decreed by Messers. Shakespear and Kemp were based on the false rubakaris mentioned above. Those officers coming fresh to the office accepted the documents as authentic, and the amla took no pains to undeceive them. The mistake was discovered in 1840 by Mr. Kemp, and applications were preferred to the Special Commissioner for retrial.[35] It would seem they were granted, for during 1841 and 1842

[32] Sbn. Commr. to Pesdy. Commr., no. 473, dated 7 Nov. 1837.

[33] Ibid., no. 425, dated 18 Nov. 1838.

[34] Ibid., 12 Dec. 1836.

[35] Presdy. Commr. to Sbn. Commr., no. 148, dated 26 Sept. 1840, and no. 170, dated 28 Oct. 1840. Mr. Kemp dismissed at least 21 cases.

a large number of cases were sent down by the Special Commissioner for local reinvestigation.

122. Results of Resumption Suits: The resumption proceedings of this period are very obscure. They do not appear to fall into any well defined groups or classes of cases. It is clear from the foregoing summary that out of the cases tried by the Sundarban Commissioner, the releases, even allowing for the erroneous decrees based on the false rubakaris, were very numerous; but his decrees had to undergo further trial before the Special Commissioner, appeals being lodged in almost all cases, and the mahalls, that were eventually resumed, were so few in number, that it is hard to name any. The Special Commissioner does not seem to have been over-exacting, for the local inquiries had not been conducted with such thoroughness as to survive a searching scrutiny,[36] and in instances where the Government claim, though feebly handled, appeared to have some justice, as in Tildanga, Pankhali, Chunkuri, & c, he expressly recorded in his faisalas that the release would be no bar to future proceedings should Government be able to put forward a stronger case after further local inquiries. Perikhali was released on 3rd September 1845.

123. Lands Resumed, 1836-45: Among the resumptions during this period in Jessore may be mentioned Sibnagar, where the Special Commissioner about the year 1837 confirmed the Board's order of resumption of 1826, and Kalajangal (*alias* Parmandartala), where the Board's order of 1826 was upheld on 31st October 1838. On the same date also was resumed the adjoining mahall Bayarsinga (including Taltala and Sadhuarghata). Other cases were Sandkhali (4,745 bighas) resumed on 13th September 1838, which the Collector appears to have first decreed: Suarnal was decreed on 19th August 1845. Bilgudara appears to have been resumed about 1844. Kinukati in lot 216 was decreed in 1843 by the Sundarban Commissioner; Bhairabghata and Bankeswar[37] similarly on 17th July 1843, and upheld by the Special Commissioner about 1848.

124. Resumption Suits in Bakarganj, 1836-44: The right of

[36] An account of the confusion in lot 216, for example, is given in Smith to Sbn. Commr., no. 72, dated 28 Apr. 1858.

[37] They had, however, been brought under settlement before, see paragraph 100.

Government to increased revenue from the unadjusted kharija mahalls in Buzurgummedpur had been under consideration since 1836. They were Bhayang Kakrabuniya, Kolshakati, Juta-buniya, and Basunda, and also the three-fourths share of Auliyapur, where the fraud referred to in paragraph 88 was discovered by Mr. Kemp in 1839. He proceeded with the approval of Mr. Dampier, the Presidency Commissioner, to enforce the right of Government against Auliyapur under section 5 of Regulation IX of 1825 (which was, however, inapplicable, since the land was reclaimed Sundarban forest and not a portion of Buzurgummedpur), instead of under Regulations II of 1819 and III of 1828. The three-fourths share was decreed in 1839, but the proceedings being irregular, Government in 1842 ordered restoration of the property and directed the institution of fresh proceedings under Regulations II and III. The Sundarban Commissioner again decreed the share, but the Special Commissioner on appeal reversed it on 15th January 1848 and cast the Government in damages.[38] The Presidency Commissioner directed Mr. Kemp in 1840[39] to proceed against the other kharija mahalls under section 5 of Regulation IX of 1825, but to invite compromises. Bhayang Kakrabuniya was resumed by Mr. Shawe on 7th March 1842,[40] but it is not clear what happened in the three other cases. Resumption proceedings had been in hand regarding the same large mahall, Buzurgummedpur, chiefly in respect of small parcels of cultivation and chars. A large number of chars were resumed,[41] but the other lands, such as Badura, Bauliya, and Pakhiya, were released by the Special Commissioner in 1842.[42] Char Londah lying north of Bara Basdiya, was discovered in 1839, and Mr. Kemp wished to compromise, but the Presidency Commissioner insisted on resumption proceedings. It was then resumed on 12th August 1840.[43] Ragua,

[38] Sbn. Commr. to Presdy. Commr., no. 280, dated 20, and no. 281, dated 22 Aug. 1840. Presdy. Commr. to Sbn. Commr., no. 21, dated 14 May 1842, and no. 156, dated 19 July 1848.

[39] Sbn. Commr. to Presdy. Commr., no. 4, dated 3 Jan. 1840. Presdy. Commr. to Sbn. Commr., no. 10, dated 15 idem.

[40] Ibid., no. 318, dated 28 Sept. 1842.

[41] See Presdy. Commr.'s statement, dated 31 March 1842.

[42] See Sbn. Commr. to Presdy. Commr., no. 239, dated 7 Aug. 1840.

[43] Presdy. Commr. to Sbn. Commr., no. 125, dated 1 Aug. 1840.

which had been resumed in 1832 and brought under assessment and settlement, with an area of 3,310 bighas, was at length released by the special Commissioner about 1844.[44] A claim over 981 bighas of taufir in Charwa was decreed by him on 21st December 1837.

125. Resumption Suits in Pargana Sahosh, 1837-42: Among the resumption suits were five for five chaks in pargana Sahosh, viz., Tildanga (adjoining lot 221), Pankhali and Lakhikhola (adjoining lot 222), Chunkuri (adjoining lot 223), and Kamarkhola (adjoining lot 224). Government claimed them as Sundarban land cleared subsequent to the decennial settlement; but from the quinquennial papers of 1791 and the jama-wasil-baki papers of 1202 (1795-96) it appeared that there were asli mauzas with those names in the pargana though their original areas were not specified. One Shah Mohammed Sarang, who held Pankhali and the neighbouring land under the zamindar Raja Srikantha, and who had unsuccessfully tried to get a patta from the Collector for it as being Sundarban land, was dispossessed, and sued the zamindar and Government about 1810 to regain possession. The Collector replied that the land belonged to the zamindar and not to Government, and the suit was dismissed in 1815. On the Raja's death his grandson Barada Kantha succeeded, but being a minor was taken care of by the Court of Wards. The Collector in 1232 (1825-26) measured the pargana, prepared a list of the villages and lands it comprised, and drew up a jamabandi and English abstract: the Board approved the settlement on 6th February 1827. Those papers were drawn up entirely in the interest of the ward, and claimed all the cultivated and forest lands in this locality and also the rivers as belonging to him. Lastly Mr. Dampier in defining the boundary in 1829 had thrown the five mauzas outside. On these grounds Mr. Kemp dismissed all the suits in 1839, and on appeals being preferred by Government, the Special Commissioner also dismissed them on 19th August 1842, but declared that, as the lands were surrounded by Sundarban jungle to which Government had an undoubted right. Government was at liberty, if it could prove that the zamindar had usurped any Sundarban land as part and parcel of his settled mauzas, to institute fresh suits to assess such land, to which this decision would

[44] Ibid., no. 546, dated 29 Nov. 1844; but see paragraph 239.

be no bar. The strongest evidence against Government lay in the admissions the Collector had made that the lands were the property of the zamindars; but the Special Commissioner held that as those admissions were made in documents drawn up entirely in the interest of the ward, they were not to be unduly pressed to the discomfiture of Government.[45]

126. Lands Resumed but Unidentified, 1841-46: As a result of the inconsiderate resumption proceedings set on foot, there existed 46 cases in 1841 where the lands appeared to have been resumed, but the boundaries were not discovered; and besides them there were Ikrabuniya, Khakrabuniya, Gauripur, and Seilabuniya in Bakarganj which Mr. Dampier had resumed in 1834, also Tetulbariya and Kakerthot resumed about the same time, and Baluibuniya and Sriramba[46]—all calling for inquiry. The first four had been granted by Henckell, but the pattadars were dispossessed by the zamindars, who held the lands fraudulently under different names. All those cases were assigned to Mr. Ross, Deputy Collector, in season 1841-42. He discovered, measured, and assessed the first three and the last two, their total area being 4,974 bighas and ultimate rental Rs. 7,062.[47] During the next season he undertook the 46 undiscovered cases, which were increased by additions to 62, and also 21 others that the Special Commissioner had committed to him for local investigation.[48] These cases appear to have been mostly in pargana Jamira. Apart from them apparently were 27 cases which a former Deputy Collector had reported to be Government property, and these too were made over to him for inquiry the same season. He completed 44 of the 62 cases, and the Special Commissioner proceeded to dispose of the appeals that were pending before him. During August and September. 1843 the Special Commissioner released Gobra, Ujanibarthal,

[45] Special Commr.'s statement of decrees for Aug. 1842. Sbn. Commr. to Bd. Rev., no. 54, dated 27 Apr. 1882.

[46] Sbn. Commr. to Presdy. Commr., no. 473, dated 7 Nov. 1837, and no. 85, dated 28 Apr. 1841.

[47] Ross to Sbn. Commr., 10 Mar.; and his statement, dated 27 May 1842. Sbn. Commr. to Presdy. Commr., no. 286, dated 8 Sept. 1842.

[48] Sbn. Commr. to Presdy. Commr., no. 318, dated 28 Sept. 1842. Presdy. Commr. to Sbn. Commr., no. 85, dated 21 July 1843.

Partabnagar, Kaliyanpur, Bishtupur, Fakirertakiya, Bogha, Srirampur, Madarbariya, Maharajpur, Merukhali, Panchpota, Majirdanga, Goalbati, Kumarkhali, Rampur, Matbari, Ramkishtapur, Hayatkhali. Hogalkati, Bhowanipur, Sirsiya, &c. All of these were small parcels of land, the first four only being estimated at more than 1,000 bighas, and many of them not exceeding 500 bighas,[49] During 1842 he had released a number of char and jungle cases: Kotbil, Jaliyakhali, Bhaghold, Mirzapur, Aluni, and Nayakhali—all small plots of 800 bighas or less. Among the resumption cases were suits for Nurpur and Amirpur, which were estimated at 389 bighas only, but according to their boundaries comprised the portion of lot 216 lying north of the Ghoshkhali khal. The case for Government was feebly managed, and the claim was dismissed by the Special Commissioner on 10th June 1842, though the right of Government was beyond all doubt, since the lands lay within the Sundarban boundary and formed part of lot 216.[50] The same area under the name Kanakhali was resumed by the Sundarban Commissioner in 1839, but released on appeal about 1843.[51] Little but the bare names of the cases can be given, and even they are incomplete. There remained undisposed of in 1843 18 of the 62 cases, and all the 21 sent by the Special Commissioner.[52] What became of them is uncertain, but it seems that on the break up of the Commission the year after, those relating to Bakarganj were sent to the Collector, while the others remained with Uma Kanta Babu. They were probably all struck off or dropped, for he appears on the revival of the office in 1846 to have commenced his resumption investigations on a new system, while about that time Special Commissioners were abolished.

127. Resumption Suits, 1843-46: There were 39 resumption suits pending before the Sundarban Commissioner in September 1843, and more seem to have been instituted the year after, but very few ended successfully. On the 'abolition of the office in 1844, the Bakarganj suits

[49] Ibid., no. 177, dated 22 July 1841; no. 174, dated 15 June 1846; and no. 469, dated 13 Oct. 1847. Statement dated 19 Nov. 1845.

[50] Ibid., no. 9, dated 14 Jan. 1856.

[51] Smith to Sbn. Commr., no. 672, dated 28 Apr. 1858.

[52] Ross to Sbn. Commr., 24 Feb. 1843; Sbn. Commr. to Presdy. Commr., no. 369, dated 28 July 1843; Presdy. Commr. to Sbn. Commr., no. 85, dated 21 July 1843.

were transferred to the Collector, and he dismissed 17 or more of them during 1845 and 1846.[53] Others were dismissed by Uma Kanta Babu and the Collector of Jessore.[54] Among those lost may be mentioned Ghoshkhali, Baliyapota, and others.[55] To the same series would seem to belong the following which the Special Commissioner dismissed in October and November 1847—Pasarbuniya, Rajpasa, Hantaliya, & c.[56] A few cases were carried on after the revival of the office.[57]

[53] Presdy. Commr. to Sbn. Commr., no. 19, dated 18 March, and no. 54, dated 28 May 1846.

[54] Ibid., no. 138, dated 22 Dec. 1846.

[55] See Sbn. Commr. to Presdy. Commr., no. 265, dated 14 Aug., and no. 294, dated 10 Sept. 1844.

[56] Statement dated 1 Dec. 1847.

[57] See list in Sbn. Commr. to Presdy. Commr., no. 334, dated 8 Aug. 1853.

CHAPTER XI

Settlements

1836-1844

128. Sicca Superseded by Company's Coinage, 30th December 1835: In the early settlements of the resumed mahalls, putting aside the patitabadi mahalls and Henckell's taluks, which had their own peculiar terms, the assessments were made in sicca money according to the pargana rates and standards of measurements, and jamabandis were prepared for all tenants who possessed a hereditary right. At the end of 1835 the Government ordered that all land revenue should in future be expressed in Company's coinage.[1] No change was made in the method of assessment; the jama was computed as before in sicca money, which was then converted into Company's money.

129. Settlements in Jessore, 1835-43: Gumantali, Jabakhali and Betangi which had been resumed together in 1834 with an estimated area of 10,000 bighas were brought under settlement in 1835, but on remeasurement were found to contain only 1,839 bighas. They were settled in 1839 for 20 years.[2] During 1835-36 Mr. Grant settled Chandmukhi, which was divided into three portions, and his settlement with a gross area of 838 bighas and jama of Rs. 446 was confirmed in 1841.[3] At the same time were settled Kalmibuniya and Bogara, total 2,493 bighas, Rs. 560. The appeal in the case of Sibnagar, which was resumed by the Board in 1826, was decided about 1837, and the chak was at once brought under settlement. It was found to comprise Ghazinagar, and also apparently Ghuruniya

[1] From 1936 the coinage (except when otherwise described) is expressed in the Company's standard under Government order to Accountant-General, no. 1267, dated 30 Dec. 1835, that all future settlements of land revenue were to be expressed in Company's rupees and not sicca rupees (Presdy. Commr. to Sbn. Commr., no. 16, dated 22 Feb. 1836).

[2] Sbn. Commr. to Presdy. Commr., no. 356, dated 21 Aug. 1847.

[3] Sbn. Commr. to Jessore Collr., no. 341, dated 22 Aug. 1846.

and Bagarder, with a total area of 1,600 bighas. All these chaks were settled in 1838 at a total jama of Rs. 883.[4] Jharjhariya was settled in 1837, Nasimabad in 1839, and Mukamiya in 1840.[5] The settlements were made at 10 or 12 annas sicca per the 55-yard bigha, 15 per cent, was allowed for expenses, and then 10 per cent, on the remainder for malikana,[6] equivalent to a whole deduction of 23½ per cent. The jama was converted into Company's money, in which all land revenue after 1835 was to be expressed. Other settlements in and near lots 217-220 were made by the Collector of Jessore during these years. They came to the Sundarban Commissioner's notice about 1841, and formed the subject of continued attention as explained in chapter XIV. About the year 1836 the Collector resettled several of the resumed mahalls situated around lot 220, such as Putimari and Suargudi.

130. Settlement of Phulhata and Adjacent Chaks, 1835-41: The six contiguous chaks Phulhata, Jeodhara, Sonirjhor, Deotala, Baharbuniya, and Ghusiyakhali when resumed by Mr. Dampier in 1834 were brought under measurement and assessment during seasons 1834-36 by Mr. Grant. Their aggregate area was 9,429 bighas, of which 7,600 bighas were assessed with a rental of Rs. 3,755 at 8 annas sicca per standard bigha; but they remained khass pending the decision on appeal. When the Special Commissioner confirmed the resumption, the haoladars and other chief tenants recused and the mahalls deteriorated.[7] In 1837-38 Mr. Herklots reckoned their gross area at 9,581 bighas and remeasuring the cultivation prepared a hastabud of it, fixing the total jama at Rs. 1,888. As the owners still recused, the mahalls were farmed out to Nanda Kumar Bagis in 1839 at a yearly revenue of Rs. 1,900 for 20 years[8] The owners then

[4] Sbn. Commr. to Presdy. Commr., nos. 87, 88, 89, and 90, all dated 27 March 1843. Presdy. Commr. to Sbn. Commr., no. 69, dated 10th July 1843, and nos. 88, 92, and 93, all dated 26 idem.

[5] Ibid., no. 151, dated 22 June 1841.

[6] Bd. Rev.'s no. 40, dated 22 Aug. 1836, is cited as the authority.

[7] Sbn. Commr. to Presdy. Commr., no. 328, dated 17 Aug. 1838, and no. 118, dated 18 May 1841.

[8] Ibid., no. 493, dated 16 [. . .] 1839; nos. 190 and 191, dated 28 June 1840, and no. 283, dated 11 Oct. 1841. Presdy. Commr. to Sbn. Commr., no. 194, dated 4 Dec. 1839, and no. 109, dated 13 Oct. 1841.

repented, the farm was cancelled, and the mahalls were assessed at 8 annas per bigha and settled with them in 1841 in three groups for 20 years retrospectively from 1836[9]—Jeodhara, area 228 bighas and jama Rs.101 ultimately;[10] Phulhata (one portion) with Baharbuniya, 1,710 bighas, Rs. 793;[11] and Phulhata (second portion), together with the other estates, 8,372 bighas, Rs. 3,800.[12]

131. Settlements in Pargana Salimabad, 1837-39: The 36 mahalls adjoining pargana Salimabad, resumed by the Special Commissioner on 29th August 1837, and the other resumed mahalls of that locality, were measured and assessed by Mr. Shakespear and his deputy Mr. Herklots during seasons 1837-39.[13] The rate was fixed at Re. 1 sicca (but in a few mahalls 12 and 14 annas) per 55-yard bigha for cultivated land, and also ultimately for the jungle; while 25 per cent, was deducted for the settlement allowances. But the assessment was excessive, especially on the jungle land, and the owners recused except in eight cases. Those eight were Betkata,[14] Sannyasi,[15] Jeolmari,[16] Bansbariya,[17] Narendrapur,[18] Teliganti with Bhatkhali, Betibuniya, and Ghazirghata[19] with a total area of 11,856 bighas and full jama of Rs. 8,108. The period was 20 years from 1838. The rate in the first two and in Narendrapur was 14 annas sicca, in Bansbariya 12 annas, and in the others Re.1. But even in these cases the assessment was burdensome. Thus Sannyasi fell into arrears and was sold, and its

[9] The Settlement reports of this period are constantly misleading; the assessed area is often given instead of the total area, and the gross jama instead of the sadar jama.

[10] Sbn. Commr. to Presdy. Commr., no. 203, dated 20 Aug, 1841.

[11] Ibid., no. 210, dated 23 Aug. 1841.

[12] Ibid., no. 209, dated 23 Aug. 1841.

[13] Ibid., no. 89, dated 9 Feb. 1838.

[14] Ibid., no. 169, dated 14 July 1841. Presdy. Commr. to Sbn. Commr., no. 109, dated 13 Oct. 1841.

[15] Sbn. Commr. to Presdy. Commr., no. 170, dated 14th July 1841.

[16] Ibid., no. 299, dated 19 Sept. 1842, and Presdy. Commr. to Sbn. Commr., no. 90, dated 26 July 1843.

[17] Sbn. Commr. to Presdy. Commr., no. 436, dated 30 Oct. 1840.

[18] Ibid., no. 435, dated 29 Oct. 1840.

[19] Sbn. Commr.'s statement, dated 15 Nov. 1838, and Herklots' statement dated 2 Nov. 1838, approved by Sbn. Commr., 15 Nov. 1838.

settlement was revised in 1841, the rate being reduced to 12 annas.[20] Similarly Jeolmari was revised in 1845, and its rate reduced to 14 annas.[21] So, too Betkata was revised in 1847, and its rate reduced to 8 annas.[22] The other estates were attached and held khass, but khass management proved unsatisfactory, for the raiyats deserted, and the lands deteriorated through neglect. Endeavours were made to lease them out, Mr. Kemp proposing to reduce the rate if it were too high, or farm out the mahalls, if the fault lay in the recusancy of the owners[23] Seventeen mahalls on the same assessment, but with a diminished allowance of 20 per cent., were farmed out to Nil Chandra Sen and Bhairab Chandra Raha in 1839 for 20 years the area being about 15,000 bighas and annual jama rising from Rs. 2,075 to Rs. 10,552 ultimately—Abdulrasulpur, Kaliya (two, Bara and Chota), Mallikber, Debraj, Harganti, Khondokarber, Nazirdiya Dhuliganti, Bhistupur, Haldaha, Nalbuniya (two), Kumariyajola, and Kakarbil from among the above estates, and also Narsinghdattber and Gazaliyarber, two neighbouring estates. But Nil Chandra Sen was convicted of forgery in the matter of the lease in 1840, the farm was cancelled in February 1841, and the mahalls again held khass.[24] The other resumed mahalls appear to have been jungle or to have relapsed into that condition, and no settlements were made of them before 1840.

132. Jangalburi Settlements in Pargana Salimabad, 1840-42: The southern resumed mahalls being for the most part jungle, and ordinary settlements being impracticable, Mr. Kemp took measures in 1840 for leasing them out otherwise. Thus on 4th January 1840 without local inquiry he gave one Kali Prasad Sen an amalnama for eight chaks—Fakirtakiya, Sutaluri, Gazaliya, Bhatkhali, Kharoikhali, Mahischaraniya, Gatipur, and Baintala—with an aggregate estimated area of about 33,000 bighas, promising him a patta if some progress

[20] Sbn. Commr. to Presdy. Commr., no. 244, dated 8 Sept. 1841, and no. 228, dated 14 May 1843.

[21] Ibid., no. 192, dated 20 June 1846.

[22] Ibid., no. 124, dated 21 June 1848.

[23] Ibid., no. 375, dated 3 Sept. 1839.

[24] Ibid., no. 536, dated 10 Dec. 1839, and no. 272, dated 6 Oct. 1841. Collr., Bakarganj, to Sbn. Commr., no. 249, dated 24 Dec. 1840, and Accountant-General to Sbn. Commr., no. 253, dated 31 Aug. 1843.

should have been made in clearing the lands, which appear to have been all jungle except where a small colony of fakirs had settled in Fakirtakiya.[25] Nine or ten other mahalls, which had almost relapsed into jungle and could not be settled raiyatwari, nor yet dealt with as forest grants, were leased out by him in 1841 on jangalburi terms, viz. Nazirdiya and Dhuliganti (together),[26] Khondakarber, Manikkhola, and Baintala (three together),[27] Putikhali,[28] Panchakaran,[29] Debraj,[30] and Harganti.[31] Departing from a hard-and-fast set of terms, he judiciously adapted the stipulations regarding the revenue-free and progressive periods, the allowances, &c, to the condition of the several mahalls. This was the introduction of a method, which, while based on the grant rules and the jangalburi terms accorded to the unreclaimed lands in the resumed Bakarganj mahalls, possessed great elasticity and has been used since with marked advantage. Mr. Kemp assigned a revenue-free period varying from 10 to 15 years, a rasad of two years at 4 and 6 annas, and thereafter in perpetuity the full assessment of 8 annas per standard bigha, which was the full rate under the Sundarban grant rules. One-fourth of the area was exempted from assessment in lieu of all allowances, and a clearing condition of one-fourth the area on pain of resumption was generally imposed, with the view of defeating a practice on the part of lessees who took lands rent-free with no intention of clearing them but in the hope of selling them. It was sometimes provided that the costs of inspection should be paid by the lessees and a deposit of a sum equal to the first yearly rental was generally demanded as security. The leases were approved by the Presidency Commissioner,[32] and given for all the chaks in 1842, except

[25] Sbn. Commr. to Presdy. Commr., no. 226, dated 19 Dec. 1845. Smith, Dy. Collr., to Sbn. Commr., no. 16, dated 31 July 1848.

[26] Sbn. Commr. to Presdy. Commr., no. 105, dated 14 May 1841.

[27] Ibid., no. 109, dated 14 May 1841.

[28] Ibid., no. 108, dated 14 May 1841.

[29] Ibid., no. 110, dated 14 May 1841.

[30] Ibid., no. 112, dated 14 May 1841.

[31] Ibid., no. 113, dated 14 May 1841.

[32] Presdy. Commr. to Sbn. Commr., no. 27, dated 23 May 1842.

Debraj, where a delay occurred pending a claim put forward to it as being comprised in one of Henckell's pattas.[33]

133. Grant of amalnamas for Jungle Lands in Pargana Salimabad, 1840-42: The practice introduced by Mr. Dampier of granting amalnamas was continued by his successors and employed by them in cases where there seems to have been no occasion for deviating from the regular methods. That Messers. Grant and Shakespear should have done so is intelligible, as they had no means of surveying jungle lands; but from the beginning of 1839 and onwards a surveyor was always attached to the office, and the surveys required were not extensive. The later amalnamas were given almost exclusively for resumed mahalls which were all waste. Thus Mr. Kemp gave one Kali Prasad Sen an amalnama in 1840 for eight of the resumed Salimabad mahalls, as mentioned in paragraph 132. In Kukua the cleared lands had been settled by Mr. Dampier in 1834, and Mr. Kemp (following Mr. Grant's precedent in Gulsakhali) gave the talukdar an amalnama for the jungle lands on 28th January 1840. Similarly he gave an amalnama in 1840 to Nand Kumar Bagis for Madardiya, which had relapsed into jungle through the recusancy of the owners at Herklots' assessment; and another in 1841 for Haldaha, which was in the same condition. So, too, in Kumariyajola he divided the lands into two portions, and gave an amalnama for one and a parwana for the other in 1842.[34] The amalnamas appear to have been drawn up on the same terms as the jangalburi pattas given for Harganti, &c. It does not appear why pattas were not given for these too; but possibly too little was known of the boundaries and areas of the chaks to render that course safe.

134. Other Settlements in Pargana Salimabad, 1838-45: Mallikber was farmed out in 1841 on the recusancy of the owners but they repented, and under the Presidency Commissioner's order the farm was quashed and a revised settlement made with them in 1845 at an ultimate rate of 14 annas.[35] Two other mahalls—Kaliya (two estates) apparently—were settled with the haoladars in 1841.[36]

[33] Sbn. Commr. to Presdy. Commr., no. 469, dated 27 Sept. 1850. The pattas, however, for the others appear not to have been delivered till 1845— see old register.

[34] Ibid., no. 397, dated 30 Dec. 1842, and no. 658, dated 28 Dec. 1850.

[35] Presdy. Commr. to Babu U.K. Sen, no. 61, dated 5 Dec. 1845.

[36] Sbn. Commr. to Presdy. Commr., nos. 106 and 107, dated 14 May 1841.

Charadaha, with an area of 287 bighas, was brought under assessment in 1842.[37] The other mahalls—Abdulrasulpur, Koyardiya Kapalibanda, Bishtupur, Kakarbil, Nalbuniya, Narsinghdattber, Kalyapara, and Gazaliyarber—appear to have been waste, and nothing was done towards their settlement till about 1845. Two chars in the river Baleswar were settled—Ghazir char in 1838[38] and Burir char in 1839.

135. Settlements in Pargana Aurangpur, 1835-44: Kalibari, Bazarghona, and Patukhali, which were resumed together in 1834, and also Chalitabimiya, Pakhiya, Charwa, and Ragua, were measured during season 1835-36, but revision of measurement and the recusancy of the owners protracted the settlement during the two following seasons. The first three were settled in 1839, the rate being Rs. 1-2 sicca per 57½ -yard bigha, and the allowances being first 10 per cent, for expenses and then 15 for malikana. But confusion being found to exist between the lands of the estates, Mr. Shawe remeasured Kalibari in 1841-42, and the Presidency Commissioner directed him in 1843 to revise the settlements of all three. That was carried out by Uma Kanta Babu in 1843-44, and the total area became 4,295 bighas, of which 4,007 were malguzari. The rate and the allowances remained the same, but the aggregate sadar jama became Company's Rs. 3,679. The rate was approved as it was almost equivalent to the Sundarban rate of 8 annas per standard bigha, and the settlements were confirmed for 20 years from 1844.[39] Charwa appears to have been settled in 1839. Ragua was farmed out in 1842,[40] but a portion of it was released by the Special Commissioner about 1844, and, after a further resumption order by Uma Kanta Babu on 13th August 1847, the lands were brought under settlement in 1854. Chalitabuniya and Pakhiya were settled in 1838, but their areas were corrected and the settlement revised in 1840. In these settlements the method was almost the same as Mr. Dampier had observed in his Bakarganj settlements. There

[37] Ibid., no. 286, dated 8 Sept. 1842.

[38] Presdy. Commr. to Sbn. Commr., no. 61, dated 25 May 1838.

[39] Sbn. Commr. to Presdy. Commr., no. 202, dated 29 June 1842, and no. 298, dated 19 Sept. 1842, nos. 223, 224, and 225, all dated 26 July 1844. Presdy. Commr. to Sbn. Commr., no. 91, dated 26th July 1843; nos. 354, 356, and 358, all dated 3 Aug. 1844.

[40] Sbn. Commr. to Presdy. Commr., no. 397, dated 30 Dec. 1842.

were four classes of raiyats—(1) ausat talukdars (nim-ausat talukdars in Pakhiya), who were the sadar malguzars; (2) haoladars; (3) nim-haoladars; and (4) karshas. Those alone were pronounced maurasi raiyats who could produce pattas or other documents to prove that they had actually reclaimed the land. Such were the haoladars. and they formed the basis of the jamabandi, while all below them were held to be tenants-at-will and were left out. In Pakhiya there were a few nim-haoladars who held direct under the sadar malguzars, and they were treated as haoladars. The haoladars were assessed at Rs. 1-2 sicca per 57½ yard bigha, and the sadar nim-haoladars in Pakhiya at Rs. 1-8 sicca. The engagements were concluded with the ausat talukdars, who received a percentage on the gross jama.[41]

136. Buzurgummedpur Khass Mahall, 1836-44: The settlement of Buzurgummedpur khass mahall did not give satisfaction, for the tenantry proved recusant. The papers were sent to the Collector of Bakarganj, and the estate made over to him in 1835-36, under the impression that the Sundarban Commissioner was on the verge of abolition. The Collector appears to have managed the estate for two or three years though the Sundarban Commissioner also retained a control over it as regarded resumptions, settlements, and such like matters. Mr. Pigou, the Presidency Commissioner, revised the arrangements in 1836, prescribing rules to secure efficient administration;[42] the Collector was ordered to resettle or resume the chars; talukdars who had not signed dowls for Mr. Grant's assessment received their lands back at their former rentals; salt and other lands were released; and in 1837 the farm of the 73 petty mahalls was cancelled.[43] The changes introduced no improvement, and Mr. Dampier on succeeding him disallowed and reversed them in 1838. The Collector had measured the chars in 1837 and farmed them out, but the arrangements were lax; the chars with other lands were retransferred to the Sundarban Commissioner at the beginning of 1839 and managed khass; and the whole mahall again came under Mr. Kemp's charge.[44] Those talukdars only who had objected to Mr. Grant's assessment and kadim

[41] Sbn. Commr. to Presdy. Commr., no. 223, dated 26 July 1844.
[42] Presdy. Commr. to Sbn. Commr., no. 177, dated 10 Dec. 1836.
[43] Sbn. Commr. to Dy. Collr., no. 481, dated 19 Dec. 1838.
[44] See. Presdy. Commr.'s remarks on operation report for 1838-39.

khudkasht raiyats were allowed to hold on at their former jamas pending decision of their objections; but all others were subjected to that assessment. Fifteen of the mahalls that had been farmed out were settled with their owners at an aggregate jama of Rs. 4,327 and a proposal to renew the farm over the 58 others at a rental of Rs. 2,435 was approved in 1839, but was not carried into effect. The rate was reduced in some cases to Rs. 4 per kani in 1839.[45] The result of Mr. Dampier's revision in 1838 was to fix the total area at 57,002 bighas, and the total jama at Rs. 42,564. But the area was increased by some subsequent resumptions, Mr. Grant's assessments where objected to were revised, and the petty mahalls of all kinds were being continually brought under revision of settlement.[46] The estate remained under khass management, though other arrangements were suggested, and the results were most unsatisfactory. Rents were not punctually collected, enormous arrears accumulated and had to be remitted to the amount of Rs. 79,017 in 1841, the Presidency Commissioner attributing the unfavourable condition to Mr. Grant's injudicious arrangements, though overassessment in some cases and recusancy on the part of the tenants in many cases were the causes of much failure.[47] In 1842 he ordered the assessment to be reduced in the places where the measurements were incorrect, where the tenants had thrown up their lands, and where the mahalls were deteriorating.[48] In 1843 Uma Kanta Babu proposed to transfer to the Collector of Bakarganj 200 of the petty mahalls with a sadar jama of Rs. 28,598 for all of which dowls had been signed,[49] and he submitted two applications for the farm of the five khass mahalls—Buzurgummedpur, Surmahall, Siddokati, Manpasa, and Darichar (which together made up the entire

[45] Presdy. Commr. to Sbn. Commr., no. 150, dated 22, no. 151, dated 24 Nov. 1838, and letter dated 31 Aug. 1839. Sbn. Commr. to Presdy. Commr., no. 363, dated 28 Aug. 1839, no. 218, dated 16 July 1840, and no. 77, dated 17 Apr. 1841.

[46] Presdy. Commr. to Sbn. Commr., no. 62, dated 13 July, and no. 109, dated 13 Oct. 1841.

[47] Ibid., no. 49, dated 28 June 1841.

[48] Sbn. Commr. to Presdy. Commr., no. 224, dated 15 July, and Presdy. Commr. to Sbn. Commr., no. 79, dated 23 Aug. 1842.

[49] Sbn. Commr. to Presdy Commr., no. 345, dated 14 July 1843.

khass mahall)—the total jama of which was Rs. 43,891.[50] No orders appear to have been passed on the proposals, but in 1844 the mahall with all the other Bakarganj estates was transferred to the Collector of that district or the abolition of the Sundarban Commission, and when the Commission was re-established in 1846, Buzurgummedpur was expressly retained under the Collector's control.

137. Settlements in Pargana Saiyadpur, 1834-40: Mr. Tottenham brought the 56 resumed mahalls in pargana Saiyadpur, viz. Tushkhali, &c, under settlement in 1833-34. He recorded all the grades of tenants and raiyats in his chittas, and made the assessment on the ausat talukdars at the rates that he found current. Pending the decision of the appeals the mahalls were managed khass through a tahsildar, but the ausat talukdars were never really dispossessed, and the tenantry recused, combining to upset the arrangements by obstruction and chicanery. Mr. Pigou drew up rules in 1836 to secure efficient management in the khass mahalls,[51] but weakened the hold of Government over this mahall by applying the Board's orders regarding khudkasht raiyats in Buzurgummedpur to tenants here who had no permanent right of occupancy in their lands. The revenue fell heavily into arrears for the people did not pay even the demand fixed in the hastabud previous to the settlement. Strict measures were adopted to realize the rents, especially by Mr. Dampier, when Revenue Commissioner, during the years 1838 and 1839, but were defeated by the resistance of the people. Favourable conditions of adjustment were then proffered with the warning that in case of refusal the estate would be farmed out, the ausat talukdari and haoladari rates being abolished, and the rents collected at the raiyati rates; but the chief ausat talukdars refused to come to terms,[52] and the Presidency Commissioner declined to accept a partial surrender.[53] The penalty was thereupon enforced and the whole estate farmed out to Debnath Rai in 1839 for 20 years—a period during which he could acquire influence and improve the lands. The cultivated area was 38,203 bighas, the rate 15 annas per bigha of

[50] Ibid., no. 441, dated 12, and no. 456, dated 19 Sept. 1843.

[51] Presdy. Commr. to Sbn. Commr., no. 177, dated 10 Dec. 1836.

[52] Ibid., no. 41, dated 20 Feb. 1839, and to Sadr. Bd. Rev., no. 354, dated 7 Nov. 1839. Sbn. Commr. to Presdy. Commr., no. 179, dated 18 June 1840.

[53] Ibid., no. 92, dated 7 May 1839.

55 yards square, and the initial revenue Rs. 34,829. Lands amounting to 5,401 bighas had been settled on progressive terms, and the total ultimate revenue was Rs. 38,097. The name Tushkhali was given to the collective mahalls.[54] The dense forest in the estate had not been measured, and was allowed free of revenue during the currency of the lease, liberty being expressly given to the farmer to reclaim it.[55] The arrears were written off, for they could not be demanded from the ausat talukdars who had not been in possession, but from the haoladars ,who had avowedly retained possession, and the only method open at that stage was by suit in the civil court, which was impracticable.[56] Halta, containing a cleared area of 5,383 bighas, was included in the farm.

138. Special Rules of Settlement in the Case of Tenants: It was laid down as a rule in the management of Buzurgummedpur that parties who had protested against a new assessment could not be held responsible for the difference between the old and new rates until the new settlement was confirmed. This rule was extended to the Saiyadpur mahalls and made applicable to all cases where the settlement was formed with kadim khudkhasht raiyats, but not to those of ordinary lease-holders;[57] and it was further explained that a recusant haoladar or other tenant in a taufir estate, who had not before paid rent to Government at a fixed rate, could be dispossessed of his lands, and the rents collected from his undertenants pending consideration of the new settlement, since he could not be held to be a kadim khudkhasht raiyat.[58]

139. Resettlement of Ramna Bamna, 1840-44: Mr. Dampier's settlement of Ramna Bamna expired in 1841, and the Sundarban Commissioner was directed to resettle it. The mahall was remeasured

[54] The Board said the name was given for the purpose of preserving to the zaminder of Saiyadpur a claim to the settlement in future. Presdy. Commr. to Sbn. Commr., no. 311, dated 18 March 1856.

[55] Sbn. Commr. to Presdy. Commr., no. 418, dated 17 Sept. 1839. Presdy. Commr. to Sbn. Commr., no. 147, dated 21 idem, and no. 267, dated 16 Feb. 1856.

[56] Sbn. Commr. to Presdy. Commr., no. 179, dated 18 June 1840. Presdy. Commr. to Sbn. Commr., no. 59, dated 23 July 1841. There is some indistinctness as to talukdars and ausat talukdars.

[57] Presdy. Commr. to Sbn. Commr., no. 151, dated 9 June 1837.

[58] Ibid., no. 28, dated 3 Mar. 1838—see, too, Sbn. Commr. to Presdy. Commr., no. 180, dated 10 Mar. 1838.

and reassessed during seasons 1840-42. The total area was drons 645-1 (equivalent to 53,742 standard bighas), of which drons 607-9 (comprising drons 540-8 of cultivation) were assessable. Mr. Dampier's assessment had been lenient, and the soil being fertile cultivation had thriven. Mr. Shawe raised the rate of rent, fixing the ausat talukdari rate at Rs. 3 per kani (and in some cases Rs. 4), since the pargana rates for raiyats ranged from Rs. 4 to, Rs. 8. The gross jama was Rs. 29,172. The majority of the ausat talukdars agreed and signed, while those who recused did so from fear of the arrears being demanded.[59] But some of them appealed and the Presidency Commissioner reduced the rate in certain cases and ordered a revision, which Babu U. K. Sen carried out in season 1843-44. The new assessed area was drons 572-7. There were 84 ausat taluks which, by agreement of parties, were converted into patni taluks and assessed at Rs. 2-10 per kani, equivalent to 8 (Company's) annas per standard bigha. Khass management was deprecated, so the excluded talukdars—the heirs of Mohammad Shafi—were admitted to engage for the estate. They were allowed two successive deductions of 10 per cent, for expenses and malikana, and the remainder was taken as the Government revenue, which amounted ultimately to Company's Rs. 19,488. The settlement was confirmed in perpetuity from 1844.[60]

140. Resettlements in Bakarganj, 1840-44: Messers. Kemp and Shawe remeasured Chota Basdiya and revised its settlement during seasons 1840-42, computing its area at drons 240-11 (equal to 31,368 bighas), and raising its ultimate jama to Company's Rs. 8,341.[61] During 1841 Mr. Shawe reported Mr. Dampier's settlements of Char Chila[62] and Bara Basdiya,[63] the latter of which still-continued khass under the control of a sazawul on account of the recusancy of the owners and in 1842 he reported Mr. Dampier's settlements of Baliyatali

[59] Sbn. Commr. to Presdy. Commr., 14 Jan. and no. 181, dated 31 Mar. 1843.

[60] Babu U.K. Sen.. Dy. Collr., to Presdy. Commr., no. 341, dated 15 Oct. 1844, and no. 388, dated 18 Sept. 1845. Presdy. Commr. to Babu U.K. Sen, no. 542, dated 28 Nov. 1844.

[61] Sbn. Commr. to Presdy. Commr., no. 393, dated 27th Dec. 1842.

[62] Ibid., no. 211, dated 23 Aug. 1841.

[63] Ibid., no. 213, dated 23 Aug. 1841.

(two estates).[64] During season 1842-43 Mr. Shawe, and the following season Uma Kanta Babu remeasured a large number of the mahalls in Bakarganj and revised their settlements. Their reason for doing so is not clear, and it was besides opposed to the instructions of the Presidency Commissioner who had remarked in 1840 that he could not sanction the remeasurement of newly cleared lands on the skirts of the jungle, a long period having been originally fixed in order to encourage reclamation.[65] In some instances the period of settlement may have expired, and in others the free period for the jungle. They, however, considered a general remeasurement and readjustment of revenue desirable. Thus Mr. Shawe in season 1842-43 remeasured Taktabuniya, Kukua, Debpur, Nishanbariya, Dhankhali, Char Chila, Tiyakhali, Lalua, Baliyatali (2), and Rangabali; and his settlement proceedings in those eleven estates appear to have been completed the following season by Uma Kanta Babu who also then remeasured and resettled the neighbouring estates— Sonauta, Dhalashar, and Bara Basdiya, besides the more distant Charwa, Bara Bighai, Keorabuniya, and Marichbuniya. He appears to have maintained the old rates, and merely adjusted the assessment according to the extent of cultivation. The settlement of Charwa, with an area of drons 173-5 and jama of Rs. 5,915, was confirmed for 20 years from 1844;[66] but the other settlements were disapproved chiefly with reference to the rates, and orders were issued for their revision. The Commission was abolished that year and the duties assigned to the Collector of Bakarganj, but when the office was revived in 1846, these settlements re-engaged the Sundarban Commissioner's attention. They will be referred to in their place later on, but the question of the rates introduced important changes of principle which deserve notice here.

141. New Rules Regarding Rates of Assessment in Bakarganj, 1844: Mr. Dampier had adopted in his Bakarganj settlements the rates he found current, and computed the Government revenue at the talukdari rate of Rs. 1-12 per kani. Below that was the ordinary haoladari rate of Rs. 2-8. Mr Shawe and Uma Kanta Babu proceeded

64 Ibid., no. 265, dated 11 Aug., and no. 302. dated 20 Sept. 1842.

65 Presdy. Commr. to Sbn. Commr., no. 25, dated 29 Jan. 1840.

66 Sbn. Commr. to Presdy. Commr., no. 240, dated 31 July, and Presdy. Commr. to Sbn. Commr., no. 460, dated 24 Sept. 1844.

to reassess at the previous rates. Rs. 2-8 per kani was equivalent to 5 annas per 40-yard bigha. Mr. Harvey, the Presidency Commissioner, when reviewing the settlements observed, that he could find no reason why resumed Sundarban lands should be assessed at a lighter rate than Sundarban grants, for which Government had prescribed 8 annas per 40-yard bigha universally as the full assessment; while to make the rates less was unjust to the grantees and impolitic, as inviting fresh usurpations by outsiders. He held therefore that the lands ought to be assessed at the 8-anna rate, but, being deterred by the previous low rental and the exposed situation of the mahalls near the sea from enforcing the rate at one stroke, and believing that no revenue officer was competent of his own motion to assess such lands at a lower rate, he referred the point for the orders of the Board. Subinfeudation, he urged, could not affect the conditions so as to reduce the assessment below that rate. He proposed to make the assessment according to the bigha and enhance it gradually up to the Sundarban rate, retaining the rate of 5 annas for the year 1252 (1845-46) till when the old settlements held good, then allowing a rasad of 6 and 7 annas for five year each, and thereafter assessing at the full rate of 8 annas, the holders being allowed a deduction of 20 or 25 per cent. The Board approved his terms.[67] Mr. Harvey ordered that the settlements (including that of Chota Basdiya) should be revised accordingly, and the estates farmed out if the parties recused; in which event they would receive no malikana, as they have not been constituted maliks nor derived any grant from Government in whom, by virtue of section 13 of Regulation III of 1828, the property of the soil in the Sundarbans was vested.[68] The results of those orders were that measurements were made in standard bighas instead of drons and kanis; 8 annas per bighas was laid down as the invariable rate of

[67] Presdy. Commr. to Sbn. Commr., no. 432, dated 14 Sept., and no. 503, dated 31 Oct. 1844.

[68] Ibid., no. 368 (Nishanbariya), and no. 369 (Sonauta), both dated 9 Aug. 1844; no. 371 (Debpur), dated 13 Aug. 1844; no. 410 (Dhankhali) and no. 411 (Taktabuniya), both dated and Sept. 1844; no. 432 (Rangabali), dated 14 Sept. 1844; no. 503 (Char Chilla, Lalua, Baliyatali—two estates—and Dhalashar), dated 31 Oct. 1844; and no. 433 (Chota Basdiya), dated 14 Sept. 1844.

full assessment for all lands; settlement holders received a percentage allowance instead of paying at a fixed rate per bigha, and an opinion was enunciated about the maliki right in the resumed mahalls which brought that subject up for subsequent discussion.

142. Sundarban Rate of 8 Annas per 40-yard Bigha: In the foregoing correspondence Mr. Harvey held 8 annas per bigha of 40-yards square, which had been fixed by Government, as the rate for Sundarban grants, to be general rate, which was in equity to be imposed on all Sundarban lands, and he treated any lower assessment as a deviation which required special sanction. The Board tacitly accepting that way of stating the question replied in their no. 215, dated 10th September 1844, that under the circumstances represented they had no objection to the terms suggested, and accordingly sanctioned the conclusion of the settlements agreeably thereto, "particularly with advertence to the fact that in all regular grants of Sundarban waste, the grantees are allowed a term of 20 years free from all rent." The qualification seems to mean that a free period of 20 years should precede the imposition of the 8 annas rate. That order by implication affirmed Mr. Harvey's proposition that 8 annas was the general rate for all Sundarban lands; and he enforced it in other correspondence about numerous other mahalls. His view was thus accepted without question, and 8 annas per the 40-yard bigha became the established rate for all Sundarban lands. There does not appear to have been any positive resolution by the Government to that effect. During Mr. Smelt's operations in 1816 the Board had proposed to fix 8 annas sicca as a universal Sundarban rate, but the Government, while accepting it as fair, declined at that stage to formulate any such rule. That fact, however, was only nominally apposite, for the bigha to which the rate applied was 55-yards square, and the rate was actually equivalent to one of 4¼ (Company's) annas per 40-yard bigha. In the patitabadi settlements 8 annas per the 40-yard bigha was the general though not invariable rate. The rate of 8 annas per standard bigha had been laid down as the ultimate rate for all grants, and that seems to be the only class of lands for which it had been positively prescribed. Mr. Harvey in giving the rate general prevalence desired to treat all lands alike fairly; but there appears to be no authority declaring the rate universally applicable.

143. Growth of Under Tenures in Bakarganj and Eastern Jessore: Another point to be noticed is the large development of undertenures at these resettlements, especially in the eastern estates in Bakarganj. The early conditions have been explained in paragraphs 104 and 105. But soon after Mr. Dampier's settlements, ausat ("intermediate") haolas were created between the haolas and nim-haolas, and a little later on ausat nim-haolas were interposed between the nim-haolas and karshas. Nim ausat taluks were created between ausat taluks and haolas. This seems to have been the general course of creation, though naturally no marked separations can be drawn, and in after years all the tenures increased together. By about 1850 all the tenants below the haoladars seems to have made good their claims to the rights of alienation, sub-division, and succession, which were at first acknowledged in the haolas alone, and the resettlements made about that time were extended to and included the nim-haolas in many cases, and the ausat nim-haolas in a few; but in subsequent resettlements there has been no uniformity in the method, so that the jamabandis in some instances have dealt with every one down to the kharshas, and in others discarded all except the haoladars. From Bakarganj this system of tenures spread westwards into the present Bagherhat subdivision, but it did not attain the same development there.

144. Rules Regarding Taujih Accounts, 1842: The khass management by the Sundarban Commissioner of estates in other districts created complications and confusion in the Collector's accounts, especially in Bakarganj, with the large mahalls in parganas Buzurgummedpur and Saiyadpur. The Sundarban mahalls under khass management were of three kinds—(1) those resumed and settled by the Sundarban Commissioner and made over to the Collector with merely a kistbandi dowl; (2) mahalls resumed but not settled, and retained meanwhile under the Commissioner's khass control: the Collector did not know even their names or the demand from them; and (3) mahalls bought by Government and held under the Commissioner's management: these remained on the district rent-roll. For the first he was directed in future to supply the Collector with information whether the settlement had been confirmed or not, whether it was permanent or temporary, and whether it was a proprietary settlement or a farm; and for both the latter kinds he was required to furnish the

Collector at the beginning of each year with a jamabandi to enable him to make the correct credits in his books, and quarterly with jama-wasil-bakis for incorporation in the Collector's own explanations of balances.[69]

145. Subdivision of Mahalls: As a rule Sundarban mahalls were not partitioned, though no prohibition appears to have been issued.[70] Subdivision, however, in other ways was not rare. Lots when too large were divided, and each part disposed of separately: or different parties might have begun reclaiming in the same block of land, and then for the sake of convenience and expediency, each received settlement of his own portion, as in Lalua, Dhankali, & c. So, too, in lots 217-20 which were made up of a large number of natural chaks held by different persons, and where each chak was constituted a separate estate. Or, again, when grants were resumed, the cleared portion was often settled with the late grantee and the jungle disposed of separately, as in lot 62, & c, but the abadkars at times recused, in which event the cleared lands after assessment were together with the jungle given out as one estate. Similar to this were the cases of Gulsakhali and Kukua, where the owners of the cultivated portions got the lease of the adjoining jungle, but as separate estates on different terms. In 1841 permission was given that when resumed lands were found to be in the possession of different person, they might claim separate settlements,[71] but it was seldom acted on. Tiyakhali, however, was partitioned in 1857.[72]

69 Presdy. Commr. to Sbn. Commr., no. 52, dated 22 July 1842.
70 See Presdy. Commr. to Sbn. Commr., no. 131, dated 20 Aug. 1856.
71 Presdy. Commr. to Sbn. Commr., no. 112, dated 18 Oct. 1841.
72 Ibid., no. 28 Ct., dated 7 Aug. 1857.

CHAPTER XII

Forest Grants, Grant Rules, and Boundary Difficulties
1836-1844

146. Inspections and Resumptions, 1836-44: Most of the grants having been leased out in 1830 and 1831, the clearance Condition fell due in 1836 and 1837. The Sundarban Commissioner was required to inspect them himself or by his Deputy Collector, reports by amins not being allowed. On failure in the condition, the procedure prescribed was that he should call upon the grantees to shew cause why their grant should not be resumed, and after hearing their representations, report the result with his opinion for the final decision of the Board.[1] Good progress had been made, though much damage had been inflicted by the storm and wave of 21st May 1833, which visited the mouth of the Hugli and inundated the country on both sides. There was a subsequent but less calamitous gale and inundation in June 1842 in 24-Parganas. Lot 42 was resumed and transferred to the Salt Department in 1836.[2] Lots 28, 29, 66, 70, 71, 73, 85, 90 and 98 were also resumed in 24-Parganas during 1837 and 1838. A grant had been made of lots 217, 218, and 219 together in Jessore with an area of 55,000 bighas in 1830, but it was afterwards found that a great part of the land was in cultivation before, and that the grant contained part of the khass mahall Chandkhali, some resumed mahalls, and a quantity of land measured by Mr. Smelt in 1816, which was claimed by the Raja of Jessore as lakhiraj of the *brit* Syam Rai Thakur, and for which the Sundarban Commissioner had instituted suits under Regulation III of 1828. The mistake appeared to have arisen from the fact that Hodges copied the Sundarban boundary from Gobra to the northern

[1] Sadr. Bd. Rev. to Sbn. Commr., 14 Sept. 1835, and Presdy. Commr. to Sbn. Commr., 4 Nov. 1836.

[2] Sbn. Commr. to Presdy. Commr., 2 Aug. 1836.

corner of lot 217 from Morrieson's map of 1814, since which time reclamation had been progressing to the north of the rivers Menus and Sipsa, while an extensive tract on the Kabadak and Kayra rivers had relapsed into jungle. Another lease had been granted in 1831 for lots 220, 221, and 224 together with an area of 121,000 bighas, where the circumstances were similar, besides that there were disputes about the first two of these lots.[3] The grant of lots 217, 218, and 219 was therefore cancelled in 1840;[4] and also the latter grant as regarded lot 220 in 1839.[5] Lot 82 was resumed in 1840 and lot 19 relinquished by the grantee: lot 225 was resumed in 1841; and lot 36 in 1843.

147. New Grants, 1836-44: After the first eager competition for grants of the forest, the applications fell off, seemingly because there remained few attractive lots, but they revived about the middle of 1839. Resumed lots were regranted, and a few new grants were made. Lot 220 was divided up into separate chaks. Lot 73 was regranted in 1836; lots 70 and 98 in 1837; lot 19 in 1838; lots 37, 39, 136 and 216 and Deluti (in lot 220) in 1839; lots 82, 217, 218, 219, and Munkiya and Godardanga (both in lot 220) in 1840; lots 173 and 225 and the khass mahall Barthal,[6] which was all waste, in 1841; lots 60 and 169 (part) in 1843; and during the same year revised pattas appear to have been given for lots 88, 89, and 93-97.[7] Lot 28 (excluding 7,000 bighas reserved for the Salt Department)[8] was granted out in 1844; and also Chakamoya, Amtali, Arpangasiya, and Pachakuraliya in Bakarganj.[9]

148. Amalnama Grants in Jessore and Bakarganj, 1836-41: Mr. Dampier, as mentioned in paragraph 96, gave an amalnama in 1834 for land west of the river Bhola and south of Perikhali, estimated at 7,000 bighas. Clearings were found in it, and the amalnama was cancelled in 1838 and the land divided between the grantee and the unauthorised reclaimer. The northern half (consisting of the present lot 237 and the north portions of lots 238 and 239) was given to the former, and

3 Ibid., 31 Jan. 1836.
4 Presdy. Commr. to Sbn. Commr., no. 108, dated 14 July 1840.
5 Ibid., no. 164, dated 1 Oct. 1839.
6 Ibid., no. 86, dated 13 June 1840.
7 *Vide* Register.
8 Presdy. Commr. to Sbn. Commr., no. 271, dated 11 June 1844.
9 Sbn. Commr. to Presdy. Commr., no. 336, dated 5 Oct. 1844.

the southern half (consisting of the south portions of lots 238 and 293) to the latter.[10] Mr. Kemp proposed to lay down the boundary between Perikhali and the northern grant, but it does not seem to have been done.[11] The tongue of land lying between the Bhola and Baleswar and known as Khaoliya Barisal was resumed by Mr. Grant in 1834 and finally by the Special Commissioner on 8th December 1836.[12] Its area was estimated at 150,000 bighas. A rough plan of it was made in 1838 with the view of breaking it up into lots, but the dividing streams could not be traced.[13] Applications were received, but were detained on a suspicion that clearances existed in it. An amalnama for the whole seems to have been granted in 1840 without authority, and was cancelled in 1841. Meanwhile an enquiry was made, the tract was divided into two blocks by the Chipa-Baroikhali, Khajurbariya-Doaniya, and Kumarkhali khals running through the middle, no smaller partitions being feasible, and the grant of both portions on the usual terms was sanctioned in 1841.[14]

149. Proposals to Survey the Bakarganj Forest, 1830-40: As mentioned in paragraph 96, no survey had been made of the region east of the Pasar, though, after the forest boundary had been defined, Mr. Dampier, in 1830, urged that Hodges should survey that tract as far as the Rabanabad Islands in detail for purposes of allotment. The suggestion was approved, but the duty was postponed for the survey of the resumed mahalls and the Bakarganj khass mahalls.[15] Other matters afterward supervened and the project received no further notice till 1835, when attention was drawn to it in consequence of frequent applications being made for grants there, and the Board proposed to

[10] Sbn. Commr. to Presdy. Commr., 18 Sept. 1837, no. 475, dated 7 Dec. 1838, and letter 26 Dec. 1838. Presdy. Commr. to Sbn. Commr., no. 191, dated 29 Nov. 1839. In some of the correspondence the total area is stated at 70,000 bighas.

[11] Sbn. Commr. to Presdy. Commr., 22 July 1839.

[12] Presdy. Commr. to Sbn. Commr., 20 March 1837.

[13] Sbn. Commr. to Presdy. Commr., 26 July 1838.

[14] Presdy. Commr. to Sbn. Commr., no. 47, dated 13 Apr. 1840; no. 50, dated 12 July, and no. 89, dated 11 Sept. 1841 Sbn. Commr. to Presdy. Commr., no. 531, dated 7 Dec. 1846.

[15] Sbn. Commr. to Presdy. Commr., 8 May 1830. Presdy. Commr. to Sbn. Commr., no. 1437, dated 4 Sept. 1830.

Government to allot and grant it out, but nothing was done.[16] The next year again the Presidency Commissioner recommended a survey of the Bakarganj forest, for, the soil being fertile applications promised to be abundant and the terms might be rendered more favourable to Government.[17] Again, in 1837 the Government considered the project desirable for the purpose of determining what fresh lands had been reclaimed there recently, as well as of plotting out fresh grants, and suggested whether the survey might not be combined with the revision of the boundary in Jessore; the Government also expressed its readiness to modify the grant terms thereon the ground of the superior value of the lands.[18] The survey was at once asked for as applications had been received for the jungle; but it was not undertaken, and pending the reconsideration of the general question of Sundarban grants, the minor one of modifying the terms in Bakarganj seems to have been dropped. The lots in Bakarganj have never been numbered; at an early period they had acquired names by which they were well known, and have been since always designated.

150. Amalnamas for Bakarganj Forest Lands, 1840-43: Although the forest in Bakarganj was not surveyed, and regular grants could not be made, yet Mr. Dampier's plan of bestowing amalnamas was feasible. Thus three parties applied for the lease of Nilganj and also of Abuganj-Mithaganj in the years 1840-42. Mr. Shawe visited the chaks in February 1843, and after hearing the opposing claims gave amalnamas to certain Mags for the chaks.[19] Three other Mags applied to him there for a grant of certain lands which comprised Chandokhali, Kachupatra, and Bogi, and he gave them an amalnama for the spot where they had begun reclaiming.[20] In these cases he promised that an inspection would be made two years afterwards and pattas given them if they had cleared the lands.

151. Reconsideration of the Grant Terms, 1841-44: A number of Sundarban grantees submitted a memorial to the Government in 1841 asking for a modification of their terms in a more liberal direction as

16 Presdy. Commr. to Sbn. Commr., 29 Oct. 1835, and 27 Oct. 1836.

17 Presdy. Commr. to Sadr. Bd. Rev., 22 Oct. 1836.

18 Presdy. Commr. to Sbn. Commr., 2 March and 29 Aug. 1837.

19 Smith, Dy. Collr. to Sbn. Commr., 25 and 26 Aug. 1847.

20 Ibid., no. 11, dated 30 June 1847.

they had met with serious difficulties, and had been obstructed by the zamindars with whom they had frequent and expensive disputes, and as the grants had been damaged by the hurricane of 1833. A report was called for and submitted. From 1830 till 1843, 138 lots with an area of 2,022,732 bighas had been granted out to 95 persons. Reclamation had been carried on by means of woodcutters and labourers procured from Hazaribagh and Mag coolies from the eastern frontier. The storm of 1833 had ruined the grants from Saugor Island to the Bidyadhari, though the raiyats driven from the southern grants had settled down in the northern grants. Twenty-six of the grants had been forfeited and some resigned. In 96 grants inspected by the surveyor, out of an area of 1,422,792 bighas, 201,910 bighas had been brought under cultivation and 28,450 bighas were low jungle, while the other grants were all forest. The lots in the 24-Parganas were surrounded by small creeks supplying fresh water during half the year and obtained enough raiyats, but those near the sea had not those advantages and were liable to inundation. The only important produce was rice; some of the grantees had tried sugarcane and coconut, but had failed; and the manufacture of salt was confined to the limits prescribed by Government. Some, however, had not undertaken reclamation, but merely realized an income from the natural products. The average rate of rent paid by raiyats was Re. 1 per bigha; half went to Government as revenue and the other half formed the grantee's income subject to expenses and losses. On the whole reclamation advanced, stood still, or receded much according to individual character and circumstances; but some of the grants had been too large to admit of successful management. Various modifications were suggested, but the Government decided in 1844 to introduce no change. The Government was disposed to view with favourable consideration the case of all grantees who had really exerted themselves to fulfil the condition of their grants, and whose failure had arisen from circumstances beyond their control, and expressed its readiness to extend the rent-free term of their leases, according to the circumstances of each, to any period not exceeding ten years beyond the original duration.[21] These promises afforded great relief and were called into frequent exercise during the following years.

[21] Presdy. Commr. to Sbn. Commr., no. 4 Ct, dated 29 Feb. 1842. Sbn. Commr.

152. Suggestions for Revision of Grant Rules, 1842: The Court of Directors reviewed the subject of the Sundarban grants at the beginning of 1842. They held it to be an objectionable feature that non-fulfilment of the contract involved no penalty, for forfeiture of land, on which no expenditure had been incurred, could scarcely be considered such; and they thought that if a premium were paid on all grants above a certain area, the contingent forfeiture would tend to confine speculation within reasonable limits. They suggested therefore the desirability of adding rules to provide for the systematic leasing out of the Sundarbans and to secure the following points—(1) that grants should not exceed 4,000 acres, equivalent to 12,100 bighas of 40 yards square, Government, however, having a discretion to bestow more on payment of an acreage price for it; (2) that no grants should be made without previous survey and determination of boundaries; (3) that they should be disposed of by public competition; (4) that grants should not be treated as real property, but be subject at the expiration of the lease to the ordinary assessment of the district; (5) that grants until reclaimed should be considered as personal and hereditary only, and be incapable of sale or transfer; (6) that certain areas should be reserved by Government for timber, and all streams and canals be under the control of Government; (7) that until lands were actually brought into cultivation, the ancient common rights of the people should not be abrogated.[22] Mr. Shawe thought some penalty should be inflicted on persons who did not cultivate their grants within the specified time, as otherwise people took grants merely to sell them, and he suggested that conditions should be imposed of clearing one-fourth in five years half in ten, and the whole in 20 years while the grantee should be at liberty to sell if he complied with the conditions.[23] The Presidency Commissioner and the Board held that in the case of a transfer forfeiture would be a penalty to a purchaser if not to the original grantee, while such transfers would be an earnest of reclamation; and although the payment of a premium

to Presdy. Commr., no. 384, dated 13 Dec. 1842. Mullins to Sbn. Commr., 10 Oct. 1843. Sbn. Commr. to Presdy. Commr., no. 500, dated 9 Nov. 1843. Presdy. Commr. to Sbn. Commr., no. 112, dated 28 Nov. 1844.

[22] Ibid., no. 45, dated 11 July 1842.

[23] Sbn. Commr. to Presdy. Commr., no. 235, dated 25 July 1842.

would strengthen the motive for reclamation; yet fearing lest it might deter speculators they opposed the proposition. Besides they thought that when the grantees had applied for more favourable terms, the Government could scarcely render the terms harder. They disapproved of the limitation of the grants to 4,000 acres, since the grants must be regulated by the natural features. On the whole they dissented from the modifications suggested by the Court of Director,[24] and the subject lay in abeyance for several years.

153. Miscellaneous Rules Regarding Grants, 1836-40: The Board had pronounced in 1829 that the grants did not convey the right of fishery in the surrounding khals, and they further explained in 1836 that the khals between the grants were public ground; but the decision was a one-sided one against the grantee when his grant bordered on permanently-settled land.[25] The question again arose in 1838 in the case of Mr. Heatly who had received a block of eight grants together—lots 87-89 and 93-97—and the right was again denied, the fact of his owning the land on both sides giving him no exclusive right over the khal between.[26] The claims of other persons were faced in 1837, when the Sundarban Commissioner was informed that if the owner or occupier of a jalkar extended his rights to rivers not comprised in his patta and lying within the Sundarban boundary, he might resume the usurpation and leave the defendant to appeal to the Special Commissioner.[27] A new clause was prescribed in 1836 for all future grants that the bank of a navigable-channel should be available as a two-path or road.[28] The question of giving the grantee possession caused some trouble, and it was laid down in 1837 that the Sundarban Commissioner should put the grantee in full possession when making the grant, but that afterwards it was the duty of the Magistrate to maintain him therein.[29]

154. Boundary Disputes in Grants, 1837-39: After Mr. Dampier's demarcation of the Sundarban boundary in the 24-Parganas; disputes

[24] Presdy. Commr. to Sbn. Commr., no. 84, dated 31 Aug. 1842.
[25] Ibid., 7 Dec. 1836.
[26] Ibid., 28 July 1838, and no. 169, dated 4 Oct. 1839.
[27] Ibid., no. 28, dated 11 Feb. 1837.
[28] Ibid., no. 176, dated 7 Dec. 1836.
[29] Ibid., no. 81, dated 7 Apr., and no. 176. dated 4 July 1837.

between the zamindars and border grantees ceased, and matters went on peacefully for a few years until the grantees' clearings reached the zamindari lands. Border grants were frequently defined as bounded by the cultivated lands of the permanently-settled estates. Mr. Dampier's bamboos, however, along the boundary were removed; no traces remained; the boundary could no longer be identified, and disputes sprang up afresh.[30] The grantees appealed to Government to protect them in their rights by again determining their boundaries, and the subject was complicated by the fact that some of them had never been formally put in possession of their grants. Such oversights were remedied,[31] but the boundary disputes were serious and difficult, for, besides other contentions, they involved the question whether a grantee was entitled to the whole area that was originally included in his lot, or merely to what was actual jungle at the time he got the grant. The Board decided in 1837 that the grantee of a lot with definite boundaries was entitled to the whole of the land inside the boundaries, notwithstanding that a portion of it, though waste in Prinsep's time, had been brought into cultivation prior to the date of his grant[32] but this ruling did not dispose of cases where there were no definite boundaries. Further, in cases where lands were concerned which had been decreed by the Special Commissioner, he declined to determine the limits fixed in his own decrees, though the Board had notified that boundary disputes in such lands were to be disposed of under his direction, he being alone competent to superintend the execution of his own decrees. The Government thereupon ordered, on 11th September 1838, that in all such cases application for decision of the disputes should be made to the resumption tribunal, which would either determine the matter summarily or direct the institution of a new suit.[33] The difficulties were enhanced in a report which Mr. Shakespear made in 1837 on the demarcation of the Sundarban

[30] Ibid., 22 Oct. 1837, and no. 10, dated 24 Jan. 1839. Sbn. Commr. to Presdy. Commr., no. 82, dated 22 Apr. 1840.

[31] Presdy. Commr. to Sbn. Commr., no. 65, dated 19 June 1838 and no. 79. dated 6 June 1840.

[32] Ibid., no. 55, dated 9 March 1837.

[33] Sbn. Commr. to Presdy. Commr., no. 18, dated 17 Jan., and no. 67, dated 28 Feb. 1837. Presdy. Commr. to Sbn. Commr., no. 159, dated 31 Oct. 1838.

boundary,[34] where he mistakenly represented that the boundary in the 24-Parganas from the Hugli to the Jabuna had never been properly defined under Regulation III of 1828, and that there were many places which did not appear to have been visited by Mr. Dampier; but Mr. Dampier when Revenue Commissioner in 1839 rectified the error,[35] and, pointing out the encroachments of the zamindar, Munshi Amir, proposed that the boundary should be surveyed and permanent land marks erected. Other disputes were relegated to the decision of the civil courts, but those affecting the boundary could not be settled except by a resurvey.

155. Surveys of Boundaries of Grants, 1830-40: Accordingly, Mr. Turner, a Surveyor, was employed in March 1839, and his duties were to resurvey Mr. Dampier's Sundarban boundary in certain specified lots, and point it out to the grantees, whose duty it then became to construct durable marks along it, while both parties would be bound down to abide by his line.[36] The lots assigned him were Nos. 46, 47, 57, 65-73, 75-77, 79-82, 89, 93-98, and 101-03, that is, omitting the first two lots, he was directed to resurvey the whole of the Sundarban boundary (except along lots 58, 63, and 88) in the present Basirhat subdivision. During 1839 he defined lots 68, 79, and 80, and during 1840 lots 46, 47, 94, 95, and 97;[37] but Mr. Elias, the principal zamindar, impugned the correctness of his surveys. The orders to Turner were suspended in 1840, and he died at the end of that year.

156. Disputes in Lots 57 and 67, 1838-43: Messers. Broadhead and others, who had obtained lots 57 and 67 arid were in dispute with Mr. Elias, applied for the relay of their boundaries, but Mr. Dampier held that no relay was required as the boundary had been defined in 1833. The grantees appealed to the Board and the decision was specially assigned to Mr. Kemp in 1840. He was directed to define the Sundarban boundary, acting de novo, and not merely relaying Prinsep's boundary which Mr. Dampier had confirmed when Sundarban

[34] Sbn. Commr. to Presdy. Commr., no. 5, dated 11 Jan. 1837.

[35] Presdy. Commr. to Sbn. Commr., no. 10, dated 24 Jan. 1839, and no. 76, dated 4 June 1840.

[36] Sbn. Commr. to Turner, 25 Oct. and 1 Nov. 1839, and 25 March 1840. Presdy. Commr. to Sbn. Commr., no. 131, dated 19 Aug. 1840.

[37] Turner to Sbn. Commr., 29 Aug. 1839. 9 May, and 13 July 1840.

Commissioner. Prinsep's map would be evidence as to the boundary, but it was not more and would not be conclusive.[38] He was instructed to hold regular proceedings under section 13 of Regulation III of 1828, recording the particulars of his inquiries and the grounds of his decision, and then have the boundary so determined by him laid down by survey.[39] He visited the lots with Mr. Mullins, the new Surveyor, in January 1841, held regular proceedings, and decided that Prinsep's boundary was correct. Thereupon Mullins surveyed it according to Prinsep's field-book in Mr. Kemp's presence, and the line was marked out by the grantees with a bund.[40] Mr. Kemp had, however, varied from Mr. Dampier's line and deprived Mr. Elias of a part of his land; so, on appeal by Mr. Elias, the Special Commissioner in December 1842 set aside the proceedings, confirmed Mr. Dampier's boundary, and ordered that Mr. Elias should be restored to whatever land he had been deprived of. Mr. Ross, Deputy Collector, carried out the order in season 1842-43, but did not employ a surveyor to demarcate his line, and the omission led to renewed difficulties.[41]

157. Difficulties in Lots 217, 218, 219, 220, 221, and 224, 1837: Besides those difficulties, there was serious confusion regarding the grants of lots 217-21 and 224 in Jessore. The character of the Sundarban boundary there has been explained in paragraph 65. Mr. Shakespear, when reporting on the boundary in 1837, mentioned the tract from Gobra to Orabuniya and lot 220 as places where he could not find that Mr. Dampier had gone or had defined the boundary according to the Board's orders. The Board then informed the Government that the line of waste as drawn in Morrieson's map between Gobra and Orabuniya—a distance of 78 miles— had been laid down, but they could not ascertain whether the limits of the existing waste had been marked out as ordered by them, and a record formed of the distance between the two; that no explanation had

[38] Presdy. Commr. to Sbn. Commr., no. 149, dated 28 Sept., and no. 151, dated 10 Oct. 1840.

[39] Sadr. Bd. Rev. to Presdy. Commr., no. 219, dated 28 Aug. 1840.

[40] Sbn. Commr. to Presdy. Commr., 261. dated 28 Sept. 1841.

[41] Sbn. Commr. to Special Commissioner, no. 277, dated 23 Aug. 1842. Presdy. Commr. to Sbn. Commr., no. 21, dated 7 Apr. 1843. and no. 24, dated 2 Apr. 1846—See paragraph 211.

been given regarding the portion of the boundary between Orabuniya and Lakhikhola—a distance of 34 miles; but that the part of the line beyond Lakhikhola had been surveyed by Morrieson.[42] Lot 220 was in a great measure, if not wholly, situated outside the forest as delineated by Rennell.[43] It was proposed in 1837 to complete the shortcomings in the boundary at once, but the project was not carried out, and difficulties were afterwards solved piecemeal.

158. Resumptions and Settlements in Lots 217, 218, and 219 by Collector of Jessore, 1836-42: Lots 217, 218, and 219, after resumption in 1839, were notwithstanding those inconveniences, again granted out in 1840 in one lease to Mahes Chandra Banerji and others, without any inquiry and merely on their incorrect representations that the lands were all waste. Persons had obtained pattas from the Collector of Jessore both before and after Hodges' survey of 1829 for small chaks, but they had cleared the greater part of three lots, which contained an estimated area of 55,000 standard bighas. Chak Khaliya had been resumed in 1826 and was at length settled by the Collector in 1836 with an area of 901 bighas and jama of Rs. 381. Other resumption proceedings had been in progress under the Special Deputy Collector of Jessore, who, on 16th January 1838, resumed, as being invalid lakiraj, taraf Madhukhali and chaks Anandatala and Harijhipatan, which two latter comprised 4,745 bighas. His decrees were confirmed by the Special Commissioner in appeal on 13th September 1838. Taraf Madhukhali contained three chaks—Hetalbuniya, Lakhikhola, and Haripur—lying in lots 217 and 218, and thirteen other little chaks situated about lot 220 and the river Bhadar.[44] Similarly chak Khariya-Dhamsakhali, containing 5,708 bighas, was resumed by him as taufir appertaining to the invalid lakhiraj chak Anandatala in 1839, and by the Special Commissioner in appeal on 14th December 1841, although the new grantees intervened to assert their rights. Mr. Stopford, the Deputy Collector, at once measured and settled the chaks, farming out Anandatala-Haripur,

[42] Presdy. Commr. to Sbn. Commr., 29 Aug 1837.

[43] Ibid., no. 228, dated 7 Sept. 1837. Sbn. Commr. to Presdy. Commr., no. 430, dated 3 Oct. 1837.

[44] Babu J.N. Das, Dy. Collr., to Sbn. Commr., no. 152, dated 19 Dec. 1853, and Sbn. Commr. to Presdy. Commr., no. 185, dated 22 Jan. 1853.

Lakhikhola and Hetalbuniya for ten years in May 1840, and giving a talukdari lease for Khariya-Dhamsakhali in April 1842.[45] The fact of the Collector having given leases for chaks inside these lots coming to Mr. Shawe's knowledge, he directed Mr. Mullins to make an inquiry. Mr. Mullins visited the lots in season 1841-42 and surveyed their boundaries, but did not put the grantees in possession. He reported that Bagura and Kalmibuniya lay in lot 217, and Orabuniya, Khaliya, and Harijhipatan in lot 219; and suggested that the leases already granted for those chaks should be upheld and the remainder of the lots reserved for the grantees. Harikhali, however, which the Collector had also settled, lay outside lot 219. Hodges in fact had surveyed as lot 219 Hanjhipatan, part of Khaliya, Soladana, Sonamukhi, Kainmukhi, Digia, Amurkata, Sonakhali, Birjapha, & c.[46] The grantees then resorted to the civil court and brought a suit at Jessore against Government and other parties to gain possession of 14,200 bighas in lot 219. The conflicting claims coming to his notice Mr. Harvey, the Presidency Commissioner, withheld his confirmation from Mr. Stopford's settlements and ordered Uma Kanta Babu to make a local inquiry in 1843. The office was abolished before the orders could be carried out, but they were subsequently attended to as explained in Chapter XIV.

[45] Babu U.K. Sen to Presdy. Commr., no. 152, dated 23 Aug., and no. 165, dated 6 Sept. 1845. Presdy. Commr. to Sbn. Commr., no. 138, dated 2 Sept. 1846.

[46] Mullins to Sbn. Commr., 18 Feb. and 31 May 1842.

CHAPTER XIII

Abolition and Re-Establishment of the Sundarban Commission
1844-1846

159. Temporary Nature of Sundarban Commission, 1820-42: The question of the abolition of the Commission was an ever-present one, and had been mooted from time to time soon after the office was first established. It seems to have been retained as an object to be worked up to. Reports were frequently called for as to the state of business, but the decision had been averted as often as the question was raised through the necessity for carrying out some particular duty. In 1830 the Board had remarked that the Commission could not be abolished as long as lands remained to be resumed.[1] Again, when Mr. Dampier quitted the Sundarbans in 1834, the plan was reconsidered, but was put aside as there existed ample business to be completed, and numerous resumptions and settlements soon afterwards cropped up for disposal. Mr. Shakespear suggested in 1838 that the Commission should be broken up and divided among the several Collectors,[2] but it was thought impracticable at the time. In answer to a renewed call in 1841, Mr. Kemp proposed either that the office should be abolished and divided among the Collectors, or that the Commissioner should be retained on a lower salary, recommending the latter course for a year during which the main business then in hand might be disposed of;[3] but the Presidency Commissioner pronounced that that was not a fit time to abolish the office,[4] and the alternative does not appear to have been adopted. The next year, however, considering the work accomplished to be very trifling, and the Sundarban field too wide

[1] Presdy. Commr. to Sbn. Commr., no. 1437, dated 4 Sept. 1830.
[2] Sbn. Commr. to Presdy. Commr., no. 425, dated 18 Nov. 1838.
[3] Ibid., no. 34, dated 27 Feb. 1841.
[4] Presdy. Commr. to Sbn. Commr., no. 42, dated 3 June 1841.

and multifarious, the Presidency Commissioner recommended the abolition of the office and its partition among the Collectors.[5] Mr. Shawe took this as a censure on himself, and entered into a description and justification of his work.[6] This seems to have had something to do with the numerous resettlements undertaken by him and Uma Kanta Babu, and the inspections made by Mr. Mullins during that and the succeeding season. Mr. Dampier's successors had received Rs. 1,000 salary per mensem, and a saving was effected by the appointment of Uma Kanta Babu on Rs. 750.

160. Commission Abolished, 1844: Mr. Harvey, who formed decided opinions on Sundarban matters, recommended the abolition of the Commission on the ground that the distribution of the jurisdiction among the Collectors would secure a saving in expenditure, greater convenience to the people, and a more efficient check over the tahsildars.[7] The Board acquiesced in his views and supported the proposal. The Government thereupon by an order, dated 18th December 1843, abolished the office, believing that, apart from the saving effected in expenditure, and the inconvenience obviated, the work in hand was trifling and not such as to require the continued existance of the office. The abolition was timed to 1st May 1844, but was delayed by the great labour in separating the records of 32 years and was not carried into effect till 18th October following.[8] The records were divided among the three districts. Babu U.K. Sen, Deputy Collector, was retained as special officer in the Sundarbans of 24-Parganas and Jessore under the Collectors of those districts, especially of the former district, and Mr. Ross, Deputy Collector, was transferred to Bakarganj[9] and placed under the Collector, who received the sole charge of the Sundarbans in his district. Mr. Mullins, the Surveyor, was intended to work under both, but was entirely occupied with the business under Uma Kanta Babu.

[5] Ibid., no. 157, dated 14 Dec. 1842.

[6] Sbn. Commr. to Presdy. Commr., no. 397, dated 30 Dec. 1842.

[7] Presdy. Commr. to Bd. Rev., no. 195, dated 19 Sept. 1843.

[8] Presdy. Commr. to Sbn. Commr., no. 35, dated 4 Apr., and no. 320, dated 11 July 1844. Collr., 24-Parganas, to Presdy. Commr., 19 Dec. 1844.

[9] He appears to have been discharged from Govt. service in 1845, and he then took the farm of Baro Basdiya.

161. Sundarban Operations, 1844-46: The duties assigned to Uma Kanta Babu were the survey and settlement of the encroachments and clearances on Sundarban lots, the remeasurement and resettlement of Henckell's mahalls and resumed estates, and the measurement, investigation, and settlement of all the lands measured and assessed by Smelt in 1816, with special reference to the 135 mahalls of Donnelly's list of 1836.[10] The Presidency Commissioner proposed that the Baleswar and Haringhata, which had formed the east boundary of Jessore in Henckell's time, should be now taken as the boundary between Jessore and Bakarganj as far as regarded the Sundarbans. The Dacca Commissioner appears to have concurred, and Uma Kanta Babu was instructed accordingly.[11] The Board disapproved of the arrangement, but it seems to have held good during the interval of abolition, and on the re-establishment of the office the point was of no practical significance.[12] The abolition was more nominal than real, for Uma Kanta Babu corresponded direct with the Presidency Commissioner, and in consideration of his high qualifications received the same salary as before. He thus reverted practically to his former position, and performed to all intents and purposes exactly the same duties as before, the only difference being that Bakarganj was divorced from his jurisdiction. As the operations went on much the same as previously, and the interval lasted about 16 months only, no separate notice will be bestowed on them here, but they will fall into their places in the ordinary course of the history.

162. Abolition Found to be Unsatisfactory and Merely Nominal: The abolition of the office left Uma Kanta Babu with nothing but a Deputy Collector's usual staff, which was inadequate to his peculiar circumstances; and on his asking for a special establishment, Mr. Harvey refused it in December 1844, believing that he was sufficiently provided for. Mr. Davidson, however, on re-assuming the Revenue Commissioner's office, supported the application in January 1845, explaining that Uma Kanta Babu was a Deputy Collector in name merely. The Board allowed an establishment at a monthly charge of

[10] Presdy. Commr. to Babu U.K. Sen, no. 549, dated 2 Dec, and Babu U.K. Sen to Presdy. Commr., no. 2, dated 13 Dec. 1844.

[11] Ibid., no. 8, dated 27 Jan. 1845.

[12] Sbn. Commr. to Presdy. Commr., no. 502, dated 18 Nov. 1851.

Rs. 307, but the Government, describing the proposal as amounting to the virtual revival of the office in two districts for the purpose of making investigations, the necessity for which had not become apparent, remanded it for reconsideration.[13] A report was called for in June 1845 as to the nature and quantity of work still to be done, the establishment required, the establishment then entertained, and the length of time the duties in hand would occupy.[14] Uma Kanta Babu replied with reference to 24-Parganas and Jessore Sundarbans, no information being available regarding Bakarganj as all the papers had gone. He stated that there were 364 mahalls with an area of 3,24, 852 bighas in Henckell's, Donnelly's, and Shakespear's statements which required measurement and settlement, but his figures were vitiated as regarded about one-third of those mahalls, by the fact that the results of the operations conducted from Henckell's time down to his own day were ignored. Besides those lands, there were 143 grants that needed measurement and settlement, and 93 lots that were available for grants. He then had an establishment of Rs. 222 per mensem, exclusive of collateral charges, but required one of Rs. 307, and he estimated that he could finish the duties in ten years.[15] The report as a summary of results and a forecast of duties is of no value, and it is chiefly remarkable as revealing what was then known concerning Sundarban history. He had acquired two years' experience, but his ignorance of English shut him out from the information collected or recorded by his predecessors.

163. Commission Re-established, 1846: The Presidency Commissioner explained the circumstances to the Board.[16] He did not think that Mr. Harvey's arrangements would work well, and the Collectors of 24-Parganas and Jessore had their misgivings. They doubted whether there would be any saving of expense or diminished inconvenience. They were both in favour of covenanted agency, and deprecated the

[13] Bd. Rev. to Govt., no. 57, dated 11 Feb., and Govt. to Bd. Rev., no. 227, dated 19 March 1845.

[14] Bd. Rev. to Presdy. Commr., no. 120, dated 16 May, and Presdy. Commr. to Babu U.K. Sen, 9 June 1845.

[15] Babu U.K. Sen to 24-Parganas Collr., no. 129, dated 25 June, and no. 136, dated July 1845.

[16] Presdy. Commr. to Bd. Rev., no. 192. dated 6 Aug. 1845.

plan which left one uncovenanted Deputy Collector under three masters and without an establishment to carry their requisitions into effect. But the Presidency Commissioner, contrasting the work accomplished by Uma Kanta Babu and his predecessors, was not in favour of covenanted agency. There was in his opinion copious work to be done, and he recommended the revival of the Commission, and Uma Kanta Babu's appointment as Commissioner, with an establishment of Rs. 307, over the whole of the Sundarbans, the Bakarganj portion being brought back under his charge. The Board supported the proposal, and the Supreme Government re-established the office in Bengal Government letter, no. 1083, to the Board, of date 14th December 1845.[17] The orders were received by Uma Kanta Babu about 20th January 1846, from which time it may be taken that they came into force. The jurisdiction was restored to what it had been before, except that Buzurgummedpur was specially excluded and remained under the Collector of Bakarganj. Alipur was fixed as the headquarters, a suggestion that the office should be located at some more central spot such as Jessore or Khulna, being negatived.[18] The records were re-collected from the several districts; those relating to permanently settled estates were retained by the Collectors, and as a rule only those concerning temporarily settled estates were made over to the Sundarban office,[19] but the transfers appear to have entailed much confusion, and the classification and arrangement of the records was a duty which was not satisfactorily performed for many years afterwards.

[17] Presdy. Commr. to Babu U.K. Sen, no. 1, dated 17 Jan. 1846.
[18] Presdy. Coramr. to Sbn. Commr., no. 37, dated 30 Apr. 1846.
[19] Ibid., no. 6, dated 9 Feb. 1846.

CHAPTER XIV

Inquiries, Surveys, Resumptions and Settlements in Connection with Lots 216-230

1844-1857

164. Inquiries and Surveys in Lots 217, 218 and 219, 1844-45: The inquiries referred to in paragraph 158 were carried on to remedy the confusion in lots 217, 218, and 219. In fact they formed but a portion of the large subject of encroachments on the Sundarban lands to which Uma Kanta Babu's attention was directed in 1844.[1] Parties often claimed such lands under pattas from the Collectors, but did not produce them when called upon, or, if they did produce them, they had usurped more than the patta authorised. In other cases the usurpers pretended that the land encroached upon belonged to their zamindars. Mr. Mullins surveyed lots 218 and 219 in season 1844-45, ascertaining their boundaries and separating them into their component chaks.[2] Lot 218 had been estimated to contain 18,000 bighas, and lot 219 19,000 bighas. The results of his survey were these—

Lot	*Chaks*	*Cultivation*	*Jungle etc.*	*Total*	*Total of lot*
		Bighas			
218	Khariya Dhamakhali	10,746	4900	15646	17,3161[3]
	Anandatala-Haripur	1,579	91	1,670	
219	Harijhipatan	9,063	4,707	13,770	25,3633[5]
	Amurkata, Digia, and Sonakhali	2,458	6,271	8,729	
	Khaliya (part)[4]	1,240	1,624	2,864	

[1] Presdy. Commr. to Babu U.K. Sen, no. 549, dated 2 Dec. 1844.

[2] Mullins to Babu U.K. Sen, no. 40, dated 12 and no. 43, dated 13 Feb. 1845.

[3] Ibid., no. 63, dated 20 Mar., no. 81, dated 14 May and letter dated 31 July 1845.

[4] The remainder of Khaliya lay outside the lot.

[5] Mullins to Babu U.K. Sen, no. 47, dated 20 Feb., and letter, dated 25 July 1845.

He does not appear to have surveyed lot 217, which had been estimated at 18,000 bighas. It included the following chaks, which had been already settled in the ordinary way before Mahes Chandra Banerji's grant, the areas being bighas of 55 yards square —Kalmibuniya 453 bighas, Bagura 2,040 bighas, Chandmukhi (three estates), 1,571 bighas (all settled in 1836) and Lakhikhola and Hetalbuniya 1,839 bighas (in 1840), the total area thus being 6,903 bighas, equal to 13,051 bighas of 40 yards square.[6] Uma Kanta Babu holding that Mr. Stopford had no authority to settle the chaks, and finding there were more lands than that officer had assessed, went beyond his instructions and concluded fresh settlements of the chaks according to the survey. He submitted his proceedings for confirmation in supersession of the arrangements made by Mr. Stopford, but the Presidency Commissioner kept them back until the other conflicting questions had been decided.[7]

165. Resumption of Grant of Lots 217, 218 and 219, 1845-46: A reply was filed in the civil court, and the suit brought by the grantees mentioned in paragraph 158 was struck off, but the difficulties of the grant still remained. The grantees had obtained the patta from Mr. Kemp by misrepresenting that the lots were all jungle, besides which they had done nothing towards reclamation for five years. Under those circumstances the Presidency Commissioner recommended the cancelment of the grant. The Board ruled that the settlements being prior to the grant held good, and the grant was void *ab initio.* Government then cancelled the patta in January 1846. The Board, considering the grantees deserving of some indulgence as the Government officers had been party in fault, promised to bestow on them an equal quantity of land elsewhere, and left the question of other compensation dependent on an investigation into the honesty of the grantees' conduct.[8] They, however, put in no claim for eight years till after the rules of 1853 had been issued. Money compensation was then refused, as they had laid out nothing in reclamation, and the law charges they had incurred had been the consequence of their

[6] Babu U.K. Sen to Presdy. Commr., no. 152, dated 23 Aug., and no. 165, dated 6 Sept. 1845.

[7] Presdy. Commr. to Babu U.K. Sen, no. 33, dated 22 Sept. 1845.

[8] Presdy. Commr. to Sbn. Commr., no. 1, dated 28 Jan. 1846.

own dishonesty;[9] while, with respect to the promised grant, difference of opinion between the Board and the Presidency, Commissioner led to a reference to Government, and it was decided that the grantees' silence for eight years, during which the grant rules had been altered, amounted to a refusal of the offer. The grant was therefore denied.[10]

166. Settlements in Lots 217, 218, and 219, 1845-46: On the cancelment of the patta for the three lots, the Presidency Commissioner disallowed Mr. Stopford's settlements in March 1846, and confirmed those made by Uma Kanta Babu for 20 years viz., Khariya-Dhamsakhali, Anandatala-Haripur, Harijhipatan,[11] and Khaliya,[12] total area 38,981 bighas, and ultimate sadar jama Rs. 16,628; and also Katamari—a chak that Mr. Mullins had discovered outside the lots—463 bighas, Rs. 281.[13] The lands were assessed at the Sundarban rate of 8 annas per 40-yard bigha. The Raja of Jessore objected to that rate on the ground that the lands had been resumed as invalid lakhiraj and not as Sundarban land, but his plea was disallowed, since they fell inside the lots.[14] The settlements were made with the parties in occupation as jangalburi abadkars.[15]

167. Settlements of Taufir in Resumed Mahalls within Lots 217-20, 1845-52: The estates comprised in or bordering on lots 217-20 which had been settled by the Collector of Jessore, as mentioned in paragraph 73, were transferred to the Sundarban Commissioner about the years 1845-47, and he sent for the papers of the various chaks in 1846 and ordered resettlement. In some cases the settlements do not appear to have terminated, and in others it seems they were permanent. The Collector objected to his proceedings, but Mr. Harvey, the Presidency Commissioner, decided in 1846 that even if the lands brought under assessment in these chaks were settled in perpetuity, that did not bar the right of Government to measure and assess subsequent

[9] Ibid., no. 313, dated 19 Mar. 1856.
[10] Ibid., no. 27, dated 9 June 1857.
[11] Ibid., no. 20, dated 12 Mar. 1846 (corrected).
[12] Ibid., no. 21, dated 12 Mar. 1846 (corrected).
[13] Ibid., no. 18, dated 12 Mar. 1846.
[14] Ibid., no. 138. dated 2 Sept. 1846.
[15] Ibid., no. 15, dated 14 Mar. 1846.

cultivation which was paying no revenue,[16] and again that by the use of the words "full jama" (which the Collector seems to have relied on as debarring revision) in the previous settlement it was not intended that any increase of assessment should be made on the lands measured, but if more lands were included in the chaks than had been measured and settled, there was no objection to the remeasurement and settlement of such new lands.[17] Mr. Smith then proceeded under Uma Kanta Babu's orders to remeasure and assess the taufir in such estates. The whole of each chak was remeasured, the settled area deducted from the total area, and the remainder was assessed at the Sundarban rate enforced by Mr. Harvey—8 annas per the 40-yard bigha. The new jama was added to the former and the whole secured by one dowl. Resettlements were so made in Koipukuriya, Singjor, Beharibhita, Basakhali, and Magurkhali in 1846; Hetalbuniya in 1847; Hariya, Siberbati, Bharbhariya, and Orabuniya in 1848; Samukpota in 1849; Khagrabuniya, Putimari, Andarmanik, and Bagura in 1851; and Parmagurkhali in 1852. The earlier of these settlements were confirmed for 20 years, but those of 1851 and 1852 were confirmed in perpetuity.[18]

168. Settlements in Lots 217-20, 1845-52: In other cases, however, the whole of the lands were after remeasurement assessed at the 8-anna rate. Many of them were first settlement, the mahalls having been newly resumed, such as Alakdiya in 1845; Bayarsinga in 1847; Kalmibuniya and Lashkarber in 1848; Kataliya in 1849;[19] Digaliya in 1852; and Geubuniya, Charkhi-Bargi, Charkhali, and Dhoramari in 1853. In the other cases the mahalls were similar to those mentioned in the last paragraph, but it does not appear on what grounds they were treated differently: they were Pana, Nangalmora, and Bakhardair in 1846; Kalajangal, Jharjhariya, and Bahirbuniya in 1847; Alladipur, Suargudi, and Bhairabdanga in 1849; Guasoba in 1850; Suarnal and Korakata in 1852. Several of these settlements were

[16] Presdy. Commr. to Jessore Collr., no. 76. dated 5 Mar. 1846. with Jessore Collr. to Sbn. Commr., no. 137, dated 18 idem.

[17] Presdy. Commr.'s no. 246, dated 16 May 1846, in case of Hetalbuniya.

[18] I have not found any orders prescribing permanent settlements.

[19] Kataliya was discovered in 1846 during the resettlement of Koipukuriya, and falling within the boundaries of Sibnagar was taken possession of without formal proceedings. Smith, Dy. Collr., to Sbn. Commr., no. 41, dated 9 July 1849.

almost immediately afterwards revised, and Uma Kanta Babu displayed a good deal of interference, reopening and altering settlements on slight grounds, so that the Presidency Commissioner informed him in 1852 that it was not expedient or just to make fresh settlements until the expiration of those already subsisting.[20] The settlements confirmed in and after 1851 were generally concluded in perpetuity.[21]

169. Settlement of Taraf Madhukhali, 1846-57: Taraf Madhukhali, resumed as invalid lakhiraj in 1838, consisted of 13 little chaks situated about lot 220 and river Bhadar, besides Lakhikhola and Hetalbuniya in lot 217. Settlements were made by Mr. Stopford under the Collector of Jessore in 1841, but were disapproved,[22] and the mahalls were made over in 1846 to the Sundarban office, where two resumption suits were then pending for these mahalls. Lakhikhola and Hetalbuniya were at length settled in 1851 at 8 annas per standard bigha, and the taraf, restricted to the 13 chaks, was after some unsatisfactory proceedings settled in 1857, Government obtaining only half of the assessment which had been fixed at 6 annas per standard bigha.[23]

170. Survey of Lot 220, 1848-49: Mr. Dampier gave an amalnama for Andarmanik, a portion of lot 220, in 1832. The holders began clearing and afterwards asked for a patta. Local inquiries were made in 1841-42 and subsequent years, but the Presidency Commissioner ordered a survey of the whole lot in 1845, and the order after being reiterated in 1846[24] was at length complied with by Mr. Smith, who in 1848-49 made a survey of the entire tract lying between the Gengrail and Shalta rivers. He found it comprised a total area of 40,471 bighas, divided among the following chaks[25]—

[20] In case of Pana, Presdy. Commr. to Sbn. Commr., no.155, dated 8 July 1852.

[21] These Jessore settlements were protracted and are not free from obscurity, and sometimes the English correspondence appears to vary from the vernacular papers.

[22] Presdy. Commr. to Sbn. Commr., no. 27, dated 10 Apr 1846.

[23] Ibid., no. 16 Ct., dated 10 July 1858.

[24] Ibid., no. 137, dated 2 Sept. 1846; also Sbn. Commr. to Presdy. Commr., no. 339, dated 20 Aug. 1846.

[25] Smith, Deputy Collr., to Sbn. Commr., no. 44, dated 21 July 1849. Sbn. Commr. to Presdy. Commr., no. 451, dated 14, and no. 460, dated 16 Aug. 1849.

	Bighas		Bighas
Gobardanga	2,646	Tetultala	2,745
Guasoba	1,844	Andarmanik	5,733
Samukpota	969	Digaliya	1,015
Bahirbuniya	697	Charkhi-Bargi	663
Munkiya	5,149	Geubuniya	1,849
Pana	1,773	Jirbuniya	3,482
Hariya	5,100	Deluti	5,451
Sankardana	1,355	Total area	40,471

The nature of the settlements of most of these mahalls has been explained above. Jirbuniya and Deluti were pronounced open to resumption. Proceedings were begun and these chaks were resumed by the Presidency Commissioner on 29th October 1857 as falling within the Sundarban boundary,[26] but the Raja brought a civil suit to regain possession, and won it on 22nd July 1859.

171. Survey of Lot 217, 1857-58: It may be mentioned here that Mr. Smith made a detailed survey of lot 217 during 1857-58, and found it contained 16 chaks with a total area of 19,369 bighas—Kalmibuniya, Bagura-Romardanga, Badiyarkona, Chandmukhi (three estates), Hetalbuniya, Lakhikhola, Mohammedabad (the 10 annas share in five portions), and four new chaks—Boalmari, Kumibuniya, Singjor, and Helakhardanga—which were discovered to fall within certain limits resumed by the Presidency Commissioner on 19th May 1854. The latter were at once brought under settlement, minus 60 bighas released as lakhiraj.[27]

172. Orders Regarding Rates of Assessment, 1846-50: Under the early system initiated by Henckell and continued by Steer, reclaimed lands were assessed as 8 annas sicca per the 55-yard bigha, but after the definition of the forest, settlements appear to have been made at the rates found current, till Mr. Harvey became Presidency Commissioner

[26] Sbn. Commr. to Presdy. Commr., no. 93, dated 27 Aug. 1857.

[27] Smith to Sbn. Commr., no. 136, dated 27 Oct. 1858. Sbn. Commr. to Presdy. Commr., no. 188, dated 5 Apr. 1859; and no. 128, dated 21 Dec. 1859.

and enforced the rate of 8 annas per the 40-yard bigha everywhere. In the cases of Atliya, Khaliya, &c, reclaimed lands which fell within the Sundarban boundary were assessed at that rate about 1846-47, but the owners of Atliya appealed, claiming to hold at the old rate, 8 annas per the 55-yard bigha. Mr. Harvey decided against them,[28] but the Board overruling his arguments laid down that the old rate should be retained for the cultivation, while the new or Sundarban rate was declared to apply to the waste.[29] In the cases of Henckell's mahalls and Kaikhali, the discussions led to the arrangement that, while old cultivation should be assessed at the old rate, and the other original terms maintained, future cultivation would be assessed at the new or Sundarban rate.[30] For all other estates it seems that Mr. Harvey's decision held good, that resumed lands which fell inside the Sundarban boundary were assessable at the Sundarban rate. These orders were communicated to the talukdars. The old rate being equivalent to 4½ Company's annas per the 40-yard bigha seems to have been alluded to at times as the half-rental assessment.

173. Incidence of Assessment in Jessore: All these settlements were carried out by Mr. Deputy Collector Smith, but he experienced much difficulty in effecting stable settlements on the rate of 8 annas per the 40-yard bigha since it was almost double the old rate. The Board ordered in their Circular no. 48, dated 23rd November 1849, that local bighas should be set aside, and the Bengal bigha of 40 yards square, or 14,400 square feet, should be adopted as the standard in survey and settlement operations.[31] Further, in the early settlements the measurements had been rough, and the reclaimed area alone assessed, and the holders in enjoying the jungle lands free obtained an increased margin of profit; but in these resettlements the measurements were exact and were usually tested by a professional survey, strict

[28] Sbn. Commr. to Presdy. Commr., no. 327, dated 4 Aug. 1847. Presdy. Commr. to Sbn. Commr., no. 114, dated 21 June 1848.

[29] Presdy. Commr. to Sbn. Commr., no. 15, dated 25 Jan. 1848. Sbn. Commr. to Presdy. Commr., no. 316, dated 26 July 1850.

[30] Ibid., no. 63, dated 30 Dec. 1845, regarding Ramzannagar, and no. 16, dated 14 Mar. 1846, regarding Pranpur. Presdy. Commr. to Sbn. Commr., no. 260, dated 30 Oct. 1848.

[31] Also paragraph 17 of Circular no. 843, dated 26 Dec. 1850.

orders having been issued that all Sundarban estates should be properly surveyed before being settled. Thus no land escaped. The whole cultivable area, whether cleared or jungle, was brought under assessment at 8 annas, the former at once, and the latter after longer or shorter rent-free and progressive periods. The Board ordered in 1851 that when the standard bigha was used in supersession of the local bigha the rates were to be adjusted proportionally so as to make the actual rents the same;[32] but the order seems never to have obtained currency in the Sundarbans, and the 8-anna rate prevailed universally. The new settlements therefore were far more stringent, and the holders were limited to their prescribed allowances, unless they could increase their receipts by enhancing their raiyats' rents. In Pana, Alladipur and Korakata the holders refused the terms, and the lands were farmed out. In Korakata and Kalajangal the cultivation relapsed into waste. It seems in fact that the raiyats' rents in this locality varied from about 7 to 8 annas per standard bigha at this period, so that the mahalls could scarcely sustain their rentals, especially when the full rate was reached throughout.[33] Mr. Smith submitted a report on the matter in 1851, in which he gave it as his opinion that the mahalls could bear the 8-anna rate when the cultivated lands alone were assessed, but could not bear it subject to the rigorous exactitude of a scientific survey. He did not recommend a general reduction of the rate throughout the Sundarbans, as some mahalls could bear the rate, but he urged that some other mode of reduction should be adopted, and suggested that settlement officers should be allowed a discretion to grant an abatement beyond the ordinary amount of 30 per cent, in special cases. He pronounced some relaxation necessary, for the change from the 55-yard to the 40-yard bigha would entail desertion and deterioration, especially in Jessore.[34] Uma Kanta Babu appears to have taken no notice of these representations, and matters continued as they were, but Mr. Smith's prognostications were verified in several of these mahalls.

[32] Bd. Rev., C.O. no. 28, dated 29 Aug. 1851.

[33] Sbn. Commr. to Bd. Rev., no. 121, dated 13 June 1883. There seem to be reasons for thinking that physical deterioration has been in progress in the lands north of lot 220.

[34] Smith, Dy. Collr., to Sbn. Commr., no. 16, dated 2 July, and no. 31, dated 25 Aug. 1851.

174. Difficulties in Lot 216, 1839-58: Haris Chandra Mittra got the grant of the portion of lot 216 south of the Ghoshkhali Khal in 1839, *i.e.*, according to the boundaries specified; but the area was stated in the patta to be 52,000 bighas, which was the area of the whole lot. Pran Nath Chaudhuri, zamindar of pargana Malai, encroached on it, claiming that he had held the land as part of his zamindari before the date of the grant, and, instituting a suit before the Joint-Magistrate of Khulna, under Act IV of 1840, obtained an order on 31st December 1846 supporting him in possession. Uma Kanta Babu reported the result, expressing his disapproval of the proceedings, and the Presidency Commissioner directed him to visit the lot and inquire with a view to adopting legal remedies.[35] He proceeded there in 1847-48, and had the lot surveyed by Mullins and its boundaries ascertained. He found the zamindar to have encroached upon 15,320 bighas of the lot, and, acting under a ruling of the Board to the effect that *bona fide* abadkars were to be considered proprietors *de jure* of the lands cleared by them,[36] again reported the circumstances. The Board replied that Government could not exclude the cleared lands from the lot, nor could it interfere as the zamindar was in possession under the Magistrate's order.[37] All proceedings were consequently stopped in 1850 and the grantee left to his remedy by the ordinary course of law. The grantee then brought a civil suit to set aside the Magistrate's order and regain possession, and Government being made a defendant, as proprietor of the Sundarbans, supported his claim. The Judge following the areas and not the boundaries decreed the whole lot to the grantee in 1857, minus the 389 bighas released by the Special Commissioner in 1842.[38] During 1856-58 Mr. Smith made enquiries and surveys in the lot, and found the north portion, where the zamindar had encroached, contained the following chaks with a total area of 23,312 bighas—Nurpur-Amirpur, Talbariya,

[35] Sbn. Commr to Presdy. Commr., no. 311, dated 27 July 1847. Presdy. Commr. to Sbn. Commr., no. 175; dated 21 Sept. 1847, and no. 111, dated 24 June 1847.

[36] Bd. Rev. to Dacca Commr., no. 241, dated 26 Oct. 1849, with Bd. Rev. to Sbn. Commr., no. 474, dated 26 idem.

[37] Presdy. Commr. to Sbn. Commr., no. 33, dated 4 March 1850.

[38] Ibid., no. 47, dated 22 Nov. 1855. Sbn. Commr. to Presdy. Commr., no. 121, dated 16 Oct. 1857.

Hatiyadanga, Kinukati-Barebare, Harikati, Churnamalla, and Goalbariya.[39] The case, however, was carried up to the High Court on appeal. Mr. Dampier's line was disallowed, the portion south of Ghoshkhali khal decreed to the grantees, and the north portion restored to the zamindar.[40]

175. Settlement in Lots 221 and 224, 1849-56: The resumption suits for mauzas Tildanga and Kamarkhola had been dismissed by the Special Commissioner in 1842 as explained in paragraph 122, but the Raja claimed also lots 221 and 224 under the names chaks Tildanga and Kamarkhola respectively on the strength of the Collector's statement of 1826. Mr. Smith taking up these cases disallowed the Raja's claim in 1849, and made a settlement of the lot lands,[41] but as the Raja also grounded his claim on the Special Commissioner's faisala of 1842 which in a measure countenanced his rights, Uma Kanta Babu cancelled the settlements and proposed to institute fresh resumption proceedings. The Commissioner, however, counselled an amicable arrangement, and the conflicting claims were at length brought to an end in 1855 by the grant of both lots to the Raja under the rules of 1853.[42] Some difficulty arose from the fact that the Collector as Court of Wards had given two leases for the lots during the Raja's minority, the lessees had been reclaiming, and the Board required that their rights should be respected to which the Raja demurred.[43] At length, however, an agreement was concluded, and the lots were settled with the Raja in 1856 for 99 years, the cleared lands at 6 annas less 30 per cent. allowance, and the jungle at 3 annas, according to the spirit of the new rules. The Government claim to the two mauzas was definitely relinquished.[44]

[39] Smith to Sbn. Commr., no. 72, dated 28 Apr. 1858.

[40] Presdy. Commr. to Sbn. Commr., no. 122 Ct., dated 3 Apr. 1860.

[41] Sbn. Commr. to Presdy. Commr., no. 65, dated 9 March 1850.

[42] Ibid., no. 138, dated 25 Apr. 1855.

[43] Presdy. Commr. to Sbn. Commr., no. 236, dated 12 Jan., and no. 340, dated 5 Apr. 1853.

[44] Sbn. Commr. to Presdy. Commr., no. 425, dated 16 Dec. 1856. Presdy. Commr. to Sbn. Commr., no. 12, dated 19 May 1857. But there were subsequent disputes and litigation, in which the civil court appears to have altered these arrangements. Sbn. Commr. to Presdy, Commr., no. 80, dated 21 Sept. 1859, and no. 186, dated 28 March 1860.

176. Settlements and Grants in Lots 223, 225, 226, 229 and 230, 1845-54: The Collector of Jessore, with the permission of the Board, had given one Maulavi Abdullah in 1827 an amalnama under the then Sundarban rules for a large tract of country with boundaries specified, but no area. The grantee began clearing, but came into collision with the talukdars of pargana Hogla. This led to a suit under Regulation III of 1828 in which the Special Commissioner decreed a portion of the amalnama land in favour of the talukdars on 23rd September 1845. Lot 225 had been granted out separately in 1841, and Mr. Smith was ordered to inspect it about the year 1848. He found Sakhira Khatun (the widow of the Maulvi, who died about 1846) and others in possession under the amalnama of 1,54,000 bighas comprising lots 223, 225, 226, 229, and 230, but only a small portion of lots 223 and 225 had been cleared.[45] As neither the amalnamadar, nor the grantee of lot 225 had complied with the clearing condition, the Board cancelled both the amalnama and the patta in April 1850, and ordered that the cleared lands should be settled with the abadkars and the other lands sub-divided and disposed of separately.[46] Bighas 885 had been reclaimed in Bajua, the south-east portion of lot 223, and were settled with Sakhira Khatun for 20 years from 1851. The jungle area—24,028 bighas—was reserved for sale under the grant rules.[47] Mr. Smith appears to have surveyed the lot in 1851, and, instead of the mere forest line that Hodges had copied from Morrieson, fixed the Bajua khal, which practically coincides with that line, as the eastern boundary of the lot.[48] East of it lay abad Chunkuri, the resumption suit for which had failed in 1842 as mentioned in paragraph 122. The difficulties attending it appeared to have discouraged further investigation. Lot 225, with an area of 34,396 bighas, was applied for, and the Board sanctioned the grant of an amalnama in 1851. But 603 bighas had been cleared in it and after some dispute 99 bighas were settled with abadkars Sakhira Khatun, &c, in 1853-54, and the

[45] Sbn. Commr. to Presdy. Commr., no. 551, dated 3 Oct. 1849.

[46] Presdy. Commr. to Sbn. Commr., no. 45, dated 5 Apr. 1850. Smith to Sbn. Commr., no. 5, dated 29 Feb. 1852.

[47] Ibid., no. 116, dated 29 June 1852.

[48] Smith to Sbn. Commr., no. 19, dated 9 Apr. 1852.

remainder with the amalnamadars. The other lots—226, 229, and 230—being all jungle were kept for disposal under the grant rules.

177. Lot 222: In lot 222 or Pankhali nothing could be attempted. Resumption suits had been instituted, and had failed as already explained.

CHAPTER XV

Settlements and Rights of Settlement
1844-1857

178. Settlements of Henckell's Mahalls and in Lots 164, 165, and 166, 1844-52: Among the duties assigned to Uma Kanta Babu in 1844 were the measurement and assessment of Henckell's mahalls and of the encroachments on lots 164, 165, 166. To a certain extent these duties were identical, for Kaikhali was an encroachment on lot 164, and Ramzannagar, Bhairabnagar and Bansipur on lot 165. Those four and also Pranpur and Ismailpur were surveyed during 1844-45, and the increased cultivation found in Pranpur,[1] Kaikhali,[2] and Ramzannagar[3] was assessed in 1845 according to the terms of the leases. In Bhairabnagar[4] cultivation had retrograded and the former dowl was simply renewed, while no settlement seems to have been made of Ismailpur, which contained only 310 bighas. At the settlement of Bansipur in 1836 the talukdars had recused, but now they came forward and no taufir being found, the settlement was concluded with them with effect from 1835.[5] The total encroachment on lot 165 was 8,382 bighas.[6] All the foregoing settlements were made for 20 years. The Collector began remeasuring Gokulnagar and Ballabhpur, which were amalgamated in one estate, in 1844-45, but the work was transferred to Uma Kanta Babu in 1845. The talukdars of this estate claimed Sannyasi, Betibuniya, Phulhata, Betkata, Mallikber, Khondakarber, Kharkariya, Manikkhola, and Amratala as having once appertained to their estate, and instituted suits to regain them, but when those mahalls were resumed by Government in 1836 and

[1] Presdy. Commr. to Sbn. Commr., no. 226, dated 15 Dec. 1846.

[2] Ibid., no. 134, dated 20 July 1849.

[3] Ibid., no. 68, dated 30 Dec. 1845.

[4] Sbn. Commr. to Presdy. Commr., no. 453, dated 12 Oct. 1847.

[5] Presdy. Commr. to Sbn. Commr., no. 151, dated 19 July 1848.

[6] Ibid., no. 68, dated 30 Dec. 1845.

1837, the suits were struck off.[7] Gokulnagar-Ballabhpur[8] was settled in 1850 as also Chandipur, now known as Kalaran Chandipur,[9] which had increased by alluvion. The others of Henckell's mahalls had practically lost their peculiar character, for Asmatpur being surrounded by well cultivated zamindari lands had been confirmed in perpetuity in 1840 with an area of 4,262 bighas and sadar jama of Rs. 1,602[10] Kalidaspur, Chandkhali, and Mohammedabad were all khass, and Babupur and Banchanagar dense jungle,[11] the persons to whom they were to be leased out in 1836 not having taken them.[12] Atliya, a portion of lot 166, leased out in 1827 one Henckell's terms was remeasured in 1846-47. Its total area was found to be 35,499 standard bighas, of which 12,630 (equivalent to 6,037 bighas of 55 yards) were reclaimed. Mr. Harvey ordered that the reclaimed area should be settled on the old terms, and the rest which was forest on the grant terms, since the pattadars could have no claim to a continuation of the old favourable terms for the latter. They, however, appealed, and after some misunderstanding and considerable discussion, Government decided that the block jungle and as much of the interlaced jungle as possible should be separated, the reclaimed lands settled on the old terms, and the jungle that could not be separated left with them. Those orders were carried out in 1851, the total area given them being 13,192 bighas.[13] Bill Gudara, another portion of lot 166, was settled in 1851 with an area of 624 bighas.[14]

179. Resettlement in Bakarganj Mahalls, 1844-48: The resettlements in the resumed Bakarganj estates that had been commenced in 1843 were carried out in agreement with the Presidency Commissioner's orders explained in paragraph 141. The Sundarban Commission being then abolished, the Collector took them in

[7] Smith to Sbn. Commr., no. 51, dated 6 Aug. 1849.

[8] Presdy. Commr. to Sbn. Commr., no. 46, dated 27 Feb. 1851.

[9] Ibid., no. 4, dated 3 Jan. 1852.

[10] Ibid., no. 93, dated 16 Sept. 1842.

[11] Jessore Collr. to Sbn. Commr., dated 24 Aug. 1848.

[12] Smith to Sbn. Commr., no. 46, dated 5 Aug. 1852.

[13] Presdy. Commr. to Sbn. Commr., no. 74, dated 3 May, nos. 116 and 117, both dated 10 July 1851.

[14] Ibid., no. 156, dated 16 Aug. 1851.

hand in 1845, and partially effected them, but on the revival of the Commission, they were referred to Uma Kanta Babu for completion in 1846. They were carried out on Mr. Dampier's lines of 1833 and possess no interest from a historical point of view. Cultivation had spread, and of course the Government revenue increased; but the assessment was confined to the reclaimed area only, and such follow and jungle as were intermixed with it: the blocks of dense jungle were excluded. The system of undertenures described in paragraph 143 had become firmly established.

180. Settlement of Amalnama Lands in Bakarganj, 1844-46: Contemporaneously with the revision of the settlements in Bakarganj, Uma Kanta Babu took in hand the settlement of lands in that district cleared under the amalnamas granted by his predecessors. Mr. D'Silva, the talukdar, had begun reclaiming Eliyatiyakhali, the jungle portion of Gulsakhali. Gulsakhali was surveyed by Mullins in 1843-44, and the total area found to be 26,824 bighas, of which 14,761 had been settled in 1834, and the rest was the amalnama land. The whole was assessed at 12 annas per the 57½ yard bigha, which had been the sadar malguzari rate in the 1834 settlements of the estates in that locality, but the talukdar protested against interference during the period of his lease and appealed. Government, though denying Mr. Grant's authority to give the amalnama, yet disallowed these proceedings, maintained the former engagement, and reinstated the talukdar on the old terms in 1845, with orders that the whole of the Gulsakhali lands should be settled at 8 annas—the Sundarban rate—at the expiration of the lease in 1856.[15] Accordingly, after some misapplication of the orders, the area of the grant portion was fixed at 12,062 bighas, and a patta was given for it in 1846.[16] Similarly in Kukua, the lands cleared under the amalnama were measured during the same season, and the Presidency Commissioner ordered the revision of Mr. Dampier's engagements, but the Board overruled his order in 1844, and confirmed the grant with effect from 1840—the date of the amalnama.[17] Its area was fixed at

[15] Ibid., no. 469, dated 20 Sept. 1844. Dacca Commr. to Bakarganj Collr., no. 193, dated 20 June 1845.

[16] Presdy. Commr. to Sbn. Commr., no. 194, dated 19 Nov. 1846.

[17] Ibid., no. 470, dated 26 Sept. 1844 and no. 5, dated 23 Jan. 1845.

13,355 bighas in 1848.[18] Mullins surveyed Gyanpara the same season and computed its area at the ridiculously small quantity of 19,800 bighas. Uma Kanta Babu proceeded to settle it in the ordinary way, but the Board disallowed his proceedings in 1845 and confirmed the grant, the area of which was put down at 20,000 bighas.[19] The owners of Ramna Bamna afterwards advanced a claim to this chak, but it was rejected in 1848.[20]

181. Settlements in Pargana Salimabad, 1845-52: Taking up the Salimabad estates that remained undisposed of, Uma Kanta Babu had Kakarbil, Gazalyarber, and Narsinghdattber measured in 1844-45, and Koyardiya and Bara Nalbuniya the next season. The progress gained under the jangalburi leases granted by Mr. Kemp, described in paragraph 132, seems to have attracted applicants for these chaks. Kakarbil[21] was settled in 1845; and following Mr. Kemp's plan, Uma Kanta Babu, in 1845, proposed to give leases for Gazaliyarber,[22] Narsinghdattber,[23] Panchamalerber,[24] and Kapalibanda.[25] The suggestion was approved in the case of the first and it was leased out at once,[26] but no sanction being conveyed regarding the others, he copied the former practice and gave amalnamas for Narsinghdattber and Panchamalerber that year. On his subsequently recommending in 1847 the bestowal of a patta for Panchamalerber, the Presidency Commissioner's attention was drawn to the practice, and the bestowal of amalnamas without the cognizance of the higher authorities was prohibited.[27] Uma Kanta Babu had wished to dispose of Koyardiya[28] and Bara Nalbuniya[29] under jangalburi pattas in 1846, but the former

[18] Ibid., 15 June 1848.

[19] Sbn. Commr. to Presdy. Commr., no. 306, dated 21 Sept. 1844. Presdy. Commr., to Babu U.K. Sen, no. 9, dated 1 Feb. 1845.

[20] Smith to Sbn. Commr., no. 2, dated 29 May 1848.

[21] Presdy. Commr. to Babu U.K. Sen, no. 62, dated 9 Dec. 1845.

[22] Babu U.K. Sen to Presdy. Commr., no. 97, dated 2 May 1845.

[23] Ibid., no. 98, dated 9 May 1845.

[24] Ibid., no. 147, dated 13 Aug. 1845.

[25] Ibid., no. 158, dated 2 Sept. 1845.

[26] Presdy. Commr. to Babu U.K. Sen, no. 22 dated 21 July 1845.

[27] Sbn. Commr. to Presdy. Commr., no. 476, dated 26 Oct. 1847.

[28] Ibid., 7 Nov. 1846.

[29] Ibid., no. 278, dated 21 July 1846.

remained khas till 1848. Outsiders then reclaimed it, and it was settled with them in 1852.[30] Bara Talbuniya was disposed of as a grant in 1851. Kapalibanda remained unattended to till 1857. Badanhaldarber, which was all waste, was settled in 1852 with an outsider,[31] and Kalkibari, a portion of Mallikber, in 1850 for 20 years,[32] but Bishtupur in 1851 in perpetuity, apparently on the same terms as Dhuliganti.[33]

182. Settlement of Amalnama Lands in Pargana Salimabad, 1845-52: Kali Prasad Sen had obtained an amalnama for Fakirtakiya and seven other adjacent chaks in 1840 as mentioned in paragraph 132. He began clearing, and Uma Kanta Babu wished to give him separate pattas for them in 1845, but Rabiullah Kazi, Mohammed Hafiz and other fakirs resident in Baroikhali applied for the settlement of that chak. No mufassil investigation had been made into the circumstances of the Salimabad mahalls prior to resumption, except the cursory visit of Mr. Houstoun and Lieutenant Goldie. Hence the boundaries set out in the faisalas were inexact and confused as subsequent inquiries proved. A local investigation was made in Fakirtakiya under the Presidency Commissioner's orders in 1845-46, and it was discovered that that chak and Baroikhali were one and the same, and that the cultivation in it had been the labour of the fakirs.[34] Mr. Harvey at once cancelled the amalnama and directed that the chaks named in it should be surveyed; that the fakirs as abadkars should get settlement of whatever they had cleared, and Kali Prasad of whatever he had cleared. The orders were not carried out intelligently, and Hafiz objected to the area assigned him. Mr. Smith surveyed the lands in 1847-48, when the area claimed by Hafiz as Baroikhali was calculated at 21,572 bighas, including Sutaluri, Gatipur, and other lands. He settled Baroikhali proper with an area of 4,556 bighas with the fakirs,[35] but under the Presidency Commissioner's orders the settlement was

[30] Smith to Sbn. Commr., no. 39, dated 28 June 1852.

[31] Sbn. Commr. to Presdy. Commr., no. 270, dated 14 July 1852.

[32] Presdy. Commr. to Sbn. Commr., no. 218, dated 1 Nov. 1850.

[33] Ibid., no. 67, dated 5 May 1854—see paragraph 185.

[34] Presdy. Commr. to Babu U.K. Sen, No. 64, dated 23 Dec. 1845. Sbn. Commr. to Presdy. Commr., no. 530, dated 7 Dec. 1846.

[35] Sbn. Commr. to Presdy. Commr., no. 23, dated 28 Jan. 1848. Smith to Sbn. Commr., no. 16. dated 31 July 1848.

concluded with Hafiz alone in 1848 for 24 years.[36] Matters as regarded Putikhali and Sutaluri were involved in confusion, for apart from the inaccuracy of the faisalas, the landowners had fraudulently falsified the local appellations. There were two Putikhalis distinguished by the additions of Sonakhali and Mehdipur. Both were resumed in the general faisala of 1837 relating to all 65 chaks, but in the separate faisalas only the latter was resumed. Mr. Kemp gave an amalnama for Putikhali Sonakhali in 1841, and it was paying revenue, but by the collusion of the zamindars and the Sundarban amala the other chak escaped free. Mr. Smith discovered the fraud in 1848, and further enquiries were made. Applications were then presented to the Judge of Bakarganj to rectify the error, but were dismissed in 1854 and 1858. Further efforts were made to regain possession from 1859 to 1864, but without success, and the right of Government to Putikhali Mehdipur was eventually lost.[37] The chak known at present as Sutaluri having an area of 17,016 bighas was settled in 1848 with Kali Prasad, who had cleared 206 bighas in it, on his former jangalburi terms,[38] and the sanction of Government was accorded in 1850.[39] The other chaks of the amalnama were Bhatkhali, Baintala, Kharoikhali, Gazaliya, Mahishcharaniya, and Gatipur. The first was found to have been united with Teliganti and settled with it in 1838.[40] The second had also been included in the patta given for Khondakarber and Manikkhola in 1842, the latter engagement was upheld and the chak removed from Kali Prasad's lands. Kharoikhali was disposed of in connexion with Panchakaran. A patta, according to the former jangalburi terms, was

[36] Sbn. Commr. to Presdy. Commr., no. 487, dated 10, and no. 512, dated 21 Aug. 1848. Presdy. Commr. to Sbn. Commr., no. 197, dated 26 Aug. 1848, and Sbn. Commr. to Presdy. Commr., no. 305, dated 20 July 1850.

[37] Ibid., no. 191, dated 12 May 1848, and no. 161, dated 10 Feb. 1859, Presdy. Commr. to Sbn. Commr., no. 13 Ct., dated 11 June 1859, no. 9, dated 30 idem, and no. 109, dated 28 Sept. 1863; and Sbn. Commr. to Presdy. Commr., no. 59, dated 20 July 1864. The subjects is obscure, and the accounts differ.

[38] Smith to Sbn. Commr., no. 33. dated 14 Sept. 1848. Sbn. Commr. to Presdy. Commr., no. 676. dated 24 Oct. 1848.

[39] Sbn. Commr. to Presdy. Commr., no. 75-2, dated 17 March 1854.

[40] Smith to Sbn. Commr., no. 58, dated 23 Dec. 1851.

executed for Gazaliya on 30th October 1848, and a similar patta for Mahishcharaniya on 30th April 1852.[41]

183. Settlement of Jangalburi Patta Lands in Pargana Salimabad, 1846-56: The inaccuracy of the faisala boundaries created most confusion in Kumariyajola and the neighbouring chaks. The investigations were carried out by Mr. Smith. Panchakaran had been resumed without boundaries, but they were defined by an amin in 1837. Mr. Shawe divided it into two portions and granted out the south portion in 1842 as Kumariyajola *alias* Panchakaran Garardiya, while he reserved the northern for settlement with the talukdar of Debraj. Boundary disputes sprang up between the holders of Kumariyajola, Debraj, and a new chak called Mistridanga, which had been discovered by the enquiry amins in 1837-38. Mullins surveyed the lands in 1846-47,[42] and found they consisted of five parcels. Mr. Smith decided the disputes and constituted the three chaks thus—Parcels 1, 3 and 5, amounting to 4,916 bighas, Kumariyajola (the portion that was granted out by Mr. Shawe in 1842); parcel 2, bighas 2,300 Debraj; and parcel 4, bighas 2,031, Mistridanga. At the same time he resumed the last named chak, for which no proceedings had been taken before, and his decree was upheld by the appellate court on 20th August 1849. The faisala boundaries of Kharoikhali did not correspond with the actual boundaries and the measurements conducted by Mr. Herklots in 1838 had not disclosed nor removed the discrepancies. The holders of that chak and Panchakaran had been disputing and the latter had won. Mr. Smith inquired into that matter at the same time and found that the northern part of Kharoikhali fell within Kumariyajola, and the southern within Panchakaran. The former portion he continued with the holder of Kumariyajola in 1848; the latter he settled with Kali Prasad Sen, in whose amalnama Kharoikhali had been inserted. But Uma Kanta Babu disapproved of his proceedings, so Mr. Smith revised them in 1849-50. He removed Kali Prasad and settled the south portion with the real abadkar, calling it second Kumariyajola, but in the main he adhered to his former

[41] Presdy. Commr. to Sbn. Commr., no. 233, dated 20 Dec. 1852.

[42] See Sbn. Commr. to Presdy. Commr., no. 460, dated 11 Nov. 1846. Presdy. Commr. to Sbn. Commr., 25 idem.

arrangements.[43] Uma Kanta Babu again disagreed,[44] but Mr. Smith's arrangements appear to have been in the main approved. Debraj, the opposing claim of the alleged pattadar being rejected, received its patta in 1850 on the previous terms with retrospective effect from 1841.[45] Mistridanga was settled for ten years in 1850 at a jama of Rs. 716.[46] A patta for Kharoikhali on Mr. Kemp's terms was given to Kali Prasad on 10th December 1851 with retrospective effect. The leases of the two portions of Kumariyajola, as Mr. Kemp had proposed, were confirmed in 1850 for 20 years; the north portion, 3,711 bighas, Rs. 1,392 ultimately; and the south portion (which appears to have been the parcel that Mr. Smith removed from Kharoikhali), 1,072 bighas, Rs. 382.[47] But the dividing line between the portions was imperfect and caused a difficulty when the south portion came into the hands of Government by purchase in 1853. To obviate it the south portion was sold to the holder of the northern, and the whole of the lands reconstituted into one estate in 1856.[48]

184. Settlements in Pargana Salimabad, 1847-53: In Madardiya and Haldaha the amalnamadars had been reclaiming and Uma Kanta Babu proposed to give them pattas on their previous terms in 1845. The recommendation was approved in the case of Madardiya. and a patta given for it in 1847 after a survey by Mullins.[49] Haldaha remained as before, but retrograded. Both chaks were inspected by Mr. Smith in 1850-51. The clearing condition was fulfilled in Madardiya and a resettlement was made;[50] but Haldaha being found all waste, the amalnama was cancelled in 1853.[51] Panchamalerber was the instance which attracted the attention of the higher authorities to the practice

[43] Smith to Sbn. Commr., no. 23, dated 29 June 1850, and no. 36, dated 30 July 1850.

[44] Sbn. Commr. to Presdy. Commr., no. 658, dated 28 Dec. 1850.

[45] Ibid., no. 469, dated 27 Sept. 1850.

[46] Presdy. Commr. to Sbn. Commr., no. 145, dated 19 Aug. 1850.

[47] Ibid., no. 79, dated 29 Apr. 1851.

[48] Sbn. Commr. to Presdy. Commr., no. 540, dated 15 Dec. 1855. Presdy. Commr. to Sbn. Commr., no. 53Ct., dated 30 Sept. 1857.

[49] Babu U.K. Sen to Presdy. Commr., no. 162, dated 2 Sept. 1845. Presdy. Commr. to Sbn. Commr., no. 5, dated 13 Jan. 1847.

[50] Presdy. Commr. to Sbn. Commr., no. 162, dated 4 Sept. 1851.

[51] Ibid., no. 266, dated 18 Oct. 1853.

of granting amalnamas. The holder was found to have reclaimed 621 bighas in 1847, out of a total area of 1,850 bighas. The Board ordered that the terms of the amalnama should stand good *quoad* the area, 378 bighas, mentioned in it; that the excess cultivation should be assessed at the Sundarban rate 8 annas, and the jungle granted out on the ordinary terms—a modification in favour perhaps of the lessee.[52] The settlement was accordingly made in 1850 for 22 years.[53] Gazaliyarber and Narsinghdattber were found to be in process of reclamation by Mr. Smith in 1851-52. A fresh patta was given for the former,[54] but a delay occurred in the settlement of the latter[55] and brought it under the operation of the revised rules of assessment issued in 1856.

185. Inspections in Jangalburi Patta Lands in Pargana Salimabad, 1849-51: Harganti, Dhuliganti and Nazirdiya were made over to Mr. Smith in 1849-50 to carry out the condition of the pattas. He surveyed and assessed them according to the terms in the pattas, but the Sundarban Commissioner ordered him to deduct first the unculturable land, and then exempt one-fourth and assess the remainder according to the patta rates, allowing the jungle a suitable extension of the free period. Uma Kanta Babu justified the variation from the terms fixed by Mr. Kemp by the explanation that those terms were stricter than the grant terms, and, when indulgences had been conceded in the latter, the former were deserving of lenient treatment.[56] The Presidency Commissioner appears to have been satisfied with the reply, and the settlements held good in perpetuity.[57]

186. Boundary Dispute in Manikkhola and Phulhata, 1848-53: Boundary disputes occurred between Nanda Kumar Bagis, who got the lease of Phulhata, Deotala, and two other chaks, and Durga Prasad Chaudhuri, who got the lease of Manikkhola, Khondakarber, and Baintala. The disputes were inevitable, for the chaks were resumed without boundaries or with incorrect boundaries, though

52 Ibid., no. 43, dated 18 Mar. 1848.

53 Sbn. Commr. to Presdy. Commr., no. 303, dated 18 July. Presdy. Commr. to Sbn. Commr., no. 155, dated 16 Aug. 1851.

54 Presdy. Commr. to Sbn. Commr., no. 166, dated 2 Aug. 1852.

55 Sbn. Commr. to Presdy. Commr., no. 203, dated 9 June 1853.

56 Ibid., no. 256, dated 11 June 1853.

57 Presdy. Commr. to Sbn. Commr., no. 68, dated 5 May 1854 (Dhuliganti).

an attempt appears to have been made to assign their boundaries in 1836-38. Mr. Smith surveyed them in 1848-9 and computed the area of Manikkhola at 10,082 bighas, but Durga Prasad claimed 25,152 bighas as composing its area. The dispute involved the determination of the boundary which was an imaginary line between Manikkhola on the one side and Phulhata and Deotala on the other. Mr. Harvey, the Revenue Commissioner, in December 1849, admitted Durga Prasad's claim as to the former quantity, and viewed it with favour as to the larger area. In putting Durga Prasad in possession and defining the boundary, Mr. Smith gave him 13,409 bighas,[58] and the Presidency Commissioner ordered in 1851 that the claimant should be put in possession of the whole area,[59] thus increasing his land and reducing that of Nanda Kumar out of all agreement with the quantities originally assigned them. On appeal the Board disallowed the later proceedings, and fixed the area of Manikkhola at 10,082 bighas.[60] The boundary was then revised and laid down in 1853, so as to give that chak the authorised area.[61]

187. Miscellaneous Settlements, 1844-56: Bhayang Kakrabuniya, which was resumed in 1842, was soon afterwards brought under settlement operations. It consisted of two portions. An assessment was made in 1846, but the proceedings dragged on for several years.[62] One portion was at length released, and a settlement was concluded in 1854 for the other for 20 years from 1851—5,904 bighas, Rs. 2,277[63] Pattamara, which had been resumed in 1832, was first taken in hand by the Collector of Bakarganj, then made over to the Sundarban Commissioner in 1846, and at length after many vicissitudes settled with the zamindar in 1850 in perpetuity at the Sundarban rate—10,723 bighas, Rs. 3,674.[64] Dihi Batgachi in 24-Parganas was resumed,

[58] Smith to Sbn. Commr., no. 47, dated 18 Sept. 1850.

[59] Presdy. Commr. to Sbn. Commr., no. 38, dated 18 Feb. 1851.

[60] Ibid., no. 200, dated 14 Oct. 1851.

[61] Smith to Sbn. Commr., no. 63, dated 20 Sept. 1853.

[62] Sbn. Commr. to Presdy. Commr., no. 341, dated 26, and no. 344, dated 28 June 1849. Presdy. Commr. to Sbn. Commr., letter dated 16 Nov. 1849.

[63] Presdy. Commr. to Sbn. Commr., no. 74, dated 11 May 1854.

[64] Sbn. Commr. to Presdy. Commr., no. 448, dated 10 Aug. 1849. Presdy. Commr. to Sbn. Commr., no. 87, dated 12 June, and no. 112, dated 13 July 1850.

and after several attempts settled finally in 1851 in perpetuity,[65] also the patitabadi mahall Madhabpur-Nandanpur in 1852 in perpetuity[66] after disputes with Ramchandrapur and Sultanpur had been decided; so too, Basudebpur, Dargatala, and Saranpur in 1854, and Baropota, which was all waste, in 1855.[67] Char Londah was resumed and at length settled permanently in 1856;[68] Gobindapur-Mastafapur was also resumed and settled temporarily.

188. Method of Settlements after 1850: Mr. Harvey had laid it down that the rate of 8 annas per the 40-yard bigha (which was made the standard in 1849[69]) was to apply to all Sundarban lands. This rule disregarded the widely different conditions of the resumed mahalls. Some like Bara and Chota Basidya contained large tracts of cultivated land and a largely developed body of tenantry. In others, such as the better reclaimed mahalls in Salimabad merely one class of tenants, generally haoladars, was found between the raiyats and the sadar malguzar. In others again, such as Alladipur and neighbouring estates in Jessore, there were few or no tenants or resident raiyats, but the settlement holder cultivated the lands through paekasht raiyats. The rate was applied indifferently to all these lands, and it meant that after excluding the unculturable portions, the rest was to be assessed at 8 annas, and the usual allowances for the settlement holder deducted. The allowances were 15 per cent, for expenses and 10 per cent, on the remainder for profits, equal to a gross deduction of 23½ per cent, and though the Board in 1850 fixed 30 per cent, for the case of mahalls assessed at the full jama,[70] yet those allowances were commonly adhered to. Under such a plan it was needless to inquire into and record the circumstances of the tenants and raiyats; it was enough to ascertain the assessable and unassessable quantities of land (a proper survey was strictly enjoined by the Board) and to draw up a dowl. The Board had notified that it was not necessary to repeat the full process of

[65] Presdy. Commr. to Sbn. Commr., no. 132, dated 21 July 1851.

[66] Ibid., no. 26, Apr. 1853.

[67] Ibid., no. 131, dated 26 Sept. 1855.

[68] Ibid., no. 207, dated 24 Oct. 1856.

[69] Bd. Rev., Cir. no. 48, dated 23 Nov. 1849, and paragraph 17 of Bd. Rev., Cir. no. 843, dated 26 Dec. 1850.

[70] Bd. Rev. no. 78, dated 19 Nov. 1850.

settlement on the expiration of a temporary settlement.[71] The process, however, was simplified even more by the mere exemption of one-fourth area on account of unculturable land and settlement holder's allowances, and the assessment of the remainder at the fixed rate. At first Mr. Harvey's order made little difference, and the jamabandis and proceedings were prepared more or less completely, but such records were soon perceived to be superfluous and were discontinued. The change produced its full effect about 1855, and thenceforward a settlement was the simplest routine.

189. Duration of Settlements after 1852: Until 1852 it was the custom in the Sundarbans, on account of the uncertainty as to the period for which a settlement might be confirmed, to avoid in drawing up dowls all mention of the period, and after confirmation to communicate the results to the parties.[72] But in the case of Bara Basdiya the Presidency Commissioner pronounced the custom objectionable and disallowed it;[73] a fresh dowl was therefore taken, and thenceforward it seems the period was generally mentioned in the dowl. Settlements were usually made for 20 years even in the case of farms, for which seven years were held to be insufficient. Mr. Harvey's ruling regarding malikana were observed, and except in indisputable cases the word was usually eschewed, and *munafa* or "profits" employed instead.

190. Sundarban Commissioner's Jurisdictions as to Resettlements, 1850-57: It was the practice for the Collectors to make over Sundarban mahalls to the Commissioner for resettlement when the previous settlements expired. The Board ordered in 1850 that "all mahalls of whatever description when settled should be transferred to the Collectors to be thenceforward managed by them,"[74] and the question was raised in 1852 whether, after estates had been resumed and once settled, the subsequent precedings might not remain with the Collectors. The change entailed extra work and continual local enquiries, for which they would probably have required deputies to help them. On those considerations the Board decided in 1852

[71] Bd. Rev., Cir. no. 6, dated 16 Apr. 1852.
[72] Sbn. Commr. to Presdy. Commr., no. 87, dated 25 March 1852.
[73] Presdy. Commr. to Sbn. Commr., no. 43, dated 5 Apr. 1852.
[74] Ibid., no. 139, dated 29 July 1851.

that there was no sufficient reason for making a change.[75] All the resettlements therefore of the Jessore and Bakarganj districts came back to the Sundarban Commissioner, but the Collector of 24-Parganas retained in his own hands the resettlements, whenever from any cause they became necessary, of the patitabadi mahalls, which were the only lands in that district resumed and settled. Those mahalls, when once their capacity for growth ceased through the granting out of the forest, approximated to the character of permanently-settled estates. Uma Kanta Babu made a representation about them, and the Board directed in 1852 that the work should be conducted as before. The Collector then sent him a few cases for resettlement, but the year after settled Kadua himself which had encroached on lot 14, and on Uma Kanta Babu's remonstrating, the Presidency Commissioner ordered that in future the Collector should communicate with the Sundarban Commissioner prior to renewing the settlements of patitabadi mahalls.[76] In 1855, however, when Uma Kanta Babu asked for Bansidharpur on the ground that he was empowered by the Government orders of 1829 to resettle such estates, the Presidency Commissioner dissented, the Sundarban Commissioner not being the sole authority and having quite enough to do besides, and prohibited him from applying to the Collectors of the three districts, without special reference to the Presidency Commissioner, for the transfer to him of the resettlement of mahalls which had once been settled and borne on their taujihs.[77] But again in 1857, on Mr. Reily's representation in the case of Bara Basdiya, the Board directed that all revisions of settlements in Sundarban estates were to be made through the Sundarban Commissioner.[78] Since then the practice has always been that all Sundarban lands have been made over to the Sundarban office when their settlements from any cause required renewal or revision.

191. Maliki Rights in Sundarban Mahalls, 1844-46: Mr. Harvey, who had been occupied in the settlement of the noabad lands in Chittagong, of which Government was the proprietor, became

[75] Ibid., no. 165, dated 20 Dec. 1852.

[76] Ibid., no. 291, dated 18, no. 1853.

[77] Ibid., no. 158, dated 31 Jan., and no. 35, dated 23 May 1855.

[78] Ibid., no. 44, dated 30 June 1857.

Commissioner of the Presidency Division about March 1843. He looked narrowly at the claims of the holders of Sundarban lands to be considered maliks and receive malikana. Hitherto, although the zamindars had been ousted under the resumption proceedings, and the settlements had been concluded with the talukdars or other highest tenants, yet the status of the latter had not been closely examined or defined, and the allowance granted them had been generally loosely designated malikana. But Mr. Harvey laid it down in the case of Rangabali (as mentioned in paragraph 141) that the holders in the event of recusancy were not entitled to malikana as they had not been constituted maliks, nor had derived any grant from Government in whom by virtue of section 13 of Regulation III of 1828 the property of the soil in the Sundarbans was vested;[79] and the same principle was applied to other estates. On this principle in the case of Lakhikhola and Hetalbuniya in 1847 he disallowed the claim of the zamindar to get the settlement, and directed that it should be concluded with the abadkari undertenants, and his order was upheld by the Board;[80] while even abadkari undertenants lost all their rights on the relapse of cultivation into waste through neglect.[81] Before that in Rangabali, Tepura, and other estates in that locality the holders had recused and Government had allowed them malikana, but Mr. Harvey had impugned their right in the case of Tepura.[82] In the subsequent resettlement of those mahalls, the maliki right, it appears, was stated to be vested in Government except in the case of Bara Basdiya where the holders were determined in their recusancy, and where after the mahall had remained khass for about 15 years, Government for special reasons conceded them that right about 1846.

192. Orders Regarding Maliki Rights in Pattamara, 1849: The question of maliki rights, including the right to engage for the settlement, next arose and was discussed at length in the case of Pattamara—an estate lying at the confluence of the Panguchi and

[79] Ibid., no. 432, dated 14 Sept. 1844.

[80] Ibid., no. 155, dated 21 Aug. 1847.

[81] In Bayarsinga, Presdy. Commr. to Sbn. Commr., no. 216, dated 10 Nov. 1847; in Harijhipatan, Presdy. Commr. to Sbn. Commr., no. 6 Ct., dated 14 Feb. 1854, which contains the final orders.

[82] Presdy. Commr. to Sbn. Commr., no. 524, dated 20 Nov. 1844.

Baleswar rivers—resumed by the Special Commissioner in 1832. In his faisala that officer directed that the settlement was to be made with the zamindar as the party in possession. The Collector began settlement operations, but after some delay the papers were transferred to the Sundarban office in 1846 for disposal. Uma Kanta Babu settled the mahall with the zamindar in 1847,[83] but Mr. Harvey disapproved his proceedings on the ground that the zamindar had no right to the lands and all his leases were void, and remanded the case with orders to settle with certain other persons.[84] The zamindar appealed to the Board, who took the matter up in 1849. The Members, Messrs Gordon and Ricketts, were divided in opinion. Mr. Gordon, who held that, the lands being Sundarban, Government could settle with whom it pleased, put aside the zamindar as being a usurper and not the real abadkar, and proposed to make the settlement with the abadkari tenants, to whom the objection regarding usurpation did not apply.[85] Mr. Ricketts held that the zamindar was entitled to the settlement, for the resumption decree did not oust him, but merely gave Government power to assess the lands. The zamindar who had long held possession could not be dispossessed by a resumption suit, and had Government desired to oust him a suit should have been brought in the civil court; and Mr. Ricketts did not understand how the revenue authorities could recognize a right on the part of the tenants to settlement, and yet not recognize that of their superior from whom their titles were derived. The question was referred to the Government and decided by the Deputy Governor on 28th May 1849. By the decision in the suit, Government had acquired the proprietary right in the land, as being Sundarban land, and had acknowledged the zamindar and no one else to be the party in possession. The order of the Special Commissioner that the settlement should be concluded with the zamindar was not binding on Government, and could not affect the rights of third parties; but as the tenants had not appealed against the settlement with the zamindar, the Deputy Governor held that that settlement should

[83] Sbn. Commr. to Presdy. Commr., no. 429, dated 29 Sept. 1847.

[84] Ibid., no. 56, dated 22 Feb. 1848. Presdy. Commr. to Sbn. Commr., no. 174, dated 7 Aug. 1848.

[85] There was a third claim by certain of Henckell's pattadars, but it was palpably groundless.

stand so as to create no disputes. He discussed, however, the grounds on which it was proposed to exclude the zamindar: (1) usurpation; but the ousted holders of Mr. Henckell's pattas had no right then, and the fact that Sundarban land was the property of Government was not of practical importance nor a reason for depriving the zamindar of his profits and giving them to the tenants: (2) the real abadkars were not the zamindar but the tenants; but as the tenants did not complain, there was no reason for disturbing existing relations: (3) the inexpediency of upholding the complicated system of undertenures; but this being a question of expediency did not need discussion. In conclusion he ruled that if the revenue authorities wished to dispossess the zamindar, they should have gone to the civil court.[86]

193. Orders Regarding Maliki Rights in Chota Basdiya, 1850: The question was raised the same year in the case of Chota Basdiya, and a decision was enunciated by the Government regarding the status of Sundarban abadkars and their right to malikana in case of recusancy, after full discussion between the Board and the Presidency Commissioner, who differed in opinion. The zamindars of pargana Chandradwip reclaimed Chota Basdiya without a grant, and, after it had been resumed by Government in 1833 under Regulation III of 1828, declined engaging for it because malikana was not allowed them. Mr. Harvey, as mentioned in paragraph 141, had ruled in 1844 that they possessed no maliki right. Some difference of opinion seems to have occurred, and the Commissioner of Dacca made a reference to the Board, soliciting their decision on the general question of the right of Sundarban clearers to malikana in case of recusancy. The Board held, in their no. 241, dated 26th October 1849, that a Sundarban squatter without a grant was entitled to settlement for his cleared land, and to the usual deduction on account of malikana, whether he settled or recused; excepting where the resumption decree declared that he had no right or interest whatever in the land, that it was the property of Government, and that the revenue authorities

[86] Presdy. Commr. to Sbn. Commr., no. 100, dated 23 June 1849. The decision proceeds on considerations of expediency, and does not expound the law. It was because the civil courts had been tried and found wanting that Regulation III of 1828 with its special provisions was enacted. The case does not appear to have been cited as a precedent in later cases.

might oust him. It was true as stated by Mr. Harvey, that under section 13 of Regulation III of 1828, the Sundarbans were declared to be the property of the State, but that the Board conceived meant that Government had a right to assess the occupied part and to grant out the unoccupied jungle, but not to oust possessors or cancel interests created by clearing jungle, that is, confiscate the capital laid out in making the soil fruitful. The Board held the intention was to regard those who had occupied and broken up the soil as Lakhirajdars, whose lands were open to resumption and assessment. That view was strengthened, they thought, by the correspondence of 1816, namely, where the Collector of Jessore had been directed in the event of the zamindars not agreeing to an equitable assessment on lands which they had reclaimed from the Sundarbans, to attach the lands until the claimants proved their right to exemption;[87] where the Government had instructed the Board to assimilate Sundarban taluks to the tenures of zamindari talukdars under Regulations VIII and XIV of 1793;[88] where the Board had proposed to class all reclaimers alike;[89] and where Government had laid it down that generally speaking there could exist no sufficient reason for asserting on the part of Government more than the right to an equitable jama, and that it would be expedient in ordinary cases formally to recognize the right of property in the person who might be found in possession of the land.[90] It followed therefore, the Board held, that a squatter without a grant was not entitled to settlement on special Sundarban terms, but only on the usual jangalburi terms, as otherwise he would be placed in a better position than a grantee.[91] In case of recusancy the Board ruled that Sundarban squatters without grants were not entitled to anything more than malikana. These orders the Board communicated to Mr. Harvey, the Presidency Commissioner, for information and guidance,

[87] Bd. Rev. to Collr., Jessore, 30 Apr. 1816—see paragraph 14 *supra.* 'In some instances..right to exemption.'

[88] Govt, to Bd. Rev., no. 434, dated 22 July 1816.

[89] Bd. Rev. to Govt., 6 Aug. 1816.

[90] Govt, to Bd. Rev., no. 523, dated 30 Aug. 1816.

[91] The Board decided in the particular instance of Chota Basdiya that malikana should be given on the original jama, but not on the increased cultivation attained under khass management with which the zamindars had had nothing to do.

but disagreeing with their views, he asked for a reconsideration. Their decisions, he stated, amounted to these two rulings—(1) that a Sundarban squatter without a grant is *de facto* malik or zamindar of the lands cultivated by him, and therefore entitled to malikana in case of recusancy: and (2) that Government cannot oust squatters on the State property of the Sundarbans nor grant pattas for such lands to other parties. These decisions, he submitted, were directly opposed to former declarations of the Sadar Board and decrees passed in the courts of justice, and he cited three cases from the civil courts where the abadkars had been ousted. The Board's decisions were also, he contended, opposed to the law—Regulation III of 1828—by virtue of which Government was entitled not only to revenue from, but also to the property in, the Sundarbans. That law was subsequent to the instructions issued in 1816, and must therefore be held to overrule them. Mr. Harvey therefore solicited a reference to the Government on the whole question, which he propounded thus—(1) "Does usurpation by cultivation on the Government property of the Sundarbans, declared to belong to Government by clause 1, section 13, Regulation III of 1828, entitle a party to a right of property as zamindar, and consequently to malikana, if recusant to the settlement offered to him; and, if so, by what law ?" (2) "Does clause 1, section 13, Regulation III of 1828, vest Government simply with a right to revenue of lands in the Sundarbans, or does it not also confer an absolute right of property in the soil, and constitute the Government malik of all the lands of the Sundarbans?" (3) "If Government is not malik of all the lands of the Sundarbans, how does it make grants constituting maliks and selling the pattas of such grants?" "If Government is malik of the lands, how come the usurpers of this property without such grant to be admitted as maliks by the Sadar Board ? Either the one position or the other appears untenable." Mr. Harvey looked upon a squatter as nothing more than a mere raiyat, subject to assessment of rent. That had been till then the universal usage, and to depart from the usage would be productive of the utmost litigation, and he placed on record his protest against the departure from that principle. The Board, which was composed of Messers. Gordon and Ricketts, submitted the matter to Government. They saw no reason to alter their opinion, and they pronounced Mr. Harvey's objection to be founded "on a want of ordinary discrimination, inasmuch as it confounded the obvious distinction of disavowing the claims of parties holding by virtue of usurpation of rights legally conferred on others, and the recognition of rights founded on long possession and clearing of the soil without injury to any other private party, and with benefit to the community in the reclamation of waste and the payment of revenue to the State.The Board dwelt on the advantage of reclamation and the hardship of confiscation. The law, it was true, declared the Sundarbans to be the property of the State, but it did not say that reclaimers were to be ousted and their property confiscated. On the contrary, clause 2 of section 13 related to clearances within the Sundarbans, and provided that if resumed they should be simply subjected to assessment, with no allusion to dispossession or confiscation or usurpation. The Government announced its decision in its No. 611, dated 25th June 1850. The Deputy Governor concurred with the Board. The squatter was at the time of the decree of resumption in possession, not as a raiyat, as Mr. Harvey maintained, but as a proprietor receiving rent. He could not be ousted from possession except by a decree of court, and that decree did not say he was liable to be ousted or say anything about title, but merely said that the land was liable to assessment of revenue. "Therefore as the person in possession as proprietor at the time of the settlement, the squatter had a right to engage if he chose, and there is no doubt that a *right* to engage involves the right to malikana on refusing to engage at the jama assessed." Mr. Harvey's first two questions were, the Deputy Governor held, broader than those involved in the present case, and he pronounced no decision on them, though he was not prepared to contend that Mr. Harvey's views as to questions of *right* were erroneous. He entirely concurred in the Board's views relative to the treatment deserved by reclaimers, and he conceived "the just and enlightened principle of the expediency in all ordinary cases of formally recognizing the right of property in the person who may be found in possession of the land, laid down by Government in 1816 to be the principle by which the Government has been guided up to this day." The three cases cited by Mr. Harvey did not, in his opinion, bear upon the real question in the present case though they did certainly bear upon it as a dry question of title.[92]

194. Views of Court of Directors as to Maliki Rights, 1851: The question would appear to have been referred to the decision of the Court of Directors, for in a despatch no. 7, dated 3rd September 1851, the Directors express the following views:

Paragraph 69. We have always been desirous of affording every reasonable encouragement to those who expend labour, skill and capital in the reclamation of waste land, whether they were grantees under Government or not.

Paragraph 70. In further instances therefore, which may appear to you deserving of special indulgence, we do not object to the grant of malikana to squatters, and a sound discretion must be exercised with reference to the length of time and circumstances of the occupation; but as a" general rule it would be inexpedient to place them on an equal footing with those who have received grants from Government.[93]

195. Results of Foregoing Orders: The result of these decisions was that the provisions of Regulation III were put on one side, and the principle of 1816 enunciated a new, namely, that the party in possession was ordinarily to be recognized as the proprietor, and was therefore entitled to malikana in recusant. Almost all the resumed mahalls had been settled once if not twice by this time, and any such claims set at rest long before, hence the new ruling was applicable only to fresh resumptions. They, however, were insignificant, and the principle seems to have been little observed until about twenty years afterwards; when the Sundarban Commissioner in discussing in his settlement reports the question, to whom the proprietary right

[92] Presdy. Commr. to Sbn. Commr., no. 111, dated 10 July 1850. It would not be easy to prove the statement regarding the principle, or even to reconcile it with the history, and the fact urged by Mr. Harvey that different principles had been especially enacted in 1828 might have suggested a doubt. Mr. Dampier is the best authority on this matter, and his remarks will be found in the case of Tushkhali (Presdy. Commr. to Sbn. Commr., no. 267, dated 16 Feb. 1856). The decision is disappointing. Mr. Harvey raised the legal question, and a ruling on it would not have debarred the Govt, from an indulgent policy. His propositions were not answered, but his views were more than substantiated afterwards by the rulings of the Sadar Court.

[93] Presdy. Commr. to Sbn. Commr., no. 22 Ct, dated 25 Nov. 1851.

in an estate belonged, constantly cited this ruling and construed it rather liberally. In case of Tarabuniya in Bakarganj, which had been resumed and settled by Mr. Dampier, and was again settled in 1854, the abadkari talukdars, who had been put aside for recusancy for many years, were admitted to settlement in 1855 on the ground of equity, but were refused malikana.[94] The same questions were agitated in the civil courts. There the claims asserted on behalf of Government were thorough-going to the last degree, and the rulings laid down by the Sadar Court placed the rights of Government in a position far different from that which the Board and the Deputy Governor had contemplated.

196. Civil Suits about Maliki Rights and Rights of Settlement, 1850-57: Several suits were instituted in Bakarganj about 1850 by parties who claimed to have settlement of resumed Sundarban lands in virtue of a jangalburi title as tenants under leases given them by the neighbouring zamindars before resumption. Government, as being the proprietor of the Sundarbans, was always made a defendant, and replies were field mostly in 1853 after approval by the Legal Remembrancer and Revenue Commissioner.[95] The grounds taken on behalf of Government, when it was held to have an interest in the case, were these—(1) Government became by resumption the absolute proprietor of the Sundarbans, and might settle the lands with any one it pleased; (2) the zamindars had no power to grant leases for Sundarban lands, and therefore titles derived from them were, after resumption, null and void; and (3) even a jangalburi title as haoladar or nim-haoladar could not give an undertenant a right of settlement with Government, since Government was the absolute proprietor. Various cases might be cited,[96] but two will be sufficient, which were appealed to the Sadar Court and decided on a full consideration of the points in dispute.

[94] Presdy. Commr. to Sbn. Commr., no. 77, dated 25 June 1855. Sbn. Commr. to Presdy. Commr., no. 335, dated 12 Sept. 1856.

[95] Mr. Harvey quitted the Presidency Division about the end of 1850, so the pleas did not specially express his views.

[96] See Presdy. Commr. to Sbn. Commr., no. 12, dated 30 Jan., and no. 14, dated 31 Jan. 1852; no. 108, dated 9 May, no. 170, dated 7 July, and no. 195, dated 27 July 1853.

197. Sadar Court Ruling in Case of Baroikhali, 1857: The first is the case of Baroikhali, which was decided by the Sadar Court on 23rd March 1857. Rabiullah Kazi and the other fakirs who had been excluded sued to be admitted to participation in the settlement which the Presidency Commissioner had given to Mohammed Hafiz alone as mentioned in paragraph 182. The court held that the terms of section 13, Regulation III of 1828 justified Government in selecting its own grantee and did not bind it to respect the claims of any party to settlement on the plea of previous occupancy or on any other plea; but looking to the obvious policy of the law, viz., reclamation of the Sundarban jungles and the rights which all parties acquire in this country through occupancy of the soil, the court doubted whether the law could be applied to the entire dispossession of an abadkar in possession, and whether his acts would not entitle him to retain possession of his cleared lands *under* a Government lessee. But that point was not involved in the legal question before the court, because the plaintiffs sought to participate in the lease granted by Government on equal terms with its own lessee, and the court held that the civil tribunals could not interfere to that extent. There was a second issue, which was also decided against the plaintiffs, and the claim was dismissed.[97]

198. Sadar Court Ruling in Case of Tushkhali, 1857: The point which was left doubtful in that case was decided in a suit regarding Tushkhali. The tenants there had been hopelessly stubborn and recusant, and in consequence the mahall had been farmed out to Debnath Rai, and their tenures cancelled. They then brought suits in the civil court to establish their claims. In one case the plaintiff sued to recover possession of 12 haolas and five nim-haolas, and the court of first instance, finding that he had been in possession of one haola and three nim-haolas before the resumption and had reclaimed the land, held that his rights in them were not annulled by the resumption decree, and decreed his claim to those four tenures. Government and three other parties appealed, and the appeals were decided together by the Sadar Court on 30th April 1857. The court held that as one person

[97] Presdy. Commr. to Sbn. Commr., no. 12 Ct, dated 28 Nov. 1853, and no. 300, dated 21 Apr. 1850.

could not give another a greater interest than he himself possessed, and the zamindar's title ceased under the resumption decree, therefore the plaintiffs derivative title also ceased at the same time, and though Government was competent to confirm his title, yet that had never been formally done. The plaintiff contended that even if his derivative title were insufficient, still the object for which it had been created, namely, the clearance of Jungle, gave him a good title in law, or at any rate on the ground of public benefit and policy. The court held, however, that a legal title was presumed even in the case of jangalburi tenures, and if no such title existed, no object, however praiseworthy or advantageous; could by law supply the deficiency; while as to the ground of public benefit and policy, they declined to entertain it, considering themselves bound to determine questions of private right strictly according to law. The claim was therefore dismissed.[98]

[98] Ibid., no. 48, dated 2 July 1857.

CHAPTER XVI

Forest Grants
1844-1853

199. Inspections in Grants, 1844-52: Inspections continued to be made in the grants, and where the clearing condition was not fulfilled, the Sundarban Commissioner reported, recommending either resumption of the grant or an extension of the revenue-free period to enable the grantees to bring their clearances up to the requirement, in accordance with the promise held out by Government in 1844. The usual reasons for default were natural calamities, and the hostility of the zamindars, who, though their pretensions had been curbed, still clandestinely encroached on the border grants and harrassed the grantees in the courts of law. A favourite weapon of theirs was Act IV of 1840, and by means of it they inflicted much harm on the grantees. Having got possession by encroachment, they invoked the aid of the Magistrate as soon as the grantee claimed the land, and the faujdari courts trying the matter in a summary sort of way passed orders maintaining the usurpers in possession, and the grantees had to fight out their claims at a disadvantage in the civil courts. The Joint-Magistrate of Baraset, in whose district many of the lots fell, seems to have been slow to support the grantees' claims, though the Sundarban Commissioner invoked his help; while the police were ready in the zamindars' interests. In 1847 the grantees petitioned for the transfer of pargana Paikhati and the neighbouring grants from Baraset to the 24-Parganas Magistracy, but the prayer does not appear to have been complied with.[1] A gale and inundation occurred in June 1842 in the 24-Parganas district and again in October, 1848, both of which inflicted much damage on the more exposed grants. A hurricane and rain occurred in October 1851, and a hurricane and inundation on

[1] Presdy. Commr. to Sbn. Commr., no. 159, dated 28 Aug. 1847. Sbn. Commr. to Presdy. Commr., no. 20, dated 21 Jan. 1848.

14th May 1852, but neither seem to have been severe.

200. Extensions of Free Period, 1844-53: The extensions of the free term conferred were ordinarily for ten years, and when a second extension was conceded it was generally for five years. Extensions were granted in lots 68 and 80 in 1844; in lots 45-49 and 74 in 1845; lots 54, 68, 79, and 80 in 1847; lots 13, 23-26, 81, 84, 91, 92, and 100 in 1848; lot 67 in 1849; lots 58, 63, 101, and 102 in 1850; lots 30, 32, 33, 40 and 76 in 1851;[2] lot 72[3] and 77[4] in 1853. In the case of Mr. Heatly's eight lots—87-89 and 93-97—where disputes with the zamindars had been unceasing so that he did not get possession till 1843, resumption was waived, and new pattas were given for four of the lots with effect from the date of possession.[5] In lots 48 and 49 the question of resuming for non-compliance with the clearing condition was raised after extension had been allowed, but the Board held in 1850 that, as it had been given without conditions, the penalty could not be enforced, and they declared that in future cases they would consider the propriety of annexing conditions stipulating for gradual cultivation.[6] At first the extension given was an extension of the free period, but after a time it was perceived that Government was perhaps needlessly foregoing its revenue, and in some of the later cases the extension was merely a lengthening of the period allowed for clearing the required area, the Government revenue falling due as originally stipulated.

201. Resumptions, 1845-53: Lots to which nothing had been done were generally resumed and in such cases the Sundarban Commissioner was directed always to record a formal proceedings.[7] In 1847 the Presidency Commissioner ordered that surveys should be made during the ensuing season, and all grants liable to resumption reported,[8] the enforcement of the clearing condition not having been regularly observed. A large number of grants were liable to

[2] Presdy. Commr.'s Statement, dated 7 Oct. 1847 and *passim.*
[3] Presdy. Commr. to Sbn. Commr., no. 26, dated 16 May 1856.
[4] Ibid., no. 150, dated 6 Sept. 1856.
[5] Ibid., 13 July 1849, and Sbn. Commr. to Presdy. Commr., 29 June 1850.
[6] Ibid., no. 176, dated 12 Sept. 1850.
[7] Ibid., no. 123, dated 7 July 1847.
[8] Ibid., no. 245, dated 24 Dec. 1847.

resumption,[9] but some received extensions, and in the following only was the penalty inflicted. Lots 104, 107 and 109[10] were resumed in 1845; lots 18, 50, 66, 122, and 123 in 1846; lots 1-7, 57 (middle part), 69, and 90 in 1847; lot 70 in 1848; lots 37, 62, 83, 105, 136, 137, 221, and 224 in 1849; and the amalnama given by Mr. Grant in 1835 for lots 211 and 212 was cancelled this year;[11] lot 57 (part) in 1850; lots 13, 108[12] and 172 in 1851; lot 99 in 1852; lots 43, 59, 106, 110-15, 123, 129, 130, 135, 138, 140, 142, and 143 in 1853. In the case of lot 216, where the encroaching zamindar had cleared more than the required area, but the grantee had done nothing, Uma Kanta Babu proposed to resume the grant, but the Presidency Commissioner held in 1849 that if the required area had been cleared, no matter by whom, Government could not intervene to resume, but the remedy would be that, if the revenue were not paid at the end of the free term, the lot could be sold.[13]

202. Settlements in Resumed Grants, 1848-53: In some instances where lots had been resumed it happened that a small portion had been reclaimed, and for such the Board laid it down in 1848 as a general rule that the late grantee should not be dispossessed, but that the cleared land should be settled with him in the ordinary way if he agreed to the terms, and only the untouched forest should be disposed of under the grant rules.[14] Thus the cleared portions of lots 13,[15] 62,[16] 63,[17] and 108[18] appear to have been settled in the years 1849-52, at the full grant rate of 8 annas, the backward lands being allowed a short rasad.

203. Orders Prescribing Public Sale of Grants, 1846: Grants

[9] Mullins to Sbn. Commr., no. 110, dated 16 June 1848.

[10] The resumption of lots 101-03 and 108 ordered in 1842 was revoked in 1845. Presdy. Commr. to Collr., 24-Parganas, no. 74, dated 17 Mar. 1845 and letter 9 May 1845.

[11] Presdy. Commr. to Sbn. Commr., no. 46, dated 18 Apr. 1849.

[12] Ibid., no. 23, dated 31 Jan. 1851.

[13] Ibid., no. 31, dated 22 May 1855.

[14] Ibid., no. 281, dated 24 Nov. 1848.

[15] Sbn. Commr. to Presdy. Commr., no. 9, dated 3 Jan. 1851.

[16] Presdy. Commr. to Sbn. Commr., no. 182, dated 25 Aug. 1849.

[17] Ibid., no. 220, dated 2 Nov. 1850.

[18] Ibid., no. 91, dated 27 Apr. 1853.

had at first been bestowed according to priority of application, but a new principle of selection was introduced in 1846. Several persons asked for lots 70, 71, 81 and 84,[19] and Mr. Harvey feeling it a delicate matter to prefer one applicant to another advocated that those lots, and lots generally, should be sold by public auction to the highest bidder—a course that would give the purchaser an interest in the improvement of his grant and provide against people taking grants for the mere purpose of making a gain out of the natural products, and one also "by which the best man (that is the man who values the lot most highly and is prepared to pay the most for the grant at public sale) shall be recognized as the grantee." The Board approved the proposal as the fairest way of determining who should have the preference. They remarked that though the price would add to the cost of reclamation, yet it would not be paid unless the lot were capable of yielding a good return; while on the other hand though the sale (it might be said) might lessen the right of Government to resume yet payment of a small sum in competition would not confer on the purchaser a right of making a distinct bargain with Government, nor would it strengthen his claim to get possession. The Government in its letter 821, dated 4th November 1846, sanctioned the general rule of public sale on the clear understanding that before proceeding to sale the Sundarban Commissioner should satisfy himself of his ability to give possession without embarrassment to Government. He was instructed to sell lots by public auction in all cases, after due notice publicly given.[20] And the further rule was added in 1847 that the sales should be always advertised not less than 15 days beforehand in the *Calcutta Gazette* and at the local offices.[21] Instructions were issued the same year that lots should be surveyed before sale, their boundaries determined, and the lots broken up if they were too large to be conveniently leased in their entirety. The Sundarban Commissioner was in all cases to give possession to the grantees in person, defining the boundaries and erecting sufficient permanent land-marks, and

[19] Lots 81 and 84 were, however, withdrawn, resumption being waived and an extension granted. Presdy. Commr. to Sbn. Commr., no. 239, dated 31 Dec. 1846.

[20] Presdy. Commr. to Sbn. Commr., no. 198, dated 23 Nov., and no. 233, dated 17 Dec. 1846.

[21] Ibid., no. 12, dated 18 Jan. 1847.

to record the particulars in a proceeding and survey map and notify the facts to all officers concerned.[22] It seems doubtful whether these last instructions were obeyed, except for a short time in the case of the border grants in 24-Parganas,[23] and to a limited extent in the Bakarganj district where a survey was a necessary preliminary amid the little known forest tracts.

204. New Grants and Regrants, 1847-52: The following new grants and regrants were made during this period—lots 18, 29, 66, 71, 133 and Chilla[24] in 1847, and a revised patta executed for lot 58;[25] lots 1-7 and 36 in 1848; lots 37, 83, 211, 212, and Nos. 1-7 Khaoliya Barisal (excluding the cleared lands in Nos. 1 and 3[26]) in 1849; lots 11, 12, 42, and 137 in 1850; lot 108 (jungle portion) and Nalbuniya in 1851; and lot 86 in 1852. The further sale of grants was suspended in 1852 pending the reconsideration of the rules for grants of the Sundarban waste lands.[27]

205. Grants in Bakarganj, 1844-51: Grants had been made of Chakamoya, Amtali, Arpangasiya, and Pachakuraliya—four chaks in Bakarganj—in 1844, and the boundaries were specified though the areas were nominal. Government allowed the grants, but required that they should be surveyed during season 1844-45, their areas and boundaries correctly assigned, and revised pattas given.[28] The Sundarban Commission having just then been abolished, this duty was made over to the Collector of Bakarganj. He applied for a surveyor to survey those grants and other jungle lands, and asked that such an officer might be permanently attached to the district, explaining the advantages, since amins could not be trusted, and referring to Phuljhuri and Aila Teorkhali, where the rights of Government had been squandered through a short-sighted policy. The Dacca Commissioner did not fall in with his views, thinking that a Deputy Collector might

[22] Ibid., no. 252, dated 31 Dec. 1847.

[23] Sbn. Commr. to Predy. Commr., no. 63, dated 8 Mar. 1850.

[24] Mr. Smith surveyed Chila in 1846-47.

[25] Presdy. Commr. to Sbn. Commr., 24 Nov. 1847.

[26] Sbn. Commr. to Presdy. Commr., no. 486, dated 28 Aug. 1849.

[27] Presdy. Commr. to Sbn. Commr., no. 184, dated 19 Aug. 1852. The revised rules were issued in 1853.

[28] Presdy. Commr. to Babu U.K. Sen, no. 10, dated 5 Feb. 1845.

do the work. Thereupon the Collector mentioned Aila (comprising seven chaks), Auliyapur, Chandokhali, Kachupatra, and Gyanpara, which with the above chaks aggregated 2,55,300 bighas by estimate, all requiring to be surveyed; besides which there were resumption cases and the khass mahall Buzurgummedpur to be attended to. In short, in his opinion, the whole district needed to be surveyed, nothing having been done since Rennell surveyed its rivers in 1782. The Commissioner was induced to ask for the services of a surveyor for the next season, but the Sundarban Commission being on the point of revival, the whole matter was transferred to it for disposal.[29] Nilgunj and Abuganj-Mithaganj also came up at the same time for adjustment. Mr. Shawe had given amalnamas for those chaks to certain Mags, but the other claimants appealed, and the Revenue Commissioner ordered a settlement of the lands. The Collector took the cases in hand in season 1844-45, but the Mags in their turn appealed, and these cases, too, were made over to the Sundarban Commissioner in January 1846. Mr. Smith, Deputy Collector, surveyed the six chaks above mentioned and also Chandokhali, Kachupatra, and Bogi in season 1846-47,[30] and proposed an adjustment, but the Presidency Commissioner negatived his suggestions, and ordered that the cleared and jungle lands in Nilganj[31] and Abuganj-Mithaganj[32] should be settled regularly in the same way as in the adjoining mahall Baliyatali, and that the other lands should be resurveyed.[33] Mr. Mullins accordingly surveyed the latter chaks in season 1847-48 with these results—Chakamoya 12,880 bighas, Amtali 7,960 bighas, Arpangasiya 13,950 bighas, Pachakuraliya 6,760 bighas, Chandokhali 8,120 bighas, Kachupatra 10,820 bighas, and also Karaibariya 9,000 bighas. The boundaries mentioned in the patta of Pachakuraliya included Chandokhali and Kachupatra, but they were separated, and all the six chaks (Karaibariya being omitted) were granted out separately.[34] Nilganj, with a cultivated

[29] Presdy. Commr. to Sbn. Commr., no. 5, dated Feb. 1846.

[30] Smith to Sbn. Commr., 25 and 26 Aug. 1847.

[31] Presdy. Commr. to Sbn. Commr., no. 191, dated 28 Sept. 1847.

[32] Ibid., no. 185, dated 25 Sept. 1847.

[33] Ibid., no. 168, dated 6 Sept. 1847.

[34] Sbn. Commr. to Presdy. Commr., no. 714, dated 7 Nov. 1848. Presdy. Commr. to Sbn. Commr., no. 275, dated 10 Nov. 1848.

area of 1,552 bighas, was settled in 1848 for 20 years,[35] and Abuganj-Mithaganj, with a total area of 15,270 bighas, in 1849 for 24 years,[36] the ultimate rate of assessment being 8 annas.

206. Grants in Khaoliya Barisal, 1846-52: The persons to whom *amalnamas* were granted in 1841 for the two portions for Khaoliya Barisal never executed the leases nor took part in its reclamation. There was some cultivation at the north of the tract which was anterior to the grants. The clearing condition being broken, those *amalnamas* as well as that given in 1840 were formally cancelled in 1846,[37] and fresh proposals called for regarding the disposal of the land. The whole tract was surveyed in 1846-48 and divided into seven portions, very nearly as they now exist, the total area being 2,39,806 bighas, and the cleared portion 2,194 bighas, apparently exclusive of the former. The Board approved the division and ordered that the allotments should be disposed of by public sale in the regular way, the cleared lands, however, being kept apart and settled separately.[38] The lots were sold on 28th August 1849, the first three being purchased by Messers. R. and T.H. Morrell.[39] The cleared area—2,194 bighas—was settled with the abadkars by Mr. Smith, but the Morrells objected to it as they had bought all lots 1-3 except the cultivation, and the area once cleared had partially relapsed, so that when they took possession in 1849-50 there were only 889 bighas under cultivation. Their contention was allowed, and only that area—889 bighas—was settled with the abadkars, the Morrells getting all the rest.[40] The 2,194 bighas occupied the fine river frontages: to have allowed it to remain jungle in the hands of the abadkar would have placed the Morrells at his mercy. They displayed great activity in clearing their lands, especially lot No. 1. They established a town and mart, which they named after

[35] Presdy. Commr. to Sbn. Commr., 9 Dec. 1848.

[36] Ibid., no. 6 Ct, dated 31 Oct. 1851.

[37] Ibid., no. 223, dated 11 Dec. 1846.

[38] Mullins to Sbn. Commr., no. 35, dated 2 Apr. 1849. Presdy. Commr. to Sbn. Commr., no. 119, dated 10 July 1849.

[39] Sbn. Commr. to Presdy. Commr., no. 626, dated 27 Nov. 1849.

[40] Presdy. Commr. to Sbn. Commr., no. 56, dated 21 March 1851, and no. 244, dated 31 Dec. 1852.

themselves Morrellganj,[41] at the north-east corner of that lot. The town possesses a fine situation at the confluence of three rivers, and it rose under their care to the leading position in that locality. It now contains a good brick house, a police station, subregistration office, and dispensary.

207. Grant in Tatibuniya, 1846-51: In the case of Tatibuniya neither of the grantees executed their leases or reclaimed the land; their grants were therefore resumed. Mr. Mullins surveyed the area in 1846 and found it to contain 58,724 bighas. The Presidency Commissioner ordered that it should be sub-divided into small equal allotments and the portions sold separately;[42] but Mr. Smith, who calculated its size at 34,025 bighas, failed *to* divide it, and recommended its sale in one block;[43] and, though four parts were afterwards made of it, it was granted out as a whole in 1851.[44]

208. Settlement of Grants on Expiry of Free Period, 1850-53: The revenue-free periods of the earliest grants, where no extension had been given, expired in 1850. The pattas and kabuliyats had been executed in 1830, and kistbandis at the same time or soon after, the revenue being calculated upon Hodges' areas, which were fairly correct. All that was necessary was to make the grants over to the Collector for the realization of the revenue already assessed. Uma Kanta Babu, however, considered that some fresh arrangements was indispensable, and feeling uncertain applied to the Presidency Commissioner for instructions how he was to make the settlements. The Board directed that the total area, unless fixed at the time of the grant, should be ascertained and assessed at the patta rates; while, if a measurement had been made at that time, remeasurement was unnecessary, and the rates should simply be assessed on the area already known.[45] These plain instructions were, however, strangely misunderstood, and Uma Kanta Babu impressed with the idea that *settlements* were necessary, proceeded to measure, assess, and conclude engagements for the

41 Saraliya is the name by which it is commonly known among the people.
42 Presdy. Commr. to Sbn. Commr., no. 8, dated 14 Jan. 1847.
43 Sbn. Commr. to Presdy. Commr., no. 638, dated 1 Dec. 1849.
44 Presdy. Commr. to Sbn. Commr., no. 179, dated 19 Sept. 1851.
45 Ibid., no. 264, dated 16 Dec. 1850.

cleared portions. He acted thus in lot 56 (north portion[46]) and lot 65 in 1851, and in the latter case the Presidency Commissioner confirmed the settlement.[47] Before, however, serious confusion could be effected the new rules of 1853 came out and radically changed the system of Sundarban grants. Still the idea that settlements were indispensable on the expiry of the free period maintained its position in his mind. Even in 1855 he insisted upon the necessity of making a settlement of lot 216, which had changed hands, and the Presidency Commissioner in reply informed him that there was no settlement to be made, that having been done when the grant was originally made.[48]

209. Salt Lands in Jessore and 24-Parganas, 1848-50: In 1848 the salt lands of 24-Parganas and Jessore were made over to the Sundarban Commissioner. Government had long before leased pargana Raimangal from the zamindar for the manufacture of salt, paying him annually Rs. 1,893 sicca as proprietary profits, lands had also been taken in parganas Malai and Jamira for salt khalaris. The salt manufacture in Jessore seems to have been given up in 1826, and the Collector was instructed to settle the lands. The lands being Sundarban were made over to the Sundarban office about 1848. Mr. Smith, Deputy Collector, inquired and identified them during 1848-49, but no one would take them, since they were all waste and situated in the heart of the forest.[49] The Salt Agency in the 24-Parganas seems to have been abolished in 1848 or 1849, and the Sundarban Commissioner was directed in December 1848 to take charge of its salt lands in trust for the department, but not to settle or lease them out without reference to the Salt Authorities. He took them over in January 1849, and Mullins was ordered to survey them, noting their extent, position, and boundaries in order to guard against future confusion. They consisted of eight hoodahs with an area of 17,061 bighas.[50] An

[46] Sbn. Commr. to Presdy. Commr., no. 402, dated 12 Sept. 1851.

[47] Presdy. Commr. to Sbn. Commr., no. 225, dated 20 Dec. 1851.

[48] Ibid., no. 31, dated 22 May 1855.

[49] Smith to Sbn. Commr., no. 69, dated 15 Sept. 1849. Sbn. Commr. to Presdy. Commr., no. 665, dated 30 Dec. 1850. See, too, Sbn. Commr. to Presdy. Commr., no. 71, dated 8 Sept. 1859.

[50] Presdy. Commr. to Sbn. Commr., no. 301, dated 9 Dec. 1848; and no. 95, dated 20 June 1849.

application by a Mr. Presgrave for a lease of all forest rights over this tract was refused in 1850 on the ground that it would constitute an objectionable monopoly.[51]

[51] Ibid., no. 67, dated 22 May 1850.

CHAPTER XVII

Resurvey and Adjustment of the Sundarban Boundary in the 24-Parganas 1844-1856

210. Boundary Disputes in 24-Parganas: The encroachments of the zamindars and the disputes between them and the border grantees in 24-Parganas district continued to cause much trouble, for Turner's and Mullins' surveys described in paragraphs 155 and 156 had but partially alleviated the friction. There was besides similar difficulties with regard to lots 217, 218, and 219, the history of which has been narrated in chapter XIV. When the Commission was abolished in 1844, the investigation into such encroachments both in 24-Parganas and Jessore, the determination of the disputes, and the settlement of the lands formed one of the subjects to which Uma Kanta Babu's attention was specially directed;[1] and it was laid down that if part of a lot had been cleared without authority the cultivated part should be assessed and the uncultivated part granted out, so much as might be expedient.[2]

211. Inquiries Regarding Boundary Disputes, 1844-49: In the case of lots 57 and 67, as mentioned in paragraph 156, Mr. Ross' neglect to employ a surveyor to mark off his line was a fatal defect. Mullins was employed in season 1844-45 to survey the line, but finding Mr. Ross' marks gone he could not make an accurate survey, and both parties objected. It was found that Mr. Ross had not kept to Mr. Dampier's line, so the Board ordered Uma Kanta Babu to mark out that line with the aid of the surveyor in the presence of both parties.[3] On the zamindar, however, objecting, the proceedings were stopped, and Government filed a petition in the Sadar Court

[1] Presdy. Commr. to Babu U.K. Sen, no. 519, dated 2 Dec. 1844.

[2] Ibid., no. 578, dated 19 Dec. 1844.

[3] Mullins to Collector, 24-Parganas, no. 9, dated 19 Jan. 1845. Presdy. Commr. to Sbn. Commr., no. 24, dated 2 Apr. 1846.

for an injunction on the Sundarban Commissioner to lay down Mr. Dampier's boundary.[4] The line was then surveyed and laid down in season 1846-47,[5] and Government in consideration of the difficulties the grantees has experienced, renewed their pattas from 1847.[6] In lots 44 and 45 the patitabadi talukdar of Bantra and Dharmtala had been encroaching. During season 1847-48 Mr. Smith seems to have made a survey and attempted a solution of the conflicting claims,[7] but the Presidency Commissioner ordered a fresh survey and definition of the boundary in 1848.[8] Mr. Mullins then made a survey and apportionment of the lands, but no decision appears to have been come to.[9] Also in lot 31 the zamindar, the Rani Sankari Dasi, was alleged to have been encroaching. Mr. Mullins made a survey in 1845-46 apparently, but she impugned its accuracy, and the Presidency Commissioner not feeling satisfied ordered a resurvey by Mr. Smith in the presence of Uma Kanta Babu in 1848.[10] Here again, however, the disputes not seem to have been decided. Other places where similar encroachments and disputes existed were lots 20 and 21[11]; 55, 57, 61, 63-67 and 80;[12] and 81.[13] Mullins appears to have made inquiries or surveys in all these places, and copies of his maps were furnished to various grantees in 1847 in order to enable them to adjust their boundary disputes, but no reliance can be placed on his surveys or maps, for, apart from the intricacy of the claims raised, his work was tested by the Revenue Survey authorities in 1851, and pronounced untrustworthy.[14]

212. Resurvey of Sundarban Boundary in 24-Parganas Ordered, 1849: Prinsep's line was the acknowledged boundary of the

[4] Presdy. Commr. to Sbn. Commr., no. 43, dated 18 May 1846.

[5] Mullins to Sbn. Commr., no. 30, dated 20 Feb., and no. 173, dated 15 Nov. 1847.

[6] Presdy. Commr. to Sbn. Commr., no. 203, dated 26 Oct. 1847.

[7] Smith to Sbn. Commr., no. 39, dated 18 Sept. 1848.

[8] Presdy. Commr. to Sbn. Commr., no. 305, dated 9 Dec. 1848.

[9] Mullins to Sbn. Commr., no. 84, dated 14 June 1849.

[10] Presdy. Commr. to Sbn. Commr., no. 169, dated 3 Aug. 1848.

[11] Sbn. Commr. to Presdy. Commr., 7 Sept. 1847.

[12] Mullins to Sbn. Commr., no. 99, dated 15 June 1847.

[13] Ibid., no. 112, dated 22 June 1846.

[14] See paragraph 219.

Sundarbans in the 24-Parganas. It had been laid down in the years 1822 and 1823, but had been departed from or lost during the 25 years or more that had elapsed. For the patitabadi mahalls had more or less continued to grow at the expense of the forest, and when they were all settled about the year 1834 many of them spread across the line. Again, decisions had been passed subsequent to his survey, by which grantees had, it seems, in some instance been placed in possession of non-Sundarban land. Besides such authorized modifications, marked changes had been wrought by the encroachment of the zamindars and grantees on each other. The numerous disputes all along the frontier, and the extremely puzzling issues involved, at length induced the Board in 1849 to apply for a resurvey and demarcation of Prinsep's boundary by scientific means. The survey was carried out by the Survey Department, and Captain R. Smyth was selected for the duty. The instructions issued to him were to trace out and survey Prinsep's boundary, ascertaining it by means of Prinsep's field-books. He was to uphold it as defined in Turner's and Mullins' maps, unless he found that they had not delineated it truly, in which event he was to note the divergence between them. As the survey went on, he was required to erect mounds for land-marks at all the angles.[15] The Superintendent of Survey was ordered to attend Captain Smyth in order to lay down the boundary whenever Prinsep's or Hodges' boundary could not be discovered.[16] Mullins also was ordered to give all the help in his power.

213. Survey Operations by Captain Smyth, 1850: Captain Smyth began his operations in January 1850 at the bank of the Hugli. After considerable difficulty he secured satisfactory starting points, and working along Prinsep's bearings and distances found every particular of the boundary fall in correctly. But by the time he had traversed ten miles, he found the limits of possession vary greatly from it, for the zamindars had encroached beyond the line, and Mr. Dampier had settled such clearances with them. They were dissatisfied with Captain Smyth's proceedings, for they claimed land in the heart of the forest

[15] Presdy. Commr. to Sbn. Commr., no. 8. dated 11 Jan. 1850.

[16] Ibid., no. 38, dated 14 March 1850. Rules for the thakbast and khasra operations were drawn up by the Board in Oct. 1850 and issued with instructions to Presdy. Commr. in letter no. 586, dated 8 Oct. 1850 (see Presdy. Commr. to Sbn. Commr., no, 169, dated 17 idem).

besides what Mr. Dampier had given them settlement of. The grantees on the other hand claimed all land up to Prinsep's line. Captain Smyth, there-upon asked, in February 1850, for instructions whether Prinsep's boundary was to be upheld or Mr. Dampier's limits of settlement. The Board issued *ad interim* orders to him to go on laying down Prinsep's boundary since that was the basis of all subsequent operations, and also at the same time to note the limits of Mr. Dampier's settlements, in order that there might be means of deciding the disputes. The people were informed that the survey was merely for the purpose of ascertaining boundaries and would not disturb possession.[17]

214. Orders Regarding Boundary to be Surveyed, 1850: The Board then called for a report as to whether Mr. Dampier was supposed to have been guided in all instances by Prinsep's boundary, or whether he departed from it as he saw fit on investigation, and whether the line that he assumed was invariably laid down by survey. The whole question embraced was—What was the real boundary of the Sundarbans as it then existed according to all decisions up to that period; and if that boundary was not truly represented by Prinsep's survey, what were the deviations, and how were they to be traced ? Prinsep's skeleton map displayed three lines—green (the limit of the Sundarban forest), red, and yellow: Hodges' map, two lines—one the limit of the Sundarban forest, green, and the other the boundary of the patitabadi lands. It appeared that both officers separated the patitabadi lands from the forest. Mr. Dampier's settlements all lay outside the green forest line and his grants all inside. On these considerations, the Presidency Commissioner recommended that Captain Smyth should define the boundary according to Prinsep's and Hodges' green line, leaving out the patitabadi mahalls, which ought to be surveyed separately like other distinct estates. The Board approved the suggestion and despatched orders to Captain Smyth in March 1850 to survey the green line depicted by Hodges who had followed Prinsep.[18] As that line was Prinsep's boundary, the order confirmed that first laid down, and the survey proceeded as before. Uma Kanta Babu reported, after the issue of the order, that although

[17] Ibid., no. 28, dated 21 Feb. 1850; and no. 2, dated 7 Jan. 1857.

[18] Ibid., no. 51, dated 9 March 1850.

Prinsep's line had always been acknowledged as the authority for the Sundarban boundary, yet portions of several Sundarban grants had been included in the patitabadi lands, and Prinsep's map and Mr. Dampier's rubakaris should be taken together as the guide.[19]

215. Extent of Survey, 1850 and 1851: During the first four months of 1850, Captain Smyth surveyed from the Hugli to Ballugachi on the river Piyali, 90 miles of Prinsep's line and 150 miles of Mr. Dampier's settlement limits, and constructed pillars at all the corners of Prinsep's line. During the following season he continued his survey as far as the river Kabadak opposite Gobra.

216. Character of Boundary Disputes as Ascertained during Survey: In the tract traversed the first season there were few grantees in possession, and the lands cleared beyond Prinsep's boundary were chiefly encroachments by the zamindars on the jungle. During the next season, however, the circumstances were different, for almost all the grants adjoining the 24-Parganas district, especially in parganas Paikhati and Balanda, were cleared and more or less cultivated, while some of them were entirely reclaimed. Here Captain Smyth had to deal with parties claiming and disputing on each side. They applied to him to put them in possession of such lands as fell within their zamindaries or grants, but he refused, it being his duty merely to demarcate the boundary. The consequence was that the losing party refused to acknowledge the boundary defined and still disputed possession, and within a few days the boundary pillars disappeared. Fearing lest his labour should thus be thrown away, he urged that the only remedy was to decide the disputes and give possession at once. In some cases, as in lots 66-70 and 80, where the boundaries of possession did not tally with Prinsep's line, and the grantees appeared to have encroached on the zamindari lands, they objected to any deviation from the existing boundaries, which they maintained were the true boundaries *de jure* and *de facto* under Regulation III of 1928; they also protested against the erection of pillars on their lands. In those cases and in another where the Special Commissioner had defined the boundary in supersession of Prinsep's line, Captain Smyth asked for instructions in order not to be delayed, and the Board modified, in March 1851,

[19] Sbn. Commr. to Presdy. Commr., no. 63, dated 8 March 1850.

the orders previously issued. They directed him to trace out and map Prinsep's boundary, but where occupied lots were met with to survey and map the boundary according to possession; while in cases where possession was disputed, the Superintendent of Survey was to decide, and the boundary was to be laid down according to his decision. All cases in which it appeared that the zamindars had encroached upon occupied grants were to be reported by the Superintendent to the Sundarban Commissioner.[20]

217. Results of Survey: His map of the first season's work shews Prinsep's boundary line, and the line that was determined after his own (Captain Smyth's) survey. Besides these it shews the boundaries of the villages bordering Prinsep's line, the then limit of the dense forest, the Government bund. & c. The boundaries of each chakdar were marked in, and all the chaks of each village included within a coloured line: Prinsep's line is coloured yellow and Captain Smyth's line red. The latter, in this region, generally falls further south than the former, thereby indicating that the patitabadi talukdars and the zamindars had been the aggressors. Mr. Dampier's settlements appeared to have no reference to Prinsep's line: the chaks ran on both sides of it. All the claims of adjoining villages to land alleged to have been settled in their favour by Mr. Dampier were marked in, but claims to jungle were merely noted down—a survey being impracticable.[21] The Board ordered, in December 1850, that copies of the maps should be supplied to the Collectors, Superintendent of Survey, and Sundarban Commissioner. The Superintendent was directed to adjust the claims on both sides of the line, and the Collector to maintain the pillars every year.[22] The maps of the second year's survey shew the two lines, the limits of the forest, and the village boundaries, but do not record details of the chaks and claims. The two lines differ here continually, but do not diverge so seriously as before. Prinsep's line more often falls further south than Smyth's line, thus indicating that the grantees had been the aggressors. Between the Kalindi and Kabadak they vary greatly, and this arises partly from the fact that Prinsep excluded and

[20] Presdy. Commr. to Sbn. Commr., no. 60, dated 2 Apr. 1851.

[21] Ibid., no. 2 dated 7 Jan. 1851.

[22] Ibid., no. 166, dated 19 Sept. 1851, and no. 87, dated 31 May 1852.

Smyth included Henckell's mahalls in that quarter, and partly to the zamindars' encroachments on the forest.

218. Instructions to Sundarban Surveyors, 1852: On the completion of the survey the Deputy Surveyor-General advised that the Sundarban surveyors should take up and connect convenient points of Captain Smyth's survey, so that some sort of connected map might be made and check obtained, for the continuous and complete survey of the entire 24-Parganas district with the portion of the Sundarbans attached would act as a sort of base on which the desultory or detached surveys of grants might be strung or verified. The Board approved the suggestion and directed that it should be observed.[23]

219. Value of Mullins' Surveys, 1841-52: It appears that the Board had not been satisfied with Mullins' work, and entertaining a suspicion of his competency as a surveyor, they directed Captain Thuillier, the Deputy Surveyor-General, in 1849 or 1850 to examine his work. The revenue survey by Captain Smyth afforded an excellent opportunity, for Mullins had made numerous surveys in the border grants, and had been directed to assist that officer in the revenue survey. Captain Thuillier reported in 1851 that the Sundarban boundary delineated in Mullins maps seldom agreed with Prinsep's boundary; that when it did agree with Prinsep's boundary, the line demarcated in the field and given to the grantees by Mullins did not agree with his own maps; and that Mullins' boundary was not to be depended on, and his maps were wanting in full and useful topographical detail. He pronounced Mullins' maps to be entirely worthless for revenue purposes.[24] Mullins was allowed a vindication, but failed, and was removed from the Sundarbans in September 1852 on the ground of the inaccuracy of his work.[25]

220. Decision of Boundary Disputes, 1850-55: The boundary lands having been thus surveyed, and copies of Smyth's survey in five maps sent to Uma Kanta Babu, he proceeded to determine the disputes and settle the lands along the border—a subject on which

[23] Presdy. Commr. to Sbn. Commr., no. 87, dated 31 May 1852.

[24] Dy. Surveyor-General to Bd. Rev., no. 27, dated 19 Dec. 1851.

[25] Presdy. Commr. to Sbn. Commr., no. 44, dated 6 Apr.; no. 73, dated 11 May; and no. 16 Ct., dated 9 Sept. 1852. See, too, Presdy. Commr. to Sbn. Commr., no. 64 Ct., dated 27 Aug. 1858.

he had been occupied during previous years. The Board in 1852 ordered that lands south of Prinsep's boundary, cleared and held by parties without title, should be brought under assessment. Such lands were of two kinds—(1) those held by owners of resumed Sundarban mahalls, that is, patitabadi talukdars; and (2) those held by the zamindars of permanently-settled estates. In the case of the former, which prevailed west of the river Bidyadhari, Uma Kanta Babu was directed to survey and assess the taufir. As to the former, which lay chiefly east of that river, it was necessary to resume the lands first.[26] He took up the investigation in season 1852-53 employing Mr. Beckett, one of his surveyors, to point out the boundaries, since the properties were so intermixed as to render it difficult to identify them without professional aid.[27] The adjustments effected are here briefly explained, beginning at the west and proceeding eastwards.

221. Lots 1, 4, 5, and 9 and Belpukhuriya: Belpukhuriya, a patitabadi mahall, contained 532 bighas at the decennial settlement, but the talukdars extended their cultivation into the jungle. It was measured in 1816 and 7,244 bighas taufir discovered, which were made the subject of resumption proceedings, and were finally decreed by the Special Commissioner on 24th December 1829. The mahall was against measured in 1824-25 when 7,117 bighas fresh taufir were discovered, for which also proceedings were instituted, and ended in favour of Government of 15th March 1830. The talukdars, however, encroached further after 1825 on the lands which Prinsep had divided into lots 1, 4, 5 and 9 (following Hodges' numbering), and four resumption suits for an aggregate area of 22,000 bighas in those lots were begun, which were decreed in favour of Government by the Special Commissioner's court on 12th February 1850. This last area included the 7,117 bighas above mentioned, which were thus decreed twice over. Lots 1, 4, and 5 were granted out in 1830 without inquiry into their condition. Mr. Reily, the Assistant, detected further encroachments in 1831, and adding them to the above two parcels of taufir, 14,362 bighas, proceeded to settle the whole 17,709 bighas; but

[26] Presdy. Commr. to Sbn. Commr., no. 31Ct., dated 22 Nov. 1852, and no. 16, dated 22 Jan. 1853.

[27] Sbn. Commr. to Presdy. Commr., no. 485, dated 12 Nov. 1853.

Mr. Dampier disapproved; and ordered that the lot lands should be excluded. The lots, however, had been abandoned by the grantees, and at the settlement in 1834 the confusion was only partially remedied. The taufir—14,362 bighas—and the cleared portions of the lots were amalgamated, and the mahall with a total area of 17,515 bighas was settled by Mr. Dampier as two estates—Nij Belpukhuriya (15,329 bighas) and Arunnagar (2,186 bighas). Nij Belpukhuriya was sold for arrears of revenue and bought by Government in 1837-38 and held khass by the Collector, but partially deteriorated. He farmed it out in 1846. The grants of lots 1, 4, and 5 were cancelled in 1847 and the lots were sold afresh in 1848 professedly exclusive of the cultivated portions that were annexed to Belpukhuriya. But boundary disputes arose and the grantee of lot 4 sued the farmer and got a decree for a certain quantity of land. Uma Kanta Babu had the lands surveyed, and investigating the disputes found that Belpukhuriya contained 8,654 bighas of lot lands in 1851, viz. 1,681 bighas of lot 1,1,206 bighas of lost 4,2,932 bighas of lot 5, and 2,835 bighas of lot 9.[28] The Board held that the lots had been really sold in their original entirety and decided the disputes by ordering that the above cleared portions of lots 1, 4, and 5 should be made over to the grantees; the farm of Belpukuriya adjusted; and the lands of lot 9 reincorporated with that lot, and the whole granted to the farmer. These arrangements were carried into effect from 1851. The clearances in lots 1, 4 and 5 were assessed at once with revenue and settled for 20 years: the farm was readjusted and fixed for 29 years: but in lot 9 the arrangements were modified, for 871 bighas of it had been settled with Lakhipur, and 2,835 bighas with Belpukhuriya in 1834. Those portions were left unaltered, and the remainder 5,294 bighas (of which 1,178 were newly reclaimed), was settled with the farmer of Belpukhuriya in perpetuity—the reclaimed land under a raiyatwari assessment and the forest on jangalburi terms.[29]

[28] Ibid., no. 218, dated 11 June, and no. 529, dated 2 Nov. 1850; no. 177, dated 8 May, no. 236, dated 17 June, and no. 306, dated 23 July 1851. Mullins' statement dated 5 June 1850.

[29] Ibid., no. 407, dated 15 Sept. 1851. Presdy. Commr. to Sbn. Commr., no. 102, dated 3 July, and no. 19 Ct., dated 17 Nov. 1851; no. 8, dated 17 Jan., and no. 22, dated 10 Feb. 1852. Sbn. Commr. to Presdy. Commr., no. 514, dated 28 Nov. 1853.

222. Lots 10, 13, and 14: Lots 10 had not been granted out, but 944 bighas of it were found reclaimed at the survey in 1850. The cleared portion was settled on the usual jangalburi terms with the abadkar in 1851, and the forest portion disposed of under the grant rules of 1853.[30] There appear to have been no special proceedings about lot 13. Lot 14 had been encroached on by Kadua, and the Collector settled the reclaimed portion with the mahall in 1852-53. Uma Kanta Babu remonstrated, but the Presidency Commissioner decided that the proceedings having been completed could not be reopened.[31]

223. Lot 16 and Bhajna: Bhajna, which bordered on lot 16, had been settled in 1838 with an area of 4,141 bighas, which comprised part of the lot. According to Smyth's survey, the talukdar held 1,338 bighas outside and 1,596 bighas inside the lot. The Presidency Commissioner ordered in 1854 that the deficiency, 1,207 bighas, should be supplemented from the waste land of the lot, and the remainder of the lot disposed of under the grant rules.[32] The portion 1,207 bighas appears to have been demarcated off in 1855-56 by Mr. Surveyor Joseph.

224. Lot 17 and Gangadharpur: Gangadharpur, which had been settled in 1833 with an area of 6,676 bighas, was found in 1850 to have encroached on lot 17. It then contained 9,361 bighas, that is 2,685 bighas taufir, while 6,653 bighas of the mahall were lands of the lot. The whole area, old and taufir, was settled with the talukdar in 1852 in perpetuity from 1851, and Gangadharpur appears to have swallowed up the lot.[33]

225. Lots 19 and 20, and Bhagabanpur and Sarasbariya: Sarasbariya and first Bhagabanpur adjoined lot 19, and had encroached on it, so Mr. Dampier included portions of it in those mahalls at the settlement of 1834. The lot was granted out in 1838 and relinquished in 1840. Meanwhile the mahalls remained khas under the Collector till 1847, when they were farmed out together, with a total area of

[30] Presdy. Commr. to Sbn. Commr., no. 36, dated 17 Feb. 1852 and no. 172, dated 5 Aug. 1852.

[31] Ibid., no. 291, dated 8 Nov. 1853.

[32] Ibid., no. 2, dated 4 Jan. 1854.

[33] Ibid., no. 97, dated 4 June 1852.

5,752 bighas. Smyth's survey shewed that the farmer held only 4,505 bighas outside the lot, but claimed 910 bighas or more inside it, and the Deputy Collector of Survey incorporated this land in first Bhagabanpur. The full area of the mahall appears to have been made good from the lands of the lot, and the remainder of the lot also to have been settled with the farmer in 1854-55.[34] Part of lot 20 also, 357 bighas, was found by the Babu in 1850 to have been reclaimed by the same farmer. It was left as a portion of first Bhagabanpur, and the remainder, 1,643 bighas, was also settled with him in 1851 in perpetuity.[35]

226. Lot 21, and Kishtarampur: Part of lot 21 was found in 1850 to have been cleared under leases from the talukdars of Kishtarampur. Settlement of the lot was offered them, but they refused. The cultivated portion, 1,569 bighas, was then settled with the abadkar in 1851 in perpetuity, and the jungle portion was disposed of on the promulgation of the 1853 rules.[36]

227. Lots 22, 23, 24, 26, and 27, and Khari: Khari had been originally settled with an area of 8,258 bighas, but the talukdar encroached on the jungle, and 6,819 bighas were resumed as *taufir* in 1830. It was settled with him by Mr. Dampier, who granted him lot 27 also. He cleared the north portion of the lot, but Khari, that is, the taufir estate, was sold in 1849, and the purchaser appears to have taken possession of the cleared land in lot 27 as part of the mahall. Taufir Khari had been encroaching on the other jungle lands around, and the Collector resettled it in 1850 with an area of 13,425 bighas. This area was found by Smyth's survey to be composed as explained below:

[34] Sbn. Commr. to Presdy. Commr., no. 62, dated 21 Feb. 1854. Presdy. Commr. to Sbn. Commr., no. 129, dated 5 Jan., and no. 208, dated 4 Apr. 1855.

[35] Sbn. Commr. to Presdy. Commr., no. 528, dated 2 Nov. 1850. Presdy. Commr. to Sbn. Commr., no. 94, dated 17 June and no. 133, dated 28 July 1851.

[36] Sbn. Commr. to Presdy. Commr., no. 528, dated 2 Nov. 1850, and no. 531, dated 6 Dec. 1851. Presdy. Commr. to Sbn. Commr., no. 94, dated 17 June 1851; no. 131, dated 8 July; and no. 167, dated 2 Aug. 1852.

			Bighas
Taufir Khari			5,079
Lands of lot	22		2,296
Ditto	23		2,627
Lands of lots	24 and 26		500
Lands of lot	27		3,763
		Total	14,265

The grantee of lot 22 at once claimed the land of which he had been deprived, and the inquiry was committed to the Sundarban Commissioner.[37] In deciding that matter, the case as regarded the other lots was brought into prominence. The difficulty in lot 22 was disposed of by the Board offering the grantee, whose lot was liable to resumption, ten years' extension of the free period on condition he renounced all claim to the portion in Khari. He accepted the terms, and the dispute was silenced in 1851.[38] The encroachments in lots 23, 24 and 26 do not appear to have received any attention, and matters remained as they were. As regards lot 27, the Government bund which cut off the 3,763 bighas in dispute from the lot was taken as the boundary between Khari and the lot: the land remained with the talukdar, and the grantee received a commuted patta under the rules 1853.[39]

228. Lot 31 and Kharbil: The Rani Sankari Dasi, zamindar of Kharbil, and Baidyanath Bose who got 1,001 bighas of resumed lakhiraj had both cleared parts of lot 31 and received settlement of their portions in November 1832. The latter, however, continued to encroach. The lot was surveyed by Mullins in 1847, but the Rani impugned the accuracy of his survey, and the Presidency Commissioner ordered a resurvey by Mr. Smith in the presence of the Sundarban

[37] Presdy. Commr. to Sbn. Commr., no. 165, dated 4 Sept. 1850.

[38] Sbn. Commr. to Presdy. Commr., no. 489, dated 7 Oct. 1850, and no. 550, dated 16 Dec. 1851. Collr. 24-Parganas, to Sbn. Commr., no. 168A, dated 13 March 1851. Presdy. Commr., to Sbn. Commr., no. 28, dated 8 Feb. 1851, and nos. 185 and 187, both dated 21 Aug. 1852.

[39] Presdy. Commr. to Sbn. Commr., no. 299, dated 17 Nov. 1853, and no. 105, dated 16 Nov. 1854. I have excluded the original area of Khari and adjusted the other areas.

Commissioner. During 1849-50 the boundary of the lot was defined by Uma Kanta Babu and surveyed by Captain Smyth. Bighas 1,198 of new clearance were settled with the abadkar in 1850 for 24 years.[40]

229. Lots 30, 32, and 33, and Shahzadpur: Lots 30, 32, and 33 were granted out in 1830, but Mr. Dampier afterwards settled 6,266 bighas of the lands of the lots in Shahzadpur. On survey in 1849-50 the talukdar was found to be in possession of 8,253 bighas (of which 2,346 were in lot 30 and 5,907 in lot 32), while the grantee had the remainder of the lots; but matters were left unaltered, there being no dispute. In 1853, however, the Presidency Commissioner ordered that 7,389 bighas should be included in the mahall, and the rest remain with the grantee. Subsequently one party ousted the other, and litigation ensued.[41]

230. Lots 34, 35, and 41, and Bantra and Rajapur: Lots 34 and 35 had been encroached upon by patitabadi taluk Bantra, and were altogether included in that estate by Mr. Dampier's settlement. The lots were thus practically removed from the Sundarban area, but for the sake of uniformity were shewn in Captain Smyth's survey as appertaining to the Sundarbans. Taluks Bantra and Rajapur Karabag also encroached on the adjacent lot 41, which was ungranted, and were found in 1852-53 to hold 1,112 and 551 bighas respectively of the lot land. Under the Presidency Commissioner's orders 3,468 bighas were given up from the lot to make good the proper areas of the taluks, and the rest of the lot separated by a defined boundary was to be granted ijmali to both talukdars. Mr. Reily, Sundarbans Commissioner, found, however, in 1856 that they held 7,544 bighas more land than was mentioned in their dowl, and the settlement appears to have been revised in 1856-57.[42]

231. Lots 44 and 45, and Bantra and Dharmtala: Bantra (with mauza Dharmtala containing 1,068 bighas) was settled in 1835; lot 44 was granted out in 1830, but the grantee did not take possession,

[40] Sbn. Commr. to Presdy. Commr., no. 527, dated 2 Nov. 1850, and no. 302, dated 18 July 1851. Presdy. Commr. to Sbn. Commr., dated 18 Dec. 1850.

[41] Sbn. Commr. to Presdy. Commr., no. 495, dated 23 Oct. 1850. Presdy. Commr. to Sbn. Commr., no. 97, dated 21 Feb. 1851.

[42] Presdy. Commr. to Sbn. Commr., no. 3 Ct., dated 13 Feb. 1854, and no. 199, dated 7 Oct. 1856.

and meanwhile the talukdar of Bantra encroached on it calling the clearance chak Dharmtala, and the holder of the chak under the talukdar in his turn encroached on lot 45, which had also been granted out in 1830-31. Disputes then arose and inquiries were made by Smith and Mullins in 1848, and by Uma Kanta Babu in 1849. The talukdar was found to have 1,893 bighas new taufir in Dharmtala and to have encroached on lot 44 to the extent of 3,942 bighas. Uma Kanta Babu defined the boundaries of both lots in 1849, settled the two parcels of encroachment with the talukdar in 1850, and gave the grantee of lot 44 (which seems to have been resumed) a new patta for the jungle area 6,558 bighas. The Sadar Court, which then exercised the powers of the Special Commissioner, confirmed his definition of the boundaries, and under its orders he recorded a formal resumption of the above mentioned 1,893 bighas.[43]

232. Lot 45 and Kalajangal: Nayan Chand Bose, a patitabadi talukdar, encroached on lot 45 which had been granted out in 1830-31, and also on lot 51 which was ungranted, and his clearances were settled in 1836 as a separate mahall under the name Kalajangal with an area of 4,129 bighas. Mr. Adams, the grantee of lot 45, sued the talukdar of Kalajangal in the civil court to recover possession of 2,295 bighas as appertaining to his lot and gained a decree in 1845, Government admitting his claim. On the execution of the decree the taluk fell into arrears, and the talukdar applied for remission. The Presidency Commissioner ordered in 1847 or 1848 that the remainder of the mahall—1,830 bighas—should be settled with the talukdar, but he declined (though Mr. Smith offered him a fair readjustment in 1848) and brought a suit against Government for 1,437 bighas. It failed entirely, being dismissed on appeal in 1856. The Presidency Commissioner then ordered a survey of the three lots 45, 46 and 51.[44] There was also a dispute regarding 1,438 bighas between the grantee

[43] Sbn. Commr. to Presdy. Commr., no. 317, dated 26 July 1850; no. 237, dated 17 June 1851; and no. 214, dated 21 May 1853. There were further resumption and settlement proceedings regarding Dharmtala in 1858—see Sbn. Commr. to Presdy. Commr., no. 4, dated 30 Apr. 1858, and no. 171, dated 7 March 1859.

[44] Sbn. Commr. to Presdy. Commr., no. 279, dated 19 Aug. 1840; no. 208, dated 28 Apr. 1849; and no. 291, dated 12 July 1853. Presdy. Commr. to Sbn. Commr., no. 40, dated 23 May 1856.

of lot 51 and the grantee of lots 45, 46, and 47, which was decided against the former by the civil court in 1856.[45]

233. Lot 52 and Zamindari Lands: In lot 52 there was a dispute regarding three small patches of land. One piece of 110 bighas was assigned to the lot and the others to the zamindar, and the grant was revised in 1852.[46]

234. Boundary Disputes East of the River Bidyadhari; and the Attitude Maintained by Government in Civil Suits: Beyond the Bidyadhari the boundary ran through cleared lands where the zamindars and grantees were alike fully alive to their rights, as mentioned in paragraph 197, and there was no scope for amicable adjustment by Government. Both sides therefore were left to the usual remedies in the civil court. Still Government, being generally made a party to the suits in its character of proprietor of the Sundarbans, was able to support whichever side appeared to be in the right. This principle of action was established in the case of lot 76, one of the first instances where litigation had followed Mr. Mullins' demarcation of the boundary in 1842. Some of the disputes between the zamindar and grantee were carried into the civil court,[47] but one claim for 16 bighas was decided by the Presidency Commissioner in favour of the grantee, and the zamindar at once brought a civil suit to establish his title. The Legal Remembrancer then expressed his opinion that "all squabbles between zamindars and abadkars after these last have once been put in possession of their grants should be settled in the civil courts, to which tribunal parties petitioning the revenue authorities should be referred."[48] His view was approved and communicated to the Sundarban Commissioner. Disputes of this kind arose in the cases of lots 55,[49] 61,[50] 71, 72, 73,[51] 76,[52] and 98[53] and in some of them efforts were made to

[45] Presdy. Commr. to Sbn. Commr., no. 347, dated 9 Apr. 1856.
[46] Ibid., no. 193, dated 23 July 1853.
[47] Ibid., no. 217, dated 13 Aug., and no. 14 Ct., dated 30 Nov. 1853.
[48] Ibid., no. 20 Ct., dated 21 Dec. 1853.
[49] Ibid., no. 42 Ct., dated 3 Sept. 1857.
[50] Sbn. Commr. to Presdy. Commr., no. 84, dated 11 Sept. 1860.
[51] Presdy. Commr. to Sbn. Commr., no. 124, dated 11 Aug. 1856.
[52] Ibid., no. 217, dated 13 Aug. 1853.
[53] Sbn. Commr. to Presdy Commr., no. 18, dated 10 Jan. 1854.

settle the disputes by means of surveys, but as neither party was bound thereby, the attempt was dropped, the Board laying it down in the cases of lots 71-73 in 1856 that it was the province of the civil court to decide disputes, and the duty of Government merely extended to the production of the requisite maps in court. These principles have guided the Sundarban officers since, and when a dispute has arisen in which Government has been implicated, an inquiry or survey has been made to ascertain the state of matters and the position of Government as regarded them.

235. Boundary Disputes between Grantees: Very similar to these were disputes between grantees regarding their common boundaries, one party in the course of reclamation having advanced beyond a common line boundary, or the existence of two khals at the boundary rendering it open to dispute. Of the former description was the dispute between the grantees of lots 56 and 60, where, at the request of the latter grantee, the boundary was defined in 1852, and the former grantee protested. The Board pronounced the action irregular, observing that "after possession of a lot has been given and the settlement sanctioned, the Commissioner of the Sundarbans has no longer any authority to interfere." But they modified the order in 1853 by permitting him to define the boundary of one lot, provided he did not interfere with that of the other, or in other words they allowed him to survey the *de facto* boundary between the lots.[54] Among disputes regarding khal boundaries, the case of lots 100 and 104 is the most important. These lots were declared to be devided by the Kakradoaniya khal, but two channels existed to which that name was given, and between them lay a parcel of land containing about bighas 8,000, which the grantee of lot 104 had taken possession of. The grantee of lot 100 applied to have the boundary defined, and surveys were made. The Presidency Commissioner, acting on the above ruling, held that the matter was one for the civil court alone,[55] but the Board here ruled in 1857 that no suit having been instituted, the Sundarban Commissioner had power to and should decide the dispute under section 2, clause (3) of Regulation IX of 1825, there being no legal difference between

[54] Ibid., no. 171, dated 4 Aug. 1852, and no. 31, dated 5 Feb. 1853.

[55] Ibid., no. 135. dated 21 Aug. 1856.

granted and ungranted Sundarban lands, since section 2, clause (6) and the 33 following sections of Regulation VII of 1822 applied to all Sundarban lands, whether under settlement or not.[56] Mr. Gomess then surveyed and reported that the disputed land belonged to lot 100. The parties, however, went to law, and the litigation was protracted till 1880, when the Privy Council finally adjudged the land to lot 104. The Legal Remembrancer repeated his advice in 1855 that after possession had once been obtained by abadkars, Government should not interfere, but that all disputes should be left to the decision of the civil courts.[57] This course was thenceforward observed, and in fact a decision by the Sundarban Commissioner had no binding force on the parties, and might involve Government in law-suits.[58]

[56] Ibid., no. 34 Ct., dated 3 March 1857.

[57] Ibid., no. 219, dated 4 Jan. 1856.

[58] See Presdy. Commr. to Sbn. Commr., no. 126 Ct., dated 25 Dec. 1857; and also Presdy. Commr. to Sbn. Commr., no. 8 Ct., dated 14 June 1858, where Govt. was condemned in its own costs for not remaining neutral.

CHAPTER XVIII

Resumptions, Inquiries, Jurisdiction, etc.
1844-1857

236. Sundarban and Presidency Officers, 1846-56: From 1846 the Sundarban Commissioner always had abundance of help. Mr. A.T. Smith, Deputy Collector, was appointed to the Sundarbans in April 1846, and remained for years, and being a professional surveyor he was a doubly useful officer. A second Deputy Collector was provided in 1848, and for many years afterwards, though the individuals were incessantly changing. Babu Isan Chandra Datt served from February to July 1848. Mr. Allan followed him from December 1848 to August 1849. Mr. Caspersz came next in September 1849 till about the middle of 1850. Mr. Ross returned to the Sundarbans from December 1850 to June 1851. After a few days' charge by Mr. Hough in October 1851, Babu Jay Narayan Das came in December 1851 and remained for some time, Mr. Mullins was the surveyor all these years till 1852. Mr. Harvey was Presidency Commissioner till nearly the end of 1850. After a short interval Mr. Bruce became Commissioner in March 1851 and held the office till October 1853. He was succeeded by Mr. Bidwell, who retained it (except during the latter part of 1855) till March 1856. Mr. Grote succeeded him. Mr. W. Dampier became Member of the Board of Revenue about the middle of 1855, and his thorough local knowledge was most beneficial in deciding questions of boundaries and other difficult matters.

237. Resumption Jurisdiction, 1846: On the abolition of the office in 1844 one of the chief subjects to which Uma Kanta Babu's attention was directed[1] was the identification resumption, and assessment of the 135 mahalls contained in Mr. Donnelly's list of 1836,[2] but pressure of other duties, which he had to carry out single-handed

[1] Presdy. Commr. to Sbn. Commr., no. 549, dated 2 Dec. 1844.

[2] See paragraphs 115 and 116.

prevented him from taking them up. The Government announced its earnest desire in August 1845 that the harassing operations under the resumption laws should be brought to a close.[3] On the re-establishment of the Commission in 1846, the list of pending resumption suits was overhauled. All suits regarding alluvial lands were stopped in January 1846.[4] In March Government ordered that the Revenue Commissioners should examine the resumption files of their subordinates and stop all cases unless there was clear evidence of the right of Government. Collectors were instructed to decide all pending suits by the close of the year, and no fresh suits were to be instituted without the Board's previous sanction.[5] The total then pending before the Sundarban Commissioner was 55 of which 20 were struck off, and the remainder ordered to be quickly disposed of,[6] but 16 new cases were sanctioned.[7] The jurisdiction of the Special Commissioner appears to have been largely curtailed in 1845-46, though it was not abolished till April 1852. The Government in its resolution dated 15th April 1852 announced that from the date of its promulgation, "the jurisdiction of Special Commissioners appointed under Regulation III of 1828 shall cease, except in regard to the disposal of such cases as may be on that date pending before them, or in regard to disputes originating in the execution of decrees that may have been passed by them," and that the procedure would thenceforth be governed by Regulation II of 1819.[8] During the interval, however, the Sadar Court at first and afterwards the District Judges exercised the powers of the Special Commissioners, though these officers continued to dispose of small routine arrears. After their abolition their jurisdiction appears to have been exercised by the District Judges.

238. Henckell's and Donnelly's Mahalls, 1846: Uma Kanta Babu without, it seems, any direct sanction brought upon the Sundarban

[3] Bd. Rev., Cir. no. 16, dated 18 Aug. 1845.
[4] Presdy. Commr. to Sbn. Commr., no. 3, dated 14 Jan. 1846.
[5] Ibid., no. 33, dated 28 March 1846.
[6] Ibid., no. 32, dated 21 Apr. 1846.
[7] Ibid., no. 34, dated 22 Apr. 1846.
[8] Bd. Rev., Cir. No. 9, dated 4 May 1852.

statements all the mahalls mentioned in Mr. Donnelly's lists of 1832.[9] Most of them needed identification and resumption, till when they could scarcely be under his jurisdiction except in name. He appears to make no reference to Mr. Donnelly's revised list of 1836, which had been sent to him in 1844 for investigation. The preference of the former had nothing, as far as can be perceived, to support it. The volume of ostensible work was increased, the 1832 lists being much fuller, but they were in a measure obsolete, for many of the mahalls named in them had been already resumed. The mahalls were thenceforward designated "Donnelly's mahalls." Their total was 241, but it is not clear how it was made up, for the mahalls in the 1832 lists, on the fullest computation that the present documents permit, do not exceed 183 in number. Besides them Uma Kanta Babu also brought on a large quantity of Henckell's patta lands, to the number of about 102 (including the well-known mahalls), but here again it is uncertain how the figures were obtained, for Mr. Henckell granted away not less than 150 pattas. Although these mahalls of both kinds had been the subject of much investigation by Uma Kanta Babu's predecessors, yet the fact is not noticed, nor does it seem to have had any bearing on his proceedings. He was not acquainted with English, yet that does not constitute a full explanation, for he had Deputy Collectors under him who knew English well. The old correspondence, however, that Mr. Grant had amassed appears to have been neglected after Mr. Kemp's departure.

239. Resumption Proceedings, 1846-50: The investigation of Henckell's and Donnelly's mahalls was one of the ordinary duties of the Sundarban officers during the years 1846-50, but little appears to have been achieved, other matters generally getting the preference. In fact the subject, though constituting an imposing branch of their duties and demanding persevering efforts, received no diligent attention. It does not appear that any of the mahalls were identified during those years. As regards resumption suits, a few only were decreed in favour of Government; but even in those cases, the practical gain was insignificant. Raghunathdih in Bakarganj was resumed on 17th March

[9] Sbn. Commr. to Presdy. Commr., no. 75, dated 20 March 1850—see paragraph 84.

1846, without any preliminary investigation, as one of Henckell's patta mahalls, and no appeal being preferred, the resumption became final. The mahall was identified according to its boundaries, and found to comprise 24,000 bighas, while Henckell's patta was for 85 bighas merely. Up to 1857 six Deputy Collectors had failed to execute the decree and on the case being then reported, the Board at once quashed all the proceedings and released the lands.[10] Bowliyaghata was resumed by the Special Commissioner on 14th January 1848, without boundaries, and so also Neapota, Dowli, Boaliya and Rajpur about the same time. The four latter were found after inquiry in 1856 to be in lots 209, 212, and 214 and only the first to lie outside lot 212, but all were dense jungle and incapable of settlement.[11] Nagarjamira, just outside lot 212, was resumed by the Sundarban Commissioner on 29th July 1850; and on 27th December 1850 Badanhaldarber in Salimabad which Mr. Smith discovered while surveying Kharoikhali. Ragua appears to have been resumed a second time by Uma Kanta Babu in 1847, but portions of it were released by the Revenue Commissioner in 1857, 1861, and 1864, leaving, however, a part which was brought under settlement in 1865.

240. Position of Resumption Proceedings, 1850: The Government had re-established the Commission since its abolition had brought no advantage, still its working was closely watched and the outturn of work citicized and contrasted with the money expended. The results did not satisfy the Government. In 1850 the Board called for a report on the operations in the Sundarbans.[12] Uma Kanta Babu replied to the best of his knowledge,[13] but the information was very little fuller than what he had given in 1845, and reveals what trifling progress had been made in the knowledge of Henckell's and Donnelly's mahalls, though they had been under consideration for nearly six years. All his knowledge of Henckell's mahalls was derived from the register of Henckell's pattas and the resettlements which he had recently conducted of Henckell's well-known taluks, that is the

[10] Presdy. Commr. to Sbn. Commr., no. 30 Ct., dated 14 Feb. 1857.

[11] Sbn. Commr., to Presdy. Commr., no. 353, dated 27 Sept. 1856. Presdy. Commr. to Sbn. Commr., no. 293, dated 11 Apr. 1857.

[12] Presdy. Commr. to Sbn. Commr., no. 96, dated 1 July 1850.

[13] Sbn. Commr. to Presdy. Commr., no. 298, dated 15 July 1850.

earliest and latest facts, while all intermediate operations were wrapped in oblivion. His knowledge of Donnelly's mahalls was gained from Donnelly's lists and the circumstances of a few of the mahalls which had been resumed. Donnelly's mahalls were, he explained, more numerous than Henckell's, but smaller in size, though the areas of those that had been discovered exceeded Donnelly's estimate. Their number, 241, as brought on the Sundarban statements in 1846 was reduced by corrections to 229, of which five had been resumed and two released, leaving 222 for inquiry in 1850. The identification of Henckell's and Donnelly's mahalls was an undertaking of great difficulty, for their boundaries were not always specified, and even when specified were often uncertain or indefinite. He described the endless local inquiries, measurements, and surveys which were indispensable preliminaries, and after the land had been identified, the perplexing and frequently unsuccessful resumption proceedings. He recommended the completion of the investigations, and, deprecating the employment of highly paid Deputy Collectors and professional surveyors, urged that amins should be used in all matters of measurement, except where grants had to be made and estates permanently settled.

241. Review and Report by the Board, 1850: The Board submitted their Report No. 612, regarding the operations in the Sundarbans to Government on 20th December 1850. They noticed that the cost of the staff had increased through the employment of an extra Deputy Collector and then proceeded to review the state of business. They divided all Sundarban mahalls under six heads, thus:

I. Henckell's mahalls, total 102, of which 17 were settled, 6 were khass, and 79 remained for identification and resumption. Regarding these, they summarized Uma Kanta Babu's remarks, and expressed their opinion that the inquiries should be either forwarded vigorously or abandoned altogether. Meanwhile as a tentative measure they propose to employ five amins to inquire into a selected case.

II. Sundarban grants, total number granted 141.

III. Lots not yet granted, 95 in number.

IV. Mahalls cultivated by persons without grants, and resumed under the Regulations; total 323. These were all settled in one way or another, except 10 which were jungle and 2 which could not be traced. With reference to these the Board authorised the Sundarban Commissioner to dispense with the professional survey that had been insisted upon prior to settlement, and admitted the sufficiency of a measurement by amins.

V. Mahalls for which abadkari *amalnamas* had been granted without the authority of Government, 20 in number, and in Bakarganj. These were in course of regular settlement or grant.

VI. Donnelly's mahalls, total 229, of which seven had been disposed of and 222 remained for identification and resumption. Here the Board summarized Uma Kanta Babu's remarks and urged that these mahalls should be dealt with like Henckell's mahalls. They proposed to have five cases inquired into by amins as a tentative measure.

The then Sundarban revenue amounted to Rs. 3,08,214, and the cost of the Commissioner was about 10 per cent on it. There was in the Board's opinion abundance of work, especially in the way of surveys, so they recommended the appointment of two more surveyors.[14]

242. Orders of Government; Fresh Surveyors Appointed, 1851: The President in Council was not satisfied with the work done, but sanctioned, in May 1851, the employment of two assistant surveyors and five amins from year to year, to dispose of the business speedily.[15] The Board had already, in January 1851, ordered the Sundarban Commissioner to entertain five amins to trace out the mahalls at once, and to leave nothing undone that it was important to do quickly.[16] Messrs. Beckett and Gomess were appointed assistant surveyors and joined their posts in November and December 1851, and their services being found indispensable they were continued for several years. Mr. Beckett was transferred in October 1853. Mr. Mullins having been removed, Mr. Gomess succeeded to the substantive post of Sundarban Surveyor, and Mr. Joseph replaced Mr. Beckett in December 1853, and remained till 1856.

[14] Presdy. Commr. to Sbn. Commr., no. 15, dated 22 Jan. 1851.
[15] Ibid., no. 100, dated 3 July 1851.
[16] Ibid., no. 15, dated 22 Jan. 1851.

243. Classification of Sundarban Estates, 1851: Till that time all Sundarban mahalls had been divided into two classes—"mahalls the property of Government," and "mahalls not the property of Government;" but the import attached to the word *property* is not quite clear. They were so classed in the annual returns in two statements A and B respectively, whence they were also called A and B mahalls. After the foregoing report by the Board, however, the arrangement was revised in 1851. Government directed that "Sundarban mahalls when settled with the abadkars or other parties entitled to settlement shall be dealt with as the property of individuals. These when settled and transferred to the Collectors were excluded from the Sundarban returns and appeared in the district returns. The mahalls that remained were included in one statement and arranged under the six heads described by the Board. A reconsideration of the statement shewed that the concurrent but independent operations of the Collector and Sundarban Commissioner[17] in the locality of lots 217-220 had led to the counting of 61 of Donnelly's mahalls twice over; so Donnelly's list was revised. The number of both kinds of mahalls then stood thus in 1851—Henckell's mahalls, 81 for investigation; Donnelly's mahalls, 165 for investigation.[18]

244. Inquiries by Amins, 1851-53: The five amins sanctioned in January 1851 were employed that season. They traced out eight Henckell's and eleven Donnelly's mahalls that had been selected for investigation. The former consisted of 16 chaks, for seven of which resumption suits were instituted, while the rest were doubtful as they lay beyond the Sundarban boundary. Similarly suits were begun for nine of the Donnelly's mahalls, and two were doubtful. The Board ordered that the eleven doubtful cases should be brought on the file and disposed of according to rule.[19] The amins were re-employed the next season and identified 20 of Henckell's mahalls (of which six cases comprised 17 chaks) with an area of 73,725 bighas, and 48 of Donnelly's mahalls with an area of 55,790 bighas: 18 and 36 were

[17] Ibid., no. 86, dated 31 May, and no. 139, dated 29 July 1851.

[18] Sbn. Commr. to Presdy. Commr., no. 349, dated 19th Aug. 1851.

[19] Ibid., no. 397, dated 10 Sept. 1851. Presdy. Commr. to Sbn. Commr., no. 3 Ct., dated 23 Oct., and no. 25 Ct., dated 28 Nov. 1851.

respectively likely to be resumed.[20] They were again employed in season 1852-53 and identified, it seems, 39 of Henckell's and 74 of Donnelly's mahalls, of which nine (1,59,900 bighas) and 19 (23,600 bighas) respectively were likely to be resumed.[21] During these years Uma Kanta Babu and Mr. Smith had also been making inquiries, while tahsildars and informers had contributed their aid, and by the end of season 1852-53 the preliminary investigations had been carried out in all except 33 of Henckell's and Donnelly's mahalls.[22]

245. Suits, and Orders Regarding Them, 1851-54: Suits were next instituted for the lands, and the number under trial at the beginning of the year 1853-54 was—Henckell's mahalls, 56 for an estimated area of 2,99,550 bighas; Donnelly's mahalls, 101 for an area of 94,585 bighas; and other mahalls (cleared clandestinely or taufir), 35 for an area of 1,03,990 bighas.[23] There remained, however, 28 of Henckell's and 33 of Donnelly's mahalls, which though identified were not then brought on the resumption file.[24] The Board and the Government were kept fully informed of the progress attained and were acquainted with the character of the undertaking. In 1852 the Board reported to the Government that a number of the suits were likely to be successful from the circumstance that the lands bordered resumed Sundarban estates, while the rest were doubtful, since the lands were situated at a distance from the Sundarban boundary; but the liability of all the mahalls to assessment depended entirely on the failure of their holders to prove their exemption, either on the score of the lands being already included in the decennial settlement, or on other similar cogent grounds.[25] The preliminary inquiries having been carried through, and the lands brought to the next stage—that of trial by suits—the Board endeavoured to expedite these proceedings in September 1853. There were eight appeals pending before the

[20] Ibid., no. 213, dated 16 June, and no. 411, dated 24 Sept. 1852. Presdy. Commr. to Sbn. Commr., no. 10 Ct., dated 2 Sept. 1852.

[21] Sbn. Commr. to Presdy. Commr., no. 281, dated 7 July 1853.

[22] See list in Sbn. Commr. to Presdy. Commr., no. 334, dated 8 Aug. 1853.

[23] Sbn. Commr. to Presdy. Commr., no. 228, dated 5 June 1853, which gives a fair analysis of the cases.

[24] Presdy, Commr. to Sbn. Commr., no. 261. dated 18 Oct. 1853.

[25] Ibid., no. 228, dated 9 Dec. 1852.

Presidency Commissioner, and the Board directed him to dispose of them forthwith so as to acquaint himself with the nature of these resumption cases, and form an opinion on their value, and according to the issue of those appeals to have all the other cases (whether instituted or to be instituted) prosecuted without delay or abandoned. The Board were not satisfied with the Sundarban administration. Hence Mr. Bruce, the Presidency Commissioner, who thought otherwise, ordered, in October 1853, that diaries should be kept by Sundarban officers of their business while in the field for submission to the Board.[26] The Board subsequently ordered, in 1854, that the proceedings regarding the unidentified mahalls should lie over until the revenue survey reached Jessore.[27]

246. Resumption Proceedings, etc., 1853-57: The resumption suits were proceeded with and now received considerable attention. The duties required were to ascertain the circumstances of the mahalls, discover what evidence could be adduced on behalf of Government, hear the evidence offered by the parties in possession, and decide whether the lands were resumable or not. The suits were distributed among the Sundarban Commissioner and his Deputies, each of whom appears to have conducted all the proceedings up to the adjudication; for the Presidency Commissioner insisted, in December 1854, that these local inquiries should be made by the Sundarban Commissioner or some trustworthy officer, as otherwise he could not decide the cases.[28] But till then nothing solid seems to have been effected. Mr. Bidwell, who succeeded Mr. Bruce as Presidency Commissioner, in October 1853, was not satisfied with Uma Kanta Babu, and proposed, in 1854, to abolish the Commission and divide the duties among the collectorates; but it was too late that year to make any change. During the early years of his tenure of the Sundarbans, Uma Kanta Babu, who had gained the appointment on account of his ability and excellent character, was energetic and busied himself throughout his district, but after he obtained the services of two Deputies continuously, he divided the work, assigning Jessore as a rule to Mr. Smith, making

[26] Ibid., no. 261, dated 18 Oct. 1853.

[27] Bd. Rev. to Presdy. Commr., no. 469, dated 1 Dec. 1854.

[28] Presdy. Commr. to Sbn. Commr., no. 11 Ct, dated 12 Dec. 1854.

arrangements for Bakarganj between the two Deputies and reserving the 24-Parganas for himself. After the year 1849 he rarely went beyond the Kalindi, and his camp was generally pitched at Baroipur; his business during this period was the rectification of the Sundarban boundary in 24-Parganas and the settlement of lands west of the Kalindi.[29] Mr. Bidwell in 1855, modifying his opinion, asked for a new and able officer.[30] The Board agreed with him, and in a report to Government reviewed the requirements of the Sundarbans.[31] Uma Kanta Babu was retired on pension, and Mr. J.H. Reily, Deputy Collector, who had served many years in Jessore and Bakarganj with distinction, succeeded him on 11th October 1855.[32] Better progress was made during the years 1854-55 and 1855-56, and at the end of the latter year the list of suits was reduced to 72, of which 39 were for Henckell's and 31 for Donnelly's mahalls.[33] Mr. Smith was engaged during those seasons and also in 1856-57 in investigating the cases in pargana Jamira and lots 209-16; Cultivation in this region had attained its most flourishing state about 1816, after which all the tract along the rivers Kabadak and Kayra had relapsed into jungle, almost as far north as the Ghoshkhali. The investigations were therefore well-nigh hopeless, 40-years ruin having obliterated all reliable knowledge of names, villages, and boundaries.[34] He succeeded, however, in localizing various mahalls in various portions of the jungle, either inside or outside the Sundarban boundary, but as nothing could be effected, the suits were struck off and the proceedings stayed with the intention, in some instances of renewing them when the lands should be reclaimed in the future.[35] Most of the mahalls sued for were lost. Few appear to

[29] He once went as far as Asasuni The resumption operations lay almost wholly to the east, and he appears to have exercised no real supervision over them.

[30] Uma Kanta Babu held cutchery in the native fashion, reclining on cushions. Sbn. Commr. to Presdy. Commr., no. 86, dated 18 Mar. 1856.

[31] Bd. Rev. to Govt., no. 230A, dated 29 June 1855.

[32] From this time the Sundarban Commissionership carried no fixed pay. It was held by Dy. Collrs. who drew the ordinary pay of their grade and got promotion in the grades in the ordinary way.

[33] Sbn. Commr. to Presdy. Commr., no. 337, dated 13 Sept. 1856.

[34] Morrieson's map is the best guide.

[35] Smith to Sbn. Commr., no. 24. dated 7 Nov. 1857. Presdy. Commr. to Sbn. Commr., no. 82 Ct., dated 17th idem.

have been decreed by the Sundarban officers, and fewer still, if any, on appeal. The evidence on which Henckell's mahalls were released was that they had been included in the Permanent Settlement, that the pattadars were out of possession, and that the lands lay outside Hodges' boundary; but the last was no proof that the lands had been assessed at the decennial settlement.[36] Some new suits were instituted during 1856-57, and the number pending trial at the end of that year was 83, of which 4 were for Sundarban mahalls, 31 for Henckell's and 48 for Donnelly's mahalls; besides which there would seem to have been 72 suits pending then before the Presidency Commissioner, which had been sent up for final adjudication.[37] Alluding to the Board's orders mentioned in paragraph 245, staying the inquiries in the undiscovered lands, Mr. Reily proposed in 1857 to postpone the investigations in those cases till the revenue survey should have been carried into Jessore and Bakarganj, where the greater portion of the mahalls lay, and lists of the mahalls were forwarded to the Superintendent of Survey to see if their boundaries could be traced at the time of survey;[38] but as the Board observed the boundaries of Henckell's mahalls could not be depended on, for they were assigned on *ex parte* statements, the pattadars rarely obtained possession, and most of them were included within the limits of estates permanently settled a few years afterwards.[39]

247. Resumption Rules: In 1854, the six months' grace in cases of resumption allowed by Board's circular no. 7, dated 8th March 1831, was withdrawn from the date on which the office of Special Commissioner for the district was declared to expire, and the assessment was to take effect immediately from the date of the Commissioner's order declaring the lands liable to assessment.[40]

[36] Sbn. Commr. to Presdy. Commr., no. 257, dated 1 July 1856.

[37] Presdy. Commr. to Sbn. Commr., no. 84 Ct, dated 17 Nov. 1857.

[38] Sbn. Commr. to Presdy. Commr., no. 64, dated 18 July 1857.

[39] In the case of Ragunathdih. Presdy. Commr. to Sbn. Commr., no. 30 Ct., dated 14 Feb. 1857.

[40] Presdy. Commr. to Sbn. Commr., no. 28 Ct., dated 24 Feb. 1854.

CHAPTER XIX

Revised Sundarban Grant Rules of 24th September 1853

248. State of Sundarban Grants, 1852: The Board had had the state of the Sundarbans repeatedly under consideration. In connexion with an application for extension of the free period in lots 56 and 72, they called, in May 1852, for a statement of all grants in the Jessore district, and in June following for a statement of all grants in the Sundarbans. The latter was at once submitted by the Sundarban Commissioner, shewing a total of 264 allotments, of which 173 had been granted out, while the rest were undisposed of. The grants were classified thus:[1]

	24-Parganas	*Jessore*	*Bakarganj*	*Total*
Free period expired, assessed and settled	6	4	3	13
Free period expired under settlement	5	1	–	6
Free period extended	37	–	3	40
Original grants unmodified	45	4	19	68
Original pattas cancelled, new grants made	36	3	–	39
Original pattas cancelled, not regranted	5	2	–	7
Total once granted out	134	14	25	173
Ungranted allotments	53	38	–	91
Total allotments	187	52	25	264

[1] Sbn. Commr. to Presdy. Commr., no. 229, dated 26 June 1852. This table is complete for the country as far as the river Pasar (excluding the sea-face), but not beyond that, where no survey had been carried out. Hence no ungranted allotments are assigned to the Bakarganj district, though it contained abundant forest lands undisposed of.

The Presidency Commissioner and Board took these facts into consideration, but meanwhile, when reporting to Government in December 1852 on the annual returns of the Sundarbans, the Board observed that the system of grants had certainly not answered. Clearances had been less than was anticipated; many settlements had broken down; the rent-free term had been extended in nearly all cases where it had expired, and the rents derived from the grants had been next to nothing. Extensive inquiries had been made and were in progress, and the Board hoped shortly to lay before the Government a revised scheme for Sundarban lands.[2]

249. Modifications in Grant Rules Proposed by the Presidency Commissioner, 1852: The Presidency Commissioner Mr. Bruce, in forwarding the foregoing statement to the Board, reviewed the system in force. He disapproved of the long free period as raising illusory expectations in the minds of grantees. The assessment in a great part of the Sundarbans was higher than in the adjacent permanently-settled estates—a circumstance that hampered reclamation in the first instance and also led to the relapse of cultivation and the ruin of the grantee. Two remedies were open, either a general extension of the free period or a reduction of the Government demand. The former was unsatisfactory as no mere extension would reduce the final rate of assessment to a proper standard, while in the interim Government would receive nothing. He therefore preferred the latter remedy. The reduction of the rate from 8 to 4 annas was absolutely necessary in the Jessore portion of the Sundarbans; while a reduction to 5 annas would, he thought, be sufficient in the 24-Parganas where access was readier and the markets nearer, and to 5½ annas in Bakarganj, where, though the markets were distant, reclamation was easier, the water sweeter, and the crops more plentiful. These modifications he recommended as desirable alike in the interests of the Government and the grantees.

250. Modifications Proposed by Grantees: The Board agreed generally with Mr. Bruce's views, but before submitting the matter to Government gave the grantees an opportunity of expressing their sentiments. Some 40 grantees laid a petition before the Board, in which they declared that unless more liberal terms were accorded,

[2] Presdy. Commr. to Sbn. Commr., no. 228, dated 9 Dec. 1852.

Government could never look forward to the general clearance of the Sundarbans in the face of the expense, labour, and risk incurred by the grantees, and the manifest failure of the rules then extant. They asked for the following terms—a free period of 20 years; then an assessment of one anna on half the area for ten years; and thereafter the assessment of the whole area (deducting the irreclaimable portion) at 1 anna for ten years, at 1/2 anna for the next ten years, and afterwards at 2 annas, the maximum rate, in perpetuity: the grant to be liable to forfeiture if one-eighth of the area were not cleared in five years.

251. Review of Sundarban Grant Scheme by the Board, 1852: The Board—Messrs. Gordon, Ricketts, and E. Currie—submitted their Report No. 461 to Government on 14th December 1852, reviewing the history of the grants from the commencement and considering all the views that had been propounded. They began with the proposal put forward by the Board in 1816 to fix 8 annas as the Sundarban rate per the bigha of 110 cubits or 55 yards, which proposal, however, had led to nothing. Next followed the terms of 1819 which were approved by the Government on 19th March 1819, but were not promulgated till 24th March 1825. Those the Board summarized, remarking with regard to the assessment that the ultimate net rate was 8 annas "upon what may be presumed to have been the bigha of 100 [110] cubits measurement". Those rules were in force till 1829 when, on the Board's report, the Government amended them on 8th September. The Board set out the amended rules as advertized on 23rd March 1830. The ultimate rate was 8 annas per bigha, which, though not defined in the rules, was stated in the remeasurement clause of the kabuliyat to be of 80 cubits or 40 yards. Hence the Board remarked "that if the bigha formerly in use was, as has been supposed, one of 110 cubits, the change was in effect tantamount to nearly doubling the rate of assessment proposed by the Board in 1816".[3] These terms

[3] The first rules, promulgated in 1825, had, as far as I can discover, special, if not sole, reference to the allotments in the 24-Parganas. It was the intention of the Govt, that the Sundarban Commissioner should first settle the claims of the State in that district before proceeding east to Jessore and Bakarganj, and in fact Smelt's operations were stopped by orders to that effect. The Board's orders prohibiting the practice of giving leases for forest lands in Jessore were most strict until 1817; and though the prohibition was relaxed in that year as mentioned in paragraph 38, and

applied especially to grants of waste lands in the Sundarbans, but there were besides lands reclaimed from the Sundarbans which had been resumed and assessed at what appeared to have been taken as the rates prevailing in the adjoining parganas, which were generally very low. It was not till 1844 that the Commissioner, Mr. Harvey, represented the anomaly of such lands being assessed at less than the Sundarban grant rate, and thence forward the Sundarban rate of 8 annas per the 40-yard bigha was the rate fixed either immediately or ultimately upon all resumed Sundarban lands open to permanent settlement. Nearly 23 years had elapsed since the rules came into force, but the scheme had proved a total failure. Clearances had been less than was anticipated and the revenue next to nothing; applications for a prolonged rent-free period had been numerous; grants had been repeatedly resumed for failure to cultivate; and the disinclination of parties to take up fresh grants was as great as ever. These facts and certain circumstances reported by the Collector of Jessore had induced the Board to reconsider the whole subject. The results in the resumed mahalls had been markedly different. The Board summed up those results, shewing that the assessment in those mahalls had fairly stood; but they agreed with Mr. Bruce in holding that the resumed mahalls were no criterion by which to judge of the grants proper, since the

---

the Collectors after that again granted leases for the jungle, yet they appear to have acted not upon a definite system, but to have given pattas or *amalnamas* somewhat irregularly for lands within such and such boundaries, as in the case of Maulavi Abdullah mentioned in paragraph 73. For these reasons I cannot help thinking that the Board's statements are mistaken. At any rate the 110-cubit bigha was not generally current in the 24-Parganas, where the prevalent measure was the bigha of 80 cubits or 40 yards square. The 24-Parganas Sundarbans were first divided into allotments by Prinsep in 1822 and 1823, while those in Jessore were not lotted out till 1829 or 1830 by Hodges. Prinsep's bighas were all 40 yards square and so too were Hodges'. The grants in the 24-Parganas were made on Prinsep's areas; hence it seems that the Board's remarks, if correct as to Jessore and Bakarganj, cannot hold good for the grants in the 24-Parganas which, as the table in paragraph 248 shews, constituted more than three-fourths of the total number. To that extent therefore the considerations on which the rules of 1853 were based proceeded from a mistaken view of the circumstances. Smelt's operations of 1816 strictly have no connexion with the subject of Sundarban grants. They were directed to lands reclaimed with or without Henckell's pattas, and his assessment—8 annas per the 55-yards bigha—was imposed on lands that had been actually brought into cultivation and not on jungle lands.

former were generally small, all more or less cultivated prior to the resumption and mostly adjacent to permanently-settled estates by the holders of which they had been reclaimed—in fact they bore little analogy to ordinary Sundarban lands. The Board discussed his views and expressed their general agreement with them. Turning to the proposals put forward by the grantees, the Board pronounced the rates too low, there being nothing in the circumstances to warrant so great a reduction, though many of the grantees' arguments, the failure of the existing system, and the Commissioner's remarks regarding the rates current, all proved that a considerable reduction was necessary. The Government letter, dated 6th August 1816, and the fact that many resumed lands had been measured in 110 cubit bighas both proved in their opinion that the area of grants had been computed in 110 cubit bighas before 1830. The size of the bigha in grants subsequent to 1830 was little more than half the measure current between 1816 and 1830. Under those circumstances it was to the grantees' interest to retain grants during the free period only, and not afterwards; though it was true that, after the demand for security had been withdrawn, there had been a good deal of mere speculation. Cases *of bona fide* reclamation were the exception, and success, where it had been secured, had been entirely due to the peculiar advantages of particular grants.

252. Modification Proposed by the Board, 1853: The Board pronounced it hopeless to look for the clearance of the Sundarbans so long as the existing rates were demanded. They therefore proposed revised rules with the following terms—(I) that grants should not exceed 10,000 bighas of 40 yards square (equal to about 3,200 acres) in order to check mere speculation, and the free period should be ten years; (2) that one-fourth should be cleared in five years on pain of forfeiture; (3) that one-fourth should be exempted from assessment as before; (4) that the remainder should be assessed at 1/2 anna for ten years, then at 1 anna for five years, at 2 annas for the next five years, at 3 annas for five years more, and thereafter at 4 annas, the full rate; (5) that the above rates should apply to the Sundarbans of 24-Parganas and Jessore, the peculiar advantages of which were about on a par, while the corresponding rates in Bakarganj should be 25 per cent, higher on account of the superior advantages of the lands there. The 6th condition provided for the recovery of the revenue; the

7th for demanding security, if necessary; and the 8th indicated the procedure for obtaining grants, applications being ordinarily made to the Sundarban Commissioner. They held that the old grants should be admitted to the benefit of the new rules, and proposed conditions of admission; while as to resumed mahalls, all that the Board believed to be necessary was that their assessment should in future be regulated by the rates current in the neighbourhood instead of the general rate of 8 annas, subject, however, to the maximum of 8 annas everywhere, and a minimum of 4 annas in 24-Parganas and Jessore, and 5 annas in Bakarganj.[4]

253. Remarks by Grantees on the Board's Proposal: The Government communicated the Board's proposals to Messrs. Begg and Rose, two of the grantees, at the desire of the others, and they were allowed to offer their remarks thereon. They objected to the limitation of the size of grants to 10,000 bighas as overriding the natural division of the country, and as being futile, since no restriction was placed on the number of grants a speculator might buy. Instead of the clearing condition recommended by the Board, they preferred one of clearing one-eight of the area in six years to be strictly enforced. The Board's assessment was, they considered, not liberal enough and would not succeed. The Board's ultimate rate of 4 annas per 40-yard bigha was practically the same as the old rate of 8 annas per the 55-yard bigha, so that the apparent reduction was in reality very trifling; besides, since that rate was nearly double the revenue assessment on lands included in the Permanent Settlement, the grantees would still be at a disadvantage. The increased rate in Bakarganj was objectionable because of the distance of the markets. Lastly, they urged that all grants should be publicly sold, Government would thereby get the full value of a grant favourably situated.

254. Modifications Sanctioned by the Government, 1853: The Government, after considering all these views and suggestions, announced its decision in its no. 306, dated 9th April 1853, to the Board of Revenue. Reviewing briefly the rules of 1825 and their failure, the Government passed on to those of 1829, regarding which they took it as certain that the bigha in the former rules was of 110

[4] Presdy. Commr. to Sbn. Commr., no. 154A, dated 25 June 1853.

cubits, and the bigha in the latter of 80 cubits, so that the assessment under the latter rules was nearly double that under the former. The 1829 rules had failed, and the Board's remarks and the position of affiars as to the grants were briefly recapitulated. The Governor stated Mr. Bruce's terms and contrasted them with the 1825 rules as to the 55-yard bigha; also the terms asked for by the grantees, comparing them with the rules of 1825 and 1829. The Board's remarks and terms were next considered and contrasted with the same rules, and the grantee's objections thereto were noticed. The paramount object of Government in devising the rules was declared to be the reclamation of the Sundarbans—a pestilential tract near Calcutta which afforded a home for wild animals and shelter to smugglers and pirates. The improvement of the revenue was of secondary and altogether subordinate importance. Till then it had been thought that improvement of revenue might keep pace with the clearance of jungle, without materially impeding it, but that had proved to be fallacious. Increase of revenue would of course follow reclamation, but had been looked for too soon. That principle was now abandoned, and speedy reclamation was declared to be the paramount object, Government being, however, left free to impose a moderate assessment at some future time. Keeping that object in view, the Governor accepted the terms offered by the grantees with two modifications—(1) that conditions of progressive clearance should be insisted on, such as one-eight of the area in five years, one-fourth in 10, one-half in 20, and three-fourths in 30 years; and (2) that the full assessment of 2 annas instead of being in perpetuity should be for 99 years, after which grants should be liable to reassessment on moderate terms, proprietorship and the right of settlement remaining with the grantees as in estates not permanently settled. Existing grantees would be allowed the option of throwing up their leases and taking fresh leases for 99 years under the new rules, lands already brought under assessment being subjected to the full rate of 2 annas. Where grants were resumed for failure, lands actually cultivated were to be settled separately with the cultivators on moderate terms not exceeding the maximum rate of 2 annas, so as not to cause desertion among the settlers; and the jungle remainder would be granted out afresh. The Governor did not consider the reasons sufficient for limiting grants to 10,000 bighas, nor for imposing a higher assessment in Bakarganj than in 24-Parganas or Jessore, nor for demanding security. In the concluding paragraph of the letter, viz., paragraph 25, the case of resumed lands was considered. They comprised an area of 7,96,286 bighas,[5] the whole of which, except four estates with an area of 40,692 bighas, had been assessed at 8 annas per the 40-yard bigha. The Governor sanctioned the course recommended by the Presidency Commissioner and the Board that in future settlements, instead of that uniform rate, the rates found to prevail in neighbouring zamindaris should be adopted, provided they in no case exceeded 8 or fell short of 4 annas.[6]

255. Grant Rules of 24th September 1853: Revised rules were drafted by the Sundarban Commissioner in accordance with these instructions,[7] and after amendment by the higher authorities were finally approved by the Government in its resolution no. 1803, dated 24th September, 1853,[8] and published in the *Calcutta Gazette* of 8th October 1853, page 1385. As a very large number of the then grants were commuted under these rules, as others were forfeited and regranted under the same rules, and as numerous fresh grants were made under them, the rules of 24th September 1853 govern by far the great majority of Sundarban grants. They are here set out in full:

"Rule I

"*Clause* 1.—Applications for grants of waste land in the Sundarban shall be ordinarily made to the Sundarbans Commissioner. Such applications shall be immediately entered in a register to be kept for that purpose in his office, and after being advertized for one week in the *Calcutta Gazette*,[9] shall be submitted through the Revenue

[5] A list of these was submitted with Sbn. Commr. to Presdy. Commr., no. 272, dated 1 July 1854.

[6] Presdy. Commr. to Sbn. Commr., no. 106, dated 6 May 1853. The restriction on the rate of assessment in resumed mahalls was superseded in 1866—see paragraph 278.

[7] Sbn. Commr. to Presdy. Commr., no. 293, dated 14 July 1853.

[8] Presdy. Commr. to Sbn. Commr., no. 277, dated 26 Oct. 1853.

[9] The Board ordered in 1854 that the patta should be executed in English and Bengali at the desire of the grantees (Presdy. Commr. to Sbn. Commr., no. 18, dated 23 Jan. 1854).

Commissioner for the orders of the Board of Revenue. In the absence of the Sundarbans Commissioner from Alipur, such applications will be received either by the Revenue Commissioner of the Jessore Division, or by the Board of Revenue.

"Clause 2.—Should there be more than one applicant for the same grant, it shall be put up to sale after a further advertisement in the *Calcutta Gazettee* of fifteen days, and the application of the highest bidder shall be submitted as above provided.

"Rule II

"When an application for a grant of land has received the sanction of the Board of Revenue, a patta in the following form[1] shall be drawn out on vellum or parchment, and submitted for registry in the office of the Board of Revenue.

"Form of Patta

"Under the orders of the Board of Revenue, dated 18, this patta is granted to for himself, his heirs, executors, and assigns for that portion of waste land in the Sundarbans estimated to contain bighas, described as lot no. of Captain Hodges' map, and bounded as follows:

On the North—
On the East—
On the South—
On the West—

"The terms of this grant are:

"First.—That one-fourth of the entire grant shall be forever exempted from assessment in lieu of an allowance for the sites of houses, for water-courses, creeks, nullahs, tanks, roads, the space required for the construction of embankments, dams, &c, and for irreclaimable waste land.

"Second.—That the remaining three-fourths of the grant shall be held free of assessment for twenty years from the 1st May , and shall afterward be subject to an annual revenue charge at the following rates, namely:

From the beginning of the 21st to the end of the 30th year, half an anna the bigha of 1,600 square yards.

From the beginning of the 31st to the end of the 40th year, one anna the bigha of 1,600 square yards.

From the beginning of the 41st to the end of the 50th year, one anna and a half the bigha of 1,600 square yards.

From the beginning of the 51st to the end of the 99th year, two annas the bigha of 1,600 square yards.

"*Third.*—That at any period after the expiration of the 20th and before the expiration of the 30th year, the Government may make a survey and measurement, and in like manner the grantee may require that a survey and measurement be made, with the view of ascertaining the exact area of the lands contained in the grant, and that the revenue conditioned in the preceding article shall thence forth be calculated upon the area ascertained by such survey. The expense of such survey shall be defrayed by the party at whose instance the survey may be made. Provided that until such survey be made, or if no such survey be made, the revenue conditioned in the preceding article shall be calculated on the area specified in the first clause of this patta.

"*Fourth.*—That after the 99th year, the grant shall be liable to survey and resettlement, and to such moderate assessment as may seem proper to the Government of the day, the proprietary right in the grant, and the right of engagement with Government remaining to the grantee, his heirs, executors or assigns under the conditions generally applicable to the owners of estates not permanently settled; and that revenue equal to the amount annually paid from the 51st to the 99th year shall be paid annually by the grantee, his heirs, executors or assigns, until such survey and resettlement or reassessment as is described above be effected.

"*Fifth.*—That one-eighth of the grant shall be cleared and rendered fit for cultivation by the expiration of the 5th year from the 18.

"That one-fourth of the grant shall be cleared and rendered fit for cultivation by the expiration of the 10th year from the 18.

"That one-half of the grant shall be cleared and rendered fit for cultivation by the expiration of 20th year from the 18.

"That three-fourths of the grant shall be cleared and rendered fit for cultivation by the expiration of the 30th year from the 18.

"That on failure of all or any of these four conditions (the fact of which failure shall after local inquiry conducted by the Sundarbans Commissioner or other officer be finally determined by the Board of Revenue) the entire grant shall be resumed and the grantee shall forfeit all right and interest in the lands, both those which may be yet uncleared, and those which may have been cleared and brought into cultivation.

"*Sixth.*—That the revenue payable under the third and fourth terms of the patta shall be paid into such treasury as the Government may determine, or to such Collector or other Government officer as may be appointed by the Government to receive it, on the dates specified on the reverse of the kabuliyat or counterpart of this patta; and that in default the revenue shall be recoverable from the grantee, his heirs, executors or assigns by the process that now is or hereafter may be in force for the recovery of arrears of Government revenue.

"*Seventh.*—That the grantee shall not in any way interfere with the passage of boats through any open river or nullah traversing his grant, and shall allow a sufficient space along the banks of all such rivers or nullahs for towing paths.

"Rule III

"*Clause* 1.—Grantees or their representatives holding grants or leases in perpetuity under the rules hitherto in force shall have the option of throwing up their existing leases and taking other leases according to these rules, terminable in 99 years from the date on which their existing leases commenced.

"*Clause* 2.—Grantees so electing to commute their present grants for settlements terminable in 99 years shall pay revenue at the rate of 2 annas per bigha from the commencement of the current year for all lands already brought under assessment to Government.

"*Clause* 3.—In cases in which a rent-free term was originally granted for twenty years, and that term having expired, a further rent-free term has been granted, the grantee, if he commutes as above, shall waive all claim to continued rent-free possession, and shall pay half an anna per bigha on the whole of his grant (after deducting the prescribed one-fourth) from the beginning of the ensuing year, and 1 anna per bigha from the commencement of the 31st year from the date of the original lease, and thenceforward according to the scale prescribed in rule II.

"*Clause* 4.—In cases in which a rent-free term was granted for twenty years, and that term not having expired, a further rent-free term has been promised, the grantee, if he commutes as above, shall waive all claim to such extended rent-free term, and shall pay revenue for the lands of his grant from the commencement of the 21st year according to the scale prescribed in rule II.

"*Clause* 5.—Persons desirous of availing themselves of the option given by this rule, must signify their desire by application to the Sundarbans Commissioner within one year from the date of these rules, that is to say, on or before the 24th day of September 1854.

"Rule IV

"When a grant is resumed under article 5 of the terms of the lease, the lands found to be actually under cultivation shall be measured and settled with the cultivators or under-tenants, as the case may be, at such rates as may appear equitable to the revenue authorities, reference being had to the circumstances under which the cultivators or undertenants were located; and in the event of a new lease being given for the resumed grant, the lands so settled with the occupants shall be included in, or excluded from, the lease, as may be deemed most suitable. Provided, however, that, when cultivated lands are included in a lease, the terms of assessment in Rule II shall be applicable only to the uncleared lands, and separate provision shall be made for the assessment of the cultivated land at the discretion of the Board of Revenue."

CHAPTER XX

Sundarban Grants and the Rules of 1853

1853-1862

256. Carrying into Effect of the New Rules: The promulgation of the revised rules gave a fresh impetus to Sundarban operations, which had, in a great measure, been held in abeyance pending their issue. Uma Kanta Babu proceeded to carry them out in their three directions of commutations, assessments, and new grants. At first his treatment was careful and proper, but afterwards he appears to have become confused amid the variety of claims put forward by grantees and others, and to have blundered strangely; and the mistakes were often due to his neglecting to report the cases to the Presidency Commissioner as he had been directed to do in all cases,[1] so that in many instances they passed unnoticed till Mr. Reily, his successor, by a methodical investigation, ascertained them and reported them for correction. It is unnecessary to notice the errors, except in so far as they served to elicit principles or explanations of rules and orders. The extension of the new rules to resumed mahalls was a matter where Uma Kanta Babu fell into serious perplexities. It will be noticed in the next chapter. As regards grants proper, the following are the important points regarding commutation and assessment where confusion arose and fresh instructions were laid down.

257. Instructions Regarding Commutation: Rule III prescribed the method of commutation, and the majority of grantees availed themselves of the option held out, but the determination of the assessment was not unattended with difficulties. As regarded the rate at which the assessment was to be made where grants under the former rules were paying 2 annas the bigha or more, Uma Kanta Babu failed to understand the rule, and the Presidency Commissioner was frequently

[1] Presdy. Commr. to Sbn. Commr., no. 25, dated 25 Aug. 1854; also no. 148, dated 19 Jan. 1855.

obliged to revise, correct, and remand the proceedings.[2] Much of the difficulty was due to uncertainty as to when the grants were to be considered to have commenced. It had been laid down in 1835 that the date of sanction was to be adopted as the initial date, but Uma Kanta Babu does not appear to have been aware of that order, and in several cases altered the initial dates. On inquiry it was found that the original leases had been in many instances executed some time after the date of the grant, so the Board laid it down in the case of lot 53, which had been granted in 1831, but where the kistbandi was executed in 1834, that the latter was the initial date;[3] and they decided in 1856 that the free period ordinarily ran from the date of the patta, and retrospective effect was to be given to this construction[4]—one result of which was the grantees escaped the payment of considerable sums which were due according to the order of 1835.[5] Other difficulties arose on the meaning of the words of the rules, and were referred to the Board or Government for an authoritative explanation in 1856. Thus as to the words "all lands already brought under assessment to Government" in Rule III, Clause 2, it was laid down that after the expiry of the free term, land *ipso facto* came under revenue, the grantee being bound to pay, and no steps being necessary on the part of Government.[6] The scope of the word "assessment" in the above-quoted passage was thrown into doubt by some previous demi-official correspondence, but on reference made, the Government decided that the literal meaning was correct and the word included lands paying revenue at 2, 4, 6, or 8 annas.[7] With respect to the words "from the date on which the existing leases commenced" in clause 1 of the same rule, the Board decided that if no engagement had been taken from the grantee previous to his signing the kabuliyat and kistbandi, the date of these documents, that is, the date of the patta, should be the date in

[2] Ibid., no. 292, dated 8 Nov. 1853, and no. 9, dated 16 Jan. 1854.

[3] Ibid., no. 27 Ct., dated 6 Feb, 1857.

[4] Ibid., no. 384, dated 30 Apr. 1856—see also Presdy. Commr. to Sbn. Commr., no. 49 Ct., dated 10 Mar. 1865.

[5] Sbn. Commr. to Presdy. Commr., no. 173, dated 5 May 1865.

[6] Presdy. Commr. to Sbn. Commr., no. 25, dated 16 May 1856, transmitting Bd. Rev. to Presdy. Commr., no. 208, dated 9 idem.

[7] Ibid., no. 38, dated 2 [*sic*; 22?] May 1856.

question. The promise referred to in Clause 4 of the same rule might be an implied one, but the Board would not lay down any general rule, leaving each case to be dealt with on its own merits.[8] The words "from the beginning of the ensuing year" in clause 3 had been held by the Board in 1855 to mean 1st May 1854, but in 1856, after the period of commutation has been extended in the case of lot 73, they decided the words meant the commencement of the year next ensuing after commutation, whenever that might be;[9] but on Mr. Reily's representing that through delays in commutation that construction would necessitate revisions, and the refund of revenue already paid,[10] and on the Presidency Commissioner's strongly commenting on the unsoundness of making the date a movable and not a fixed one,[11] the Board decided that the "current year" in the rule meant 1853-54, and the ensuing year 1854-55, thus making the date a fixed one and reverting to the first interpretation.[12]

258. Grants Commuted: Commuted leases were granted for the following lands during the years 1854-1856, the applications having in all cases been made in time—Lots 2, 3, 6, 7, 9, 10, 18, 21, 22, 27,[13] 28, 30, 31 (jungle portion[14] only), 32, 33, 36-40, 52, 53, 56, 57, 61-69, 72 (four portions), 75-77, 81, 82, 86, 87, 91, 92, 98, 101, 105, 108, 136, 137, 166 (four portions), 216, and 225;[15] also for the grant, portions of Gulsakhali[16] and Kukua; for Harijhipatan, Andarmanik, Munkiya and Godardanga,[17] Nalbuniya and Amtali; and lots 1-3 Khaoliya Barisal. In the case of lot 73 the application was made after the expiry of the time allowed, but commutation was allowed, the grantees being country

[8] Ibid., no. 25, dated 16 May 1856.

[9] Ibid., no. 25, dated 16 May 1856.

[10] Sbn. Commr. to Presdy. Commr., no. 213, dated 27 May 1856.

[11] Presdy. Commr. to Sbn. Commr., no. 58, dated 9 June 1856.

[12] Ibid., no. 108, dated 29 July 1856.

[13] Revised Presdy. Commr. to Sbn. Commr., no. 65, dated 12 June, and no. 18 Ct, dated 23 July 1857.

[14] Presdy. Commr. to Sbn. Commr., no. 192, dated 15 Mar. 1856.

[15] As to lot 167, see Presdy. Commr. to Sbn. Commr., no. 28, dated 4 Feb, 1853; no. 100, dated 29 July 1856; no. 104 Ct., dated 27 Nov. 1857; and no. 60, dated 10 Jan. 1858.

[16] Sbn. Commr. to Presdy. Commr., no. 440, dated 9 Jan. 1857.

[17] Presdy. Commr. to Sbn. Commr., 52 Ct., dated 29 Sept. 1857.

folk who were unacquainted with the limitation.[18] The settled land of lot 108 was, in consideration of its exposed situation, allowed an abatement of from 8 to 2 annas and a lengthened period of 99 years.[19] Gyanpara, which Mr. Gomess' Survey of 1852-53 shewed to comprise 1,12,761 bighas instead of Mullins' absurd area of 20,000 bighas, was admitted to the benefit of commutation, three-fourths of the old area being assessed at 2 annas.[20] Similarly in Kalamegha, for which the Collector of Bakarganj had given an amalnama is 1844-45, the cultivation was assessed, and the whole cultivated and jungle, 45,012 bighas, disposed of as a grant.[21] In Tushkhali, the farmer Debnath Rai had received express permission to clear the adjacent jungle in 1839, and had been reclaiming. He applied for a patta under the new rules. The area was surveyed by Mr. Gomess in 1854-55 and found to contain 83,493 bighas of unsettled land (of which 23,743 bighas were cultivated); this was settled with him under the new rules, but Mr. Reily disapproved and the Presidency Commissioner quashed all the proceedings in 1855, on the ground that Debnath as farmer had no right to the benefit.[22] In appeal the Board (of which Mr. Dampier was a Member) explained that the Bakarganj forest not having been lotted out, no formal grant had been feasible, but that Debnath got the land on the same terms as authorised grantees, and was to all intents and purposes a real grantee. They therefore admitted him to the benefit of the new rules[23] for all the jungle land north of the Saplenja Don within defined boundaries, and a patta was given him in 1857 for those lands under the name Debnathpur, no allotment number being possible since Mr. Gomess' Survey of the forest had not been carried so far at the time.[24] But a further claim by him to a lease of the land

[18] Ibid., no. 1S5, dated 4 Dec. 1855.

[19] Ibid., no. 24, dated 3 June 1857.

[20] Ibid., no. 144, dated 18 Jan. 1855; no. 70, dated 17 June 1856; and no. 45, dated 30 June 1857.

[21] Sbn. Commr. to Presdy. Commr., no. 464, dated 25 Feb. 1857, and Presdy. Commr. to Sbn. Commr., no. 4 Ct., dated 11 July 1857.

[22] Presdy. Commr. to Sbn. Commr., no. 217, dated 29 Dec. 1855.

[23] Ibid., no. 267, dated 16 Feb. 1856.

[24] Ibid., no. 69, dated 17 June, and no. 209, dated 24th Oct., and no. 14 Ct., dated 22nd Dec. 1856; and no. 107 Ct., dated 28 Nov. 1857.

south of that Don was refused by the Board.[25] Other mahalls were allowed a modified commutation, as Nilganj and Tiyakhali.

259. Extensions of Clearance Periods: The admission of grants to the easy terms of the new rules did away for a time with the demand for extensions. The change had already been inaugurated of extending merely the confiscation period without touching the revenue stipulations, and, after the issue of the revised rules, that was the invariable practice, it being so necessitated by the enforcement of gradual clearness long before the free period expired. The new shape which the bestowal of extensions took was to suspend the penalty for a year or two to enable the grantee to come up to the proportion required, as was done in lots 2, 10, 11, 12, 28, 37, 38, 105, 136,[26] and others.

260. Resumptions, 1853-67: During the first two years after the promulgation of the new rules, the penalty of resumption was not rigidly enforced, but from 1856 under Mr. Reily a stricter practice appears to have obtained. In 1859 Government ordered that the clearance conditions should be always enforced, except in extraordinary cases, in order to promote the reclamation of the Sundarbans.[27] The resumptions comprised lots 58 and 90 in 1854; lots 48 and 49[28] in 1855; lots 23-26, 78,[29] and 84; lots 4-7 of Khaoliya Barisal, Pachakuraliya, Chandokhali, and Kachupatra[30] in 1856; lots 7, 29, 36, 39, 57 (second portion), 87, 122,[31] 137, 211, and 212 in 1857; lots 18, 27 and 168, and Karaibariya in 1858; lots 11, 99, 105, 109-15, 123, 138, 140, 142, 143 in 1859; lots 59, 106, 107 and 136 in 1860; lot 227 in 1861; lots 67, 90, 121, 124-26, 163 and 172 in 1862; lots 25, 63, 242, and no. 7 Khaoliya Barisal in 1864; lots 15, 122 (north part), 135, 137 and Kukuriya Mukuriya in 1865; lots 110-14 and 139 in 1866; and lots 11 and 117 in 1867.

[25] Presdy. Commr. to Sbn. Commr., no. 69, dated 17 June 1856, and no. 49 Ct., dated 24 Sept. 1857.

[26] Ibid., no. 41 Ct., dated 31st July 1858.

[27] Ibid., no. 51 Ct., dated 2 Dec. 1859.

[28] Ibid., 231, dated 28 Apr. 1855.

[29] Ibid., no. 6, dated 3 May 1856.

[30] Ibid., no. 157, dated 15 Sept. 1856.

[31] Ibid., no. 103 Ct., dated 27 Nov. 1857.

261. Interests of the Salt Department: The reorganization of the Salt Agency, which was under discussion, was finally negatived by the Government in 1854, and no general provision regarding salt was required in the grants, but lots 127, 128, 131, 132 and 149-52 were reserved by the Board for excise manufacture.[32] Government had relinquished the salt lands in the old grants, and, none being reserved in the new, the Salt Agent was left to obtain his lands by ordinary lease, or acquire them under Regulation I of 1824,[33] though the Sundarban Commissioner was instructed always to consult him prior to bestowing new grants.[34] The Salt Agent applied for lot 148, and asked for no restrictions beyond the insertion of a special salt clause, explaining that, as this manufacture was carried on only along the banks and a breadth of 100 feet would suffice, reclamation and the manufacture could go on together.[35] The following clause was then prescribed in 1856—"Provided that in the event of the Salt Department requiring to occupy any of the lands within the grant, such lands shall be given up on demand, the revenue derivable therefrom being remitted by the Government."[36] It was to be inserted in all leases except those in Bakarganj, where there was no likelihood of the manufacture ever being renewed.[37] In 1860 the restriction on the abovementioned eight lots was withdrawn, and they became available for grants.[38]

262. New Grants and Regrants, 1853-62: On the publication of the rules, the Sundarban Commissioner proceeded to sell the grants, and the favourable character of the rules once more stimulated capitalists to embark in Sundarban reclamation. In the case of resumed grants being offered for sale, the Board directed in 1853 that the whole of the lands should be sold, both cultivated and uncultivated,

[32] Ibid., no. 85, dated 19 May 1854, and no. 145, dated 27 July 1854.

[33] Ibid., no. 171, dated 14 Nov. 1855.

[34] Ibid., no. 212, dated 24 Dec. 1855.

[35] Salt Agent to Sbn. Commr., letters dated 30 Nov. 1855, and 4 and 28 March 1856.

[36] Presdy. Commr. to Sbn. Commr., no. 28, dated 20 May, and no. 114. dated 30 July 1856; also no. 31 Ct., dated 14 Feb. 1857.

[37] Ibid., no. 56, dated 5, and no. 93, dated 28 June 1856.

[38] Ibid., no. 103 Ct., dated 2 March 1860.

the rights of the abadkari tenants being expressly safeguarded.[39] This overruled the principle laid down in 1848 as mentioned in paragraph 202. Lots 43, 59, 99, 104, 110-15, 123, 129, 130, 135, 138, 140, 142, 143, 148, 163, 168 and 226[40] were granted out in 1853; in 1854 lots 13, 14, 134, 164, 166, 223, and 227; in 1855 lots 48, 49, 58, 90 and 172 (?); in 1856 lots 23, 25, 78, 87, 121, 124-26, Halliday Island,[41] and Lata Chapli; in 1857 lots 241-51 and Khaoliya Barisal lots 4-7, Pachakuraliya, Chandokhali, Kachupatra, and Kakchira Char; in 1858 lots 7, 8, 15, 16, 29, 36, 39, 57, 87, 116, 118, 120, 122, 137, 211 (two portions), and 229-32; in 1859 lots 85 (?), 195, 196, and 210 (?); in 1860 lots 167, 168 (two parts), and 223 (?); and in 1861 lots 216 and 240. In April 1862 the further grant of waste lands was stopped pending the issue of the new waste land rules.[42] Several of the lots, such as nos. 23 and 25, were keenly competed for and realized a large price. The proceeds of the sales constituted a large fund and were devoted to the improvement of Sundarban estates.[43] The total realizations were reckoned at Rs. 1,56,066 in 1862, namely, Rs. 1,21,000 in 24-Parganas, Rs. 18,371 in Jessore, and Rs. 16,695 in Bakarganj.[44] Lot 44 was assessed ultimately at 2 annas, and incorporated with taluk Bantra.[45]

263. Settlements on Expiry of Free Term: Uma Kanta Babu's practice of measuring grants on the expiry of the free term and assessing them *de novo* was dropped, and the execution of dowls at that stage was pronounced useless.[46] A survey was not indispensable, but it was sufficient to calculate the revenue on Hodges' area, and where dowls and kabuliyats had been executed and possession given, nothing

[39] Ibid., no. 67, dated 30 March 1853.

[40] The portion Karamjal was included in the grant in 1857. Presdy. Commr. to Sbn. Commr., no. 120 Ct., dated 15 Dec. 1857.

[41] An amalnama for the island had been given to certain pilots in 1846, but was cancelled, Presdy. Commr. to Sbn. Commr., no. 233. dated 11 Jan. 1856, and no. 354, dated 12 Apr. 1856.

[42] Bd. Rev. C.O. no. 27, dated 1 Apr. and no. 41, dated 23 June 1862.

[43] See paragraph 301.

[44] Sbn. Commr. to Presdy. Commr., no. 130, dated 10 Sept. 1862.

[45] The opposition of the talukdars had prevented its reclamation. Presdy. Commr. to Sbn. Commr., no. 194, dated 4 Oct. 1856.

[46] Presdy. Commr. to Sbn. Commr., no. 251, dated 31 Jan. 1856.

further was necessary.[47] The notion, however, that something was required on the expiry of the free term to give efficacy to the revenue provisions still held its ground, and the practice of taking dowls was observed for more than twenty years afterwards. Grants as soon as made were to be brought on to the Collector's rent-roll.[48]

264. Subsidiary Rules, 1856-67: In 1859 Government ordered the words "properly embanked" should be inserted in future leases where embankments were necessary.[49] It had been questioned whether Government could resume a grant for non-clearance, if the right were not exercised at the proper time. It was decided in 1856 that if the period expired and the grant commenced to pay revenue, the right was barred, otherwise apparently delay did not destroy it. Commutation made to change in those respects.[50] The rule requiring a survey before a grant could be made was relaxed in 1867, Government declaring that a boundary road might be cut all around beforehand, and pillars erected by the grantee within three months after getting possession.[51] Government directed in 1865 that no grant should be sold for arrears of revenue without its state as regarded clearance being ascertained by a reference to the Sundarban Commissioner.[52]

[47] Ibid., no. 22, dated 10, and no. 25, dated 16 May 1856.

[48] Ibid.., no. 145, dated 30 Aug. 1856.

[49] Ibid., no. 58 Ct., dated 29 Dec. 1859.

[50] Ibid., Nos. 34 and 35, dated 22 May 1856.

[51] Ibid., no. 177, dated 30 Oct. 1867.

[52] Ibid., Memo. no. 214, dated 23 Oct. 1865, and no. 37 Ct., dated 19 March 1866.

CHAPTER XXI

Resumed Mahalls and the Rules of 1853

1853-1862

265. Effect of the 1853 Rules on the Resumed or Excluded Mahalls: "When passing the new rules for grants in 1853, the Governor had sanctioned a relaxation of the assessment upon resumed mahalls, namely, that in future they should be assessed at current rates not exceeding 8 annas and not falling below 4 annas.[1] A list of these mahalls, which, in consequence of their being expressly denied the benefit of the grant rules, were spoken of as "excluded mahalls," was prepared by Uma Kanta Babu and submitted to the higher authorities in 1854.[2] But a large body of the holders of resumed lands in the Sundarbans petitioned the Board in August 1854, representing that the indulgent rates conceded to grantees by the 1853 rules bore with great hardship on them, inasmuch as their raiyats were deserting, being tempted by the lower terms which the grantees were able to offer; they declared that they could not continue to pay the 8-anna rate, and they asked for some consideration. The Board refused to make any reduction in the case of lands that were cultivated when settled, but, thinking it might be necessary to revise the prospective assessment fixed in perpetuity on jungle lands they called for a report on the subject from the Sundarban Commissioner.[3] Uma Kanta Babu made no remarks on the questions raised by the Board, hut merely sent up a list of 70 resumed mahalls in February 1855.[4]

266. Detailed Sundarban Map, 1855: About the same time that the landowners petitioned, the Government desired to know what the state of the Sundarbans then was, and what was the proportion

[1] See parrgraph 254.

[2] Sbn. Commr. to Presdy. Commr., no. 272, dated 1 July 1854.

[3] Presdy. Commr. to Sbn. Commr., no. 82, dated 28 Oct. 1854

[4] Sbn. Commr. to Presdy. Commr., no. 55, dated 5 Feb. 1855.

between the cultivated and uncultivated land. The Presidency Commissioner directed Uma Kanta Babu in September 1854 to have a plan of the Sundarbans drawn up, each district in one sheet, exhibiting the names, numbers, and state of cultivation of each of the lots.[5] The map though pronounced most urgent was not completed till the end of 1855.[6]

267. Terms of Assessment Revised in the Resumed or Excluded Mahalls, 1855-56: Meanwhile the Presidency Commissioner forwarded the list, remarking that it shewed no strict rule had been followed in the settlement of the jungle lands of those estates. The free period varied from one to twenty years, then followed a rasad of two or three years, after which the full assessment of 8 annas was imposed. It seemed that in some recent cases the new rules had been applied to such jungle lands. He was in favour of granting the petitioners some indulgence, and suggested proposals for giving the jungle lands in the estates the benefit of the new rules. The Board, which then consisted of Messrs. Ricketts, Dampier, and Dunbar, took some time to deliberate, and submitted their report to Government in January 1856. They were divided in opinion, Mr. Dunbar desiring to offer liberal concessions with the object of having the forest reclaimed. The decision of Government was recorded in its no. 105, dated 1st February 1856. The Lieutenant-Governor, agreeing with the majority—Messrs. Rickett and Dampier—held that there was no necessity for a general reduction of the assessment in resumed mahalls, since these lands were usually more favourably situated than the mass of Sundarban lands, having been selected by the people themselves on account of their proxmity to zamindari lands or for other good reasons: but as regarded other lands differently situated, where there was reason to believe that they were likely to be affected by the lower assessment obtaining in grants, the Lieutenant-Governor decided that, where the original ábádkars were still in possession, the rate should be decreased to 4 annas; and in resumed lands, which were entirely surrounded (if any such existed) by mahalls assessed at a maximum of 2 annas, the assessment should be reduced to the same level; but in all cases local

[5] Presdy. Commr. to Sbn. Commr., no. 29, dated 1 Sept. 1854.

[6] Sbn. Commr. to Presdy. Commr., no. 539, dated 18 Dec. 1855.

inquiries were to be made. In the case of lands appertaining to resumed mahalls which were waste at the period of settlement, the assessment should be revised uniformly according to the second clause of the new leases. In sanctioning these rules, he enjoined however, that in all cases the reduction of the existing assessment should be conceded only on condition that the perpetual leases on which the lands in question were then held should be surrendered, since he conceived it to be very desirable that those parts of the Sundarban territory which were originally usurped should be liable to resettlement at a future day equally with the larger area which was embraced by the grants.[7]

268. Results of these Orders: The result of these orders was to rescind the rate of 8 annas which Mr. Harvey had uniformly established, and to make local circumstances the criterion for determining the assessment. A reduction was permitted, if necessary, in all kinds of lands. As mentioned in paragraphs 167 and 168 several settlements had been made in perpetuity. Such settlements were now prohibited, and the duration in all cases was to be temporary, but in several cases[8] the period was, as in Sundarban grants, fixed at 99 years.

269. Claims to Commutation in Resumed Mahalls, 1854-55: There was, however, a general impression among the landowners that the grant rules were intended for lands of every description, and numerous applications were sent in for commutation. Uma Kanta Babu at first acted rightly, and refused them on the ground that the lands were either resumed mahalls or lay outside Hodges' Sundarban boundary. But towards the end of 1854 he appears to have modified his views, and considered that lands which fell within that boundary were admissible to the benefit of the rules, even though they were resumed or "excluded" mahalls. Thus he allowed commutation in lots which had been incorporated with patitábádi mahalls, such as Nos. 17, 20, &c.; in resumed estates which composed lots 216-220, such as Khaliya, Hariya, *&c.*; and in other resumed estates falling inside the boundary, such as Gulsakhali. Some of Henckell's talukdars applied for admission, and commutation was allowed in Pránpur by the Presidency Commissioner on the ground that it was reclaimed

[7] Presdy. Commr. to Sbn. Commr., no. 262, dated 12 Feb. 1856.
[8] E.g., Tarabuniya. Sbn. Commr. to Presdy. Commr., no. 508, dated 5 Dec. 1855.

land;[9] so also in Ramzannagar[10] and Atliya.[11] But when commutation was recommended in Ballabhpur, Mr. Stainforth, the Presidency Commissioner, noticing its circumstances, refused since it was one of the mahalls excluded by paragraph 25 of the Government orders.[12] In the case of not a few Sundarban mahalls, however, Uma Kanta Babu had commuted the terms and bestowed fresh pattas, either without the previous sanction declared to be indispensable, or in cases which were not entitled to the benefit of the grant rules. Such irregularities were detected in 1855, and much of Mr. Reily's time for two years was occupied in rectifying the errors, which frequently involved serious diminutions of land revenue. It had been ordered in 1853 that on the presentation of applications for commutation immediate information should be sent to the Collector with the request that, pending the adjustment of the settlement, he would receive payment of the revenue according to the new rules.[13] A reduced revenue was thus being paid by the mahalls which had been improperly admitted to commutation, and when the irregular proceedings were quashed and the revenue restored to its former amount, a sum of arrears became due, which the Board allowed to be liquidated by instalments during one or two years.

270. Claims to Commutation in Jungle Mahalls in Bakarganj, 1854-57: The absence, of a detailed survey in the Bakarganj district had rendered the application of the grant rules almost inoperative, and the question arose in 1854 whether lands there, especially in pargana Salimábad, were entitled to commutation under the new rules, the talukdars of Putikhali, Panchakaran, Debraj, Dhuliganti, Harganti, Nazirdiya, and Madardiya having applied to commute.[14] Commuted pattas were given for the first three and were confirmed by the Board in 1855, the free term remaining 15 years as before.[15] In the case of Gulsakhali the Board laid it down in 1855 that the

[9] Presdy. Commr. to Sbn. Commr., no. 17, dated 22 Aug. 1854.
[10] Ibid., no. 18, dated 22 Aug. 1854.
[11] Ibid., no. 16, dated 22 Aug. 1854.
[12] Ibid., no. 214, dated 24 Dec. 1855—see paragraph 254 above.
[13] Ibid., no. 279, dated 27 Oct. 1853.
[14] See Sbn. Commr. to Presdy. Commr., no. 273, dated 11 July 1856.
[15] Presdy. Commr. to Sbn. Commr., no. 210, dated 16 Apr. 1855.

new rules applied only to grants and not to resumed estates.[16] But resumed mahalls, especially in pargana Salimábad, were of various kinds, and lay both within and without the Sundarban forest; and Mr. Reily suggested that the fact whether the lands lay without or within the Sundarban boundary should be taken as the criterion for deciding claims to commutation, only those within having a reasonable claim.[17] The Presidency Commissioner held that the new rules did not apply to resumed estates whether within or without the boundary. He informed Mr. Reily that Government could not demand a higher rate than was specified in the pattas, and that, if none were mentioned, the assessment might be made at the pargana rates.[18] The assessment was not to be fixed at 8 annas, merely because that had till then been the uniform rate, but it might be reduced according to local circumstances.[19] The commuted leases were then cancelled, and the mahalls were settled agreeably to local rates, some at 8, some at 6, but most at 7 annas, for a period of 99 years. Commutation had also been carried out in Khondkarber, Baintala, and Manikkhola, but the Board disallowed it, expressly declaring that resumed mahalls acquired no special character by being comprised within the Sundarban boundary.[20] The resettlement in these mahalls was, however, made at 2 annas.[21] In the six chaks—Phulhata, &c—the farmer was pronounced entitled as ábádkar to the benefit of the 1853 rules.[22]

[16] Bd. Rev. to Presdy. Commr., no. 136, dated 16 Mar. 1855.

[17] Sbn. Commr. to Presdy. Commr., no. 37, dated 16 Feb. 1856.

[18] Presdy. Commr. to Sbn. Commr., no. 10, dated 5 May, and no. 89, dated 28 June 1856.

[19] Ibid., no. 106. dated 25 July, and no. 133, dated 21 Aug. 1856.

[20] Sbn. Commr. to Presdy. Commr., no. 387, dated 10 Nov. 1856, and Presdy. Commr. to Sbn. Commr., no. 306, dated 24 Apr. 1857.

[21] Ibid., no. 16, dated 22 May 1857.

[22] Presdy. Commr. to Sbn. Commr., no. 286, dated 20 Jan. 1857.

CHAPTER XXII

Jurisdiction, Settlements, and Rights of Settlement 1853-1868

271. Sundarban Commissioner's Jurisdiction in Jessore and Bakarganj, 1858-61: Tushkhali, which came up for resettlement in 1858, raised some questions of jurisdiction. The Sundarban Commissioner was pronounced by the Board to be an independent Deputy Collector within the meaning of section 4 of Act VI of 1853 in the portions of 24-Parganas and Jessore which lay within the Sundarban boundary, but not over resumed and kháss mahalls outside that boundary.[1] It was the practice, however, that he should resettle all Sundarban estates and all resumed mahalls. Still to obviate uncertainty the Government vested Mr. Reily, under section 2 of Regulation IX of 1816, with the full powers of a Collector in the districts bordering on the Sundarbans, to enable him to exercise all the powers described in Regulations VII of 1822 and IX of 1825.[2] He then took the settlement of Tushkhali in hand, but as the mahall lay in Bakarganj, the Presidency Commissioner could not hear appeals from his proceedings, and the appeals went to the Commissioner of Dacca. The Government thereupon ordered that all appeals from the Sundarban Commissioner's orders on settlements made in Bakarganj should go to the Board.[3] This led to all Bakarganj settlements being reported direct to the Board. On a reference by the Presidency Commissioner in 1862 as to resumption proceedings, the Board decided that all Sundarban appeals lay to him, except where estates, which were the subject of the appeals, had been brought on the Bakarganj taujih, in

[1] Presdy. Commr. to Sbn. Commr., no. 99 Ct., dated 28 Aug. 1858.

[2] Govt. to Bd. Rev., no. 2560, dated 24 Nov. 1858, and Govt. to Sbn. Commr., no. 2559, dated idem.

[3] Ibid., no. 164, dated 20 Jan. 1859. Presdy. Commr. to Sbn. Commr., no. 147 Ct, dated 10 Feb. 1859.

which case they would lie to the Dacca Commissioner. The entire Sundarban forest constituted a single estate subject to the Presidency Commissioner, and resumption suits there would still come before him.[4] In 1861 Government directed, in its no. 105A of 25th January, that all Sundarban estates situated on the west bank of the Baleswar should on resettlement be transferred from Bakarganj to Jessore.[5] The river Baleswar thus became the boundary between, the two districts.

272. Summary Rent Suits in the Sundarbans, 1828-63: It had been the practice from Mr. Dampier's time for the Sundarban Commissioner to try summary suits for rent and hear appeals by the raiyats against the tahsildars under Regulations VII of 1799, V of 1812, and VIII of 1831, in khass and resumed mahalls under their care, and the practice was re-enforced in 1839, when it seems to have dropped into desuetude.[6] The summary jurisdiction, however, would seem to have been chiefly exercised in the large kháss mahalls—Buzurgummedpur, Ramna Bamna, and Tushkhali—and when they were settled or removed from his control, the number of suits was trifling, and amounted to about 30 only in the five years 1847-51. The Joint-Magistrate of Baraset had been authorised by Government in 1833 to try such suits, and he had taken up such suits in the Sundarbans, but on a representation by Uma Kanta Babu, Government decided in 1851 that the Joint-Magistrate's jurisdiction did not extend into the Sundarbans, and the Sundarban Commissioner continued to hear all suits.[7] The question was again raised in 1857, and it was then laid down that while the Sundarban Commissioner was competent to hear such suits, the trial of pending suits was not to be carried about into the districts, but should be made over to the Collectors in whose districts they lay.[8] In 1855 Babu U.K. Sen urged that the Deputy Collectors of Kaliganj, Khulna, and Perozepur should be vested with

[4] Presdy. Commr. to Sbn. Commr., no. 66, dated 1 July 1862. The orders were affirmed in 1866. Presdy. Commr. to Sbn. Commr., memo. no. 23 Ct., dated 25 Jan. 1866.

[5] Ibid., no. 53, dated 2 Mar. 1861.

[6] Ibid., no. 17, dated 4 Feb. 1839.

[7] Ibid., no. 20 Ct.. dated 18 Nov. 1851.

[8] Ibid., 110 Ct., dated 4 Dec. 1857.

jurisdiction in summary suits,[9] and it seems to have been granted, for it was laid down in 1858 that appeals from the Deputy Collector of Kaliganj should lie to the Sundarban Commissioner and not to the Deputy Collector of Baraset.[10] The Sundarban officers, however, could not readily deal with such suits since they were frequently travelling about, and their jurisdiction in this respect gradually diminished, until it died out about 1863.[11]

273. Method of Granting Settlement-holders' Allowances, 1859: The method of providing for unculturable lands, and the expenses and profits of collection by the exemption of one-fourth area from assessment, which was prescribed in the case of grants, had been utilized by Mr. Kemp in the settlement of resumed grants that were all waste, and was brought into vogue generally in after years, the remaining three-fourths being assessed at 8 annas. Mr. Smith, who had pleaded for a reduction of the rate in the Jessore mahalls, as mentioned in paragraph 173, objected to the one-fourth area exemption in those mahalls on the ground that khals and unculturable land formed so large a proportion of the area as to render that allowance inadequate. Hence he reverted to the regular method of specific deductions, and under the Government orders permitting a diminution of the rates, inclined towards under-assessment. Mr. Reily combatted his views and directed him to adhere to the one-fourth area exemption.[12] But on the question arising in the case of Sannyasi, the Board in 1859 disapproved of the practice of providing for the allowances by such exemptions in resumed mahalls, and. overruled Mr. Reily's plea of expediency.[13]

274. Confirmation of Settlements: Under the rules of 10th August 1842. Collectors were empowered to confirm settlements where the revenue did not exceed Rs. 200, and those of 11th July 1855 raised the

[9] Sbn. Commr. to Presdy. Commr., no. 428, dated 3 Oct. 1855.

[10] Presdy. Commr. to Sbn. Commr., no. 85 Ct., dated 27 Sept. 1858.

[11] Ibid., no. 81 Ct., dated 12 Oct. 1860. Sbn. Commr. to Presdy. Commr., no. 229, dated 28 Apr. 1863.

[12] Sbn. Commr. to Smith, no. 243, dated 30 March 1859. Smith to Sbn. Commr., no. 229, dated 7 Apr. 1859.

[13] Presdy. Commr. to Sbn. Commr., no. 182 Ct,, dated 15 Apr. 1859, and no. 112 Ct., dated 16 March 1860. Sbn. Commr. to Presdy. Commr., no. 49, dated 5 Aug. 1856.

limit to Rs. 500: Uma Kanta Babu had misapplied the rule to grants and revised settlements which had once been confirmed, and himself confirmed 25 such small settlements. Mr. Reily at first followed his practice in nine settlements, but, on his mooting the point in 1856, the Presidency Commissioner prohibited the practice and ordered that all Sundarban settlements required his sanction. A fresh reference was made in 1859, but the Board approved the order and directed that it should be strictly observed.[14]

275. Miscellaneous Conditions in Leases, 1858-65: It was laid down in 1858 that no rent-free terms should be given without provision being at the same time made for enforcing the gradual clearance of the land. Government decided in 1865 that no occupancy should be given except on amalnama or other authority, and that where permissive occupancy was given, the formal lease should take effect from the date of occupancy.[15]

276. Rules Regarding Period of Settlement and Malikana, 1855-56: Rules were laid down in the case of Putimari regarding the period of settlement and malikana. It had been settled in 1831, again in 1842, and was brought under resettlement in 1849 and following years, when the taufir alone was assessed, the Presidency Commissioner holding that the 1842 settlement was in perpetuity. Mr. Reily demurred to that view, and the case raised also the questions, whether, if no period were mentioned, a settlement was to be held as made in perpetuity rather than for the customary Sundarban period of 10 or 20 years, and whether the holders could demand malikana.[16] The old correspondence was consulted and also the orders of 1850 regarding malikana.[17] The Board decided the questions in their No. 256, dated 4th June 1850, pronouncing against the permanency of the 1842 settlement. The orders did not declare the right of all squatters to malikana, but each claim was to be decided on its own merits. As to

[14] Ibid., no. 62, dated 29 Aug.; no. 46 Ct.. dated 25 Nov. and no. 60 Ct., dated 30 Dec. 1859. Sbn. Commr. to Presdy. Commr., no. 59, dated 1 Sept., and no. 117, dated 29 Nov. 1859.

[15] Presdy. Commr. to Sbn. Commr., no. 49Ct., dated 10 March 1865.

[16] Sbn. Commr. to Presdy, Commr., no. 92, dated 19 March 1856.

[17] Presdy. Commr. to Sbn. Commr., no. 336, dated 4 Apr., and no. 27, dated 16 May 1856.

the period, it was laid down that "no settlement was to be considered as in perpetuity unless expressly stated to be so either in the settlement report or in the orders confirming the same."[18] The same question was raised in the case of Bhairabghata and Bankeswar settled in 1832 where the taufir was brought under assessment in 1852.[19] No period had been fixed, but the Board taking them as patitabadi taluks pronounced the settlements in such taluks to be permanent *quoad* the area assessed. Yet as the boundaries of 1832 and 1852 agreed, the Board held there had been no encroachment. The proceedings were quashed and the 1832 settlement became permanent.[20] Again, in 1862, the Presidency Commissioner prohibited the use of the word "malikana" in the dowls of Sundarban estates belonging to Government.[21]

277. Rights of Settlement in Resumed Mahalls, 1863-66: On a reference made by the Presidency Commissioner in 1863, the Board unanimously concurred in his view that the Government has full power to take resumed mahalls into its own possession, without acknowledging any right on the part of any of the occupiers; but individual hardship that this principle might involve could be remedied by recognising, as the owners of permanent hereditary tenures, held at a permanent assessment at 10 per cent, below the raiyati jamas, those who could prove they had expended capital largely in bringing the forest lands under cultivation. This principle the Board again affirmed in 1866, enunciating it once for all on a reference from the Commissioner of Dacca.[22] They defined the term "resumed mahall" as being "a mahall, the lands of which though situated within the boundary of the Sundarbans, and therefore not falling within the operations of the decennial settlement, had been usurped by the zamindars of the decennially settled estates, or by independent squatters, but which have been subsequently resumed in favour of Government under the provisions of the resumption laws." Hence, not only should undertenures be recognized in all cases where their

[18] Ibid., no. 60, dated 10 June 1856.

[19] Ibid., no. 61, dated 10 June 1856. Sbn. Commr. to Presdy Commr., no. 251, dated 27 idem.

[20] Ibid., no. 139, dated 26 Aug.. and no. 168 dated 10 Sept. 1856.

[21] Ibid., no. 170, dated 8 Nov. 1862.

[22] Bd. Rev. to Dacca Commr., no. 4387B, dated 10 Oct. 1866.

holders could shew good cause in accordance with the above ruling, but even the original usurpers might shew good cause for favourable consideration in regard to settlement of the estates with them. Each case, however, was to be decided on its merits.

278. Rules Regarding Rates of Assessment in Resumed Mahalls, 1866: On the question of assessment, the Board at the same time expressed their opinion that Government was not pledged to maintain the rate of 8 annas per bigha in all resumed mahalls. Referring to Mr. Harvey's rule and the orders passed in 1853, they held that 8 annas rate was not intended to be observed in perpetuity if the Government changed its mind. Each case, however, was to be decided according to its own circumstances. In resumed estates settled with the raiyats, the jamabandi was to be drawn up at the rates prevailing in the neighbourhood.[23] These orders, superseding the old 8-annas rate and making the surrounding rates the criterion for the assessment, permitted as often as otherwise of the rate being fixed at more than 8 annas. This permission has been largely called into practice with the marked improvement that has taken place in the country.

279. Law of Resumption and Rights of Settlement in Resumed Mahalls Discussed, 1867-68: The general question of the law of resumption and the rights of parties after resumption was reviewed by Mr. H. L. Dampier, the Presidency Commissioner, in a note in 1867. Referring to the High Court's decision in Rabiullah Kazi's case,[24] and the custom of the Board to recognise trespassing occupants and admit them to settlement in the case of resumed mahalls, he observed that no distinct rules had been laid down defining the right to be conferred by such settlements. He discussed the various kinds of ownership that might be created in such cases, and reviewed the principles that had been enunciated, beginning from 1816. It appeared therefrom that the Government and the Board took the view that a resumption decree did not *per se* relieve Government of the legal obligation to make a direct settlement with a trespassing clearer as proprietor of the lands, though the High Court had ruled otherwise in the case referred to. The history shewed that apart from the legal standpoint it was the approved *policy* of the authorities in all ordinary cases formally to recognize the

[23] Bd. Rev. to Dacca Commr., no. 4387B, dated 10 Oct. 1866.

[24] See paragraph 197.

right of property in the person who was found in possession. Squatters had been treated with all consideration and there had been no cases of recusancy. He gave it as his conclusion that trespassing occupants ought to obtain the full rights of a proprietor in a temporarily-settled estate, and that the under-tenants ought (unless for good reasons) to have their rights confirmed. In furtherance of this view he formulated a number of principles dealing with rights to settlement, rates of assessment, disposal of unreclaimed forest, & c. Mr. Chapman who succeeded him reviewed his note. He held that Government could not oust trespassers merely on a decree under the resumption laws that the lands were liable to assessment, and that if Government wished to oust them, it must resort to the civil courts. He thought it was sufficient to maintain the trespassers and assess them with the full Government revenue. The papers were submitted to the Board. Messrs. Grote and Schalch declined to lay down abstract principles in supersession of previous orders; they preferred that resettlements should be made on the lines of the old settlements, and that new settlements should be effected in the manner that should appear most fit.[25] The subject was further discussed by Mr. Chapman in an appeal regarding the settlement of chak Anandatala in 1868.[26]

280. Abolition of Sundarban Commission Reconsidered, 1861-66: It may be mentioned here that the question of the abolition of the Sundarban office was revived in 1861, and again in 1865. It was carefully considered by Mr. Dampier, the Presidency Commissioner, and the Lieutenant-Governor decided in 1866 that the abolition was then inexpedient, and not likely to entail any saving to the Government. He thought, however, that the work done was insufficient, and directed the Presidency Commissioner to give his attention to the matter.[27] Mr. Caspersz succeeded Mr. Reily as Sundarban Commissioner on 10th August 1861, and held the office (with an interval of 18 months' furlough from May 1863) till 13th December 1865. Mr. Gomess who had acted during the interval then became the Commissioner.

[25] Bd Rev. to Presdy. Commr., no. 4662, dated 27 Aug. 1867, with Presdy. Commr. to Sbn. Commr., memo. no. 145, dated 2 Sept. 1867.

[26] Presdy. Commr. to Sbn. Commr., memo. no. 21, dated 19 Sept. 1868.

[27] Bengal Govt. to Bd. Rev., no. 707, dated 20 Feb. 1866, with Presdy. Commr. to Sbn. Commr., no. 48 Ct., dated 5 March 1866.

CHAPTER XXIII

Revenue and Other Surveys, Boundary Decisions, and Resumptions

1852-1870

281. Surveys in the Bakarganj forest, 1852-55: It has been explained in the preceding pages that the Bakarganj portion of the Sundarban forest had never been surveyed in detail, the detailed survey by the brothers Morrieson having ended at the Pasar river. The need for a survey had been often urged and acknowledged. Partial surveys had been made from time to time in the eastern part by Messrs. Mullins and Smith. In the same way Mr. Gomess during 1852-53 surveyed the large block containing Gyanpara and Kalamegha, found its area to be 1,57,773 bighas, Mullins having vastly underestimated it. Mr. Smith during 1854-55 surveyed Khaprabhanga, Dabrogo-Phulbuniya, Sonatala, Karaibariya, and Bara and Chota Bogi. There were small clearings in the first four, tenanted, chiefly by Mags, but the lots were disposed of separately under the grant rules.[1] At the same time Mr. Gomess surveyed the Tushkhali tract down to the Halta Don: the total area was 1,66,954 bighas and the cultivation 1,07,204 bighas, of which only 83,461 bighas were settled. He had thus during two seasons surveyed the whole of the country on the east bank of the Baleswar.

282. Survey of Lots 237-51 and Settlements, 1855-58: Mr. Reily had been serving as Deputy Collector in Bakarganj and was acquainted with the circumstances of the forest there. On succeeding to the Sundarban Commissionership in 1855, he urged that Mr. Gomess should be employed in surveying the region east of the Pasar, and on the Board's recommendation the proposal was sanctioned.[2] Mr. Gomess was ordered to survey the forest between the Pasar and Baleswar during 1855-56, dividing it up into allotments, separately

[1] Presdy. Commr. to Sbn. Commr., no. 299, dated 13 March 1856.

[2] Ibid., no. 187, dated 8 Dec. 1855.

marking in his map such lands as had been already settled, and noting the taufir.[3] He surveyed the jungle lands between the Pasar and Bhola rivers down: to the Bari Gang, which was as far south as was advantageous then, and divided them into 15 lots with an average area of 12,000 bighas. He tried to secure natural boundaries, and where they were absent he adopted lines drawn due east and west from well defined points.[4] At the same time he surveyed Hodges' boundary along the north of that tract. Of the 15 lots, the zamindars laid claim to the first and second, but as they fell clearly within the boundary, Mr. Reily resumed them on 15th August 1856, and the order was confirmed by the Presidency Commissioner on 19th September 1856. The third and fourth lots had been already granted out by Uma Kanta Babu, and the rest were all jungle.[5] The operations were approved by the Government, and under their orders Hodges' series of numbers was carried on, and the new lots received the Nos. 237 to 251.[6] The zamindar of Hogla, however, claimed that the Chilla Chandpai river (a portion of which Mr. Dampier, as Sundarban Commissioner, had fixed as, the boundary of the forest) was the boundary as far as its junction with the Pasar, so as to bring lots 237-39 into his zamindari; but Mr. Dampier who was now a Member of the Board of Revenue, dismissed his claim in 1857.[7] Mr. Gomess defined the boundary along Perikhali according to the Board's orders in 1857-58,[8] but the orders were revised in 1858.[9] The resumed lands were settled with the zamindars for 99 years.[10]

283. Further Surveys and Settlements, 1856-66: During 1856-57 Mr. Gomess continued the survey, and examining lots 3-7 Khaoliya Barisal altered their boundaries so as to give each lot a frontage on

[3] Sbn. Commr. to Gomess, no. 563, dated 31 Dec. 1855.

[4] For the boundaries, see Gomess to Sbn. Commr., no. 49, dated 15 July 1857.

[5] Sbn. Commr. to Presdy. Commr., no. 325, dated 2 Sept. 1856. Presdy. Commr. to Sbn. Commr., no. 169, dated 19 idem.

[6] Presdy. Commr. to Sbn. Commr., no. 189, dated 1 Oct. 1856.

[7] Ibid., no. 78 Ct., dated 12 Nov. 1857.

[8] Gomess to Sbn. Commr., no. 85, dated 11 March 1858.

[9] Presdy. Commr. to Sbn. Commr., no. 87 Ct., dated 30 Sept. 1858, see paragraph 290 *infra*.

[10] Ibid., no. 113 Ct., dated 20 Nov. 1858.

the river Baleswar.[11] Lots 4 and 6 which had been resumed were then settled on jangalburi terms. The next season he continued the Tushkhali operations by surveying the country between the Saplenja Don and Gyanpara, and dividing it into four blocks—Halta, Sonakhali, Saplenja, and Noli. Hodges had partly surveyed some of these estates. Since the lands belonged to Government his boundaries were modified so as to secure water boundaries.[12] Cultivation was scattered through those estates, and they were brought under assessment in 1859-60, the total assessed area being 29,883 bighas and the Government revenue Rs. 21,255[13] No settlement could be made because of the claim of Debnath Rai to them, and they remained khass. In 1865 those claims were decided[14] and the Presidency Commissioner ordered that the estates should be disposed of. There was a civil suit pending regarding the boundary between Halta and Sonakhahi, and Tushkhali, but without waiting for its decision those two chaks were sold as Government estates under the khas mahall rules in 1866, and Noli and Saplenja were at the same time disposed of under the sale in fee-simple rules of 1863.[15]

284. Preparations for the Revenue Survey of the Jessore Sundarbans, 1856-57: The revenue survey of Jessore approached the Sundarbans in 1857, and preparations were made for its covering the south portion of that district during the following season. The Sundarban Commissioner had furnished the survey officers with all Hodges' maps from the Jabuna to the Baleswar, and a list of the lots and resumed mahalls that bordered the zamindari lands.[16] During season 1856-57 the Superintendent of Survey demarcated almost all the mahalls, and the Board ordered that the Surveyor should survey

[11] Gomess to Sbn. Commr., no. 53, dated 6 Aug. 1857. Presdy. Commr. to Sbn. Commr., no. 68 Ct., dated 2 Nov. 1857.

[12] Sbn. Commr. to Presdy. Commr., no. 132, dated 24 Nov. 1858. Presdy. Commr. to Sbn. Commr., no. 138 Ct., dated 11 Jan. 1859.

[13] Sbn. Commr. to Presdy. Commr., no. 293, dated 5 Apr. 1865.

[14] See paragraph 292.

[15] Presdy. Commr. to Sbn. Commr., no. 189, dated 16 Sept. 1865. Sbn. Commr. to Presdy. Commr., no. 254, dated 9 Feb. 1866.

[16] Sbn. Commr. to Presdy. Commr., no. 451, dated 31 Jan. 1857. Bd. Rev. to Superintendent of Survey, no. 77, dated 17 Feb. 1857.

the Sundarban estates and the cultivated portions of the grants and also demarcate Hodges' line from Pranpur eastward, which was to be followed as the boundary of the Sundarbans. Mr. Reily was ordered to co-operate and supply all the information requisite.[17] Further, a list of the unidentified Henckell's and Donnelly's mahalls was sent to the Superintendent to see whether their boundaries could be traced out.[18]

285. Revenue Survey of Jessore Sundarbans, 1857-58: The survey was carried out during season 1857-58 by Captain J. E. Gastrell, Revenue Surveyor, Mr. Smith, Deputy Collector, accompanying and assisting him in all matters that concerned the Sundarbans. It extended that season from the Kabadak as far as the Manikkhola, Putimari, and Chilla Chandpai rivers. One signal advantage under which the proceedings were conducted was that Mr. Dampier was at this time Member of the Board, and was able from his personal recollection to instruct the officers and set them right on points where they were doubtful or had gone wrong.

286. Determination of Boundaries: Great importance was attached to the correct definition of the boundaries of mahalls, for in the case of Nȃlbuniya, where the Survey Deputy Collector had laid down the boundary wrong and the Superintendent declined to reopen the matter, the Board ordered that the boundary defined in 1838 should be maintained, while as regarded Sundarban chaks lying outside Hodges' boundary, the survey officers were to take the maps and local surveys as the grounds of their demarcation.[19] Only two or three other disagreements arose,[20] for as a rule the petty mahalls

[17] Sbn. Commr. to Rev. Survr., no. 89, dated 8 Aug.; Presdy. Commr. to Sbn. Commr., no. 55 Ct., dated 7 Oct.; Sbn. Commr. to Deputy Surveyor-General, no. 130, dated 21 idem, 1857.

[18] Bd. Rev. to Presdy. Commr., no. 469, dated 1 Dec. 1854. Sbn. Commr. to Presdy. Commr., no. 64, dated 18 July 1857.

[19] Presdy. Commr. to Sbn. Commr., no. 113Ct., dated 9 Dec. 1857.

[20] In lot 220 and Bayarsinga. Sbn. Commr. to Superintendent of Survey, no. 188, dated 11 Feb. 1858. In connexion with the boundary of lot 220, Mr. Reily fell into a mistake, thinking that the Special Commissioner in decreeing certain lands west of the river Gengrail had fixed that river as the boundary in supersession of Hodges' line; but the Board explained that the decree merely went to the resumption of the lands, and did not affect the Sundarban boundary. (Sbn. Commr. to Superintendent of Survey, no. 177, dated 16 Jan., and no. 197, dated 8 March 1858. Bd. Rev. to

that abound in Jessore presented no difficulties, khals being almost invariably the boundaries between them.

287. Survey of Hodges' Line: The survey of Hodges' line was for the most part a piece of professional work merely, and did not bring in its train boundary disputes and claims such as had been experienced in the 24-Parganas, except in two places—lot 222 and Perikhali, for owing to the inquiries, resumptions, and adjustments that had been carried out during the years 1844-57, as described in chapter XIV, Hodges' boundary no longer regulated the limits of mahalls, but had become in great measure obsolete. The localities where it still, however, remained authoritative were brought by Mr. Reily to the Revenue Surveyor's notice. The first was the gap between Gobra and lot 217, where Hodges had been unable to make any survey and had copied Morrieson; and here the Board directed that, as Morrieson's marks could not be identified, the boundary should, as before, be plotted from Morrieson's map, while the limit of the cultivation should be surveyed and the jungle between it and Morrieson's boundary delineated.[21] As that part of the country was still covered with jungle, the survey officers could not carry their operations further south than the Ghoshkhali khal, and delineated the boundary merely from the vicinity of that khal northwards. Yet even there the greater portion of the lands was waste and the cultivation at the south was being deserted. At Gobra itself there was some uncertainty. Captain Gastrell defined the boundary by a line cutting off the required area 1,177 bighas,[22] and Mr. Smith demarcated the line; but the dispute was only settled by subsequent litigation.[23] The next place was lot 222 where also Hodges had been unable to survey and had copied Morrieson. The thakbast amin had included the whole of lot 222 in pargana Sahosh, and Mr. Reily pointed out that only Pankhali and Lakhikhola were

---

Superintendent of Survey, no. 125, dated 9 Apr. 1858, sent with Superintendent of Survey to Sbn. Commr., no. 147, dated 16 idem, Superintendent of Survey to Sbn. Commr., no. 166, dated 8 May 1858).

[21] Presdy. Commr. to Sbn. Commr., no. 112 Ct., dated 7 Dec. 1857.

[22] Sbn. Commr. to Presdy. Commr., no. 96, dated 21 Sept. 1858. Presdy. Commr. to Sbn. Commr., no. 85 Ct., dated 27 idem.

[23] See paragraph 289 *infra*.

excluded from it.[24] The Presidency Commissioner ordered that these two mauzas which bordered the lot on the west, north, and east should be marked off from the lot with the areas assigned them in the 1232 statement, 2,555 and 8,621 bighas respectively, and Mr. Reily and Captain Gastrell proposed to carry out the order by demarcating give-and-take straight lines from certain well defined points.[25] The starting points were fixed by Mr. Reily, and Captain Gastrell surveyed the lines so as to assign the areas approved by the Commissioner. The line for Lakhikhola was drawn from near the mouth of the Maukhali khal in a north-west direction to the river Bhadar cutting off that mouza to the south-west. The line for Pankhali was drawn due south from the junction of the Manga and Jhabjhabiya rivers to the Chunkuri khal, cutting off Pankhali to the east. Mr. Smith was ordered to demarcate these lines in season 1858-59.[26] Hodges' line here was discussed between Captain Gastrell and Mr. Reily, and the former carefully studied Hodges' field-books;[27] but no reference was made throughout their proceedings to Mr. Dampier's rubakaris, which are the real authority for fixing the boundary, and Hodges' survey, which was ancillary, was treated as the prime authority. The result was that the lines laid down were erroneous and served only to mislead. The matter does not appear to have come before the Board, so that no light was thrown upon it by Mr. Dampier.[28] In lot 223 there was a slight change. It was bounded on the east by Chunkuri abad which Mr. Dampier threw outside the Sundarban boundary, but as the abad had reverted into jungle Hodges had not surveyed it, but had copied Morrieson's line. Mr. Smith had fixed the Bajua khal (which practically coincides with that line) as the boundary between the lot and Chunkuri in 1852, and under the Presidency Commissioner's

[24] Sbn. Commr. to Superintendent of Survey, no. 188, dated 11 Feb. 1858.

[25] Sbn. Commr. to Rev. Survr., no. 193, dated 13 Feb. 1858. Sbn. Commr. to Superintendent. of Survey, no. 198, dated 8 March 1858.

[26] Rev. Survr. to Sbn. Commr., no. 33, dated 17 Dec. 1858.

[27] Rev. Survr. to Sbn. Commr., no. 1, dated 2 Oct. 1858, see note 3 to paragraph 65. He also went carefully through the Morrieson's field-books. Rev. Survr. to Sbn. Commr., no. 160, dated 25 Aug. 1858. See note 4 to paragraph 12.

[28] See paragraph 289 *infra.*

orders, the khal was thenceforward made the boundary.[29] The last place where the Sundarban boundary was doubtful was along the south of Perikhali. Hodges had surveyed the tortuous outline of the forest, but Mr. Dampier, it appears, had for convenience sake defined the boundary as running straight from the Mangla river to the Chilla Chandpai. Here the Board decided that Hodges' forest outline should be maintained as the boundary.[30]

288. Revenue Survey Stations: Captain Gastrell urged that his survey stations should be permanently marked, and the Presidency Commissioner ordered that the chief outer southern stations should be marked by pucca pillars.[31] Mr. Smith erected pucka pillars, but the boundary was not demarcated continuously as in the 24-Parganas on account of the dense jungle, nor was it marked at Gobra and other places of uncertainty where Mr. Reily considered something should be done.[32]

289. Resumption Proceedings in Lot 166, Gobra, and Lot 222, 1858-84: Out of the revenue survey arose various resumption proceedings and boundary disputes. Resumption proceedings were begun in 1858 for lands in Gobra, but in 1861 the owner of Gobra brought a suit to recover possession of 1,750 bighas south of the line demarcated by Mr. Smith and won it about 1867.[33] In lot 166 there were three resumption cases fort Biralakhi and two other mahalls. These cases and all the land of the lot south of Hodges' boundary appear to have been decreed to Government by the Presidency Commissioner in 1859.[34] After the two lines were laid down for mauzas

[29] Presdy. Commr. to Sbn. Commr., no. 138 Ct., dated 5 Feb. 1858. Sbn. Commr. to Rev. Survr., no. 193, dated 3 idem. Mr. Reily's remarks about Chunkuri in his letter to Presdy. Commr., no. 163, dated 4 Dec. 1857, are mistaken.

[30] Bd. Rev. to Superintendent of Survey, no. 125, dated 9 Apr. 1858, sent with Superintendent of Survey to Sbn. Commr., no. 147, dated 16 idem, but see paragraph 290.

[31] Presdy. Commr. to Sbn. Commr., no. 50 Ct., dated 13 Aug. 1858, and no. 63 Ct., dated 27 idem.

[32] Ibid., no. 79 Ct., dated 19 Sept. 1858; Sbn. Commr. to Presdy. Commr., no. 115, dated 23 Dec. 1861.

[33] Sbn. Commr. to Presdy. Commr., no. 65, dated 31 July 1872.

[34] Ibid., no. 83, dated 22 Sept., and Presdy. Commr. to Sbn. Commr., no. 35, Ct., dated 9 Nov. 1859.

Pankhali and Lakhikhola, Mr. Reily instituted two suits in 1859 for all the remaining land that lay between the rivers Bhadar, Manga, and Jhabjhabiya and the Chunkuri khal,[35] but the claim was untenable and was abandoned in 1867. Mr. Gomess then instituted a fresh suit for 798 bighas of reclaimed land at the mouth of the Maukhali khal, which, owing to the confusion in which lot 222 was involved, was not decided till 1882. Part of this area was resumed and part released. Following on the conclusions then laid down, a suit was instituted for the remainder of the lot, which was in the possession of Raja Barada Kantha Rai, and it was decided in favour of Government in 1883. A suit had been begun in 1852 for Khonarmet, the south-west portion of the lot, which was decreed to Government in 1866. All these lands were brought under settlement in 1883-84.[36]

290. Boundary Disputes in Jessore, 1856-67: Boundary disputes were not numerous in Jessore, for the extensive and frequent inquiries, surveys, and resumption proceedings that had been carried out had cleared away all difficulties in lots 216 to 224. Beyond the Pasar, however, there were considerable disputes regarding the boundary of Perikhali. After Mr. Gomess, following Hodges' line, surveyed the lands there in 1856, the zamindars put in a claim to 22,182 bighas as belonging to their zamindari of Perikhali, and produced two faisalas by the Special Commissioner of 1838 and 1845. But these lands being found to be different from those released under the faisalas, their claim was dismissed by the Sundarban Commissioner on 15th August 1856 and by the Presidency Commissioner on 19th September 1856. On appeal, the Board amended the decision by defining the boundary as a straight line drawn from a khal rising out of the river Bhola and flowing west to the junction of the Pasar and Mangla rivers. The zamindars were thus found to be in possession of two blocks aggregating 7,775 bighas, which were then brought under settlement. But they instituted two suits in 1861 to gain possession alleging the Nora Chilla khal to be their south boundary.[37] An attempt appears to have been made

[35] Presdy. Commr. to Sbn. Commr., no. 34 Ct., dated 9 Nov. 1859.

[36] Sbn. Commr. to Bd. Rev., no. 54, dated 27 Apr. 1882. Bd. Rev. to Sbn. Commr., no. 958A, dated 1 Nov. 1882, and no. 899A, dated 11 Sept. 1883.

[37] Sbn. Commr. to Presdy. Commr., no. 156, dated 18 March 1862. Presdy. Commr. to Sbn. Commr., no. 24, dated 27 May 1863.

to settle the dispute amicably[38] but they won their claims on appeal before the High Court in 1865[39] and the lands were given up to the zamindars, who thus gained lots 237 and 238 as part and parcel of their zamindaris. Mention may be made here of a settlement of Babupur and Banchanagar which brought about a modification of Hodges' line in lot 216. These mahalls bordered on the lot, but could not be identified as the country had reverted into jungle. A settlement was made of them for an area of 12,000 bighas without boundaries in 1867. After reclamation had begun the zamindars sued to obtain the land as belonging to pargana Talakhajra and gained part of their claim in 1881, and the civil court decreed away to them part of lot 216 between the Patnikhali and Kathaltala Doaniya khals.[40]

291. Revenue Survey of the Eastern Jessore and the Bakarganj Sundarbans, 1862-63: The revenue survey after traversing the district of Bakarganj came round to the Sundarbans of that district in 1862, and the operations there were taken up at the point where they ended in 1858, and the remainder of the Jessore Sundarbans and the whole of the Bakarganj Sundarbans were surveyed during season 1862-63 by Lieutenant W.J. Stewart—at least so much as was in process of reclamation or could well be surveyed. The dense forest was left untouched in Jessore, but the whole of the Bakarganj Sundarbans, where cultivation in many cases reached the sea, was brought within the operations. It was approved that the survey that season should deal with the forest tract between the Pasar and Baleswar rivers,[41] which Mr. Gomess had partially mapped, but the undertaking appears to have been beyond accomplishment and was not carried out. The survey stations were at the same time secured by pucca marks by Mr. Gomess.[42]

292. Boundary Disputes in Bakarganj, 1852-65: There was a boundary dispute between Debnathpur and Sonakhali, Debnath Rai

[38] Presdy. Commr. to Sbn. Commr., no. 1 Ct., dated 25 June, and no. 60, dated 9 July 1863.

[39] Sbn. Commr. to Presdy. Commr., no. 125, dated 6 Sept. 1866.

[40] Sbn. Commr. to Bd. Rev., no. 194, dated 18 Aug. 1883.

[41] Presdy. Commr. to Sbn. Commr., no. 168, dated 7 Nov. 1862.

[42] Rev. Survr. to Sbn. Commr., no. 89, dated 22 Apr. 1863. Sbn. Commr to Presdy. Commr., no. 271, dated 16 Feb. 1863.

claiming 19,495 bighas south of the Saplenja river. The point for decision was, what was cultivated when he got the patta of 1839, for he was entitled to all that was cultivated in 1850, except those parts which, like chaks Betmor and Rajpasa, had been cultivated before 18-19. He brought a civil suit and his claim was decreed by the High Court in 1865 for about 13,500 bighas, being all the land claimed, except these two chaks.[43]

293. Resumption Proceedings in Henckell's and Donnelly's Mahalls, 1857-67: As mentioned in paragraph 246 the resumption proceedings in the numerous undiscovered Henckell's and Donnelly's mahallas were stayed in 1857 until the revenue survey should have traversed Jessore and Bakarganj, when it was hoped some light might be thrown on them. At that time there were 83 cases pending before the Sundarban Commissioner, and 72, it would seem, before the Presidency Commissioner:[44] 36 cases were remanded to Mr. Reily in order to have the lands mapped. Of those before the Presidency Commissioner some appear to have been released and others returned for further investigation. What their numbers were is not clear, but at the end of the year 1863-64, when the survey operations had been concluded, there were 96 of Henckell's and Donnelly's mahallas under inquiry. Registers of these mahalls were then prepared at the Presidency Commissioner's orders.[45] During the following years up to 1867 the cases were gradually disposed of, few if any being decreed in favour of Government.[46]

294. Resumption of Bargona, Dhalua, and Naltona, 1846-70: It has been mentioned in paragraph 80 that Mr. Dampier, when Sundarban Commissioner, released from resumption mauza Phuljhuri and mauza Aila Teorkhali in Bakarganj in 1831. In 1843, however, the Collector of Bakarganj finding cultivation spreading there prepared a map dividing the tract into seven chaks—(1) Phuljhuri, (2) Keorabuniya, (3) Aila Teorkhali, (4) 'Buriswar, (5) Bargona, (6) Dhalua, and (7) Naltona. It was proposed to institute resumption

[43] Presdy. Commr, to Sbn. Commr., no. 38, dated 22 May and memo. no. 59, dated 2 June 1865.

[44] Ibid., no. 84Ct., dated 17 Nov. 1857.

[45] Ibid., no. 65, dated 11 Aug. 1864.

[46] See Presdy. Commr. to Sbn. Commr., memo. no. 145, dated 2 Sept. 1867.

proceedings for lands not included within the boundaries of the patta of 1805, under which all these chaks were claimed to be held, and suits were accordingly begun by the Sundarban Commissioner after the revival of his office in 1846. Uma Kanta Babu found that the pattadar had taken possession of land beyond the boundaries of the patta, but, holding that the question had been concluded by Mr. Dampier's decision, dismissed the Government claim in 1849. On appeal the Special Commissioner reversed the order on 17th December 1851, and remanded the case for trial on the question whether the lands in dispute were within the boundaries mentioned in the patta, or were included in Mr. Dampier's decision. After retrial the Presidency Commissioner on 25th July 1856 finally released Phuljhuri as being comprised within those boundaries, resumed the last three chaks as lying outside the boundaries, and reserved his decision as to the three others until they should have been surveyed. A survey was made by Mr. Gomess in 1857-58, and the Presidency Commissioner thereupon, concurring with Mr. Reily's opinion of 6th September 1860, decided on 10th April 1861 that, the pattadar having failed to prove these chaks were comprised in his patta, they were all resumable. Keorabuniya and Buriswar were resumed, but Aila Teorkhali was relinquished as a favour since two of its boundaries tallied with those in the patta. Khaja Abdul Ghani Mir, the pattadar, then instituted two suits in the Civil Court to set aside those two orders in 1857 and 1862 respectively, and the suits were carried up in appeal to the High Court, which decreed Bargona, Dhalua, and Naltona to Government on 11th May 1863, and Keorabuniya and Buriswar to him on 20th March 1865. He appealed against the former decree, and the Government against the latter to the Privy Council. The main question for decision was what lands were covered by the boundaries specified in the patta. Those of mauza Aila Teorkhali as mentioned in the patta were these—"Bounded on the north and east by the Aila Don, on the south by the Parwa river, on the west by the river Bhyang down to the Khak Don." These rivers did not agree with the actual rivers bounding any particular tract, and the question had been answered differently by the different courts. The Privy Council heard the appeals together and dealing with the whole description of the lands in the patta decided that the grant of mauza Aila Teorkhali embraced chaks Keorabuniya, Aila Teorkhali, and Buriswar. The Council therefore decreed those three to Abdul Ghani, and the other three—Bargona, Dhalua and Naltona—to Government on 26th January 1870.[47] Meanwhile acting on the resumption decree of 1856, Mr. Gomess brought the cleared lands in Bargona (3,462 bighas) and Dhalua (1,693 bighas) under settlement in 1857-58. Naltona was all waste. Abdul Ghani was set aside and all titles created by him extinguished,[48] but the haolas and nim-haolas were maintained.[49] These chaks have remained khass mahalls ever since, and Bargona and Dhalua have been developing under a system of haoladari settlements. Keorarbuniya and Buriswar, when resumed by the Presidency Commissioner in 1861, were also brought under settlement in 1862-63,[50] and were kept khass till restored to Abdul Ghani on the Privy Council's decision in 1870.

295. Other Proceedings in Bakarganj: Mr. Caspersz proposed in 1865 to commence resumption proceedings for a tract comprising 15,608 bighas and lying between Tushkali and Ramna Bamna which appears to have been all forest in 1830, but the Presidency Commissioner distrusted the grounds and the idea was abandoned.[51]

[47] Privy Council's decision, dated 26 Jan. 1870. Presdy. Commr. to Sbn. Commr., no. 45, dated 15 Apr. 1861.

[48] Presdy. Commr. to Sbn. Commr., no. 17 Ct., dated 17 June 1856.

[49] Dacca Commr. to Sbn. Commr., no. 572, dated 14 March 1868.

[50] Sbn. Commr. To Presdy. Commr., no. 109, dated 28 July 1865.

[51] Ibid., memo. No. 37, dated 22 May 1865. Sbn. Commr. to Presdy. Commr., no. 294, dated, 20 March 1866.

CHAPTER XXIV

Schemes of Sundarban Improvement, and Miscellaneous Matters

1853-1868

296. Improvement of Sundarban Navigation, 1853-56: In 1853 Mr. Mactier, Collector of Faridpur, brought to notice the difficulties attending the navigation between Calcutta and East Bengal along the Sundarban channels, such as the want of a towing path from Calcutta to Khulna, the delay and want of room in the Baliyaghata and Circular Canals, the obstruction from sunken boats, & c, and the want of dredging machines; and urged that measures should be taken for the improvement of the navigation. The Commissioner of Dacca endorsed his proposals, and the Government sanctioned the undertaking. Mr. Smith, the Deputy Collector in the Sundarbans, was vested with the powers of a Magistrate in the 24-Parganas, Baraset, and Jessore, and was deputed in company with a subordinate of the Public Works Department and a body of coolies (1) to report minutely on the state of the frequented channels and their banks; (2) to ascertain what was necessary to facilitate the passage of boats at all times of the tide; and (3) to remove the obstructions that more immediately impeded the navigation.[1] He entered on this duty in June 1853, and submitted his report in September following. He recommended that an officer should be located at some place about midway in the passage with magisterial powers and jurisdiction over the thanas along the route, and that police and conservancy establishments should be maintained for the chief channels between Khulna and the Salt Water Lakes.[2] Mr. Smith himself was selected for this duty. He was stationed at Kaliganj, still remaining, however, subordinate to the

[1] Presdy. Commr. to Sbn. Commr., no. 113, dated 16 May 1853.

[2] Smith to Sbn. Commr., no. 65, dated 22 Sept. 1853. Sbn. Commr. to Presdy. Commr., no. 473, dated 29 Oct. 1853.

Sundarban Commissioner, and being employed in the Sundarbans during the cold season.[3] Mr. Smith remained there till June 1856 and was succeeded by Mr. Tweedie, but the scheme does not appear to have been thoroughly satisfactory.

297. Port Canning Scheme, 1853-64: The idea was started of making a subsidiary port to Calcutta on the river Matla, and that river was surveyed by Lieutenant Ward in 1853. On 5th July 1853, Government bought lot 54 with an area of 25,000 bighas for Rs. 11,000 for the construction of a ship canal and railway connecting the Matlah and Hugli rivers. During 1854 the lands were measured and the cleared portion, 3,883 bighas, settled provisionally.[4] In 1855 the river frontage of the lot, where part had been cleared, was surveyed by Mr. Gomess under the Board's orders for six miles, and marked out into roads and lots for the construction of the new town and port, a site being chosen near the Malikhal for the railway station. The clearance of the lot was begun by contract, Rs. 4,000 being sanctioned for the clearance of the river frontage and the excavation of two tanks.[5] The provisional settlement caused much confusion, the tenants asserting various claims and rights which threatened to injure the rights of Government, hence the Supreme Government disallowed it and prohibited any alienation of the land pending the determination of the site of the proposed town, & c.[6] Lot 50, which adjoins lot 54 on the south, became open to resumption and was resumed in 1856.[7] After considerable discussion it was decided in 1857 that a square mile at the north-east' of the lot, on the river Matlah, should be reserved for Government, and the remainder was regranted to the late owner on condition that he should clear the northern side adjoining lot 54

[3] Presdy. Commr. to Sbn. Commr., no. 141, dated 15 July 1854.

[4] Sbn. Commr. to Presdy. Commr., no. 333, dated 7 Aug. Presdy. Commr. to Sbn. Commr., no. 56, dated 22 Sept. 1854.

[5] Sbn. Commr. to Presdy. Commr., no. 560, dated 31 Dec. 1855. Presdy. Commr. to Sbn. Commr., no. 252, dated 1 Feb. 1856.

[6] Presdy. Commr.. to Sbn. Commr., no. 380, dated 26 Apr., and no. 12 Ct., dated 20 Dec. 1856.

[7] Sbn. Commr. to Presdy. Commr., no. 77, dated 7 March 1856.

within a specified time.[8] Lots 43,129, and 130, which also border on the river Matla, became liable to resumption and were resumed in 1859, Government intending to reserve the valuable river frontages in the former two. But after long discussion Government restored the lots to the grantees in 1862.[9] Ellenganj and the Idu khal were suggested for the site of the port, but the former was preferred. It was at first intended to carry out all the schemes at that place under Mr. Reily's direction,[10] but the Government of India considering that the scheme and plans should be well matured appointed Mr. Leonard, C.E., independently in 1856, with orders to clear lots 50 and 54 and conduct all the operations there.[11] The settlement of the cleared lands was revised in 1857,[12] and an attempt was made, but unsuccessfully, to establish a bazar there. In 1860 the management of the Government property there was made over to the Sundarban Commissioner, with instructions to clear the jungle, lease out the land to rice cultivators, keep the embankments in repair, and collect the rents of the town. About Rs. 38,000 would seem to have been spent on the clearance of the Matla lots during years 1860-63,[13] from a fund called the "Matlah Town Improvement Fund." In 1864 a map of lot 54 was submitted to Government with an explanatory report by Mr. Caspersz, Sundarban Commissioner.[14]

298. Port Canning Municipality, 1862-83: The lands near the west bank of the Matla were reserved as town lots, while the rest remained agricultural lands; and in 1858 and 1859 the leasehold right in the town lots was sold by Government at public auction for a term of 60 years at rates varying from Rs. 8 to Rs. 20 per bigha per annum. In 1862 the Port Canning Municipality was formed and Government

[8] Presdy. Commr. to Sbn. Commr., no. 296, dated 15 Apr., and no. 108 Ct., dated 30 Nov. 1857.

[9] Ibid., no. 51 Ct., dated 2nd Dec. 1859; no. 30, dated 12 March 1861; and no. 35, dated 6 June 1862. The lots were neglected and deteriorated in the interval, and Govt, paid the grantees Rs. 28,225, compensation. Presdy. Commr. to Sbn. Commr., no. 224, dated 22 Apr. 1864.

[10] Ibid., no. 75, dated 20 June 1856.

[11] Ibid., no. 18 Ct., dated 27 Dec. 1856.

[12] Ibid., no. 29 Ct., dated 7 Aug. 1857.

[13] Sbn. Commr. to Presdy. Commr., no. 172, dated 9 Apr. 1862.

[14] Ibid., no. 43, dated 16 June 1862.

formally assigned its property in the lands to the municipality. Attempts were made to raise public loans for the improvement of the town and port, but they were not attended with success. In March 1865, however, the municipality succeeded in raising a debenture loan, and the Port Canning Company which had been recently formed subscribed Rs. 2,50,200 towards it. This loan carried the municipality through its operations during 1864-65, but the sum still fell short by Rs. 1,29,918 of its requirements for the following year. Hence on their application, Government granted the municipality, in March 1866, a loan of 4½ lakhs without interest for five years on the security of their land and other property—the port dues, however, being retained in the hands of Government. The total debentures thus seem to have been—Government Rs. 4,50,000, private individuals Rs. 1,60,700, and the Port Canning Company Rs. 2,50,200. Among the private debenture-holders were a number of the leaseholders, and they were entitled under the terms of the loan to commute their leasehold rights into free-hold titles in the town lots. Private individuals then commuted Rs. 87,600 debenture bonds for the free-hold title in 26 lots, and the Port Canning Company Rs. 2,50,200 in respect of 41 lots; but there were errors in the latter commutation, the Company repudiated it and costly litigation ensued. In 1870 the Government advanced the municipality a further loan of Rs. 22,200 on mortgage: it bore interest at 5 per cent, and was repayable in four half-yearly instalments. When half had been repaid, however, the property of the municipality was attached by the Civil Court in execution of a decree obtained by Government in respect of the loan of 4 1/2 lakhs, and the Collector of the 24-Parganas was appointed *ex-officio* manager of the estate. The net income was reckoned at about at Rs. 20,550, and was employed in paying the dividends due to Government and the private debenture-holders who were 20 in number. During the years 1877 to 1881 Government took steps to buy out these debenture-holders, offering them 50 per cent, of the par value of their bonds. Seventeen accepted the terms, and the sum paid them was Rs. 56,915, while three remained to whom the full amount due was Rs. 25,157. In 1881 Government resolved to execute the decrees it held, by bringing the estate to sale, and to buy it in. This was done and at a sale held on 5th November 1883, Government bought the municipal estate for

Rs. 50,000. Government thus acquired the right, title and interest of the municipality and became the proprietor of the whole property with the exception of the free-hold town lots.[15]

299. Port Canning Company, 1864-68: In connexion with the Port Canning scheme a Company was started called the "Port Canning Land Investment, Reclamation, and Dock Company, Limited," for the purpose of purchasing and reclaiming the waste lands bordering on the river Matla. The Company bought lots 121, 122, 124, 125, 126, 128 (part), and 132 in fee-simple, and redeemed the land revenue of lots 43, 123, 127, 128 (part), 129-31, 133, 134, and 136 in 1865. One-tenth of the money was paid down and the balance liquidated from year to year. But in 1868 the Company finding itself unable to complete the acquisitions, was permitted to relinquish lots 123, 127, and part of 128, and all the fee-simple lots except No. 132, and to carry the money that had been paid on their account to the credit of the other lots.[16]

300. East Bengal Mart Scheme, 1855-63: The Sundarbans formed the subject of a long report by the Board in 1855, and various suggestions were thrown out for their improvement.[17] One of the suggestions was the establishment of a mart on the river Baleswar or Bishkhali, independent of Calcutta, as a centre for the trade of East Bengal. The Board urged that those rivers should be surveyed to ascertain their suitability for the navigation of vessels, and Mr. Reily on being consulted supported the scheme. Soundings were taken in season 1855-56, which shewed that the Bishkhali was not adapted for navigation, and the Baleswar could be traversed by small vessels only.[18] Mr. Reily then suggested that the Sipsa should be chosen, and a mart established at the corner of lot 219 or 221,[19] but this too came to nothing. Again, in 1859, Mr. Reily urged that the navigation

[15] Govt of India Resolution No. 251A, dated 5 March 1866; Govt. of Bengal to Govt. of India, no. 853 dated 17 Sept. 1880; Bd. Rev. to Govt., no. 536A, dated 15 Aug. 1882; No. 483A, dated 2 June 1884; no. 763½, dated 1 Sept. 1884; no. 900A, dated 27 Oct. 1884, and no. 155A, dated 18 Feb. 1885.

[16] Sbn. Commr. to Presdy. Commr., no. 165, dated 14 Dec. 1868.

[17] Bd. Rev. to Govt., no. 230A, dated 29 June 1855.

[18] Presdy. Commr. to Sbn. Commr., no. 231, dated 11 Jan. 1856.

[19] Sbn. Commr. to Presdy. Commr., no. 488, dated 9 Apr. 1857.

between the rivers Pasar and Baleswar should be improved, and offered various suggestions.[20] Lieutenant Sweney surveyed the Baleswar as far as Morrellganj in season 1860-61, and reported favourably of it as navigable for vessels. Government thereupon called for a report in 1862, proposing Kachua or Morrellganj or some intermediate place as the site of the mart.[21] Mr. Caspersz, the Sundarban Commissioner, recommended Kachua, but Mr. Reily (who was also consulted) Morrellganj. Further inquiries were made, and Perozepur was then recommended in 1863.[22] But the scheme seems to have been then dropped.

301. Funds for Sundarban Improvement, 1856-64: Another scheme was the improvement of the Sundarban estates and of the raiyats occupying them, and towards that object Government sanctioned in 1856 the application of the sale proceeds of Sundarban grants. The fund was called the "Sale of Sundarban Lots Fund". It grew very rich, but owing to the restrictions imposed, not much was expended, though Rs. 3,260 were granted to Messrs. Morrell to excavate khals in Tushkhali and Sonakhali. About 1861 the fund appears to have been amalgamated with the Calcutta Canal Fund, and in 1862, when it amounted to Rs. 1,37,992, it was abolished, and the money carried to the imperial account.[23] In 1861 another fund, called the "Fund for the improvement of reserved Sundarban lots", was started, which was composed of the proceeds of the temporary settlements of Sundarban lots.[24] The lots reserved were Nos. 43, 50, 54, 128, 129, and 130 (which all lie on the river Matla), but lots 43, 129, and 130 were restored to the grantees in 1862 as mentioned in paragraph 296. The Fund appears to have grown to Rs. 11,085 in 1864.[25] I do not find, however, what became of it.

302. Destruction of Wild Animals, 1852-64: The Government

[20] Sbn. Commr. to Presdy. Commr., no. 146, dated 31 Jan., and no. 114, dated 11 Oct. 1860.

[21] Presdy. Commr, to Sbn. Commr., no, 133, dated 25 Aug. 1862.

[22] Sbn. Commr. to Presdy. Commr., no. 241, dated 2 Feb. 1863.

[23] Presdy. Commr. to Sbn. Commr., 24 Ct., dated 27 Dec. 1856, and no. 21, dated 23 May 1862. Sbn. Commr. to Presdy. Commr., no. 172, dated 9 Apr. 1862.

[24] Presdy. Commr. to Sbn. Commr., no. 143, dated 24 Dec. 1861.

[25] Sbn. Commr. to Presdy. Commr., no. 133, dated 27 Oct. 1864.

in 1852 seems to have thought that special measures were necessary for the destruction of tigers in the 24-Parganas. The Collector recommended (and the Sundarban Commissioner supported him) that the reward should be raised from Rs. 5, which afforded very little profit, to Rs. 10 and paid over promptly.[26] Government sanctioned the increase in 1853,[27] and doubled the reward in 1860, for every tiger killed near the Matla in order to aid the work of reclamation there. But it would seem that the reward was afterwards reduced to Rs. 5, for, when Government called for a report on the subject in 1864, the Sundarban Commissioner urged that the reward should be raised from Rs. 5 to Rs. 8.[28]

303. Embankments in the 24-Parganas, 1765-1857: Before the decennial settlement embankments in the 24-Parganas were in the hands of the zamindars, to whom Government made an allowance for repairs equivalent to Company's Rs. 16,786. In 1785 Government undertook the maintenance of the repairs and resumed those *pulbandi* charges. At the decennial settlement in 1791 Government resolved to throw the cost of keeping up the embankments on the zamindars, but they refused, and it was agreed that if Government decided to maintain them, the zamindars should be exonerated from all loss that might occur. Government then undertook them and they were looked after by the Salt Agent till 1803, when they were transferred to the Embankment Committee then constituted. The embankments, however, were not properly repaired, and in 1814 Government was obliged to renew them at its own expense. In 1819, again, it was determined that the zamindars themselves should estimate for and effect the necessary repairs under the supervision of the Superintendent of Embankments. This system prevailed up to 1834, when Government on 15th January ordered that the advances made from the public treasury for the repair of the embankments should be discontinued, and the interference of Government therewith withdrawn. These orders led to the general deterioration of the district and the ruin of the zamindars, who, considering that they

26 Ibid., no. 124, dated 29 March 1853.

27 Presdy. Commr. to Sbn. Commr., no. 84, dated 4 June 1853.

28 Sbn. Commr. to Presdy. Commr., no. 64, dated 2 Aug. 1864.

had a right to demand the intervention of Government and that they were aggrieved by its withdrawal, preferred throwing up their estates to incurring the necessary expense on the embankments. In 1838 therefore Government was compelled to undertake the liability of maintaining the embankments, and the work was carried out under the supervision of the Department of Public Works. In 1857, owing to the spread of cultivation, the Superintendent of Embankments raised the question whether Government was obliged to protect the Sundarban grants. Mr. Reily in reply said that Government was under no liability as regarded Sundarban grantees, for they were bound under the terms of their leases to protect their own grants, though he suggested that Government might give the grantees of lots 1-3, 6-8, and 110 some aid as their lands bordered on the Hugli and were more exposed than others. Claims by the patitábádi talukdars would need to be specially considered, as it was doubtful whether they were entitled to such aid. The results of Captain Smyth's survey would shew the boundaries of the permanently-settled portions of the 24-Parganas and would remove all uncertainty as to how far the responsibility of Government extended.[29]

304. Fisheries in the Sundarbans, 1859-68: Before 1859 no leases appear to have been given for fisheries in the Sundarbans, but in that year the Government directed that the fisheries of all navigable rivers should be taxed, and the orders were calculated with the Board's circular order No. 36, dated 8th November 1859. All the Sundarban rivers were to be divided into convenient blocks and farmed out for five years.[30] The rivers in the 24-Parganas Sundarbans were divided into seven blocks," five of which were disposed of by public auction for an annual jama of Rs. 3,530; those in Jessore were formed into three blocks and sold for Rs. 210 jama; and 11 rivers in Bakarganj between "the Bhola and Bamna were sold for Rs. 453, while no bids could be got for the rivers further east.[31] The fisheries in the 24-Parganas were the most valuable, the value of the others being affected by their greater

[29] Presdy. Commr. to Sbn. Commr., no. 20, dated 27 May; and Sbn. Commr. to Presdy. Commr., no. 29, dated 6 June 1857.

[30] Ibid., no. 44 Ct., dated 25 Nov. 1859.

[31] Sbn. Commr. to Presdy. Commr., no. 179, dated 15 March 1860, and no. 195, dated 1 March 1861. Presdy. Commr. to Sbn. Commr., no. 38, dated 18 Apr. 1861.

distance from Calcutta. There had been an old fishery and fish-drying business off Rabanabad and Char Chapli, but it had been given up.[32] The people, however, had overestimated the worth of the fisheries, and the bids had been excessive; the drawbacks being that some rivers lay amid dense forest, others suffered from the continual traffic over them, and others again were too far from the markets.[33] Four of the farmers in 24-Parganas and all those in Jessore defaulted. In the latter district none but grantees appeared inclined to take up the fisheries, and they sought only those situated near their lots in order to prevent strangers interfering with their tenants. The blocks were then sub-divided, and each river disposed of separately. Those in Jessore—now 35 in number—were farmed out for Rs. 670, and five in Bakarganj for Rs. 46 in 1862.[34] Those in the 24-Parganas were sub-divided and farmed out for Rs. 497 in 1862 and 1863.[35] These settlements were confirmed by the Presidency Commissioner, the jalkar in the Hugli being left to the Collector of Midnapur.[36] The arrangements, however, had in some cases been hastily effected, for two of the fisheries in the Puna Don and another river in Bakarganj were claimed by the zamindars.. The list was then scrutinzed, and fisheries which had been wrongly taken from private persons were restored in 1864 and 1865.[37] The jalkars did not possess much stability, though a deposit of one year's revenue had always been exacted as security. The farmers frequently defaulted and fresh settlements had to be made. In 1866, when the scheme was in fair working order, the results were these —in the 24-Parganas 65 blocks were farmed out at an annual jama of Rs. 584, in Jessore 35 blocks at Rs. 442, and in Bakarganj 24 blocks at Rs. 946, the total yearly revenue being Rs. 1,972.[38] A farmer prosecuted certain trespassers in 1867, but the Deputy Magistrate of Satkhira

[32] Sbn. Commr., to Presdy. Commr., no. 25, dated 24 May 1860.

[33] Ibid., no. 77, dated 9 Aug. 1863.

[34] Ibid., 19 Sept. and 27 Oct. 1862.

[35] Ibid., no. 139, dated 24 Nov. 1863.

[36] Presdy. Commr. to Sbn. Commr., no. 132, dated 29 Oct. 1863.

[37] Sbn. Commr. to Presdy. Commr., no. 232, dated 30 Apr. 1864. Presdy Commr. to Sbn Commr., no. 54, dated 8 Aug. 1864, and Bd. Rev. C.O. no. 1 of July 1864.

[38] Sbn. Commr. to Presdy. Commr., no. 316, dated 27 Apr.; no. 4, dated 27 June; and nos. 163 and 164, dated 11 Oct. 1866.

acquitted them on the ground that the public had a prescriptive right of fishery in the Sundarban rivers.[39] This raised the question of the right of Government to lease them out, and the Government, after reconsidering it, decided that the further lease of fisheries should be stopped,[40] and in 1868 ordered that all sums realized as jalkar from the Port- Canning Company should be refunded to them with interest. Mr. Gomess treated the order as applying generally to all farmers of fisheries from the date of the original farms in 1861.[41]

305. Lease of Banker in the Sundarbans, 1864-68: Notice has already been taken of applications for the bankar, or the farm of the forest produce of the Sundarbans. They had been always refused, such arrangements being considered inexpedient. About 1862, however, the policy of conserving the forests in Bengal came under the consideration of the Government, and Dr. Brandis, the Conservator of Forests in Burmah, drew up a preliminary memorandum on the subject on 6th January 1863.[42] Reports were called for. A statement of the extent of forest at the absolute disposal of Government was prepared in 1864, and also a list of trees in the Sundarbans. The ungranted lots contained 8,81,836 acres of forest, and Saugor Island and the unlotted lands along the seaface between Channel Creek and the Baleswar 12,95,785 acres.[43] In consequence of this change in opinion (it would seem) the Presidency Commissioner in 1863 took a favourable view of the bankar farms, and the Sundarban Commissioner advocated their trials.[44] Mr. Gomess then divided the ungranted lands in the 24-Parganas and Jessore into convenient blocks and proposed that the bankar in them should be farmed out by public auction. The Board sanctioned the scheme in 1864, provided that the farms should be liable to cancelment after six months' notice in the event of the lands

[39] Sbn. Commr. to Presdy. Commr., no. 62, dated 31 May 1867.

[40] Presdy. Commr. to Sbn. Commr., memo. no. 2 Ct., dated 23 Nov. 1867.

[41] Sbn. Commr. to Presdy. Commr., no. 146, dated 12 Nov. 1868.

[42] Presdy. Commr. to Sbn. Commr., memo. no. 76, dated 23 Aug. 1864.

[43] Sbn. Commr. to Presdy. Commr., no. 114, dated 24 Sept., and no. 169, dated 24 Nov. 1864.

[44] Presdy. Commr. to Sbn. Commr., no. 196, dated 25 Apr. 1863. Sbn. Commr. to Presdy Commr., no. 101, dated 21 Sept. 1863.

being required for grants.[45] The bankar and maukar in the Government khass mahalls Bargona, Dhalua, and Naltona were farmed out that year, but otherwise no applications were received.[46] In January 1866 he put up the bankars to public auction and disposed of them for five years, thus—24-Parganas, 26 blocks (area 11,16,844 bighas), for Rs. 7,342 annual jama; Jessore, 22 blocks (area 7,74,609 bighas) for Rs. 1,016. The Bakarganj Sundarbans were almost wholly leased out, and with the exception of the above three khass mahalls, no bankars were feasible. A deposit of one year's rent was always taken as security.[47] The Port Canning Company bought most of the farms at the auction, and within a year acquired all the rest, thereby obtaining the monopoly of the forest produce. The leases were recalled and were renewed without modification in 1867. It was intended that if Mr. Schiller floated his Sundarban Reclamation Company the leases should be cancelled, and the whole of the bankar be included in his grant. But in 1868 when his scheme fell through, Government wished to render the waste lands again available for grants, and the question was raised whether the bankar leases should not be cancelled. The Port Canning Company objected, but the Government decided that they should be cancelled on the expiry of the six months' notice.[48] The farms had been most lucrative, for the Company obtained a net profit from them of Rs. 42,849 in the year 1867-68.[49]

306. Mr. F. Schiller's Scheme of Sundarban Reclamation, 1865-68: In January 1865 Mr. Ferdinand Schiller and eight other gentlemen, European and native, applied to Government to purchase the remaining ungranted waste lands, proposing to raise a capital of not less than one million sterling and reclaim the lands by means of labour imported from China, Madras, Zanzibar, and other places. As their object was the same as Government had had in view when

[45] Presdy. Commr. to Sbn. Commr., no. 159, dated 13 Dec. 1864.

[46] Sbn. Commr. to Presdy. Commr., no. 250, dated 25 Feb. 1865.

[47] Ibid., no. 243A, dated 28 Jan. 1866. Presdy. Commr. to Sbn. Commr., memo. no. 72, dated 23rd July 1866.

[48] Presdy. Commr. to Sbn. Commr., no. 1831, dated 2 May 1867; and memo. no. 139, dated 23 Oct. 1868. Sbn. Commr. to Presdy. Commr., no. 148, dated 13 Nov., and no. 156, dated 28 Nov. 1868.

[49] Sbn. Commr. to Presdy. Commr., no. 155, dated 24 Nov. 1868.

framing the rules of 1853, the Bengal Government proposed and the Government of India sanctioned these terms in February 1865—that the unappropriated waste lands in the 24-Parganas Sundarbans, aggregating 1,186,560 acres, should be sold under the waste land rules of 1863 by public auction at Calcutta in one lot at the upset price of Rs. 2-8 per acre. The Government, however, would not encourage any intention to import labour from Africa, and would hold itself free to take measures to secure the health and protection of the labourers.[50] The sale advertisement was drafted for all the lands mentioned, except six lots which were included in the prospectus of the Port Canning Company.[51] Mr. Schiller then attempted to start the Company to reclaim the Sundarbans, with a capital of £1,800,000, but without success. In December 1865 he again applied, undertaking to float the Company, and asking to have the lands under the grants rules of 1853 with liberty to redeem afterwards, and the Board, though doubting whether a large Company would succeed where the enterprise of individuals had fallen short, supported his petition. The Company, however, could not be got together, and on his again applying in 1867, the Government allowed him time till August 1868.[52] Mr. Schiller asked to have the leases executed in his own name in anticipation of the Company being started, but this could not be conceded, though further grants were stopped meanwhile.[53] All his efforts, however, proved unsuccessful and his scheme was dropped in August 1868. That Port Canning Company then proposed a similar scheme in their favour,[54]but it was not granted.

307. Cultivation of Cotton, 1860-68: Attempts were also made to introduce new staples into the Sundarbans. Three barrels of New Orleans cotton seed were distributed by the Sundarban Commissioner

[50] Govt, of India, no. 1425, dated 15 Feb. 1865, with Presdy. Commr. to Sbn. Commr., no. 58 Ct., dated 17 March 1865.

[51] Sbn. Commr. to Presdy. Commr., no. 287, dated 27 March 1865.

[52] Govt. of India to Govt. of Bengal, no. 497, dated 17 Jan. 1867, with Presdy. Commr. to Sbn. Commr., memo. no. 27 Ct., dated 4 March 1867. Presdy. Commr. to Sbn. Commr., memo. no. 25, dated 16 Apr. 1867.

[53] Presdy. Commr. to Sbn. Commr., no. 104, dated 5 July 1867.

[54] Ibid., memo. no. 127, dated 12 Oct. 1868. Sbn. Commr. to Presdy. Commr., no. 155, dated 24 Nov. 1868.

among the grantees in 1860 under the orders of Government, and its cultivation was tried at Matla also, but the conditions were not suitable, and the attempt failed; though Mr. Reily reported that the Mags grew cotton in the extreme east of Bakarganj.[55] Further trials were made with cotton in 1867-68, but they do not seem to have been successful.

[55] Sbn. Commr. to Presdy. Commr., no. 40, dated 3 July 1860 and no. 209, dated 27 March 1861.

CHAPTER XXV

Rules for the Sale of Waste Lands Free of Land Revenue and for the Redemption of Land Revenue 1858-1870

308. Deliberations Regarding Sales in Fee-simple and Redemption of Land Revenue, 1858-60: Two measures of revenue policy were brought forward by Government about the year 1858—first, the sale of waste lands in perpetuity, discharged from all prospective demand on account of land revenue; and, secondly, permission to redeem the existing land revenue by the immediate payment of one sum equal in value to the revenue redeemed. They were generally advocated with the object of promoting the settlement of Europeans in India, and were discussed by the Secretary of State in his despatches no. 2, dated 31st December 1858, and no. 1, dated 16th March 1859. He sanctioned the commutation of the annual payments of the land revenue by one payment at the time of taking the grant, or at any future time during the currency of the lease, and a notification to that effect, dated 12th August 1859, was published in the *Calcutta. Gazette* of 17th idem, page 1907. Local officers were then called upon to report on the second measure.[1] Mr. Reily, replying for the Sundarbans, premised that, as the primary object in framing the rules of 1853 had been to promote reclamation, the measure was to be considered with reference to that object. Its influence would depend on whether redemption would extinguish the clearance conditions, and as it was proposed to retain them, the object of reclamation would be secured; hence he gave his approval to the measure, though he thought that permission to redeem should be withheld until the free period had expired and one-half of the grant was found cleared.[2] A further notification was then issued by the Government, no. 1136, dated 15th May 1860, which specified

[1] Presdy. Commr. to Sbn. Commr., no. 2844, dated 23 Nov. 1859.

[2] Sbn. Commr. to Presdy. Commr., no. 203, dated 12 Dec. 1859.

in a table the terms on which parties would be allowed to commute.[3]

309. Further Deliberations, 1860-62: The whole scheme, however, remained under deliberation during 1860 and 1861, and on 17th October 1861 the Government of India drew up a resolution sanctioning both branches of it and setting out its general features, but leaving local Governments to give legal effect thereto.[4] The resolution was submitted to the Home Government, and the Secretary of State replied in his despatch no. 14, dated 9th July 1862. While approving of the general outline of the measure for the sale of waste lands, he took objection to the uniform maximum rates of Rs. 2½ per acre for uncleared land and Rs. 5 for cleared land laid down for the whole of India, and enjoined that after due inquiry minimum prices should be fixed suited to the various descriptions of land in the several provinces; that lots should be sold by public auction at the minimum upset price; that a survey should be made preliminary to the grant; and that the sales should be advertised beforehand. As regarded the scheme of redemption the Secretary of State, among other matters, objected to the general nature of the permission to redeem. In permanently-settled estates, the proposed capitalization at 20 years' purchase would entail loss on the State, if the rate of interest fell below 5 per cent. In temporarily-settled estate the question was more serious, for the redemption would operate as a permanent settlement of the revenue on the basis of the existing assessment. He doubted the expediency of the policy of redeeming the land revenue generally, and after discussing this point at length, expressed his conclusion that the direct mode of making a permanent settlement was preferable to the indirect one of obtaining that result through redemption, and restricted the power to redeem to the case of lands required for dwelling-houses, factories, gardens, plantations, &c. This despatch was communicated to the local Governments by the Government of India in its no. 4206, dated 15th August 1862, and they were ordered to prepare rules accordingly. The rule regarding grants was formulated thus—"Grants which have already been given for a term of years at progressively increasing rents, such as those in the Sundarbans, will be treated as if the land were

[3] *Calcutta Gazette,* 19 May 1860, p. 1096.
[4] Ibid., 19 Oct. 1861, Supplement, p. 515.

permanently settled * * * at the highest rate fixed for any year during the currency of the grant".[5]

310. Waste Land Rules of 30th August 1882: The Government of Bengal then drew up a set of rules on 30th August 1862 for the sale of waste lands and the redemption of revenue (based on the draft rules prepared by the Board[6] upon the former resolution) and communicated them to the Board in its no. 377T of that date. They were published in the *Calcutta Gazette* of 27th September, Supplement, page 345, and were transmitted to the local officers in the Board's circular order no. 63, dated 14th October following. All former rules were rescinded. Tables for calculating the redemption money were given in the Board's circular order no. 63½, dated 23rd December 1862, which provided that grantees might pay down the full amount at once, or pay an instalment of 10 per cent at once, and the remainder by instalments within 10 years; but permission to redeem in no way affected the clearing conditions under the previous rules, and compliance with the conditions up to date was an indispensable prerequisite, subject, however, to leniency in special circumstances. Sales and redemptions were to be reported within a week of the completion of the transactions.[7]

311. Rules Revised and Amended, 1862 and 1863: On the publication of the notification of 15th May 1860, the grantee of lot 133 applied to redeem and deposited the costs of survey. It was permitted, and the survey of the lot ordered.[8] The grantees of lot 63 next applied in January 1862. No applications were made for the purchase of waste lands. Nothing positive, however, was done since the Board in April 1862 prohibited sales without their previous sanction,[9] and in June 1862 the making of grants was stopped till the promulgation of the new rules.[10] Permission to proceed with the sale of lots was given in November 1862.[11] The carrying out of the rules brought various points

[5] Ibid., 16 Aug. 1862, p. 2889.
[6] Bd. Rev. to Govt., no. 914, dated 28 Dec. 1861.
[7] Bd. Rev., C.O., no. 1B, dated 6 Jan. 1863.
[8] Presdy. Commr. to Sbn. Commr., no. 7Ct., dated 29 Jan. 1862.
[9] Bd. Rev., C.O., no. 27, dated 1 Apr. 1862.
[10] Bd. Rev., C.O., no. 41, dated 28 June 1862.
[11] The new excise rules for the manufacture of salt (then under correspondence with

to notice and elicited further rules in explanation and amendment. The rules contained no provision with regard to survey in the case of redemption. The Presidency Commissioner held that if the lot had been properly surveyed and the boundaries defined, no further survey was necessary.[12] On the question whether an existing grant could be redeemed in anticipation of a regular survey, he decided that no rule could be laid down; though, as the Government had declined to relax the rule requiring a survey as an essential preliminary in the case of the Sundarbans, he thought that a survey should be first made, and that the procedure should follow that laid down regarding applications for new grants under the same rules. No deposit of costs of survey, however, was to be taken in cases of doubt even in anticipation. As to the table of rates and the computation of the redemption money, since Rs. 2-8 per acre had been fixed as the minimum rate, it followed that the rates would be inoperative until a grant reached its eleventh year; before that the redemption would be at Rs. 2-8 on the whole area.[13] On 10th March 1863 was passed Act XXIII of that year to provide for the adjudication of claims to waste lands proposed to be sold on account of Government. Alterations and additions were made to the rules of October 1862, and published by the Board in their circular order no. 22, 5th May 1863: they referred to costs of survey, date of sale, claims and objections, &c.

312. Consolidated Rules of 13th October 1863: *Sale of waste lands free of land revenue.*—The rules were then revised and consolidated by the Board, and the amended rules were published with the Board's notification no. 314, dated 13th October 1863, in the *Calcutta Gazette* of 17th idem, page 2915. Their provisions were briefly these. All unassessed waste lands, in which no right of proprietorship or exclusive occupancy existed, were available for purchase with certain reservations. The maximum limit of a lot was 3,000 acres. The lot was to be first surveyed and demarcated, the applicant depositing the costs of survey and advertisement. It was then to be advertised and sold not less than three months afterwards by public auction at the

---

the Govt.) threw open to applicants for licenses all saliferous tracts in the Sundarbans. Presdy. Commr. to Sbn. Commr., no. 1319, dated 24 Nov. 1862.

[12] Presdy. Commr. to Sbn. Commr., no. 301, dated 27 Apr. 1863.

[13] Ibid., no. 105, dated 23 Sept. 1863.

minimum upset price of Rs. 2-8 per acre[14] on the *whole* area, provided all counterclaims, if any, were disposed of. On payment of one-tenth of the purchase money at once, the purchaser received a deed conveying to him the lot in full hereditary and transferable proprietary right free for ever from all demand of land revenue, but subject to all general taxes and local rates. He was bound to erect substantial boundary marks; and a tow-path, 20 feet in width, was to be reserved on either side of each stream. If the whole amount of purchase money were not paid at once, it might be paid up by instalments within 10 years with interest at 10 per cent., the whole lot remaining hypothecated as security for the amount and being liable to sale in case of default of payment:

Redemption of land revenue.—For redemptions it was provided that all grants of waste land already made for a term of years under previously existing rules, in which no right of occupancy or proprietorship existed, except that of the grantee or what was derived from him, would be treated as if the land were permanently settled at the highest annual rate of rent payable under the lease, and grantees would be permitted to redeem the future land revenue of their grants, or any compact part, in perpetuity for an amount equal to the present value of all future stipulated annual payments calculated at 5 per cent interest, provided that that amount was not less than Rs. 2-8 per acre on the whole area of which the land revenue was redeemed. The redemption money might be paid up at once or by instalments, as in the case of new grants bought; but permission to redeem did not affect the obligation of the clearance conditions, and, before a grantee could redeem, he would be bound to shew he had complied with them, subject to relaxations in special cases. Lastly, waste lands were not to be granted, nor redemption permitted in lands already granted, except in accordance with these rules. The necessary forms and tables were appended to the rules.

[14] It does not appear how this price was chosen. Mr. Reily in 1859 had suggested Rs. 2-8 per *bigha* as being 20 years' purchase of the highest rate (2 annas) imposed under the rules of 1853 (Sbn. Commr. to Presdy. Commr., no. 203, dated 12 Dec. 1859). The point was specially referred for opinion in 1862 (Bd. Rev. C.O. no. 55, dated 22 Aug. 1862), and Mr. Caspersz recommended Rs. 2-4 per acre in the 24-Parganas, Re. 1-6 in Jessore, and Rs. 2 in Bakarganj as minimum prices (Sbn. Commr. to Presdy. Commr., no. 130, dated 10 Sept. 1862).

313. Objections to the Rules and their Reconsideration, 1862-67: The rules of 30th August 1862 rescinded all previous rules, but they were not at once appreciated. No applications for fresh lands had been made under the resolution of 17th October 1861, and only a few informal petitions were presented under the rules of 30th August 1862,[15] one reason being that the price was too high, but the chief objection being the large amount of capital required to take grants under them. In May 1863 a Mr. Ladd, urging these facts, prayed for a grant under the 1853 rules with liberty to redeem under the new rules at a future period, but his petition was refused. The Government of India inquired whether any modifications were desired, and the Lieutenant-Governor recommended that, if after due advertisement there was no competition, the option should be given of taking the lands either under the new rules, or under terms similar to the former rules with liberty to the grantee to redeem at any future time. This the Government of India sanctioned in 1864.[16] The question was then mooted whether the 1853 rules should be revived, or whether any modifications should be introduced, and the Sundarban Commissioner suggested a number of changes.[17] Eight applications were filed during 1864 for new grants under the rules of 1853,[18] but no alteration was made, chiefly, it would seem, because Mr. Schiller proposed to buy up the whole of the waste lands in 1865, as mentioned in paragraph 306. In 1867 Government allowed that a purchaser might relinquish one of several lots and carry his payments on account of that lot to the credit of another lot.[19]

314. Sales of Waste Lands, 1865-70: During 1865 lot 132 (part) was sold, and in 1860 lots 121, 122, 124, 125, 126, 128 (part), 132 (part), and 137, Guasoba Island, Noli, Saplenja[20] and Kakchira char. The sale of lots was, however, kept in abeyance pending the floating

[15] Sbn. Commr. to Presdy. Commr., no. 265, dated 13 Feb. 1863.

[16] Presdy. Commr. to Sbn, Commr., memo. no. 207, dated 7 Apr. 1864. Sbn. Commr. also recommended it in his letter to Presdy. Commr., no. 204, dated 15 March 1864.

[17] Sbn. Commr. to Presdy. Commr., no. 228, dated 24 Apr. 1864.

[18] Ibid., no. 121, dated 2 Oct. 1864.

[19] Bd. Rev. to Presdy. Commr., no. 758A, dated 1 March 1867.

[20] Sbn. Commr. to Presdy. Commr., no. 254, dated 9 Feb. 1866.

of Mr. Schiller's scheme, and, when the scheme failed finally in August 1868, the Government withdrew the restriction on the sales. There was, however, no eagerness to purchase, and in fact default being made, lots 121, 122 (part); 124, 125, 126, 128 (part), and 132 (part) were sold to recover the purchase money and were bought in by Government in 1870. Guasoba Island came back in 1879. Lot 19 (part) was sold in 1870.

315. Redemptions of Land Revenue, 1865-70: As regards redemption the new rules met with more success. The grantee of lot 133 had applied to redeem in 1860; the grantees of lots 63, 67, and 163 applied in 1862; and the grantee of lot 85 in 1863. In 1864 and the subsequent years numerous applications were received, and redemption was permitted in lots 18, 43, 48, 49, 50 (part), 57 (part), 83, 91, 92, 109, 123, 127, 128 (part), 129, 130, 131, 133, 134, and 138 in 1865; and in lots 59 and 136[21] in 1866. Many of these lots belonged to the Port Canning Company. One-tenth of the redemption money was paid and the lots remained hypothecated for the balance. Redemptions also took place in lot 108 in 1870; lot 86 in 1872; and in other cases in after years. Default, however, being made, lots 123, 127, 128 (part), and 138 were resold and bought in by Government in 1870. In lot 109 permission was given to revert to the rules of 1853.

316. Orders Regarding Survey of Waste Lands Sold or Redeemed, 1864-67: The rule declaring a survey, *&c,* to be indispensable before any waste land could be granted was suspended in October 1864; and it was provided instead that when a grant was made before survey, it should remain hypothecated for any deficiency of price that might appear after survey. No application for unsurveyed land was to be received unless accompanied by a specification of its situation and probable area and a rough plan giving all available particulars.[22] The Sundarban Commissioner, however, permitted the redemption of unsurveyed grants, and sold unsurveyed waste lands without first taking the deposit for survey and clearance required by the rules. He was then ordered to enforce these conditions, but the grantees

[21] See Presdy. Commr. to Sbn. Commr., memo. no. 18, dated 15 Apr. 1867. In those two lots it seems the redemption money was calculated irregularly—see Presdy. Commr. to Sbn. Commr., no. 51, dated 13 May 1867.

[22] Bd. Rev., C.O. no. 1 of Oct. 1864. *Calcutta Gazette* of 9 Nov. 1864, p. 1957.

protested, especially Mr. Schiller, both on his own account and also on behalf of the Port Canning Company. Hodges' areas had been adopted as the basis of these proceedings, and they were held to contain a considerable percentage of error if the lots were taken separately, though sufficiently correct if all the lots were lumped together. The greater part of these lands being under forest, and no survey being feasible for some time, the Board pronounced it harsh to demand the cost of survey at that period and ordered that the matter should be postponed till the lots were cleared.[23]

[23] Sbn. Commr. to Presdy. Commr., no. 215, dated 27 Dec. 1866. Presdy. Commr. to Sbn. Commr., memo. no. 237, dated 28 Jan. 1867.

CHAPTER XXVI

History of Saugor Island

1811-1877

317. Saugor Island, though strictly falling within the Sundarbans, did not come under the Sundarban Commissioner's jurisdiction till 1850, and its history lies apart.

318. Earliest Projects of Reclamation, 1811-17: The project of clearing the island was started by the Government in 1811, but on vague and conjectural data, with the intention of benefitting the navigation of the river Hugli. A Mr. Jones in 1812 got a lease with a free period of ten years to clear and cultivate, but failed; so also did a Mr. Beaumont, who appears to have got a similar lease in 1813. Terms were published in 1812, and about 65 Europeans and natives came forward readily with applications, which mounted up to an area of 4,29,806 bighas. The area of the island being reckoned at 4,34,228 bighas according to Lieutenant Blane's survey of 1813-14, their applications were entertained. The Collector of 24-Parganas allotted them quantities of the total area proportional to their applications, and detained their amalnamas proposing to visit the island himself in order to make more satisfactory arrangements, but he was unable to do so. The applicants, however, were not eager to engage for the grants, and had merely desired to secure a nominal property that might eventually become valuable. In 1816 the Court of Directors inquired what the result of the scheme had been, and the Board reported that it had failed. As, however, it had never had a fair trial, and they approved the Collector's decision, the Board proposed to carry out his arrangements. The Governor-General in reply inquired whether the applicants wanted the land *bonâ fide* for cultivation, and how far the good faith of Government was pledged to them. It would appear that the Government was not satisfied, and that the scheme was annulled in 1817.[1]

319. Further Proposals, 1817 and 1818: The Collector, Mr. Trower, was then instructed to adopt the best means of reclaiming the island. He began clearing in a central portion, named after him Trowerland, but finding that cultivation could be better undertaken by private persons, he convened a meeting of merchants and others in Calcutta in 1818. A Committee was formed which proposed that a joint stock company should be formed, consisting of both Europeans and natives, with a capital of Rs. 2,50,000 sicca in 250 shares for the purpose of reclaiming the island, it being-thought that the whole could be cleared in three or four years at the cost of the above sum. The Collector proposed to grant out the island, free for 30 years and afterwards subject to an ultimate assessment of 4 annas per bigha. The Governor-General considered these opinions were too sanguine, as the estimated cost would, compared with the area, amount to about 8 annas per bigha, where as Lieutenant Blane's notes went to shew that the reclamation would not be so easy as was imagined. Still the attempt was not impracticable if judiciously and vigorously pursued, though success could only be attained by large capital and European direction. The attempt was one for private enterprize, and the ordinary policy of Government as to the tenure of land by Europeans did not apply in this case as the object was connected with the commercial interests of the port. The Governor-General therefore approved the scheme, transferring the land to the Society in perpetuity on the Collector's terms as to the period and rate of settlement, but declined to sanction it formally, until the whole capital of 2½ lakhs had been subscribed, and the Society regularly constituted. He left the Board and the Collector to determine what security should be provided to ensure that the instructions of the Court of Directors should be observed as to pushing the reclamation on vigorously, and to reserve to Government the power of resuming in the event of entire failure.[2]

320. Saugor Island Society Established, 1819: The Company

[1] Bd. Rev. to Governor-General, 31 Dec. 1816; Governor-General to Bd. Rev., no. 76, dated 24 Jan. 1817; and Bd. Rev. to Collr., 24-Parganas, 31 idem. Sbn. Commr. to Presdy. Commr., no. 161, dated 24 Dec. 1863.

[2] Govt. to Bd. Rev., no. 1073, dated 23 Oct. 1818.

was then started in 1819 under the name of the Saugor Island Society, and the lease was executed on 10th June 1819. The capital consisted of Rs. 2,50,000 in 250 share of Rs. 1,000 each, and the management was to be in the hands of a Committee of at least 13 trustees.[3] The Government granted the island in perpetuity to the Society as zamindars, free for 30 years from 1st January 1820 and thereafter subject to an assessment of 4 annas for every bigha capable of being cultivated except what the Society might reserve for its own use, the Society undertaking to reclaim the island energetically—25,000 bighas within five years and 1,00,000 bighas within ten years from 1st January 1829 on pain of resumption. Various stipulations were provided as to the disposal of the island in the event of non-reclamation or excessive mortality, as to the manuafcture of salt, the division of the whole into smaller grants, and the maintenance of the trust. Failure in any of the conditions entitled Government to re-enter on the island.[4]

321. Progress, 1819-49: The Society commenced reclamation, constructing embankments, clearing the land, digging tanks, and settling cultivators. Considerable progress was made in five portions called Mud Point, Ferintosh, Trowerland, Shikarpur and Dhobelat,[5] until May 1833, when the great gale and inundation occurred which destroyed almost everything and compelled the Society to throw up the scheme in despair. Four gentlemen then—Messrs Hare, Macpherson, Hunter, and Campbell— bought the four northern portions, or giants Shikarpur, Trowerland, Mud Point, and Ferintosh, and carried on the undertaking. Government had supported medical, military, and post office establishments there to protect and assist the immigrants and inhabitants; but in 1834-35 it granted in lieu thereof the privilege of making salt for Government. Those gentlemen commenced salt operations in those grants and reaped a lucrative return from the salt manufacture and rice cultivation combined.[6] Storms occurred in

[3] The names of the original Committee are mentioned in the lease.

[4] Presdy. Commr. to Sbn. Commr., no. 228, dated 13 Nov. 1856. Sbn. Commr. to Presdy Commr., no. 161, dated 24 Dec. 1863.

[5] Another portion, called Phuldobi, is said to have been cleared, which was utterly ruined by the storm of 1833. (Sbn. Commr. to Presdy. Commr., no. 161, dated 24 Dec. 1863).

[6] Presdy. Commr. to Sbn. Commr., no. 16, dated 1 Feb. 1850.

June 1842, October 1848, and again in June 1852, which inflicted serious damage.

322. Salt Manufacture, and Extension of the Free Term, 1849-54: About 1848 the Government reconsidered its salt policy and contracted its operations generally. On the report of the Board of Customs, Salt, and Opium, the Bengal Government, agreeing with the Board, decided, in 1849, that it was no longer expedient to continue the privilege of making salt to the grantees of Saugor Island, and that the manufacture must be discontinued after that season. The grantees remonstrated on the ground that it would ruin the raiyats, and throw the whole land back in jungle so as no longer to provide a place of refuge for shipwrecked sailors. Thereupon the Government ordered an inquiry in 1850 as to how far the prosperity of the island depended on the continuance of the salt manufacture.[7] Babu U.K. Sen made a perfunctory visit of one day in February 1850 in company with Mr. Fraser, the grantees' agent, and reported in their interests,[8] but his opinion was discarded. Trustworthy inquiries, however, were made by the Tumlook Salt Agent in whose district the island lay. The grantees alleged that they had spent large sums on the reclamation and improvement of their property, but he did not find their statements borne out. The embankments and tanks had for the most part been constructed by the Society before the ruin of 1833, and had not been properly maintained since then. He thought the grants had been deteriorating, and that the reason lay in mismanagement and neglect. The rents had been enhanced to exorbitant rates[9] under cover of the protection afforded by the salt manufacture, for the residents were both molungis and cultivators, and made salt when not engaged in their rice cultivation, consequently they gained little livelihood either from the manufacture or from their crops. Dhobelat had been almost entirely abandoned in 1848 for want of fresh water, and in the other giants the people were frequently deserting. The Salt Agent recommended that embankments should be constructed, rents reduced to 10 or 12 annas per bigha, and cesses abolished, with certain other proposals

[7] Presdy. Commr. to Sbn. Commr., no. 16, dated 1 Feb. 1850.

[8] Sbn. Commr. to Presdy. Commr., no. 70, dated 12 March 1850.

[9] Re. 1-4 per bigha was about the average rate.

regarding the salt manufacture. His suggestions were approved by the Board and Government,[10] but the grantees demurred. The free term having expired with 1849, the Sundarban Commissioner began to assess the land, but in 1851 the Government conceded them an extension of the free term for 30 years from 1833, the year of the great storm.[11] Meanwhile the grantees had memorialized the Court of Directors about the withdrawal of the salt manufacture. The Directors wrote out a letter in 1850 that appears to have led to the issue of the salt rules of 1853-54, under which the island prospered.

323. Settlement Proceedings and the Cyclone-wave of 1864: As the free term expired in 1863, Mr. Gomess surveyed the island in season 1862-63 with a view to its assessment. It then contained six blocks partially or wholly cleared and cultivated, *viz.,* Mud Point (all cleared), Ferintosh (partly cleared), Bamankhali (2,096 bighas cleared), Trowerland (partly cleared), Shikarpur (2,579 bighas cleared), and Dhobelat or Ganga Saugor[12] (2,311 bighas cleared), the total area cleared being 31,190 bighas. All the rest of the island was dense jungle, except the spot occupied by the light-house. Mr. Gomess proposed terms of settlement for these grants, and suggested that the remainder of the island, comprising 3,26,368 bighas, should be sub-divided and sold by public auction.[13] The grantees objected to the proposed assessment of 8 annas per bigha and asked that, since 4 annas was the rate for the island when ordinary grants paid 8 annas, it should be exempted now that grants were assessed at 2 annas only.[14] The proposals remained under the consideration of the higher authorities till the cyclone and wave of 5th October 1864 occurred, which swept over the island with full force and wrought great havoc. In December 1864 the Board deferred the settlement as inopportune. Inquiries were made, and the grantees objected to any assessment,

[10] Presdy. Commr. to Sbn. Commr., no. 149, dated 2 Aug. 1850. The Salt Agent's report contains much interesting information about population, embankments, tanks, rents, &c.

[11] Ibid., no. 208, dated 28 Oct. 1850, and no. 35, dated 13 Fob. 1851.

[12] A large mela is held here every year at the beginning of Magh, and pilgrims come from all parts of the country.

[13] Sbn. Commr. to Presdy. Commr., no. 161, dated 24 Dec. 1863.

[14] Presdy. Commr. to Sbn. Commr., memo. no. 158, dated 5 Dec. 1863.

but offered to relinquish their grant under the terms of the lease, if Government paid them Rs.5 per bigha for all the cleared land.[15] No orders were passed and the grants remained in the same condition, though Mr. Chapman, the Presidency Commissioner, suggested that high and strong embankments were indispensable in order to guard against the constantly recurring loss of life by storms on the island. On 1st and 2nd November 1867 occurred another storm and high tide, which caused great damage to the crops, and reduced the area under cultivation to 2,750 bighas.

324. Modification of the Grants in Order to Secure Protection to Human Life, 1867-71: These calamities compelled attention to the necessity of providing means of safety, especially as regarded human life. Mr. Chapman in December 1867 urged that the following protective measures should be insisted upon—that in each village a place of refuge should be provided consisting of a small tank surrounded by an embankment high and strong enough to be proof against all storm-waves, and that no habitation should be allowed beyond a fixed distance from it. He held that the island was at the absolute disposal of Government through the lapse of the rights of the then grantees, and recommended that the area then under cultivation should be regranted to them free of revenue for ever, on condition that they maintained such protecttive works.[16] The Board, however, reviewing the proceedings of 1851, held that the grantees were entitled to settlement of their cultivated lands at 4 annas per bigha (the grant of the remainder being cancelled), and that Mr. Chapman's condition could not be imposed under the terms of their deed. The Government, in its no. 1608 of 26th May 1868, agreeing with the Board, approved the proposal to settle the cultivated lands at 4 annas per bigha in perpetuity with the grantees, but at the same time offered to continue the grantees in possession of their respective grants rent free for ever, if they would provide places of refuge and reserves for fresh water as proposed by Mr. Chapman.[17] These

15 Sbn. Commr. to Presdy. Commr., no. 319, dated 30 Apr. 1866.

16 Presdy. Commr. to Bd. Rev., no. 103 Ct., dated 28 Dec. 1867, with Presdy. Commr. to Sbn. Commr., memo. no. 73, dated 14 July 1868.

17 Presdy. Commr. to Sbn. Commr., memo. no. 73, dated 14 July 1868, which transmits all the correspondence.

alternative offers were communicated to the grantees, but the proposals required elaboration.[18] In December 1868, Mr. Chapman laid before Government, in the Public Works Department, a proposal made by the proprietor of Dhobelat regarding the protective works deemed necessary for the safety of that grant. This proposal seeming to be more complete than that advocated by Mr. Chapman, the Board desired him in March 1869 to obtain the orders of Government on it, and then make the offer of the alternative terms approved by Government. Captain Mayne, Superintending Engineer, recommended that for Dhobelat the embankment surrounding the tank should be 16½ feet high, with a slope outside of 3½ to 1 and inside of 2 to 1, with a crest 5 feet broad, and that it should be terraced inside and the whole properly rammed and turfed. The cost of such a work was estimated at Rs. 7,974. The Government approved this estimate and pronounced it the lowest that would be required for any grant.[19] The grantees accepted the offer of the revenue-free tenure of their estates, with the conditions attaching therto.[20] They, however, resisted the construction placed on the words "respective grants" in the Government offer as meaning the "extent of cultivation in 1863", and claimed the grants in their original entirety. The Government disallowed this contention, but in carrying out the orders the grantees were liberally dealt with, and the areas assigned the several estates were, for convenience as regards boundaries and other reasons, increased beyond the extent of cultivation in 1863, especially in Shikarpur and Trowerland. The Government approved the arrangements in its no. 808 of 1st March 1871. Three seasons were allowed for the construction of the works; yearly inspection was to be made by the Sundarban Commissioner; additional protective works would be required as cultivation extended; and neglect to construct or maintain the work would entail resumption of the grant.[21]

325. Grants Reconstituted Revenue-free on Condition of Maintaining Protective Works, 1875-77: The preparation of the

[18] Sbn. Commr. to Presdy. Commr., no. 200, dated 1 Fob. 1869.

[19] Presdy. Commr. to Sbn. Commr., no. 4, date 5 Apr. 1869, and annexures.

[20] Sbn. Commr. to Presdy. Commr., no. 172, dated 6 Jan., and no. 152, dated 26 Nov. 1870.

[21] Presdy. Commr. to Sbn. Commr., memo. no. 201, dated 21 March 1871.

new deeds was delayed by uncertainties concerning the title deeds and various legal obstacles, and was not completed till 1875. The estates were granted out free of land revenue in perpetuity on the following conditions, the deeds being alike for all the grants:

(1) A place of refuge consisting of a tank and an embankment terraced inside surrounding it was to be constructed on a specified spot, shown on a plan attached to the deed;
(2) The dimensions were to be—the tank 200 by 150 feet, the embankment 16½ feet high with a crest 5 feet broad, and a slope of 3½ to 1 outside, and 2 to 1 inside;
(3) The embankment was to be properly rammed and turfed; and there was to be a sward of 50 feet width between it and the tank;
(4) No habitation should be erected more than one mile from the place of refuse, unless its basement were raised 16½ feet above the ground; and good bund-roads were to. be constructed connecting the place of refuge with the habitations on the estate;
(5) As cultivation extended beyond the prescribed distance, fresh protective works should be constructed;
(6) The works specified in the first three clauses were to be completed in three years, and all future new works required in clause 5 within a like period.

The next three clauses provided for maintenance and repairs and the 10th clause for navigation through the grants. Most of the deeds were at once executed in 1875-76, but a year's delay occured in the case of Shikarpur. The areas assigned the grants were these—Mud Point 11,783 bighas, Ferintosh 15,258 bighas, Shikarpur 7,486 bighas, Trowerland 7,349 bighas, Bamankhali 3,821 bighas, and Dhobelat 17,726 bighas. The remainder of the island became the absolute property of the State.

Index

www.ingramcontent.com/pod-product-compliance
Ingram Content Group UK Ltd.
Pitfield, Milton Keynes, MK11 3LW, UK
UKHW022032061126
477531UK00008B/292

9781032654423